Multicultural Education
in the U.S.

Multicultural Education
—— in the U.S. ——

A Guide to Policies and Programs in the 50 States

Bruce M. Mitchell and Robert E. Salsbury

Greenwood Press
Westport, Connecticut • London

Library of Congress Cataloging-in-Publication Data

Mitchell, Bruce M.
    Multicultural education in the U.S. : a guide to policies and
programs in the 50 states / Bruce M. Mitchell and Robert E.
Salsbury.
        p.   cm.
    Includes bibliographical references (p.   ) and index.
    ISBN 0–313–30859–4 (alk. paper)
    1. Multicultural education—United States—States.   2. Education
and state—United States—States.   I. Salsbury, Robert E.
II. Title.
LC1099.3.M59   2000
370.117′0973—dc21   99–31579

British Library Cataloguing in Publication Data is available.

Library of Congress Catalog Card Number: 99–31579
ISBN: 0–313–30859–4

First published in 2000

Greenwood Press, 88 Post Road West, Westport, CT 06881
An imprint of Greenwood Publishing Group, Inc.
www.greenwood.com

Printed in the United States of America

The paper used in this book complies with the
Permanent Paper Standard issued by the National
Information Standards Organization (Z39.48–1984).

10 9 8 7 6 5 4 3 2 1

CONTENTS

PREFACE

As the United States moves closer to the second millennium, it seems necessary to examine the issues and opportunities of multicultural education, past, present, and future. Born during the turbulent era of the 1960s, multicultural education has attempted to help students acquire a more sophisticated understanding of the pluralistic populations of the United States. Sometimes this has been difficult when students have had limited access to microcultural populations different from their own. Indeed, this issue has become even more complicated due to the "resegregation of America" which some social scientists feel has been occurring in recent years.

The idea for this book came from the authors' earlier work, *Multicultural Education: An International Guide to Research, Policies and Programs* (Greenwood, 1996). That book examined the status of multicultural education programs throughout the world. While the United States was included, the authors felt that it was necessary to address the situation in the United States in much more detail. Indeed, some writers have characterized the country as fifty separate nations with individual constitutions, legislatures, and educational systems. While a great many similarities exist between the states, there are profound differences which the authors have felt compelled to explore in their work.

Moreover, the nation is beset with deep divisions over educational programs related to affirmative action, bilingual instruction efforts, and other attempts to improve the learning potential of America's children. But in addition to the improvement of cognitive thought processes of young learners, the companion issue of instilling appropriate attitudes has become a problem for all educators. Since the intent of multicultural education programs is to help students learn to appreciate others who are different, problems related to differences of opinion about religion, politics, language, and other issues of ethnicity come into play, often causing enormous areas of disagreement.

Educators are becoming increasingly concerned over the number of students who have been taught to hate in their developmental years. Whether the hatred manifests itself in negative attitudes toward government, race, religion, or language, the ensuing problems have been addressed by teachers throughout the land in an effort to do the best job humanly possible in the education of America's youth.

Consequently, multicultural education efforts are often vilified by some groups who view it as an attempt to meddle in the values instruction which normally occurs in the homes. However, powerful images of the past, such as Nazi Germany's blatant assault against the Jews, have motivated educators to search for strategies which can help students develop more tolerant attitudes toward persons who happen to be different racially or ethnically from themselves. These efforts occur to some degree in all fifty states and the purpose of this book is to determine what multicultural programs exist.

The authors thought that it was important to provide the reader with a short multicultural history of each state. Since every state is responsible for the education of its youth, it is necessary to provide the reader with insights about the general nature of the educational programs for the children. Finally, each chapter includes the research findings based on our national survey of multicultural education. The data-gathering strategies will be discussed in the introduction chapter.

It is hoped that the final product will be useful to a wide variety of educators who are interested in examining multicultural education in the fifty states. It is also our hope that in addition to the information on multicultural education programs in each state, the book will help to provide readers with a clearer view of the complicated nature of America's education system. Unlike many other countries, there is no Ministry of Education, which directs educational efforts on a national level. Thus, the assessment of the country's educational "system" is extremely complicated. In addition, when problems such as poverty are analyzed, valid assessment becomes extremely difficult. However, it is crucial that educators and lay persons alike have a better understanding of the multicultural issues that the nation's schools have addressed and will continue to confront as the United States heads into the twenty-first century.

The research on the topic was carried out by the authors over a three-year period. In the absence of grants and special funding, we would like to thank the Department of Education, Eastern Washington University, for its excellent support. In particular, we would like to thank Department Chair, Dr. William Goetter, for his complete cooperation. In addition, we wish to give special thanks to Ms. Sherry Miller for her word processing efforts, and to Mr. Mike Montemayor, Jr. for his outstanding data-gathering contributions.

INTRODUCTION

Without a doubt, the United States of America is one of the most complicated nations on the globe. Its turbulent history has been beset by slavery and the doctrine of manifest destiny which provided some European-Americans with a rationale for taking over the lands of the native residents for themselves. Its history also made it possible for tens of millions of Europeans to flee oppressive governments and religious tyranny to start over and hopefully acquire "the American dream." Throughout the years, immigrants from Asia, Africa, South America, Southeast Asia, Europe, and many other parts of the world have provided the country with an effective labor force. Some of these persons acquired excellent educations, which propelled them into professional areas and made it possible for them to acquire vast fortunes.

However, given the capitalistic economic system the country has enjoyed throughout the years, the United States has also had to deal with enormous poverty problems. Indeed, in recent years the nation has seen a frightening increase in both the poverty culture, along with the economic culture of the wealthy. This enormous increase in the number of poor persons has created gigantic problems for educators who have the responsibility of providing equal educational opportunities for all children, a property right guaranteed by the United States Constitution.

Another phenomenon of American life compounds the problem even further. In the United States, persons of color have far greater proportions of their people who find themselves struggling in poverty. On the contrary, smaller percentages of European-Americans have had to contend with this issue. Consequently, this condition has helped contribute to the racial strife which has ravaged the land in numerous ways. For example, it is well documented that poverty is often responsible for health and physical conditions which can result in substandard intellectual performance. Throughout the history of the country, this has sometimes led to the conclusion, particularly among European-Americans, that "minorities" (persons of color) are genetically deficient in intelligence and consequently human beings of a lesser status.

Obviously, these problems have caused great difficulties for educators. For example, when considering the issue of language, the 1978 *Lau v. Nichols* Supreme Court decision led to the notion that "equal educational opportunities" could not exist unless the student had compensatory educational programs which would help the student cope with English language deficiencies. One of the most common ways to deal with this problem was through the creation of bilingual education programs. These strategies sought to provide the instruction in the student's native language as long as necessary. In the meantime, the student was provided instruction in English so that the need for bilingual education programs would disappear as the student became fluent in the two languages. Such programs exist all over the world in countries like Finland, Australia, and Brazil. The underlying philosophy is that if students need instruction in their native language and are provided it, then the odds of encountering successful educational experiences will increase dramatically.

However, in the United States, a well-orchestrated effort against the use of bilingual education programs has resulted in an "English Only" movement, which attempts to prevent the inclusion of bilingual education programs in the schools. In addition, this "English Only" movement has resulted in a number of states establishing laws which prevent the official use of any other language. Pete Wilson, Republican Governor of California, initiated an English-only testing program and has been a staunch foe of bilingual education. And while most Latino parents support bilingual education programs for their children, many other Americans have opposed them.

In addition to the "English Only" efforts, attempts to terminate affirmative action programs have occurred throughout the nation. Affirmative action measures have irritated European-American males, resulting in their attempts to end these programs. Taken together, the efforts to terminate both bilingual education and affirmative action programs have reversed many of the civil rights efforts to "level the playing field."

The United States is a highly pluralistic society, consisting of persons who enjoy different racial and ethnic backgrounds, religions, and language patterns. Not only do these differences define the country's microcultural populations, but differences in gender, age, and mental potential also occur. America's school children are exposed to a plethora of social statements daily about the value of persons who are different from themselves. These messages come not only from the media, but from conversations with their peers and statements overheard by virtually all persons with whom they come into contact.

Throughout history, Americans have heard that African-Americans were not very intelligent and were responsible for most of the country's crime; Jews had all the money; Latinos were illegal immigrants and "taking over" the western states; Italian-Americans were gangsters; Scottish-Americans were cheap; and Native-Americans were on welfare and received an automatic allotment from the United States government. These negative stereotypes have caused enormous damage to America's microcultures, and the primary goal of multicultural education is to help young students learn the folly of such stereotypical assertions.

Given these social conditions, the goal of multicultural education programs has been twofold: to provide more accurate descriptions of America's microcultural populations and to guarantee a better education for all American school children, regardless of their gender, race, ethnicity, religion, or language background. As a result, our 1998 national study of multicultural education asked the following fourteen questions pertaining to state programs:

1. Does the state have a planned multicultural education program?
2. Does the state have a person in its Office of Public Instruction who is responsible for multicultural education?
3. Does the state have funding specifically for multicultural education?
4. Does the state offer leadership to school districts in specific kinds of multicultural education programs?
5. What are the predominant microcultures in the state?
6. Does the state require special coursework and/or other microcultural experiences for teacher education?
7. Does the curriculum and instruction tend to stress cultural pluralism or cultural assimilation?
8. Does the state have special programs to teach children in their native language?
9. What desegregation strategies are being employed in the state?
10. Have racist incidents increased or decreased in the state's schools during the past five years?
11. Is the history of Native-Americans included in each state's regular curriculum?
12. Does the state's Office of Education evaluate curriculum materials, library materials and/or textbooks for racist and sexist content?
13. What are the biggest problems facing multicultural education in the state?
14. What are the biggest improvements needed in each state's multicultural education program?

Responses to the questionnaire survey were received from all but two states (Alaska and South Carolina). As is usual with any questionnaire survey, some replies are complete and usable, while others are either sketchy or nonexistent. Moreover, some respondents go to great lengths to supply the information as completely as possible, while others simply race through the exercise. The authors have attempted to supplement the information from other sources in order to provide the most valid information possible. Also, some states, such as Iowa, New Mexico, New Jersey, Florida, and Wisconsin have included valuable documents and monographs which provided us with supplemental information.

Many of the ideas for this study were based on the scholarly work of such multi-cultural education professionals as James Banks, Ronald Takaki, Hilda Hernandez, Ricardo Garcia, Donna Gollnick, Philip Chinn, and Pamela and Iris Tiedt. Their ideas helped the authors to formulate a framework for the book.

Each entry includes four sections. The first segment relates to the pre- and post-Columbian history, particularly the multicultural events which helped shape the state's present-day situation. Part two describes each state's education system briefly while the third part includes the analysis of the state's multicultural education efforts, and the fourth lists references. The written account of each state's multicultural education program is based on a combination of completed questionnaires, research documents related to the state's history and school organization, and the literature on multicultural education. It is hoped that the fifty entries will provide the reader with useful descriptions of each state's multicultural efforts. Since education in America is a federal interest, it is also hoped that the information about each state will be useful in the development of a solid national effort in multicultural education.

ALABAMA

STATE HISTORY

Archaeological discoveries of food grinding tools and other implements have suggested that human beings inhabited the territories of present-day Alabama approximately ninety-five centuries before the arrival of Columbus. Chickasaws, Cherokees, Choctaws, and Creeks dwelled in both the hilly and coastal area. European settlers found the Native-American groups involved in both agricultural and hunting pursuits.

After the termination of the American Revolution, more European-Americans moved to Alabama, causing a great deal of friction between the native residents and the new settlers. In 1786, the Chickasaws signed the Treaty of Hopewell with the United States. Under the treaty they were offered protection by the U.S. government, and the tribe sold off part of their land to the new nation. By 1832, the Chickasaws had sold all of their land and moved to Indian Territory (modern Oklahoma) under provisions of the Removal Act of 1830.

Members of the Iroquois language group, the Cherokees resided in the hill areas and the coastal plains of Alabama and other southeastern states as well. Their total population at the time of contact with the first Europeans in 1540 was about 25,000. This interaction occurred when Hernando de Soto landed at Tampa Bay, contacting Cherokees in the area. Eventually, the Cherokees were removed to present-day Oklahoma as a result of the Removal Act of 1830.

The Choctaw tribe, originally inhabiting the present-day states of Alabama, Mississippi, and Arkansas, rapidly adapted to European cultures. Linguistically, they were part of the Muskogean macroculture and were considered to be part of the "Five Civilized Tribes." As a result of the Removal Act of 1830, they also were required to give up their land and move to Indian Territory in Oklahoma.

One of their primary living sites in Alabama was the area near the confluence of the Alabama and Tombigbee Rivers. They became well known for their progressive farming, ranching, and industrial development. While it has been estimated that the Choctaw population was small in Alabama, there are now about 82,000 people, which makes them the fifth largest tribe in the United States.

Also members of the Muskogean language group are the Creeks, who moved from west of the Mississippi and occupied part of Alabama by the seventeenth century. Despite the fact that the Creeks included people from several tribal groups, they have shared a common macroculture. Their first contacts with Europeans occurred during the seventeenth century. The Creeks were adept traders, providing deerskins in exchange for European goods. This interaction precipitated a rather extensive amount of inter-marriage, resulting in considerable European-American acculturation.

However, the termination of the American Revolution created greater pressures from European-American settlers, and some Creeks chose to spurn any thoughts of assimilation in favor of maintaining their tribal traditions. Eventually a civil war erupted between the traditionalists (referred to as "Red Sticks") and the faction of Creeks who were more friendly toward European-American settlers. After suffering major defeats, many Red Sticks fled to Florida, joining the Seminoles. Many others moved to Oklahoma as a result of President Jackson's removal policies.

Due to the need for cheap labor in the cotton producing parts of the state, European-American settlers became deeply involved in the purchase of African slaves who had been captured, transported, and sold to European-Americans. Slaves in Alabama were purchased to work in the cotton fields and other farming enterprises. The first Africans in present-day United States consisted of seventeen men and three women who were brought to Jamestown, Virginia, in 1619 as indentured servants on a Dutch ship. This action precipitated the importation of African slaves who were purchased by European-Americans.

As the result of a general notion among European-Americans that Africans were of inferior intellectual status, coupled with repressive laws and limited funding resources, education opportunities for African-American students were minimal at best and led to the creation of Alabama's two-tiered educational system. Less than one-half the money budgeted for European-American students was spent on the education of African-American pupils. This formula was comparable to the budgetary structure of South Africa during that country's Apartheid era.

One of the first Alabama educators to attract national attention was Booker T. Washington, the principal of Tuskegee Institute. One of the main speakers at the Alabama Exposition of 1895, Washington helped articulate the South's efforts at describing their industrial achievements during the three decades following the termination of the Civil War. It was one of the first times that an African-American had the chance to address such a large gathering of European-American entrepreneurs.

While he argued the need for African-Americans acquiring vocational skills which would enable them to become self-supporting, many disagreed with this goal. One such critic was W.E.B. Du Bois, the first African-American to receive a Ph.D. degree from Harvard University. Du Bois believed that the curriculum for African-American students should be more well grounded in the liberal arts and that vocational programs might teach African-Americans to become more subservient. However, Washington did not believe in the movement for social equity and thought that African-Americans needed to concentrate on preparation efforts which would help them acquire the skills that would enable them to achieve economic success. He also felt that, given the racial climate in Alabama at the time, the vocational emphasis at Tuskegee would not antagonize as many European-Americans as a curriculum which stressed philosophical issues such as the morality of treating freed African-American slaves as second-class citizens.

After the Civil War, the South experienced severe economic hardships, resulting in fierce competition between African-Americans and European-Americans for low-paying jobs. Just two years after the end of that war, the Ku Klux Klan was established in northern Alabama. Composed of many low-income and sometimes illiterate European-American males, the Klan often acted as vigilantes who were on "the right side of morality." Their targets were usually Freedmen, Catholics, Jews, and according to some authors, anyone who might be perceived to be an employment threat.

In 1870 the Ku Klux Klan hanged a European-Canadian who came south to teach freed slaves. In another incident, four of the five Klan victims consisted of young African-American men. These and other actions continued throughout the years, and Alabama was also the scene of several key racial confrontations following the critical *Brown v. Board of Education* decision in 1954. These incidents included the Rosa Parks bus incident, which precipitated the Montgomery bus boycott of 1955; the bombing of Martin Luther King Jr.'s home in 1956; the 1961 bombing of a Freedom Riders' bus; the attack on civil rights demonstrators by the Birmingham police in 1963; and the 1965 march from Selma to Montgomery to protest the treatment of African-Americans in the United States.

THE EDUCATIONAL SYSTEM

Alabama does not have a long history of public education comparable to the New England states. Its public school system was initiated in 1854, but not until 1900 was there a concentrated statewide effort to provide an adequate level of support for the education of Alabama's children. The schools were segregated racially until 1963, nine years after the 9 – 0 antisegregation Supreme Court ruling in the 1954 *Brown v. Board of Education* decision. However, Alabama failed to comply with the ruling and in 1958 the voters approved a measure which allowed the use of public funds for operating private schools in order to avoid the racial integration of the state's schools.

Under this arrangement, the Alabama schools remained racially segregated until 1963 when schools with segregated European-American student populations were racially integrated under the supervision of the federal government. The event that terminated segregation in Alabama occurred at the University of Alabama when Governor George Wallace ceased his attempts to bar the entry of James Hood and Vivian Malone, two African-American students who broke the color barrier at the university with assistance from Henry Graham, the Alabama National Guard General, and federal marshals.

The state's K - 12 grade school programs are supervised by Alabama's state superintendent of schools, who is appointed by the State Board of Education. This nine-member body is elected for four-year terms. Alabama state law requires attendance between the ages of seven and sixteen years. Exemptions are allowed for church school students; children who are privately tutored by certified instructors; children with severe physical or mental conditions; children compelled to walk over two miles to attend public school; and any child who is legally and regularly employed. The state allows one minute each day for voluntary prayer or meditation.

MULTICULTURAL EDUCATION EFFORTS

Responses to the 1998 multicultural education questionnaire indicated that there was no planned multicultural education program in the state of Alabama. However, the respondent stated that the state's Board of Education did require each curriculum to reflect multicultural education where appropriate. No one in the State Office of Instruction is responsible for multicultural education programs, and there is no special funding for multicultural education.

The questionnaire respondent stated that Alabama offered leadership to school districts in specific kinds of multicultural education programs, specifically through the language arts and social studies curriculum. The respondent also stated that the predominant microcultures in the state were African-Americans, Hispanics, and Native-Americans. No special coursework and/or other multicultural experiences are required for teacher certification, and there are no special provisions for teaching children in their native language. No information pertaining to racial desegregation strategies was provided in the questionnaire responses.

The respondent was unable to tell whether racist incidents had increased or decreased in the schools during the past five years. The history of Native-Americans is included in the state's social studies curriculum and Alabama's Office of Education evaluates textbooks for racist and sexist content but does not do so for curriculum and library materials. The rest of the questionnaire queries were unanswered.

Located in Montgomery, Alabama, the Southern Poverty Law Center, founded by attorney Morris Dees, has a successful history of representing low-income clients in a wide variety of legal actions, many of them taking the form of hate crimes against poverty clients, many of whom are persons of color. In addition to the Center's monitoring the activities of the Ku Klux Klan and militia units, the Center also publishes free curriculum materials for school use by teachers through their Teaching Tolerance Division.

REFERENCES

Abernathy, Thomas P., *The Formative Years in Alabama, 1815 - 1828*. Tuscaloosa: University of Alabama Press, 1965.

Corkran, David H., *The Cherokee Frontier: Conflict and Survival, 1740 - 1762*. Norman: University of Oklahoma Press, 1962.

Finger, John R., *The Eastern Band of the Cherokee, 1819 - 1900*. Knoxville: University of Tennessee Press, 1984.

Hamilton, Virginia V., *Alabama: A History*. New York: W. W. Norton, 1984.

Harley, Sharon, *The Timetable of African-American History*. New York: Simon & Schuster, 1995.

Hudson, Charles, *The Southeastern Indians*. Knoxville: University of Tennessee Press, 1976.

Jordan, Weymouth T., *Ante-Bellum Alabama: Town and Country*. Tuscaloosa: University of Alabama Press, 1986.

Leiter, Richard, (Ed.), *National Survey of State Laws. First edition*. Detroit: *Gale Research*, 1997.

Markowitz, Harvey, *American Indians, Volume 1*. Pasadena, CA: Salem Press, 1995.

Martin, Joel W., *Sacred Revolt: The Muskogee's Struggle for a New World*. Boston: Beacon Press, 1991.

Morrison, James D., *The Social History of the Choctaw Nation, 1865 - 1907*. Durant, OK: Creative Informatics, 1987.

Takaki, Ronald, *A Different Mirror: A History of Multicultural America.* Boston: Little, Brown, 1993.

Walthall, John A., *Prehistoric Indians of the Southeast.* University of Alabama: University of Alabama Press, 1980.

ALASKA

STATE HISTORY

The largest and northernmost of the fifty states, Alaska is famous for its great geological spectacles. It is unique in its vastness (more than twice the size of Texas), which makes it highly dependent on the airplane for transportation. It is also unique among the other forty-nine states in terms of population density with the fewest people per square mile. Much of the recent growth occurred after 1970 in the Anchorage area. The first known European to explore the area was Vitus Bering, a Danish sea captain in the Russian navy.

Alaska was purchased from Russia in 1867, becoming a United States territory. The Russians who first came to Alaska were entrepreneurs who were interested in the fur trade. Eventually, the private traders had been replaced by the Russian-American company, a government-sponsored monopoly. However, by the middle of the nineteeth century, this organization encountered economic difficulties and was supported primarily by subsidies from the government. Russian leaders eventually decided that economically, control of the Alaskan area was not worth the effort, and so they sold it to the United States.

It was not until 1906 that Congress passed a measure which allowed Alaska to have one voteless representative to the United States Congress. The first attempt at acquiring statehood occurred in 1916. However, statehood was finally accomplished on January 3, 1959.

The residents of the new state included European-Americans and several groups of Native-Alaskans: Inuit (Eskimos) in the Arctic; Haidas, dwelling on Queen Charlotte Islands and the southern portion of Prince of Wales Island; Aleuts in the Aleutians and the Alaskan peninsula; Tlingits and Tsimshians in southeastern Alaska; and Athapascans, who speak a number of different dialects, residing in the interior.

Native Alaskans can trace their heritage back some 15,000 years, when they migrated to the Northwest over the Bering Sea Land Bridge, which archaeologists believe was composed of glacial ice sheets up to 1,000 miles wide. According to many accounts by archaeologists and anthropologists, these early migrants were hunting game, and their travels took them south all the way to Tierra del Fuego on the tip of South America. However, approximately 10,000 years ago, the ice receded and Siberia and Alaska became separated by about 56 miles of stormy Arctic waters. In recent years this Bering Sea Land Bridge theory has been at least partially verified through scientific studies of similarities between the blood types of Asians and Native-Americans.

The Tlingit tribe is the largest group of Native Alaskans. It is believed that they occupied their present place of residence in southeastern Alaska some 5,000 to 6,000 years ago. In this Sitka area and other northwestern locales, it is estimated that the population of the Tlingit tribe is close to 19,000. They are primarily a coastal people and are part of the Na-Dene language groups. The first known Europeans to make contact with the Tlingit were the Russians in 1741.

Shamanism is an important part of the Tlinglit culture. There is a sort of mythology connected with the Tlinglit ethos, and animal spirits are deemed to be important in the maintenance of life. The Shaman protects the spirits of animals and human beings alike. Nonideological in nature, the religion is primarily concerned with the maintenance of order, religion, and life.

The Alaskan Inuit live in centralized villages and towns which are supported with government offices, schools, retail stores, and medical facilities. The people are heavily involved in fishing and hunting, through the use of boats, snowmobiles, and state of the art hunting weapons. The Inuit religion involves the use of shamans and illnesses and diseases were thought to have been caused through violations of cultural taboos. Census figures from 1990 revealed a population of more than 44,000 Inuit.

The Haida Alaskans spoke a language which anthropologists believed to be related to that of the Athapaskan. According to some experts, they had driven out some of the Tlinglit tribes approximately two centuries before the arrival of the Europeans. They were well adapted to coastal life and used nets, fish traps, and dip nets for fishing. They also relied on harpoons with detachable shafts which were connected by a line. They also angled for cod and halibut.

It is believed that the Aleut migrated to Alaska about 6,000 years before the birth of Christ. Members of the Eskimo-Aleut language group, the Aleut consisted of two main groups, the Atka and Unalaska. According to 1990 census reports, the Aleuts had about 10,000 tribal members. After their migration to Alaska, they inhabited the Aleutian Islands. Their name was created by the Russians from a Russian word meaning "barren rock."

The Aleuts have always relied on the hunting of sea animals for their livelihood. However, in 1911, the United States Department of the Interior limited the hunting of sea lions, since they were becoming an endangered species. The sea lion has been one of the primary sources of food for Aleuts.

The Aleut religion centered around the worship of Agudar, believed to be the creator of the universe. Only adult males were allowed to participate in the sacred religious ceremonies. While death resulted in cremation for commoners and slaves, important leaders and children were mummified. Family members then laid the body in a stream, stuffed it with grass, oiled it, wrapped it in furs and then placed it in a grave.

During the 1700s, the Aleuts came into contact with the Russians. This interaction created dire consequences for this group of native Alaskans. Between 1750 and 1780, nearly 90 percent of the Aleuts died from smallpox, malnutrition, various sorts of forced labor by the Russians, and suicide. When the United States purchased Russia in 1867, the Aleut population had dwindled to about 3,000.

The 1990 census revealed a population of about 2,400 members of the Tsimshian tribe, located in southeastern Alaska. Other tribal members reside in northwestern British Columbia (Canada). Copper was considered to be a symbol of great wealth among the Tsimshian, and the tribe became famous for its artistic prowess, particularly in the creation of intricate totem poles.

Toward the end of the eighteenth century, the Tsimshian people indulged in extensive trade negotiations with Americans and Canadians. Contact between the tribe and the outside world increased because of the gold rush of 1867. Finally, in 1881 the Canadian government assumed responsibility for the people. The Tsimshian people have been successful in resisting extensive government controls.

Alaskan Athapaskan inhabit the interior of the sub-Arctic and Arctic regions. Anthropologists feel that there are similarities between the Athapaskan language and the native tongues used in Siberia. The Athapaskans use about twelve different dialects in their language systems. Linguists feel that the Athapaskan languages have a great deal of similarities with the languages used by the Apaches, Navajos, and other southwestern United States tribes.

During the latter portion of the eighteenth century, large numbers of Aleuts were killed by the Russians. However, during the early part of the nineteeth century many Aleuts joined the Russian Orthodox Church and learned the Russian language. At the end of the twentieth century there is still a fairly substantial number of Aleuts who can speak English, Aleut, and Russian.

The acquisition of Alaska by the United States in 1867 precipitated an influx of American speculators to Alaska, particularly in Sitka. However, by 1880 there were fewer Americans in the area then their Russian predecessors. Alaska became a "district" in 1884 when the Organic Act made Alaska a judicial district. This prohibited Alaska from forming a legislature, and the citizens were not subject to American taxation, since they had no right to vote in the United States. In 1912 Alaska finally became a territory. By 1940, only about half of the Alaskan population consisted of non-native Alaskans. Statehood occurred in 1958, during the second term of President Dwight D. Eisenhower.

THE EDUCATIONAL SYSTEM

Alaska's educational system during its years as a territory and before was rather sporadic. While the Russians had established schools in the 1820s, it was not until 1887 that a school for girls was opened in Wrangell. This creation got the attention of the Presbyterian Church and Sheldon Jackson, a missionary leader. Jackson was successful in establishing a system of schools for native Alaskans in southeastern and western Alaska. He also encouraged the creation of missions throughout the state. With statehood, the new Alaskan government established a system of public schools. At the present time, most of the financial support comes from the state rather than the federal government.

During the 1970s the state attempted to upgrade its rural education programs. Many parents were anxious for their children to stay home during high school and, conse-quently, more small schools were developed in the rural or "bush" areas. Many of the teachers in such areas were brought from the lower forty-eight states since Alaskan teachers were often reluctant to move from the urban to rural areas. Because of the high cost of living and the remote nature of Alaska's rural areas, there is a high turnover among rural teachers. However, the state is usually able to employ teachers in the "bush" areas because of the high salaries provided.

While the compulsory attendance age in Alaska is seven to sixteen, there are a number of other options for parents and their school-age children. Comparable education can be provided through private school or tutoring. Children can also attend schools operated by the federal government. State laws allow students to be excused from school attendance if they have physical or mental conditions which makes school attendance impractical; if they are temporarily injured or are ill; if they reside more than two miles from a public transportation route; if they are enrolled in an approved correspondence course, or if they are well served by another type of approved educational experience.

The state of Alaska has no statutory provisions relating to the use of corporal punishment or prayer in the schools. Custodial and noncustodial parents are allowed access to the school records of children. The median income per Alaskan household was $47,954, the highest in the nation. Only 7.1 percent of the population found itself below the poverty level in 1995, the lowest percentage of the fifty states. Alaska also enjoyed the highest educational expenditures (on a per capita level) for both elementary and secondary students. Alaska leads the nation with a per capita expenditure of $1,818 per student for its elementary and secondary education program. This amount is nearly twice that for the entire nation. Seven percent of Alaskan citizens are below the poverty line, compared to the national rate of nearly 14 percent.

MULTICULTURAL EDUCATION EFFORTS

Unfortunately, the state of Alaska failed to respond to numerous requests to supply the authors information pertaining to their multicultural education efforts in the schools. Consequently, there is no information pertaining to the current status of such efforts. However, Alaska did participate in the last survey of multicultural education conducted by the authors in 1991. At that time the state reported that they had certification requirements in racism/sexism and/or multicultural education. Alaska also responded that the basic themes of valuing pluralism were included in the state's curriculum and instruction programs. Finally, Alaska has provided basic instruction in the student's native language with an accompanying English as a Second Language (ESL) component.

The state has specific multicultural education requirements for certification as a teacher or school administrator. Candidates must complete three semester hours in Alaska studies and three semester hours in multicultural education or crosscultural communications. These are also required for Alaska's Type C Special Services Certificate.

REFERENCES

Alaska Department of Education, *Procedures and Requirements—Teacher Certification.* Juneau: Alaska Department of Education, 1998.

Burch, Ernest S. and Forman, Werner, *The Eskimos.* Norman: University of Oklahoma Press, 1988.

Chance, Norman A., *The Inupiat and Arctic Alaska.* Fort Worth: Holt, Rinehart and Winston, 1990.

Leiter, Richard A., (ed.), *National Survey of State Laws*. First edition. Detroit: Gale Research, 1997.

Naske, Claus M. and Slotnick, Herman E., *Alaska: A History of the 49th State*. Second Edition. Norman, OK: University of Oklahoma Press, 1987.

Pelton, Mary Helan and DiGennaro, Jacqueline, *Images of a People: Tlingit Myths and Legends*. Englewood, CO: Libraries Unlimited, 1992.

Ray, Dorothy Jean, *The Eskimos of Bering Strait, 1650 - 1898*. Seattle: University of Washington Press, 1975.

Salsbury, Robert and Mitchell, Bruce, *Multicultural Education in American Schools*. Cheney, WA: Eastern Washington University (Monograph), 1991.

United States Department of Education, *Digest of Educational Statistics*. Washington D.C.: United States Department of Education, 1997.

ARIZONA

STATE HISTORY

As a result of the 1848 Treaty of Guadalupe Hidalgo which ended the U.S. war against Mexico, the United States received the lands which constitute the present boundaries of Arizona. Later, in 1853, the territories from the Gila River to the present boundaries were acquired in the Gadsen Purchase. Arizona remained a territory until it became the forty-eighth state in 1912. However, Arizona's history has been traced back to 9,500 BC when Paleo Native-Americans inhabited the region and hunted large Pleistocene animals with spears.

Archaeologists have verified this group as being the first known humans in the Americas. These Paleo Native-Americans are believed to have crossed the land bridge from Asia, eventually ending up in present-day Arizona.

Residing in central and southern Arizona, the Hohokam Native-Americans lived from 600-1450 and are believed to be the ancestors of the present-day Pima and Tohono O'odham (Papago) tribes. Some archaeologists believe that the Hohokam may have been derived from Mesoamerica because of their ball courts and exotic trade goods. Other Hohokam contributions include the development of a complex system of irrigation canals and the farming of maize, squash and beans, which were their primary staples. By the time the Spanish arrived, the Hohokam culture had disappeared for unsubstantiated but hotly debated reasons.

One of the largest immigration periods occurred approximately 6,000 years ago when the Athapascan-speaking Navajos and Apaches started migrating southward from the northern plains. By about 1100 AD they had settled in present-day Arizona and eventually split into the two present groups (Apache and Navajo).

Another of the most famous early cultures of Arizona, located in the northern portions of the state near "Four Corners," is the Anasazi group. They are thought to have migrated to the area from 300 BC to about 1610, when they abandoned many of their dwelling sites. During the mid-sixteenth century, Francisco Vásquez de Coronado reported on encountering ten Anasazi provinces in which six different languages were spoken. Coronado and his followers were searching for the famous seven cities of gold. The Zuni, Hopi, and Navajo tribes are thought to have descended from the Anasazi culture.

A Franciscan priest, Marcos de Niza and Coronado were among the first Europeans to contact the Native-Americans who resided in Arizona. Because of the European incursions, the cultures of the original residents were forever changed.

For approximately 300 years, the Spaniards attempted to colonize the lands of Arizona. While the lure of gold motivated many of the Spanish adventurers, they also brought horses, sheep, cattle and new farming techniques to the native Arizonans. The first large city to emerge was Tucson, which was established as a Presidio in 1776.

Historically, the Native-American groups in Arizona played key roles in the state's development. The Navajo reservation is the largest in the United States, consisting of approximately 15,000,000 acres and a population of nearly 200,000 people.   The boundaries actually include a small portion of northwestern New Mexico and southeastern Utah.

The involvement of Navajo men in World War II changed Navajo life forever.   Among the tribe's major contributions to the war efforts was the creation of a code which was never broken by the Japanese during the duration of the conflict.   The Navajo language was unique and the Navajo "code talkers" created a language which greatly facilitated the Pacific war efforts. Unfortunately, the Navajo tribe has suffered from extreme poverty and the vastness of the area has sometimes created great difficulties for the people in the acquisition of appropriate food, clothing, shelter, and medical attention.

Like the Navajo, the Apache have become the other most well-known Arizona tribe. They also belong to the Athapascan language group and became feared by the Spaniards who were afraid of their guerrilla warfare tactics.   The Apache were organized into a system of clans and bands which raided the Spaniards for their supplies.   After the Mexicans obtained their freedom from Spain the Apache raids continued in even greater numbers, since the new Mexican government had difficulty in gathering forces together to thwart the raiding groups.   Thus, when northern Mexico became part of the United States in 1848, the Apache had achieved a solid reputation for being fearsome raiders.

Probably the two most famous Apache chiefs were Cochise and Geronimo. Cochise, who negotiated a pact with the United States government in 1859, attempted to help European-American settlers proceed through southern Arizona to California safely.   At this time he was the principal leader of the entire Chiricahua tribe.   However, the Apache raids continued until Cochise conceded that many of the Apache traditions should end because of the increasing number of European-American settlers. In 1872 a treaty was signed with General Oliver Otis Howard.

Geronimo is known for his fearlessness as a warrior and leader of one of the most successful encounters against the encroaching European-Americans. Also a member of the Chiricahua band of Apaches, he finally surrendered to General Miles in 1882. However, in 1885 he and a small band headed south, conducting a series of raids.   After his subsequent capture, he was sent to Florida. Eventually he left that state and was moved to Fort Sill, Oklahoma. According to some accounts, he had been promised a return to his native lands in southern Arizona, but he finally died in Oklahoma in 1909 after he came down with pneumonia.

Among the motivating factors which lured the European-Americans to Arizona during the latter part of the nineteenth century was the discovery of gold along the Gila River and silver, which was discovered later in 1877 near Tombstone. However, the silver discovery was short-lived, ending in 1886 with the flooding of many of the mines. Ironically, it was copper which proved to be the most valuable mineral. The richest copper lode was discovered in Bisbee in 1877.

After the turn of the century, Arizonans turned to the issue of statehood during their territorial history. During this era, the cattle and mining industries became the primary resources of the state's economy. In 1904 a bill was passed in the U.S. House of Representatives allowing Arizona and New Mexico to enter the Union as one large state. However, Arizona voted against the measure and statehood was not achieved until 1912 when the Arizona Statehood Bill was signed by President Howard Taft on February 14 (Valentine's Day), after his approval of the new state's constitution. One of the largest celebrations occurred in Bisbee when a dynamite charge blew off a substantial portion of one of the state's mountains.

Besides gaining notoriety as the youngest state at the time, Arizona also became the first state to vote in favor of women's suffrage when the measure was approved in 1914, granting Arizona women the right to vote. The first presidential election in which women were franchised was the successful campaign of President Warren G. Harding.

Arizona's history has had a rich multicultural flavor. The Native-American/Latino/European-American history has had a profound influence on the character of the state. That, coupled with the early right to vote for women and the appointment of the first female member of the United States Supreme Court, has caused Arizona to be viewed as a pioneer in certain multicultural areas.

Born in 1916 in Cananea, Sonora Mexico, Raul Castro graduated from the University of Arizona in 1949. He went on to practice law and became a judge. He was the Ambassador to El Salvador for four years and the Ambassador to Bolivia for one year. In 1974 he became the first Mexican-American to hold an executive office in Arizona when he was elected governor. In addition, he became the United States Ambassador to Argentina.

Henry Clay Day, started the Lazy B ranch in 1880. His granddaughter, Sandra Day, graduated from Stanford Law School in 1952. After marrying lawyer John O'Conner, she became involved in politics, and served in the state senate. After becoming a superior court judge, she was appointed to the State Court of Appeals. A conservative Republican, O'Connor became the first female member of the United States Supreme Court as a result of an appointment by president Ronald Reagan.

THE EDUCATIONAL SYSTEM

Prior to 1863, only parochial school education was available to children in Arizona. Little attention was given to the concept of public education during the state's territorial years until Governor Safford's administration from 1869 to 1877. At this time, efforts were taken to begin a system of public education.

During the 1989 - 1990 school year the average teacher's salary was $29,402, which was slightly below the national average of $32,100. While Native-American children living on the reservations often attend reservation schools or government schools in Tucson and Phoenix, many are also enrolled in the public school systems.

The compulsory attendance ages for Arizona children are from six to sixteen. However, in lieu of attending public or private school, Arizona children can receive home instruction and take a standardized achievement test. A second option is the state's allowance for school-age children who have physical or mental conditions which make school attendance impractical. Children are also excused if they are in the custody of the court or a law enforcement officer. Still another legal exclusion for school-age children is if the child lives more than two miles away from a transportation source. Finally, children can be excused from school attendance if they are enrolled in approved correspondence courses or are well served by other types of approved educational experiences.

Corporal punishment for Arizona school children is allowed as long as it is administered by adhering to prescribed state guidelines. While the state does not allow organized prayer, per se, children are entitled to participate in one minute of silence for meditation.

Arizona teachers are required to pass a basic skills test in order to become certified as teachers. Slightly over 50 percent of Arizona's teachers have a bachelor of arts degree, while about 43 percent hold a master's. Seventy-two percent of the state's teachers have taught between three and twenty years.

Arizona has one of the highest percentages of children between the ages of five and seventeen who are below the poverty level. Twenty-four percent of the state's children fall into that category compared to nineteen percent nationally. The per-capita education expenditures are slightly below the national average.

MULTICULTURAL EDUCATION EFFORTS

Responses to the authors' 1998 multicultural education survey instrument reported that Arizona has no planned multicultural education program and nobody is in charge of such an effort. Moreover, there is no special funding for such ventures, nor is the state offering leadership to school districts in the development of multicultural education programs.

The predominant minority microcultures in the state were reported to be nineteen Native-American tribes and the Mexican-American population. It was also stipulated that Arizona had no special certification requirements in multicultural education and racist incidents had increased during the years 1994-1999.

The respondents indicated that the state stressed the notion of cultural pluralism, as opposed to the assimilationist concept, in Arizona's curriculum and instruction programs and bilingual education programs were utilized when appropriate. Moreover, elementary foreign language is a course requirement.

School districts use federal funding for school desegregation by implementing magnet schools in order to maintain a system of desegregated schools. While the history of Native-Americans is not specifically included in Arizona's regular curriculum, some school districts include activities and strategies which serve to acquaint students with Native-American history in Arizona.

Finally, the respondents felt that the biggest problems facing multicultural education programs in the state were the lack of funding and the curriculum. The most needed improvements for Arizona's multicultural education efforts would be the inclusion of multicultural education into the regular curriculum, improved teacher preparation, and better funding, specifically for multicultural materials.

REFERENCES

Brody, J. J., *The Anasazi: Ancient People of the American Southwest.* New York: Rizzoli International, 1990.

Cordell, Linda S., *Prehistory of the Southwest.* Orlando: Academic Press, 1984.

Dutton, Bertha P., *American Indians of the Southwest.* Rev. ed., Albuquerque: University of New Mexico Press, 1990.

Haury, Emil, *The Hohokam.* Tucson: University of Arizona Press, 1976.

Kidder, Alfred. *An Introduction to the Study of Southwestern Archaeology.* New Haven: Yale University Press, 1962.

Leiter, Richard A., (ed.), *National Survey of State Laws.* First edition. Detroit: Gale Research, 1997.

Shadegg, Stephen C., *Arizona Politics.* Tempe: Arizona State University Press, 1986.

Trimble, Marshall, *Arizona: A Cavalcade of History.* Tucson: Treasure Chest Publications, 1989.

United States Department of Education, *Digest of Educational Statistics.* Washington D.C.: United States Department of Education, 1997.

Wagoner, Jay, *Arizona's Heritage.* Salt Lake City: Peregrine Smith, 1977.

ARKANSAS

STATE HISTORY

It is believed that the earliest residents of Arkansas were nomadic hunters who traveled throughout the state boundaries as early as 10,000 BC. Bluff dwellers are thought to have occupied bluff shelters and caves along northwestern Arkansas stream beds. Hunters and gatherers, they wove clothing and baskets from grass. They were primarily hunters and fishermen.

The pre-Columbian mound builders resided in southern Arkansas forests and built earthen mounds for their dead. They also grew vegetables, particularly corn, and made fine pottery, artistic ornaments, and created arrowheads, knives, and hoes, which were found around the Hot Springs areas. When the first European-Americans arrived in the area, they encountered three different tribes of Native-Americans: the Quapaw, Osage, and Caddo.

The primary location of the Quapaw was the mouth of the Arkansas River, close to the point at which it flows into the Mississippi. They originally migrated from the Ohio Valley. While the history of the tribe has not been clearly understood, they have been referred to as the "Downstream People. They belong to the Siouan language group.

After selling their land to the United States government for $4,000 and some annuities, they moved to the Caddo reservation in Louisiana. Their numbers were greatly diminished by smallpox. By 1833 they were provided land in northwest Oklahoma (Indian Territory at the time) but they were scattered during the Civil War. However, during the late 1800s, some of the surviving tribal members attempted to reestablish their culture on the Indian Territory reservation. Plagued with poverty and a population low of just 236 in 1895, the Quapaw fortunes took a turn for the better when zinc and nickel were discovered on their land in the 1920s. Eventually the Quapaw population increased to 1,538, as reported in the U. S. census. However, it is estimated that only about 20 percent of the tribal members are more than 25 percent Quapaw.

Members of the Arkansas Osage tribe were one of three political groups of Osage Native-Americans. The other two groups were the Great Osage and Little Osage. In 1808 the Osage ceded northern Arkansas and most of Missouri to the United States government. Later, in 1825, the Osage had ceded all of their lands to the United States and were provided a reservation in Indian Territory. During the Civil War Osage men fought on both the Northern and Southern sides.

At the end of the Civil War, the Osage tribe suffered extremely hard times due to minimal medical aid and a lack of food and clothing. They had been given some of the worst land in Indian Territory and the buffalo were gone. However, oil and gas deposits were discovered on their land and the financial hardships were somewhat relieved.

An eight-member tribal council makes the decisions affecting the lives of the Osage. Because of their relative wealth, many Osage have stepped forward to become voting citizens. Despite the comparative wealth of the tribe, the Osage have made a strong attempt to maintain their cultural values. They belong to the Siouan language group and 1990 U. S. Census figures revealed an Osage population of 9,527.

The Caddo of southwest Arkansas were members of the Caddoan language group. Known as excellent hunters, they would often venture to the plains in search of buffalo. The Caddo also became well-known for their dancing prowess. The Turkey Dance, conducted in the afternoon, involves male drummers who call the dancers through a number of songs. The women dance in a circle, moving clockwise on the balls of their feet in harmony with the earth.

The Drum Dance describes the origins of the Caddo people as they came from the world of darkness and took their place in the world of light. The dance expresses the Caddo people's belief in the significance of the sun. It also honors Caddo heroes, such as the Medicine Screech Owl, which is believed to have introduced the bow and arrow into Caddo society.

The first Europeans to enter the lands of present-day Arkansas were members of Hernando De Soto's party in 1541. Over one hundred years later, Jacques Marquette and Louise Joliet reached the mouth of the Arkansas River before turning back, heeding the advice of friendly Native-Americans. Nine years later in 1682, Rene Robert Cavelier left Canada with a party of fifty-four. They went through the area on their way to the Gulf, claiming the Mississippi River Valley for France.

The first permanent settlement in Arkansas was Arkansas Post, a French settlement, located near the mouth of the Arkansas River in 1682. By 1720, a Scottish financier named John Law established a colony of German farmers. At the time of the 1803 Louisiana Purchase, Arkansas had a population of some 1,000 European-Americans. After becoming a section of the United States at that time, it was later part of the District of Louisiana, the Louisiana Territory, and the Missouri Territory. It became separated from the Missouri Territory in 1819 and became the Arkansas Territory, with Arkansas Post serving as the capitol. In 1821 the capitol was moved to Little Rock.

When Arkansas was admitted to the Union as a slave state in 1836, the population growth picked up its pace. Joining the Native-American groups were large numbers of European-Americans and African-American slaves, who were used in the cotton fields of eastern and southern Arkansas, along with the river bottom lands of the northwest. By 1850, 47,100 African-American slaves resided in Arkansas. Following the Civil War, the state rewrote its constitution and was readmitted to the Union in 1868.

One of Arkansas's earliest schools was created for Cherokee Indian students in 1820 by a Yale College missionary. Albert Pike, a Harvard University graduate, became one of the first teachers of European-American students. Thus, Arkansas historically had a segregated school system. However, in the early days of statehood, education was a local option rather than a state requirement. By 1860 the state had but twenty-five elementary and secondary schools. These schools were segregated for European-American students and it wasn't until 1864 that the Freedman's Bureau opened schools for African-Americans. While the state took over the operation of these schools in 1868, they were badly underfunded and woefully inadequate compared to the schools for European-

American students. At this time the state finally founded the state's first tax-supported school system.

Arkansas' new 1874 Constitution required the maintenance of the public school system, but the right-leaning legislature did not provide an adequate level of funding, and the schools were faced with difficult times. In the early 1900s, a demand for better schools created a better level of funding, which resulted in improved education. In 1909 a compulsory attendance law was enacted and free textbooks were provided in 1937.

However, throughout its history, Arkansas maintained its segregated school system and the situation came to a head with the landmark *Brown v. Board of Education* Supreme Court decision in 1954, which declared racially segregated schools to be unequal and, therefore, unconstitutional. In 1957 it required over 1,000 members of the 101st Airborne Unit to enforce the integration of Little Rock High School. President Dwight Eisenhower ordered the paratroopers in when Arkansas Governor Orville Faubus defied the United States Justice Department, attempting to prevent school integration.

THE EDUCATIONAL SYSTEM

Arkansas teachers are required to pass the National Teachers Examination in order to become certified classroom practitioners. Of the state's elementary and secondary instructors, 32.5 percent hold a master's degree, compared with 42 percent at the national level. Per capita expenditures for elementary/secondary education are $707.23, which ranks 48th in the nation.

Children in Arkansas are required to attend school between the ages of five and seventeen unless they are home schooled. Home-school teachers must have at least a high school diploma. However, at the age of eight, home-schooled students are required to take a standardized achievement test. If they do not score satisfactorily, they must be enrolled in a public, private, or parochial school. Children are allowed one minute of silent meditation and reflection each day in school. Corporal punishment is still allowed in Arkansas schools as long as it is "for good cause" and is specifically authorized.

While Arkansas has lagged behind other states in the funding of its schools, it must be remembered that it is one of the poorer states economically, and consequently, generating appropriate funds for schools has been difficult. Nineteen percent of all Arkansas persons were in poverty status during 1994 - 1995. This compared with a national percentage of thirteen. However, when examining the percentage of Arkansas children (ages five through seventeen) who found themselves below the poverty level, the figure climbed to 21.7 percent, compared to the national average of 19 percent. As high as these percentages are, when examining the percentage of children under the age of five who are below the poverty level, 28.5 percent of Arkansas children found themselves in that predicament in 1995.

MULTICULTURAL EDUCATION EFFORTS

While the Arkansas respondents reported that no planned multicultural education program existed in the state, some of the public schools have multicultural education as part of their curriculum. There is a person who is responsible for multicultural education programs. Such efforts are carried out by the Arkansas Equity Assistance Office/State Department of Education. However, no state funding is directly earmarked for multicultural education.

Arkansas does provide leadership from its State Department of Education. The Equity Assistance Center has the responsibility for generating and coordinating the development of multicultural sensitivity in Arkansas' public schools. The respondents felt that it would take considerable time to accomplish this because of the sensitive issues that accompany the diverse student population, which consists of African-Americans, Asian-Americans, Native-Americans, Hispanics, and European-Americans.

The state does not have any special coursework and/or other multicultural experiences for teacher certification, and there are no special programs designed to teach children in their native language when necessary.

The respondent stated that the Equity Assistance Center's role was to promote sensitivity to cultural differences and ensure that the dominant culture's willingness to diversify or understand cultural differences was paramount to social, academic, and economic accessibility. The respondent also felt that children needed to have access to a quality education in order to maximize their abilities and talents.

All public schools in Arkansas are required to adhere to the stipulations set forth in the Civil Rights Act of 1964, Executive Order 11246, Title IX of 172, Title VI, ADA (504) and any subsequent acts relative to the Desegregation Plan. Several schools are being monitored on a regular basis for assurance of compliance with the state desegregation requirements. All public schools are required to submit a Compliance Report annually documenting the school's status of compliance.

Arkansas' Office of Education evaluates curriculum materials, library materials, and textbooks for racist and sexist content. Also, the state has attempted to include viable information about Native-American history in curriculum materials.

In responding to the question pertaining to an increase or decrease of racist incidents in the state's schools, the respondent said the following: "This question can be answered with both words (increased and decreased). Arkansas has seen some very positive changes since the beginning of the integration era. African-Americans, the initiators and the culture which stood to gain the most from systematic changes, other migrating cultures and Native-Americans have experienced some major social, academic, economic, and political changes that are indicative to increased racism. However, there is a resurgence of racism that takes on different sets of values, supported by the same political teams that declared racist incidents to be unconstitutional in the 1960s."

In the opinion of the respondent, the biggest problem facing multicultural education programs in Arkansas were the dominant culture's unwillingness to accept human differences, the exploitation of human resources for personal gain, and the failure to explore the uniqueness of population diversity and change. The biggest improvement would be the development of a "fair market" multicultural program implemented at the school level.

REFERENCES

Ashmore, Harry S., *Arkansas: A History.* New York: Norton, 1984.

Berry, Fred, and Novak, John, *The History of Arkansas.* New York: Rose, 1987.

Leiter, Richard A. (ed.), *National Survey of State Laws.* First Edition. Detroit: Gale Research, 1997.

Markowitz, Harvey (ed.), *American Indians* Volumes I, II, and III. Pasadena, CA: Salem Press, 1995.

Rollings, Willard H., *The Osage: An Ethnohistorical Study of the Hegemony on the Prairie-Plains.* Columbia: University of Missouri Press, 1991.

Tucker, David M., *Arkansas: A People and Their Reputation.* Memphis: Memphis State University Press, 1985.

United States Department of Education, *Digest of Educational Statistics.* Washington D.C.: United States Department of Education, 1997.

Williams, C. Fred, *A Documentary History of Arkansas.* Little Rock: University of Arkansas Press, 1984.

Williams, Juan, *Eyes on the Prize: America's Civil Rights Years, 1954 - 1965.* New York: Viking, 1987.

Wilson, Terry P., *The Osage.* New York: Chelsea House, 1988.

Wood, James M., *Rebellion and Realignment.* Little Rock: University of Arkansas Press, 1987.

CALIFORNIA

STATE HISTORY

California has forty identified Native-American culture areas located throughout this third largest state in the Union. At the time the Spanish/Mexican settlement began in the 1700s, the Native-American population was estimated at about 300,000 residents. By the beginning of the mid-nineteeth century gold rush, the population of Native-Americans was estimated at just 150,000. Tragically, the gold rush resulted in disease, starvation, homicide, and a decline in the Native-American birth rate, reducing the tribal population to just 30,000.

The Chumash tribe was one of the largest Native-American groups at the time of the Latino/European incursions. Particularly noteworthy was their extensive rock art and their knowledge of boat building. Residing along the coastal areas and on islands near the coast of the Ventura/Santa Barbara/San Louis Obispo areas, they were quite adept at using their canoes to reach the mainland for hunting. They were viewed as peaceful, and many of them became involved in the mission life. However, in May, 1941, Juan Justo, the last identified full-blooded Chumash, died in Santa Barbara. By 1993, just 195 persons of Chumash ancestry resided on the Santa Ynez reservation, one of the numerous small Native-American reservations in the state.

The northern Paiutes inhabited the eastern portion of Central California. To sustain a livelihood, they hunted, fished, and gathered piñon nuts. Sometimes they were derogatorily referred to as the "digger Indians" by European-American settlers. Members of the Uto-Aztecan language group, they were provided a reservation in northern Nevada, but many Paiutes have not chosen to reside there.

One of the many smaller groups of Native-Americans is the Shasta tribe in northern California. Members of the Shastan language group, this group of Native-Americans resided near the base of Mount Shasta, in northern California, and in southern Oregon's Rogue River valley. Noted for the use of obsidian in the creation of knives, the Shasta hunted deer and used the acorn as their staple diet. The Shasta practiced a form of shamanism to drive away the evil spirits. The tribe presently numbers about 584.

When Europeans discovered California, the growth of California increased dramatically. In 1540 Antonio de Mendoza, the first viceroy of Mexico (New Spain), sponsored an exploration which extended into the present-day San Diego area. His exploits were also responsible for the incursions of Francisco Vásquez de Coronado into California and other southwestern states.   Other Spanish explorations included the expedition of Vásquez de Coronado into the southwestern United States. Other adventurers and/or explorers included Juan Rodriguez Cabrillo who sailed into San Diego in 1542. Later, anchoring in the Santa Barbara/Goleta area, Cabrillo's log estimated the population of Native-Americans on Mescalatan Island off the Goleta coast to be about 10,000. He also noticed that the campfires of the Native-Americans rose for a short distance and then flattened out. It is believed that this occurred because of the temperature inversion conditions which have caused much of the smog in Southern California.

In spite of these explorations, California was not colonized until 1769 due to the exploits of Russian and British adventurers. José de Gálvez and Gaspar de Portolá were key figures in the colonization efforts in New Spain. Portolá and a contingent of sixty-four priests, muleteers, soldiers, and Native-Americans marched northward to Monterey Bay in 1769. Shortly after, Portolá was successful in establishing a settlement in Monterey Bay. In 1776, Juan Bautista de Anza, a Spanish frontier captain, led another expedition to Monterey and north to Yerba Buena (San Francisco) and established another settlement site there.

The Spaniards also relied on the establishment of Presidios (military garrisons) at San Diego, Santa Barbara, Monterey, and San Francisco. Pueblos, which were communities designed for civilian populations, were established at Los Angeles, San Jose, and Santa Cruz. Moreover, Franciscan father Junípero Serra founded twenty-one missions which were located from San Diego to Sonoma, between 1769 and 1823. They were located approximately one day's journey from each other. The purpose of the missions was to Christianize the Native-Americans. However, they also served as cultural and agricultural centers.

Perhaps no other state has surpassed the diverse multicultural history of California. Enriched by the participation of Latino groups, California also experienced a plethora of pluralistic involvement by many other microcultures. The California gold rush of 1849 created a need for mining laborers. However, California imposed a tax of $20 monthly, referred to as a "Mexican Miners Tax."

In addition to the Latino and European-American miners, were the Chinese miners who left their country by the hundreds of thousands to come to California and other parts of the western United States to work the mines. By 1870, 63,000 Chinese laborers resided in the United States, nearly 80 percent of them in California. Many Chinese-American miners were independent miners, while some of them formed small companies.

However, in addition to the mines, another western venture also attracted many Chinese laborers. The construction of the Central Pacific Railroad created an enormous need for cheap labor. Charlie Crocker, one of the principle figures in the Central Pacific venture (along with Leland Stanford, Colis Huntington, and Mark Hopkins), recruited Chinese laborers to work on the railroad. Crocker, the company superintendent, declared that there was "no danger of strikes among them. We are training them to do all kinds of labor: blasting, driving horses, handling rock, as well as pick and shovel." After the rail line was completed, many Chinese-American railroad workers went to Canada to work on their rail lines and to other parts of the United States. Many Chinese-American railroad workers settled in San Francisco and Los Angeles.

By 1852, 25,000 Chinese people resided in the state. The Chinese-Americans were subjected to severe discrimination, since they were involved in labor markets which were sometimes sought after by European-American laborers. A tax imposed on Chinese laborers, sometimes referred to as the "coolie bill," was declared unconstitutional by the California Supreme Court.

By and large the Chinese-American people felt that it was in their best interests not to complain about unfair practices which were imposed on them.

During World War II, California experienced a major African-American migration from the southern states. The African-American population in Los Angeles doubled from 75,000 to 135,000 and a similar pattern existed in the Bay Area, particularly in Oakland. In Los Angeles, the south-central portion of the city became an ethnic enclave for African-American people. The south central area known as Watts, became embroiled in one of the country's worst riots as the result of Los Angeles policemen arresting an African-American motorist in 1965.

As African-American persons in south central Los Angeles became more affluent, many of them moved to other Southern California locations and gradually, low-income Latino families took their place. The result was that the city began to see a dramatic increase in its poverty culture. At the same time, test scores declined, giving some people the impression that the public school system was losing its effectiveness. This phenomenon actually occurred in many parts of the state and consequently the test scores of the entire state commenced dropping because of the burgeoning number of poverty children.

For Japanese-Americans, times were definitely not good during World War II. Because of Executive Order 9066, even loyal Japanese-American citizens in California were forced to move to ten relocation centers, which were situated away from the Pacific Coast and as far east as Jerome and Rohwer, Arkansas. Their land and property were confiscated and, in some cases, never returned.

After the end of the Vietnam conflict, other groups of immigrants from southeast Asia commenced arriving in California, particularly in the Los Angeles and San Francisco areas. One of these groups was the Hmong from the Laotian highlands. During the war the Hmong were loyal to the United States and, when the war ended, they were provided the opportunity to come to the United States to live. Many other Southeast Asians also took advantage of the opportunity and the state became more multicultural in the process.

Among the latest groups to migrate to California have been people from eastern European countries such as Russia, Latvia, and Estonia. These immigrations occurred due to the breakup of the Soviet Union. This often created difficult times for educators who were faced with the task of providing constitutionally guaranteed equal educational opportunities for these new groups of students.

From this brief multicultural history, it can be seen that the state of California is blessed with an extremely pluralistic population. While the reasons for moving to the state often grew out of desperate circumstances, all of these microcultures have endured, prospered, and contributed mightily to the crucial developments of the state.

THE EDUCATIONAL SYSTEM

In educational circles, California has often been viewed as one of the leading states. Regardless of its huge student enrollment, many educational innovations have started there. For example, gifted/talented education programs were initiated during the late 1950s and the Fisher Bill, passed by the California legislature required each school district to craft a foreign language program for sixth grade students.

However, a great deal of racist practices also existed. Until the 1954 *Brown v. The Board of Education* Supreme Court decision, segregated schools for Mexican-American students existed in a number of areas. Often, these schools consisted of portable classrooms and the "school" was named "The Mexican School." One of the landmark Supreme Court decisions, *The Regents of the University of California v. Bakke,* addressed the issue of "reverse discrimination" as a result of the state's affirmative action programs. Even though Bakke won his case, the concept of "affirmative action" was constitutionally acceptable until 1998, when Governor Wilson ordered the University of California to terminate its affirmative action programs. As a result of this action, the participation of students of color plummeted dramatically. California voters passed Proposition 109, making all affirmative action programs illegal in the state. And in 1998, California voters opted for the termination of bilingual education programs by a 60–40 percent margin. This led to numerous lawsuits and created great difficulties for educators who are responsible for providing children with constitutionally guaranteed equal educational opportunities. The action was particularly troublesome for educators working with children who had limited English proficiency.

The California state superintendent of public instruction is an elected position. California was successful in electing one of the first African-American state superintendents in the United States Dr. Wilson Riles. Interestingly, the state did not develop its public education system until 1874, when the legislature passed a law to enforce the educational rights of children. This act was quite controversial and only applied to elementary education. However, by 1884, California became the first state to require the publication of state reading materials, which were published by the state's educational printing office.

Legally, California school children must attend school between the ages of six and eighteen. Exceptions are children attending private schools, students being tutored by a properly-credentialed person; and children with work permits. Children of fifteen years are allowed to take a leave of absence for supervised travel, study, training, or work not available to the student.

Corporal punishment is prohibited in California and the state has no statutory provisions regarding prayer or meditation in the schools. In order to become certificated, prospective teachers must pass the California Basic Education Skills Test.

In 1995, 16.7 percent of all persons were below the poverty level compared with the national average of 16.7 percent. Of all children between the ages of five and seventeen, 23.4 percent were below the poverty level in 1995. Ninety-one percent of all teachers have either a bachelor's degree or master's degree, or both.

MULTICULTURAL EDUCATION EFFORTS

The responses to the authors' 1998 questionnaire survey were sketchy, and the respondents did not supply any name or title. Nevertheless, it was indicated that California had no planned multicultural education program at the state level, and no funds were provided for such efforts. However, multicultural education is incorporated into the history/ social studies framework.

California student microcultures include 38 percent Latino, 8.7percent African-American, 8.2 percent Asian, 2.4 percent Filipino, and the rest (43 percent) are Native-Americans and European-Americans. According to the respondents figures, this means that European-American students are a minority in California schools.

California was actually one of the pioneers of bilingual education. They were put into place because the state had such large numbers of children with limited English proficiency. It was felt by educators that if children could learn in their native language first, they would understand the instruction and would not waste time with materials which made no sense to them. Then, along with receiving solid instruction in the English language, the need for receiving instruction in their native language would disappear as they became bilingual. This notion was one issue involved in the landmark *Lau v. Nichols* decision of 1974, in which a San Francisco student sued the San Francisco school district. Lau argued that his civil right to an equal educational opportunity was violated because he could not read English.

It was reported that the state had a procedure for evaluating curriculum materials and textbooks for racist and sexist content and each school district determines its own specific curriculum, but the state framework encourages the inclusion of curriculum content pertaining to the history of Native-Americans. This is especially encouraged in each district's history curricula. The respondents failed to answer any of the other questions. .

REFERENCES

Alexander, Kern and Alexander, M. David, *American School Law*. Belmont, CA: West/Wadsworth, 1998.

Bean, Walton and Rawls, J., *California: An Interpretive History*. New York: McGraw, 1982.

Beck, Warren A. and Haase, Ynez D., *Historical Atlas of California*. Norman: University of Oklahoma Press, 1974.

Bullough, et al., *The Elusive Eden: A New History of California*. New York: Alfred A. Knopf, 1987.

Camarillo, Albert, *Chicanos in a Changing Society*. Cambridge: Harvard University Press, 1979.

Chapin, J. and Messick, R., *California: People of a Region*. Fourth edition. New York: McGraw, 1984.

Cook, Sherburne F., *The Conflict Between the California Indians and White Civilization*. Berkeley: University of California Press, 1967.

Culver, John H. and Syer, John C., *Politics and Power in California*, Second edition. New York: Wiley, 1984.

Harlow, Neal, *California Conquered: War and Peace on the Pacific: 1846–1850*. Berkeley: University of California Press, 1982.

Heizer, Robert F., (ed.), *California*. In *Handbook of North American Indians* Volume 8. Washington D.C.: Smithsonian Institution, 1978.

Houston, James D., *Californians: Searching for the Golden State.* New York: Alfred A. Knopf, 1982.

Kroeber, Alfred L., "The Indians of California." In *The North American Indians,* (ed.), Roger Owen, James Deeta, and Anthony Fisher. New York: Macmillan, 1967.

Lavender, David S., *California: A Bicentennial History.* New York: Norton, 1976.

Lavender, David S., *California: Land of the New Beginnings.* Lincoln: University of Nebraska, 1987.

Leiter, Richard A., (ed.), *National Survey of State Law.* First edition. Detroit: Gale Research, 1997.

Merriam, C. Hart, *Studies of California Indians.* Berkeley: University of California Press, 1955.

Mitchell, Bruce, et al., *The Dynamic Classroom: A Creative Approach to the Teaching/Evaluation Process.* Dubuque, IA: Kendall/Hunt, 1996.

Rawls, James J., *Indians of California: The Changing Image.* Norman: University of Oklahoma Press, 1984.

Rolle, Andrew F., *California: A History.* Fourth edition. Los Angeles: Harlan Davidson, 1978.

Starr, Kevin, *Inventing the Dream.* New York: Oxford, 1985.

Takaki, Ronald, *A Different Mirror: A History of Multicultural America.* Boston: Little, Brown, 1995.

United States Department of Education, *Digest of Educational Statistics.* Washington D C.: United States Department of Education, 1997.

Weiss, Kenneth R., and Curtius, Mary, "Acceptance of Blacks, Latinos to UC Plunges." *Los Angeles Times,* April 1, 1998.

COLORADO

STATE HISTORY

Ironically, Colorado is a Spanish word meaning "colored" or "reddish." The irony is that Colorado, with a Spanish name, is one of a handful of states to pass "English only" laws which affect public and private institutions in regard to allowable language usage.

The state's history is believed to extend back to biblical times when Native-Americans are thought to have resided in the Mesa Verde portion of southwestern Colorado. They occupied the area for approximately thirteen centuries. These Anasazi residents occupied dwellings which were located along the cliffs and were sometimes four stories high. Due to the limited rainfall in the region, these pueblos included artificial reservoirs and stone check dams.

These early residents of the state were known for their ceramic bowls and mugs as well as their leather moccasins, yucca baskets, rush mats, and wooden prayer sticks which have been located in archaeological digs. Anasazi from southeastern Colorado vacated their dwellings some time before the first voyage of Columbus for reasons which have never been fully explained.

Two other large Colorado tribes were the Utes and Cheyennes. While the primary residence areas of the Cheyenne were Montana and Oklahoma, many Cheyenne moved south to Colorado when Bent's Fort was erected in southern Colorado during the late 1830s. The name *Cheyenne* was given to the tribe by the Dakota Sioux who called them "the people who speak differently."

In 1864, Colonel Chivington, a Methodist minister turned major in the Colorado cavalry, attacked about 500 Cheyenne people who were sleeping in their lodges at Sand Creek. The attack was in retaliation for clashes between the Cheyenne and the Colorado cavalry over a failed treaty. The Cheyenne were no match for the well-armed Colorado cavalry and an estimated three hundred Native-Americans lost their lives in the surprise attack. While Chivington and his soldiers were viewed as heroes in Colorado, Chivington was condemned by Washington officials, and he resigned in 1865.

Previously residing in the great basin of Nevada, the Utes migrated to Colorado after the Anasazi left. Many of the tribal members settled in western Colorado, spending the fall and summer months hunting deer and elk in the mountains and gathering nuts and berries. Often, they wintered in the river valleys of western Colorado. Some anthropologists believe that they may have been responsible for driving the Anasazi out of the region because of the competition for food.

The first encounters with Europeans occurred during the seventeenth century. A great deal of trade occurred between the two entities and by and large their involvement with each other was relatively peaceful. When the Mormons came through their lands in 1847 the influx of European-Americans created a number of confrontations between the two groups. In 1849 a treaty was consummated between the Utes and the United States government. However, as minerals were discovered in the Rockies, more and more European-Americans settled in the land of the Utes, resulting in a number of new treaties which ceded more of their lands to the encroaching Europeans.

During this time, Ouray, a Ute chief, assumed a prominent role, becoming the main spokesperson for the Ute tribe during the mid-1800s. In 1879 Nathan C. Meeker antagonized the Ute tribe by moving the White River Agency. The Utes, believing that the European-American forces were attempting to remove them to Indian Territory, attacked the U.S. forces. As a result of their actions, the Utes were forced to be relocated to the Uintah reservation in Utah. The 1990 census showed the Utes having a population of 7,293.

It is believed that the first European to enter the lands comprising the present boundaries of Colorado was Francisco Vásquez de Coronado, who reportedly entered the San Luis Valley in 1541. One of the Spanish Conquistadors' goals was to find the Seven Cities of Cibola, which was rumored to have enormous deposits of gold and silver. It is also thought that the search for the Seven Cities was responsible for introducing the horse to that region.

The northeastern regions of the state were acquired under the Louisiana Purchase, which was orchestrated by President Thomas Jefferson in 1803. One of the first European-Americans to explore the region was Zebulon Pike, who entered the area in 1806. Other European-American explorers were Stephen H. Long in 1820 and John Fremont in 1842 and 1845. The fur traders were active until 1840 and the Russell brothers and their party panned for gold in 1858 at the mouth of Dry Creek. Shortly after, the Colorado gold rush commenced and these two events caused an enormous migration of European-Americans into the area.

Just one year after the Russell brothers gold-panning exploits, the first school in Denver opened. The schoolmaster O. J. Goldrick had studied in Dublin and at Columbia University. His students included two Mexican-Americans, two Native-Americans, and nine European-Americans. His students were charged $3.00 per month for the privilege of attending his school. By 1863 plans were underway for the creation of the Denver Seminary which would later become the University of Denver.

During the summer of 1859, Colorado experienced an enormous influx of new settlers. It is estimated that some 50,000 persons came to the region. Among their numbers were young English/Irish-American farmers from Kansas and Iowa, Scotch/Irish-Americans from Kentucky, and Scotch/Welsh/German-Americans from Pennsylvania. Many African-Americans, both freemen from the East and slaves with their masters came to the area. "Aunt Clara" Brown was the first African-American woman in Central City. She was a nurse and owned a laundry. Barney Ford was the first African-American to "strike it rich" when he located a lucrative lode near Breckenridge and later was elected to the territorial legislature.

Statehood came to Colorado in 1876 after the gold-mining boom had all but ended. This created the nickname "Centennial State," since statehood was achieved 100 years after the Declaration of Independence. However, silver was responsible for the state's economy at that time. Colorado's public school system was created during the 1870s, when the office of the state superintendent was developed.

By 1921 the Ku Klux Klan had surfaced in Colorado. Dr. John Galen Locke, a Denver physician, became the grand dragon of a local chapter. They persecuted Catholics, Jews, and African-Americans, dressing up in the usual sheets and burning crosses on Pikes Peak and on top of Table Mountain near Golden. By 1924 they were strong enough to elect a governor, senator, and a Denver chief of police and mayor. However, the Klan organization died quickly when Locke resigned after being convicted on an income-tax matter.

THE EDUCATIONAL SYSTEM

In order for persons to become certified teachers in the state, it is necessary for them to pass the California Achievement Test at an acceptable level. Certification also requires classroom observations in which the prospective teacher must exhibit satisfactory levels of performance. Nearly 50 percent of Colorado teachers have finished their master's degree.

Colorado teachers are entitled to due process in regard to notification of termination prior to the granting of tenure. In a 1986 case *Dav v. Prowers County School District (RE-1, 725 P2d 14 Col. App. 1986)*, a teacher who was not given timely notice of her contract renewal, was ordered by the court to be reemployed for the fourth year and given tenure.

Compulsory school attendance is required for all children between the ages of seven and sixteen. Compulsory special education services are provided for children between the ages of three and twenty. Children are not required to attend school if they are ill or temporarily injured; if they attend a parochial school that provides "basic academic education"; if the child has a physical/mental/emotional disability; if the child is lawfully employed; if the child is in custody of court or law enforcement authorities; if the child has graduated from the twelfth grade; if the child is instructed at home; or if the youngster is suspended or expelled.

Parents who home school are not subject to the Teacher Certification Act of 1975 and must provide a minimum average of four hours of instruction each day. The home-schooling curriculum must include reading, writing, speaking, math, history, civics, literature, science, and the constitution. Parents who home school are required to notify the school district of their intent each year and home-schooled children are evaluated at grades three, five, seven, nine, and eleven.

Colorado has some year-round schools but school districts are not required to offer kindergarten programs. However, most of them do. Colorado citizens have graduated from high school at a rate of 25.5 percent compared to 30 percent nationally. Of school-age children in Colorado, 10.7 percent are in poverty compared to 19 percent nationally. The median household income for the state is $40,706 compared to $34,076 nationally. Colorado spent $923 per capita on elementary/ secondary education compared to the national average of $932 per capita.

The state has no statutory provisions for corporal punishment in the schools. Neither are there any statutory provisions for participating in school prayer. A Colorado statute allows employers or law enforcement officers to have access to school records without parental consent unless federal laws prevent it. Student records are confidential except when they should be requested by the governor or a committee of the general assembly.

MULTICULTURAL EDUCATION EFFORTS

Colorado's replies to the 1998 questionnaire items revealed that the state did not have a planned multicultural education program due to the decentralized nature of the state's educational system. However, it was stipulated that some of the school districts had such programs. Nobody in the Office of the State Superintendent had the responsibility for such efforts. It was stated that cuts in educational funding by the president caused the elimination of such a position. Also, there are no state funds budgeted for such enterprises and nobody in the superintendent's office has any direct responsibilities for multicultural education programs. A state equity team of six professional educators had been in charge of such a program, but funding cuts eliminated such efforts.

In addition to the majority European-Americans, the primary microcultures in Colorado are Latinos, African-Americans, Native-Americans, and Asian-Americans. It was also stipulated that the state has no specific multicultural education requirements for teacher certification.

Some of Colorado's school districts have special programs which are designed to teach children in their native language, and at the present time there are no school districts which are under court order to become racially desegregated.

The respondent felt that there had been an increase in racist incidents in the state's schools during the past five years. Since Colorado has no state curriculum, there are no state-sponsored attempts to teach the history of Native-Americans, although many school districts are attempting to do that in their local school programs. The State Office of Education does not evaluate curriculum materials, library holdings, or text books for racist or sexist statements.

The Colorado respondent felt that the biggest problems facing multicultural education efforts were the lack of funding and a lack of support from the United States Office of Education (USOE). The biggest improvement in Colorado's multicultural education efforts would be realized if the staffing for equity education could be re-established.

In spite of the relative lack of support for multicultural education programs in Colorado, two cases in particular are crucial to such efforts in the state and throughout the nation. And while the first case dealt with an African-American social worker, the implications for other educators are clear. A school district rehired the African-American social worker who had less seniority than a European-American social worker. The action occurred during the midst of a Reduction in Force (RIF) proceeding. The court ruled this to be a racist act since there was a lack of evidence of past discrimination which would justify remedial race-conscious affirmative action. To justify such affirmative action, it must be proven that there had been "manifest imbalance" in a traditionally segregated job category. Moreover, when such an imbalance is proven, the affirmative action plan must not "unnecessarily trammel the rights of others" *(Cunico v. Pueblo School District No. 60, 917 F.2d 431 10th Cir.1990).*

The second case related to the issue of gender discrimination. A school district policy stated that maternity leave will be granted with full pay until the teacher's sick leave days are used up. After that, the teacher will be paid at the contractual amount less the substitute teacher's regular pay. The teacher requested leave based on the language of the maternity-leave agreement. However, the Board of Trustees granted the first fifty days at full pay pursuant to its maternity leave policy but stipulated that the remainder of the leave would be without pay. The court ruled against the school district, ordering the payment of the days beyond the first fifty minus the substitute teacher's salary *(Pastor v. San Juan School District No. 1, 699P.2d418 Colo. App. 1985).*

Another Colorado gender discrimination case had to do with Title IX. The state athletic association forbade coeducational interscholastic athletic competition in events which were deemed to be "contact sports." A high school student sued the association when she was prevented from playing on the soccer team. The argument for forbidding girls to participate in soccer was to protect girls from harm. However, the court ruled that the rule violated the equal protection clause since it arbitrarily separated boys from girls without any concern for the wide range of variation within both genders.

REFERENCES

Abbott, Carl, *Colorado: A History of the Centennial State.* Boulder: Colorado Associated University Press, 1976.

Ambler, J. Richard, *The Anasazi: Prehistoric People of the Four Corners Region.* Flagstaff: Museum of Northern Arizona, 1972.

DeLaney, Robert, *The Southern Ute People.* Phoenix: Indian Tribal Series, 1974.

DeLaney, Robert, *The Ute Mountain Utes.* Albuquerque: University of New Mexico Press, 1989.

Fischer, Louis, Schimmel, and Kelly, Cynthia, *Teachers and the Law.* New York: Longman, 1995.

Hoebel, E. Adamson, *The Cheyennes: Indians of the Great Plains.* New York: Holt, Rinehart and Winston, 1978.

Leiter, Richard, *National Survey of State Laws.* First edition. Detroit: Gale Research, 1997.

Markowitz, Harvey, (ed.), *American Indians.* Pasadena, CA: Salem Press, 1995.

Sprague, Marshall, *Colorado.* New York: Norton, 1976.

Ubbelohde, Carl, Benson, Maxine and Smith, Duanne, (eds.), *A Colorado History.* Boulder, CO: Pruett Publishing Company, 1982.

United States Department of Education, *Digest of Educational Statistics.* Washington D.C.: United States Department of Education, 1997.

CONNECTICUT

STATE HISTORY

The name "Connecticut" comes from the Algonquin word *quinnehtukqut,* which means "beyond the tidal river." Approximately 20,000 Algonquians resided near the Atlantic cost in present-day Connecticut when the Europeans arrived during the early 1600s. Among other Connecticut tribes were the Pequot, who lived along the Thames River, the closely-related Mohegan who were the subjects in James Fenimore Cooper's book, *The Last of the Mohicans,* the Niantic, the Quinnipiac, and the Wangunk.

The Pequot tribe, members of the Algonquian language group, had an estimated population of approximately 13,000 at the time of the European incursions during the early 1600s. While the men were hunters, the women raised corn, beans, and squash, and were known for their horticulture prowess. Both genders harvested fish and shellfish along the Atlantic coast. However, in 1633, a smallpox outbreak decimated the tribe, reducing their numbers to an estimated 3,000. This decrease in the tribal population made it possible for the Europeans to encroach on Pequot lands in great numbers, leading to the Pequot War, which lasted from 1636–1637. The war essentially ended Pequot life as it existed prior to the Europeans and eventually the language was lost. Only two small Pequot reservations exist in the state in 1998. The Mohegan, formerly part of the Pequot tribe, formed their own entity early in the seventeenth century. The name Mohegan means "wolf." During the Pequot War, the Mohegans actually sided with the English, which helped lead to the decimation of the Pequot tribe. During King Philip's War (1675–1677), the Mohegan again were allied with the English.

Even though the Mohegans owned an estimated 4,000 acres of the James River valley in 1721, the tribe saw a substantial number of its residents leave the New England area, migrating to Wisconsin and other areas. By 1861 the state of Connecticut had taken over much of the Mohegan's native lands. Unable to stand the continual pressures of the European-Americans, the Mohegan people gradually became assimilated into the dominant culture.

The Niantic lived along the Connecticut coast and were actually considered to be a branch of the Algonquian family. The word Algonquin means "at a point of land on an estuary." Historians believe that this group of Native-Americans inhabited their lands for thousands of years prior to the arrival of the Europeans. They were not nomadic, rather choosing to live in villages and subsisting on diets of fish, seafood, maize, beans, and pumpkins. Cooking was done in clay pots which were stirred with large, wooden spoons. Also, the Niantic created excellent woven fabrics and leather goods.

The first European to come to the area was Adriaen Block, a Dutch navigator who came upon the Connecticut River in 1614. He claimed the area for the Dutch, in spite of the Native-American population which resided in the area. Thus, the concept of "Manifest Destiny" was ushered into nearby Connecticut and the other New England areas. A Dutch trading fort named the House of Hope was erected in 1633 near the location of present-day Hartford. However, it was abandoned shortly thereafter. In the meantime, English settlers from the Plymouth Colony and Massachusetts Bay Colony started settlements at Windsor and Wethersfield, in spite of the efforts of the Pequot tribe to keep them out. These two villages, along with Hartford, all founded in the Connecticut River Valley, became an important nucleus for the new English colony of Connecticut. In 1639 Connecticut adopted a constitution based on democratic principles.

John Winthrop, who became governor of the Connecticut colony in 1662, obtained a royal charter which gave the colony considerable self-government and between 1685 and 1689, James II decided to organize New England into one government. However, Connecticut refused to participate and would not relinquish its charter, which supposedly was hidden in an oak tree which later was dubbed the "Charter Oak."

In the early 1700s, Connecticut farmers commenced exporting their crops to other American colonies and the coastal towns became involved in trade enterprises with the West Indies, providing food for that region's sugarcane plantations. Because of this interaction with the West Indies, some of the first African-Americans came from Barbados to become servants or slaves. The first mention of the term "Negroes" appeared in the Connecticut Code of 1650. In 1660 the General Court ruled that neither Native-Americans or African-Americans could serve in the militia. However, in spite of this decree, both African-Americans and Native-Americans fought in several wars when their services were needed.

The Connecticut colony also commenced to acquire a reputation for fine clocks, shipbuilding, tinware, and silverware. Shortly before the American Revolution, Connecticut had an estimated population of about 200,000 residents, most of whom were eager to become independent from England. During the Revolution, Connecticut supplied about 30,000 troops to the Continental Army.

One noted participant in the Revolutionary War was Nathan Hale, a young teacher who agreed to spy on English military establishments. Disguised as a Dutch schoolmaster, he moved freely throughout British installations, creating maps and taking notes which he hid in the soles of his shoes. Just as he was ready to cross a river and head back with his information, he was captured by the British and hanged. His patriotic exploits provided a further source of motivation for the Revolution.

Throughout its early history, Connecticut utilized the services of both African-American and Native-America slaves and servants. In 1715 Connecticut forbid the importation of Native-American slaves from the Carolinas because they were believed to be hostile. And a curfew was imposed on Native-Americans and African-Americans who were required to be in their places of residence by 9:00 at night.

The formal system of education in Connecticut is thought to have been originated through the enactment of the Code of 1650. Children and apprentices were taught to read and to become catechized at least once a week. Heads of families were required to do this. In addition, part of the Code stipulated that children should be trained in an honest calling in order to contribute to the commonwealth, in addition to improving their own well-being. Also, Connecticut, like Massachusetts, called for towns of fifty households to create a reading and writing school. For towns with 100 or more households, the law required the maintenance of a grammar school which prepared boys for college. During the seventeenth and eighteenth century, parents had to provide their children with the basic necessities for school participation. In addition to the usual pens, pencils, and paper, they were even required to supply firewood in the winter months.

Another important factor in the history of Connecticut's educational system has been the influence of Yale College (now a University). Chartered as the second college in the colonies (Harvard was the first), Yale College originally trained young men to become leaders. Many of them went into the ministry, some became missionaries, and others such as Nathan Hale, acquired an interest in becoming schoolmasters.

After the American Revolution, slavery still existed in Connecticut, although a growing number of state residents opposed it. By 1848 it was abolished altogether. During the Civil War the state sent about 55,000 men to fight with the Union forces. Connecticut's burgeoning industrial base continued to expand after the war and its cities grew rather dramatically during World War I, when Connecticut became a major producer of war materials. World War II helped to revive the state's slumping economy, which was deeply affected during the nation's Great Depression of the 1930s.

During the last half of the twentieth century, Connecticut's older cities declined as manufacturers moved to other parts of the country and to other nations as well. As a result, the state has had to contend with increased social problems when crime and poverty commenced to afflict the large urban centers. But even though the state has been forced to address many complicated issues of the postindustrial society, Connecticut's per capita income level has remained strong.

The state's population has become more multicultural in recent years, with an increasing population of Latinos and Haitian-Americans. An estimated 15,000 Haitian-Americans reside in Stanford, Hartford, and Norwalk, and many Haitian-American students have argued for the inclusion of bilingual education programs in the schools. While most of the Haitian-American population still practice Catholicism, many others have switched to various Protestant sects. Haitian Creole is still the predominant language in the home.

THE EDUCATIONAL SYSTEM

Connecticut has benefited from one of the finest public education systems in the United States. The establishment of Yale University (the second higher education institution in the nation) and the early precolonial laws requiring the establishment of K–12th grade public schools, has created a positive attitude about the importance of wisdom and learning that has become part of the state's ethos. Moreover, Henry Barnard became the first United States commissioner of education, which made Connecticut one of the most influential players in the solidification of the free public education concept, which has become such an important part of the nation's history.

The compulsory attendance ages for the state's school children is from seven to sixteen, unless children are receiving an equivalent education elsewhere. Special education programs are available for age three to twenty. Children may be home schooled, but the home-schooling curriculum must include reading, writing, spelling, English grammar, geography, history, arithmetic, United States history and citizenship. All home-schooled children must receive instruction which is the equivalent to that encountered in the public schools. There is a daily $25 fine for parents who do not comply with these compulsory education laws.

There are no legal provisions statewide for the allowance of corporal punishment in the schools. Silent meditation is allowed in schools and parents are generally allowed access to the school records of their children. However, communication about drugs and/or alcohol between school nurses and individual students is considered to be privileged and nurses are not required to reveal such conversations to parents. In order for teachers to become certificated for teaching in the state, they must perform successfully on a basic skills test prepared by the state of Connecticut. In addition to acquiring a successful score on the state certification exam, teachers must also demonstrate successful classroom performance through in-class observations. Sixty-two percent of Connecticut's elementary and secondary teachers have completed the master's degree, compared to forty-two percent nationally.

Eleven percent of Connecticut citizens who are twenty-five years or older have achieved graduate or professional degrees. This compares favorably with the national rate of 7 percent and is the second highest percentage among the fifty states. Connecticut has only 10 percent of its population who find themselves below the poverty line. This compares with the national percentage of 14. However, 18 percent of Connecticut's children between the ages of five and seventeen are below the poverty line, compared with the national figure of 19 percent. The state spends $1,152 per capita for elementary and secondary education. This compares with the national figure of $931 per capita.

MULTICULTURAL EDUCATION EFFORTS

Connecticut does have a planned multicultural education program, according to the responses to the authors' 1998 national study. The State Office of Instruction also has a person who is responsible for such efforts in the state's schools. The title of that office is the Office of Urban and Priority School Districts. During the 1995–1996 school year, $15,400,000 was budgeted for such efforts.

The state provides leadership to school districts in the development and improvement of multicultural education programs. These services are provided through the Office of Urban and Priority School Districts. Some of the state's magnet schools offer a substantial multicultural education curricula.

Even though Connecticut does require teachers to pass a basic skills test in order to become certificated teachers, there is no requirement for prospective teaching candidates to complete special coursework or to acquire special experiences in multicultural education.

Connecticut does have special programs in bilingual education in order to provide the types of educational skills necessary for success among children who do not speak English as their native language. English as a Second Language (ESL) programs are also available for immigrant children and others who are not native English speakers. Questionnaire responses indicated that in addition to the European-American student population, the other major microcultures in the state's schools were African-Americans, Native-Americans, Latinos, and Haitian-Americans.

In order to comply with *the Brown v. Board of Education Supreme Court* decision of 1954, several desegregation strategies are currently being utilized in Connecticut. Magnet schools and urban/suburban transfer programs are some of the strategies being utilized for ensuring that Connecticut's schools are not racially segregated.

According to the respondent to the authors' 1998 questionnaire, racist incidents in Connecticut schools have remained about the same in number during the past five years. The history of Native-Americans is an important part of the state's regular curriculum, but Connecticut does not evaluate curriculum materials, library materials, or textbooks for racist/sexist content at the state level. Such practices are carried on in local school districts.

The respondent felt that Connecticut needed more funding for multicultural education programs. While the current programs in multicultural education were thought to meet the state's needs, additional funding would allow Connecticut educators to expand their scope.

REFERENCES

Colman, Rosalie Marson, *The Haitian Immigrant in Connecticut: A Socio-Cultural Pre-Study.* Storrs, CT: School of Education, University of Connecticut, 1985.

Cremin, Laurence A., *American Education: The Colonial Experience, 1607–1783.* New York: Harper and Row, 1970.

Lee, W. Storrs, *The Yankees of Connecticut.* New York: Henry Holt, 1954.

Leiter, Richard A., (ed.), *National Survey of State Laws.* First edition. Detroit: Gale Research, 1997.

Markowitz, Harvey, consulting editor, *American Indians.* Pasadena, CA: Salem Press, 1995.

Peters, Samuel Andrew, *General History of Connecticut.* New York: D. Appleton & Company, 1977.

Robertson, James Oliver and Robertson, Janet C., *All of Our Yesterdays: A Century of Life in an American Small Town.* New York: Harpers Collins, 1993.

Segal, Charles M. and Stinebeck, David C., *Puritans, Indians, and Manifest Destiny.* New York: G. Putnam's Sons, 1977.

Taylor, Robert J., *Colonial Connecticut: A History.* New York: KTO Press, 1979.

United States Department of Education, *Digest of Educational Statistics.* Washington D.C.: United States Department of Education, 1997.

Vaughan, Aldon T., *New England Frontier: Puritans and Indians, 1620–1675.* Boston: Little, Brown, 1965.

DELAWARE

STATE HISTORY

European settlers who first landed in present-day Delaware, encountered a tribe of Native-Americans called the Lenni Lenape. The name "Lenape" has been given a number of meanings by anthropologists: "a male of our kind," "our men," "men of the same nation," "common," "ordinary," or "real people." This was the dominant tribe in the eastern United States until about 1720. The tribe was also known as "Delaware," a name given them by European-American settlers who were unable to pronounce the original Native-America name. Among the first Europeans to arrive in the area was a group led by Sir Samuel Argall, the captain of the *Discovery*, which sailed into the De la Warre Bay, named in honor of the third Lord De la Warre, governor of the Virginia colony. The name of the state (Delaware) was an outgrowth of this Lord's name.

The Delaware were an Algonquian-speaking confederacy of Northeastern tribes, originally inhabiting Delaware, New Jersey, and parts of New York and Pennsylvania. In the first half of the eighteenth century, they commenced moving westward as the members of the Iroquois League forced them out of their original homeland. They teamed up with new allies, the Syandot and Shawnee, which helped them resist the encroaching Europeans until the Treaty of Greenville was signed in 1795. This treaty resulted in a loss of their new Ohio lands and, as a result, they became scattered into a number of bands, residing in Missouri, Arkansas, Texas, Ontario (Canada) and a small portion of Ohio.

During the earliest contacts with Europeans, the Lenape religion was not greatly affected. However, the Europeans felt that the Lenapes were Godless and some religious groups attempted to convert them to Christianity. While some tribal members did convert, many others went back to their native religious beliefs after becoming convinced that the Christian sermons made no sense to them. However, one lasting effect of the Christian conversion efforts was an annual ceremony celebrating the harvest. This involved a deer meat feast in a "big house."

In 1631, the first European settlement in Delaware was established by the Dutch West India Company, which commenced to develop a whaling industry and a tobacco-growing operation at present-day Lewes, known as Zwaanendael at that time. For obvious reasons, they were not welcomed by the original Native-American groups, and, as a result, the settlement only lasted for a year. However, in 1638, a Swedish settlement was established in present-day Wilmington. Known as Fort Christina, it became part of a colony which came to be known as New Sweden.

By 1655 the new colony became controlled by the Dutch under Peter Stuyvesant and his council at New Amsterdam. He had supreme command over officers, soldiers, and freemen. However, it was turned over to the British just nine years later, and by 1682 the area came under the proprietorship of William Penn.

During the New Sweden days, King Gustavus Adolphus advocated the establishment of a strong educational program in his colonies. He believed that such a system would help Sweden's colonies become more productive. During the Dutch and English occupation the Delaware colony was allowed to have its own teachers and clergymen. English authorities required Delaware inhabitants to instruct their children and servants in the laws of the country and religion. Children who were unruly ran the risk of having the constable or justice of the peace inflict corporal punishment on the guilty parties.

Delaware became the first new state to ratify the United States Constitution and after the American Revolution, education in Delaware increased rapidly. By 1818 a college was established when the Delaware legislature authorized a lottery for raising money for an institution of higher education at Newark. And while the education of European-American children was, at best, meager, it was denied to African-American children. Slaves were allowed to study with their masters or with children at times. However, the first segregated school for African-American children was not opened until 1814.

Even though Delaware was a slave state until the beginning of the Civil War, the slave population was less than 2,000, while the free African-Americans numbered about 20,000. By this time, the Quakers and other Protestant denominations had argued strongly for the termination of slavery altogether. And while the state as a whole was divided on the issue of slavery at the start of the Civil War, Delaware supported the Union. However, the old racist attitudes persisted and following the Civil War, rights for African-Americans were largely ignored, in spite of the fact that they had supported the Union cause. Moreover, African-Americans were disenfranchised in 1873, as a result of poll taxes and unscrupulous politics. The poll tax was replaced by a literacy test for African-American males in 1897. European-American males were not required to pass the test.

After the Civil War, Delaware grew rapidly and its strong economic growth occurred in the Wilmington area. Friendly tax laws were responsible for enticing many businesses and industries to the region. But due to the right-of-center political leanings in the state, Delaware trailed many other parts of the new nation in prison reform and other social services. During the worst part of the Great Depression, the state's unemployment insurance benefits were withdrawn.

Other microcultures which contributed to the pluralistic diversity of the state were the Finns, Germans, Poles, Italians, and other European groups. During the 1880s, the migration of Russian Jews escaping from czarist pogroms added to the population of Delaware. And throughout the years, members of the du Pont family have exerted a profound influence both industrially and politically, on the state.

THE EDUCATIONAL SYSTEM

By 1820, demands for a public system of education in Delaware became more prominent. Willard Hall, who became known as the father of public education in the state, was amazed at the poor level of public education in a state so close to the United States Capitol. Arriving in 1803 as a graduate from Harvard University, he had been used to the strong system of public education in Massachusetts and wished to create a comparable system in Delaware. After being appointed to the federal bench by President Monroe, this ex-Congressman created a plan for public education in Delaware, which passed the Delaware legislature in 1829. However, there were no requirements for determining teacher competence, and woefully inadequate textbooks were used throughout the state. Moreover, the schools utilized old-fashioned notions of pedagogy, such as forcing children to memorize terribly complicated spelling words before allowing them to learn reading. Rote memorization was carried to extremes and severe spankings were administered, whether or not children had broken any rules.

By 1866, religious organizations created pressure to improve the education of African-American children, who were not allowed to attend the state's public schools, which were for European-Americans only. In 1866, an organization known as the Delaware Association for the Moral Improvement and Education of Colored People was formed. In 1907 Delaware enacted compulsory education laws, but children from rural areas were only required to attend school for three months each year.

The student population in Delaware's elementary schools is just under 76,000, while 28,338 students are enrolled in the state's secondary schools. About 29,000 school-age children do not attend the public schools, receiving their education through various private school options.

In order to become certified in Delaware, it is necessary to pass the Preprofessional Skills Test (PPST) and be observed performing effectively in the classroom. Yearly per capita expenditures for elementary and secondary education are $973, compared to the national average of $932. Forty-three percent of Delaware's teachers hold the masters degree, compared to the national average of 42 percent. Nearly one-third of Delaware's teachers have taught for over twenty years.

The level of educational attainment in Delaware is slightly above the national average for the fifty states. One-third of all Delaware residents have received their high school diploma, while another 16 percent have some college but no degree. However, 13.7 percent have a college degree, which is above the national average of 13.1 percent.

Nationally, 19 percent of all children between the ages of five and seventeen are below the poverty line. Thus, Delaware's 16.6 percent compares rather favorably.

Children in Delaware must attend school between the ages of five and sixteen. The exceptions to this requirement include: private school attendance or mental and physical handicaps. Parents can request written documentation by a psychologist. Penalties for parents who choose to not comply with these requirements are $5 for the first offense and $25 to $50 for subsequent infractions. Special education services are provided between the ages of three and twenty. Delaware provides half-day programs for its kindergarten children.

Teachers are allowed to exercise the same authority as parents, which includes the administration of corporal punishment if necessary. Students can participate in moral, philosophical, or patriotic activity for two or three minutes on a volunteer basis. The school records of children are considered to be confidential except for authorized school personnel, the request of a student over fourteen, and a parent, or guardian.

MULTICULTURAL EDUCATION EFFORTS

Responses to the multicultural education survey revealed that Delaware did have a planned multicultural education program. Such a policy has existed since 1990. Unfortunately, there is nobody in the State Office of Instruction who is responsible for it. Moreover, there is no state funding designated for such educational programs. The state is not offering leadership to school districts in specific kinds of multicultural education programs, but technical assistance is provided to school districts by the state in regard to the implementation of Delaware's multicultural education policies.

The respondent indicated that the two predominant minority microcultures in the state were African-Americans and Latinos. Also, the survey replies stipulated that the state of Delaware does have specific certification requirements in the form of a three-credit course in multicultural education, which is required for all the state's prospective teachers.

Delaware has curriculum content standards which stress the notion of cultural pluralism, as opposed to a philosophy which stresses assimilation into the dominant European-American culture. Also, Delaware has special education programs which are designed to teach children in their native language when appropriate. One limited English proficiency program functions in one of the state's nineteen school districts.

Four of Delaware's school districts were under court order to become racially segregated until 1966. At that time, the state and the four school districts in question were able to prove the achievement of "unitary status" in the courts. This court order for desegregation was in effect for nearly twenty years.

The history of the state's Native-Americans is contained in Delaware's regular curriculum. However, the state does not evaluate curriculum materials, library materials, and textbooks for the exclusion of racist and sexist statements.

The Delaware respondent felt that the main problem facing multicultural education efforts in Delaware was the lack of understanding among many educators and the public as to the value of multicultural education programs for all students. The survey responses went on to say that the biggest improvements in Delaware's education program stems from the fact that 1998 was the first year that the state policy on multicultural education has been implemented systematically.

REFERENCES

Eckman, Jeanette, et al., (eds.), *Delaware: A Guide to the First State*. New York: Viking Press, 1938.

Hoffecker, Carol E., *Delaware: A Bicentennial History*. New York: W. W. Norton, 1977.

Leiter, Richard A., (ed.), *National Survey of State Laws*. First edition. Detroit: Gale Research, 1997.

Markowitz, Harvey, (consulting ed.), *American Indians*. Pasadena, CA: Salem Press, 1995.

Munroe, John A., *Colonial Delaware: A History*. Millwood, NY: KTO Press, 1978.

Raft, Herbert C., *The Lenape: Archaeology, History, and Ethnography*. Newark: New Jersey Historical Society, 1986.

United States Department of Education, *Digest of Educational Statistics*. Washington D.C.: United States Department of Education, 1997.

FLORIDA

STATE HISTORY

The earliest historical records show that Florida was originally inhabited by people from the Caribbean at the end of the last ice age, more than 10,000 years ago. Two of the earliest tribes to reside in the present state of Florida, were the Ais, who dwelled on the banks of eastern Florida and the Calusa, who inhabited the south Florida peninsula. Both were members of the Muskogean language group.

The Ais were fishers and gatherers who made use of dugout canoes which they used to travel the various waterways. According to some accounts, a shipwrecked Basque sailor was the first European to encounter these residents of early Florida. Records reveal that he lived among them and learned their language. While some of the tribal chiefs were baptized by the Spanish, general evangelization by the Spaniards was relatively unsuccessful.

Calusa Floridians were thought to have migrated from South America or the Caribbean area because of their cannibalism and human sacrifice. Historians have estimated their population at approximately 3,000 when the first Europeans arrived. When Ponce de Leon tried to invade the Calusa territory, he was forced to retreat because of their fierce resistance. Thus, they lived up to their name, which meant "fierce people."

But the most famous Floridian Native-American group is undoubtedly the Seminole, who were among the later southeastern tribes to inhabit the area. Their tribal name evolved from the Muskogee word *Seminole,* which actually was borrowed from the Spanish language and related to the notion of persons who were going to a rather primitive and untamed area. Anthropologists have argued that they are relatives of the Creek tribe.

Population estimates at the time of European arrival were not too accurate. They range from 100,000 to 900,000. When Ponce de Leon landed on the northeast coast of Florida in 1513 during his famous quest for gold, he claimed the region for Spain. He believed Florida was a large island which he named "Pascua la Florida" for the Spaniards' Easter feast known as the "Feast of the Flowers." Like the others, his quest for gold turned out to be fruitless. However, he did not return until 1521, when he attempted to found a Spanish colony. De Leon was unsuccessful in his efforts, giving his life in that quest. But other Spanish explorers followed, even though they were relatively unsuccessful in establishing colonies.

One of the more successful early Spanish explorers was Hernando de Soto, who became famous because of his involvement with Francisco Pizarro in Peru. He arrived in Florida in 1539 and traveled through present-day Georgia, Arkansas, Mississippi and finally, back to the mouth of the Arkansas River, where de Soto died and was buried. Their search for gold was unsuccessful, which resulted in a waning interest in Florida.

However, in 1565, Pedro Menendez de Aviles destroyed the French settlement at Saint Augustine and created a new Spanish presence in the region. In a later treaty with Britain after the Seven Years War, Spain traded Florida to Britain in exchange for Cuba. But the most famous European to explore Florida was probably Ponce de Leon.

In a treaty with Britain after the Seven Years War (1756–1763) Florida was divided into two British colonies, East Florida and West Florida. However, the lands were eventually returned to Spain in 1783, after belonging to Britain for the two previous decades as a result of the 1763 Treaty of Paris. Finally, Florida became part of the United States in 1821, after Pensacola's capture by the United States during the War of 1812. President James Monroe proclaimed the Adams-Onis Treaty, which ceded Florida to the United States in 1821. During that year Key West became known as the first city in southern Florida. Its deep-water port enabled the southern part of the state to become involved in more trade enterprises. In 1822 the U.S. Congress created a territorial government, which articulated a series of steps which would lead to statehood.

However, in 1835, the relentless European incursions and numerous attempts to dislodge the Seminoles from their native lands led to a Seminole attack on Major Francis Dade, resulting in the death of the Major and 109 members of his command. This incident led to a war (referred to as the Second Seminole War) which persisted until 1842, when many of the Seminoles were removed to Arkansas territory. During these conflicts, the Seminoles were aided by nearly 1,000 African-Americans who were subsequently returned to slavery. But even a third war was unsuccessful in removing all the Seminoles from Florida.

Statehood was eventually granted in 1845, when Florida entered the Union as a slave state. It seceded from the Union on January 10, 1861. As a member of the Confederacy, most of Florida's coastal towns were captured, but Tallahassee was able to remain a Confederate city until the end of the hostilities. One of the last Confederate victories was the Battle of Olustee, which occurred in 1864. Finally, in 1868, the state agreed on a new constitution, which gave African-American males voting rights.

During Reconstruction, Florida finally commenced to improve its economic standing because of the discovery of phosphate deposits, the draining of southern swamp lands and, consequently, the creation of new farmlands, the planting of citrus groves, and a new tourist industry. All of these factors motivated the development of new rail facilities for transportation purposes. Florida's enormous real estate booms occurred during the first quarter of the twentieth century, but the Great Depression slowed its growth quite dramatically. However, by 1930 the population of the state had grown to nearly 1,500,000.

This steady growth continued through the 1930s and even through the years of World War II when Florida's development was motivated by a number of war-related factors. By 1950 the population had reached more than 2.7 million, due to the tourist and retirement industries. Another factor which prompted the state's steady and rapid growth was the development of the aerospace industry, along with the new space projects at Cape Canaveral. However, the 1954 *Brown v. Board of Education* Supreme Court decision would create major changes as the state was forced to deal with serious civil rights issues.

Historically, racism in the United States has motivated much of its history and Florida was no exception. In 1956, shortly after the year-long Montgomery bus boycott by African-Americans, the South's second major bus boycott occurred in Tallahassee. Two students from Florida A & M University boarded the bus, paid their money, and sat in the first row. They refused to move, instead asking for their money back so they could leave the bus. They were arrested and a boycott of the Tallahassee buses occurred. Since between 60 and 70 percent of the riders were African-Americans, the boycott had a chilling effect on the bus company's economy. However, the boycott finally ended because of intense European-American resistance by the KKK, European-American fraternities from Florida State University, and even the Tallahassee police department. Despite the best efforts of Tallahassee's African-American community, the segregation policy remained intact.

Other civil rights demonstrations included lunch counter sit-ins and demonstrations at a Woolworth's department store. By 1960 Governor Collins, who denounced these civil rights demonstrations, reversed himself and issued a plea for tolerance and racial understanding, much to the chagrin of the Florida legislature. The governor also received severe criticism for vetoing a number of bills which were patterned after the segregationist actions taken by other southern states.

The Tallahassee civil rights demonstrations continued through the 1960s, and included a march by more than 1,000 African-Americans to the state capitol in support of the 1964 Civil Rights Act. As a result of the actions which occurred during the American Civil Rights movement, the city of Tallahassee and Florida would never be the same again. Thousands of Cuban refugees came to the state during the 1970s and 1980s, particularly impacting the city of Miami, which experienced rapid growth. The estimated population in 1994 was about 14,000,000.

THE EDUCATIONAL SYSTEM

Even though territorial status was granted to Florida in 1822, it was not until 1839 that the territorial legislature set aside the sixteenth section in every township of public land for schools. Residents were able to elect three trustees who would see to it that the income from these school lands would be utilized for the support of schools. Four years after Florida became a state in 1845, a new law added 5 percent of public land sales coastal property and eschewed property for the support of Florida's schools. By 1860 there were 97 schools and 8,494 students. An additional 138 private academies had 4,486 students. By 1993 the public school enrollment had grown to better than 2,000,000 children.

The compulsory attendance ages for Florida's school population are between six and sixteen. Exceptions to this law apply to students enrolled in parochial schools, as well as home-schooled children. Other exceptions include children whose physical, mental, or emotional condition prevents successful participation. Employed children who are fourteen or older can be exempted, as can children who have been granted an exemption from a circuit judge and children whose parent has no access to childcare.

Corporal punishment is still allowed in Florida's schools, although such forms of punishment are subject to approval by the building principal. Moreover, it must be administered in the presence of a witness and an explanation must be provided to the parents.

A brief period of time can be allotted for silent prayer or meditation in Florida. However, it is illegal for teachers and/or educational personnel to conduct any religious practices which would be perceived as assisting in the establishment of an official religious position.

Florida has implemented most parts of the Family Educational Records Protection Act (FERPA). Both parents and students have access to all of their existing school records. The state allows penalties for disallowing records access in the form of injunctive relief and attorney's fees.

In order for persons to become certificated teachers in the state of Florida, it is necessary that they pass a state test which measures the attainment of both basic skills and content knowledge. However, Florida is one of five states which require no in-class observations for achieving certification. Of the population, 6.3 percent receive graduate or professional degrees, compared with 7.2 percent nationally. While the national level for less than a ninth grade education is 10.4 percent, Florida's percentage is just 9.5. Compared to the national percentage of 13.1, only 12 percent of Floridians receive a bachelor's degree.

One barometer used to measure the socioeconomic health of states and nations is the percentage of children between the ages of five and seventeen who are in poverty. In Florida, 22.1 percent of these school-age children are in poverty. This compares to the national percentage of 19. Only eleven states have higher percentages of children in poverty. Florida's median household income was $29,745, a $2,294 decline since 1990. In 1995 the national median household income was $34,076.

Thirty-seven percent of all public elementary and secondary school teachers in Florida have received a master's degree compared to a national average of 42 percent. However, 1.7 percent have a doctor's degree compared with a national average of 0.7 percent. Just 24 percent of the state's teachers have taught twenty years or more, compared with nearly 30 percent nationally.

Teacher certification in Florida involves a three-step process. Candidates must hold a bachelor's degree or higher and meet specialization (subject content) requirements in a subject in which Florida offers certification. If the statement of eligibility indicates deficiencies, they must be satisfied before the issuance of the temporary certificate.

Certification candidates must obtain a 2.5 grade point average on a 4.0 scale. The second step for issuance of a two-year non-renewable temporary certificate requires a valid statement of eligibility with no noted deficiencies, employment in a Florida public, state supported school, or an approved nonpublic school, and submission of a fingerprint report. The third step (for a five-year professional certificate) requires the successful completion of the two-year probationary period, satisfaction of the professional preparation (education courses) requirement, demonstration of required professional education competence, and passing scores on a professional education test, the College-Level Academic Skills Test (COAST), and a subject test for each subject shown on the certificate.

MULTICULTURAL EDUCATION EFFORTS

Florida's multicultural education efforts are described in a 1993 report entitled *Multicultural Education in Florida* prepared by the Multicultural Education Review Task Force. The state's Multicultural Education Act of 1992 addressed the needs of its culturally diverse students and amended statutory requirements in career education, inservice training, master inservice training, instructional materials, and composition of instructional materials selection committees. For purposes of shedding light on multicultural education efforts in the state, Florida's Commission on Educational Reform measured the extent to which districts provided multicultural education for students. The commission also measured the extent of training for Florida teachers and other personnel in multicultural education and analyzed the performance of students in various cultural groups.

The major findings of the study were as follows: Survey respondents reported that instructional materials were adequate insofar as the portrayal of various cultural groups. These materials were found to reflect the cultural diversity within the United States. However, library and media resources were considered to be outdated and not representative of broad cultural diversity. Still another finding in the study revealed that school policies and guidelines addressing multicultural education were in place in the schools with promising programs and practices in existence. Educators believed that their policies were multiculturally sensitive and fostered positive interaction among different cultural groups. However, the respondents seemed unsure as to what policies were appropriate or in place.

Approximately 66 percent of the respondents agreed that family and community representatives were reflected in the cultural composition of the student population. However, about 80 percent of the respondents believed that there was a lack of minority parent involvement in the schools.

Five other findings indicated that extracurricular activities were open to all and participation reflected appropriate pluralistic involvement; students were assigned school and classroom duties fairly; discipline, likewise, was enforced fairly; guidance counselors fostered positive interaction among all cultural groups; and career-oriented programs promoted positive career opportunities for all students.

However, the study revealed that teachers disagreed with the extent of stereotyping in instructional and assessment materials, the adequacy of multicultural instructional resources, the cultural balance in course enrollment, and the adequacy of library and media center resources.

In other major findings related to teacher training of Florida teachers it was found that teacher education programs did not adequately prepare most teachers to manage multicultural issues nor design and implement related strategies in the school environment. More than one third of the teachers viewed their staff development to be either minimal or nonexistent. However, 92 percent of the teachers in schools with promising programs and practices reflected high participation in staff development/training in multicultural education.

It also was found that some school districts were not providing adequate inservice support in multicultural education.

The 1993 multicultural education review task force presented a number of key recommendations:

1. Bias-free assessment measures should be developed and instructional materials on multicultural education should be prepared for state adoption, particularly those which target the improved performance of at-risk and low-performing students.
2. Schools with promising programs in multicultural education should share their program designs and operational procedures with other schools for possible adoption.
3. Each school district should create a multicultural education task force to develop district-wide policies and guidelines.
4. Workable procedures for the recruitment of diverse parent groups should be made available to other school districts throughout the state.
5. Library/media center staffs should conduct self studies to determine needs for specific types and quantities of multicultural resources.

In summary, it should be noted that the findings show that some of Florida's efforts appeared to be only marginally successful in addressing the various parts of the Florida Multicultural Education Law of 1992. However, the state must be commended for its efforts in addressing the various multicultural issues which have baffled educators since the very beginnings of the country's modern educational systems. Other states would be well served to undertake such ambitious efforts. Part twenty of the law reads as follows: "WHEREAS the 1991 Florida Legislature recognized that in order to live, learn, and work in a pluralistic world, children of this culturally diverse state need to build an awareness of their own cultural and ethnic heritage, develop an understanding, respect, and appreciation for the history, culture, and contributions of other groups, and eliminate personal and national ethnocentrism so they understand that a specific culture is not intrinsically superior or inferior to another."

REFERENCES

Alexander, Kern and Alexander, M. David, *The Law of Schools, Students and Teachers.* St. Paul: West Publishing Company, 1995.

Boswell, Thomas, (ed.), *South Florida: The Winds of Change.* Miami: Association of American Geographers, 1991.

Florida Department of Education, *Multicultural Education in Florida.* Tallahassee: Florida Department of Education, 1993.

Leiter, Richard A., (ed.), *National Survey of State Laws.* First edition. Detroit: Gale Research, 1997.

Markowitz, Harvey, (consulting ed.), *American Indians.* Pasadena, CA: Salem Press, 1995.

Tebeau, Charlton, *A History of Florida.* Coral Gables: University of Miami Press, 1971.

United States Department of Education, *Digest of Educational Statistics.* Washington D.C.: United States Department of Education, 1997.

GEORGIA

STATE HISTORY

The first known residents of Georgia were the Cherokee and Creek Native-Americans. Cherokees, members of the Iroquois language group, encountered the first known European intruders in 1540 when Hernando de Soto first entered Cherokee country during the spring of that year. However, there are also undocumented legends of white-skinned people visiting the area in about the twelfth century.

At first, the Cherokees thought that the armor-clad Spaniards might have been sent to their lands by the gods in order to punish them for their sins. However, they quickly decided that their best course of action was to facilitate the movement of the Spaniards out of their lands as quickly as possible. When de Soto found no gold in the territory he quickly departed. Moving into Chickasaw territory, he soon died in 1542 and was buried in the Mississippi River. With the exception of a short intrusion by Juan Pardo, another Spaniard looking in vain for gold, the Cherokees enjoyed peace for about one hundred years until 1763, when they killed one of two residents from the English colony of Virginia who were sent to their land in hopes of establishing commercial ties with the tribe.

In 1730 the Cherokees signed the Articles of Friendship with England. Through this action they agreed to fight only for the English settlers. From that time on they sided with the British during the French and Indian War except for the two-year Cherokee War, which occurred between 1759–1761. The Long Island Treaty, signed in 1777, kept most of the Cherokees out of the American Revolution. In 1785 the Cherokees recognized the supreme authority of the new United States government in the Treaty of Hopewell.

The next 100 years were turbulent, to say the least. Although the United States government promised to allow them to keep their land, by 1817 they had been reduced to about seven million acres in southwest North Carolina, southeast Tennessee, the northwest portion of Alabama, and a great deal of north Georgia. During the decade of the 1930s (1830–1839) the tribe was relocated to present-day Oklahoma, even though the majority of Cherokee people opted to stay on their native lands. The Removal Act was passed during the Jackson administration after the discovery of gold in Georgia in 1828.

The Cherokee tribe was the first known group of Native-Americans to acquire a written language when Sequoyah, a Cherokee, created a workable alphabet for the tribal language. Shortly after, the tribe began to publish the *Cherokee Phoenix,* creating the first group of literate Native-Americans in the United States. Among the more famous Americans with Cherokee ancestry are Vice-President Curtis (during the Herbert Hoover administration) and Will Rogers, the famous actor and cowboy roper. According to the 1990 census, the total Cherokee population in the United States was 308,132.

Originally occupying large areas of Georgia and Alabama, the Creeks are members of the Muskogean language group. The 1990 census listed their population at 43,500. Their current tribal name was provided by the English immigrants who named the tribe after Ochesee Creek, which flows into the Ocmulgee River. Actually, the Creeks consisted of several tribes such as the Muskogees, Alabamas, Hitchitis, Shawnees, Coushattas, Natchez, and Yuchis. Primarily an agricultural group, their major crop was corn and the corn ceremony was one of the primary cultural traditions of these Native-Americans.

Creeks encountered the new European settlers during the seventeenth century. They quickly became involved in trade with the European transplants as they swapped their deerskins for clothing, weapons, and other goods. Following the American Revolution, the Creeks encountered great pressures from the European settlers, eventually resulting in their initial treaty with the new European-American residents. One major stipulation of this treaty was the ceding of some of their Georgia lands in 1790.

By 1812 the Creeks had become split into two factions and a civil war erupted. This Creek War involved the traditionalists and the National Council faction which attempted to punish Creeks who continued to attack settlers. During the War of 1812, the United States forces inflicted heavy losses on the traditionalists (known as Red Sticks) and half of the tribe's remaining lands were ceded to the United States. In 1932 the United States removed the remainder of the Creeks to Indian Territory (Oklahoma Territory). Throughout the years there was a great deal of acculturation among the Creek people. By the 1990 census, the Creek population was nearly 36,000.

In 1732, King George II of England granted a charter to a number of affluent Englishmen for the purpose of starting a colony in their new colonial territories. The group was headed by James Oglethorpe. A member of Parliament, he was aggressive, powerful, and a profoundly moral man. While he was a staunch Protestant, his brothers-in-law, nephews, and nieces were Roman Catholics. Much of his sense of duty and honor was inherited from his father, Theophilus.

The establishment of this English colony, originally populated by imprisoned debtors, as well as the poor and unemployed, precipitated the rapid growth of Georgia's European-Americans. The original voyage proceeded down the Thames, crossed the Atlantic and finally reached the Georgia coast on February 12, 1733. The colony eventually became embroiled in the American Revolution.

Originally the Georgia colony prohibited slavery and when Oglethorpe returned in 1736 after a trip to England, he reaffirmed his opposition to this practice. However, in order to circumvent the slavery ban, the Georgian colonists "rented" African-American slaves from South Carolina, paying one lump sum.

During the American Revolution, Georgia became a major battlefield. One of the first confrontations occurred when the British attempted to blockade eleven Georgia rice ships which were proceeding to the mouth of the Savannah River on the way to their markets. One of the British ships was set on fire and ran aground. This episode, dubbed the Battle of the Rice Boats, caused the removal of Georgia's provincial congress from Savannah to Augusta. At this time a written document for the government of Georgia was created.

But while the famous battles of Trenton, Princeton, Brandywine, Germantown, Saratoga, and Valley Forge were fought through the use of more conventional methods of warfare for that period of time, Georgia's involvement tended to rely more on guerrilla tactics. One of the highlights of Georgia's involvement in the Revolution was Lt. Colonel Henry Lee (known as "Light Horse Harry" who was successful in taking Fort Cornwallis at Augusta. This victory was significant in that it marked the beginning of the end for the British forces during the American Revolution.

Following the American Revolution, a new Georgia Constitution was drawn up in 1789. After the election of Abraham Lincoln, the state declared itself a free republic in order to preserve its plantation culture. By this time Georgia had established itself as one of the wealthiest states. Plantation agriculture had transformed it into a wealthy region. Successful planters had cultivated a highly envied life style. This was made possible because of the vast supply of cheap labor in the form of African-American slaves. Cotton was king and the primary cash crop on the majority of plantations.

During the Civil War, Georgia was the scene of the Battle of Chickamauga near the Tennessee border. But probably the most well-known episode was the capture of Atlanta by General William T. Sherman and his subsequent march to the sea. During this famous campaign he cut a swath through the state in order to sever the supply lines of the Confederate forces. This and other devastating losses led to the economic woes suffered by the state when it was bankrupt at the end of the Civil War. Following the war, the state was readmitted to the Union on July 15, 1870.

In the early days of Reconstruction, the Georgia legislature attempted to cope with the disruptions caused by the Civil War by passing a number of measures relating to social services for European-Americans. However, African-Americans were excluded from juries and both houses rejected the Fourteenth Amendment which extended citizenship, due process, and equality to African-American males.

By World War I, the cotton industry had been in full swing for a number of years and the price of cotton actually increased substantially because of large purchases by the British. At this time, a number of other crops were flourishing as pecan groves, peach and apple orchards, tobacco, watermelon, corn, and peanuts also became highly valuable crops.

During World War II, the state supplied 320,000 servicemen and 6,754 were killed or listed as missing in action. Between 1940 and 1972, the per-capita income throughout the state increased one thousand percent, even though it was still below the national average for that time. This was due partly to the development of many new industries which helped diversify the state's economy.

The Ku Klux Klan was organized at Stone Mountain near Atlanta in 1915. Sometimes the organization actually had considerable power. For example, at one time the Klan membership included the governor, chief justice of the supreme court, the state superintendent of education, the mayor of Atlanta, and a large number of other political figures. However, the organization declined rapidly after the mid 1920s.

The decades of the 1970s, 1980s, and 1990s brought about a number of major changes to the state. Established in 1785 as the first chartered state university in the country, the University of Georgia at Athens became known as one of the premier universities in the South. The institution has attracted famous scholars such as novelist James Dickey and E. Paul Torrance, who pioneered the intellectual measurement of creative thinking. Agriculture became even more diversified, even though a number of cotton fields between Atlanta and Athens declined, as they did in other parts of the state. Atlanta's growth became a symbol of the burgeoning prosperity in the new South. The state won the bid for the 1994 Super Bowl and hosted the 1996 Olympic Games.

THE EDUCATIONAL SYSTEM

In Georgia's earlier days, the state lagged behind its northern counterparts in the development of public education. While the northern states believed that public school systems were necessary for "Americanizing" immigrants and preparing young people for assuming different roles in the new nation, these concepts were slower to develop in states such as Georgia. The more rural South attracted far fewer European immigrants and tended not to see a great need for the creation of strong public school systems.

The schools that did exist were often "old field schools" which were private in nature and provided only a rudimentary education for children from European-American families. Educational opportunities for African-American slaves were non-existent until after the Civil War, since Georgia law prohibited the education of African-American children. Many of the existing schools were erected on unused fields and were private community-sponsored facilities. Local residents built them and hired the teachers. Affluent children often went on to the academies, which normally provided about three years of education after the "field schools."

By 1900 there were about fifty local school systems as a result of the creation of the common school system in 1870. However, even by 1905 there were only twelve public high schools in the state and most of the graduates continued their education in various colleges and universities. These racially-segregated high schools were for European-American students only. In 1910 it was determined that the state spent five times as much money for European-American students as it did for African-American pupils. Finally, in 1951 Herman Talmadge, the Georgia governor, was successful in establishing a new comprehensive public school system which was racially segregated.

The *Brown v. Board of Education* Supreme Court decision had a profound effect on the Georgia educational system. Segregationists managed to forestall the racial integration of Georgia's schools for several years and Atlanta became the first Georgia city to come under court order for desegregation. The University of Georgia became desegregated in 1961 when two qualified African-American students were admitted.

Presently, Georgia's educational system is under the direction of the Department of Education, which was created in 1868 in its state constitution. In addition to the University of Georgia and its thirty-four state-supported campuses, are many excellent private institutions such as Wesleyan College, which was founded in 1836 as the state's first women's college under the name of Georgia Female College.

The state requires teachers to pass a test in order to become certified as classroom teachers. The test measures content knowledge and basic skills. In addition to successful test performance, prospective teachers are observed in teaching situations. Of Georgians who are twenty-five years old, 29.6 percent have graduated from high school with no higher education schooling, compared to a national average of 30 percent. However, 12 percent have less than a ninth grade education, compared to the national average of 10.4 percent. The compulsory public school attendance age requirements are from seven to sixteen, unless the youngster is in a private school or is involved in home school study. Home schoolers must take reading, language arts, math, social studies, and science. Parents wishing to home school their children must at least have a high school education.

Georgia's schools allow corporal punishment, but it must not be excessive or unduly severe. It cannot be used as a first line of punishment, and it must be administered in the presence of a school official. A written explanation must be provided on request, and it may not be utilized as a punishment if a physician certifies that a child's mental or emotional stability might be affected.

The state expenditures for elementary and secondary education on a per capita basis was $859.03 in 1993, compared to the national per capita rate of $931.76. The percentage of teachers holding the bachelor's degree is 48.9, compared to the national percentage of 52.0 percent. Of the state's teachers, 42.5 percent have a Master's degree, while 7.7 percent of them have a doctorate. The state allows for a brief period of silent prayer or meditation.

One of Georgia's most noteworthy educational achievements has been the creation of the famous Foxfire program, based on the educational philosophy of John Dewey. Begun in the late 1960s, Foxfire originated in Rabun County, Georgia. Its excellent magazine and *Foxfire* books have been based on the theme of "cultural journalism," a term which relates to the procurement of local cultural history. Dewey's notion of the entire community becoming the classroom is carried out to its fullest in the *Foxfire* philosophy.

The program got its name from the students in a tenth-grade English class taught by Eliot Wiggington. His students decided to commence publishing a magazine of their writing. This publication was named after a fungus which grows in the damp undergrowth of this portion of Appalachia.

The program connects the school life of students to their out-of-school experiences in order to maximize their academic and personal growth skills. The notion is that by having students create their own literature based on their own life experiences, an intensified motivation for learning occurs which becomes transformed into improved school performance. These premises undergird the noted language experience and "whole-language" approaches to reading instruction, as well as the famous "oral history" approach to the teaching of that discipline.

Field research on Foxfire's effectiveness began in 1984. Five months worth of observations took place at Georgia's Rabun County High School, where Foxfire had been functioning since 1977. Interviews were conducted with Foxfire students, teachers, guidance counselors, and school administrators. The other part of the data-gathering process consisted of an examination of the many documents connected with the Foxfire program. Through this and other investigations, Foxfire has proven to be so successful that it has been utilized throughout the United States and overseas.

MULTICULTURAL EDUCATION EFFORTS

Responses to the authors' 1998 questionnaire were supplied by the state's coordinator of migrant/ESOL programs. Georgia does not have a planned multicultural education program in the state. Moreover, there is no person responsible for such enterprises from Georgia's State Office of Instruction and no state funding is available for such efforts. Through the utilization of an equity unit, the state is attempting to provide some leadership in multicultural education programs. The predominant microcultures in the state are Latinos, Asians, and African-Americans.

The state of Georgia does not require any special coursework and/or multicultural experiences for teacher certification and there are no state programs which attempt to teach children in their native languages when necessary. In order to comply with the 1954 *Brown v. Board of Education* case, Georgia currently relies on magnet school programs and voluntary busing. The history of Native-American students is included in the social studies curriculum.

Georgia's median income was $34,099 in 1995, compared to the national average of $34,076. The percentage of students under age seventeen who were in poverty was 15.6, compared to the national level of 19 percent.

REFERENCES

Abbott, W. W., *The Royal Governors of Georgia: 1754–1775*. Chapel Hill: University of North Carolina Press, 1959.

Avery, I. W., *The History of the State of Georgia from 1850–1881*. New York: Brown and Derby, 1881.

Bartley, Numan V., *The Creation of Modern Georgia*. Athens: University of Georgia Press, 1990.

Corkran, David H., *The Cherokee Frontier: Conflict and Survival, 1740–62*. Norman: University of Oklahoma Press, 1962.

Finger, John R., *The Eastern Band of the Cherokee, 1819–1900*. Knoxville: University of Tennessee Press, 1984.

Green, Michael D., *The Politics of Indian Removal: Creek Government and Society in Crisis*. Lincoln: University of Nebraska Press, 1982.

Leiter, Richard A., (ed.), *National Survey of State Laws*. First edition. Detroit: Gale Research, 1997.

Lumpkin, Henry, *From Savannah to Yorktown: The American Revolution in the South*. New York: Paragon House, 1981.

Malone, Henry, *Cherokees of the Old South*. Athens: University of Georgia Press, 1956.

Martin, Harold H., *Georgia: A History*. New York: W. W. Norton, 1977.

Owens, James Leggette, *The Negro in Georgia During Reconstruction, 1864-1872: A Social History*. Athens: University of Georgia Doctoral Dissertation, 1975.

Owsley, Frank L., Jr., *Struggle for the Gulf Borderlands: The Creek War and the Battle of New Orleans, 1812–1815.* Gainesville: University Presses of Florida, 1981.

Puckette, John L., *Foxfire Reconsidered: A Twenty-Year Experiment in Progressive Education.* Urbana: University of Illinois Press, 1989.

Spalding, Phinizy, *Oglethorpe in America.* Chicago: University of Chicago Press, 1977.

United States Department of Education, *Digest of Educational Statistics.* Washington,D C.: United States Department of Education, 1997.

Wilkins, Thurman, *Cherokee Tragedy.* New York: Macmillan, 1970.

HAWAII

STATE HISTORY

Becoming the fiftieth state in 1959, Hawaii is the only part of the United States which is located out of North America. Rising from depths of more than 15,000 feet, most of the eight volcanic land areas are actually under water. It has been estimated that the islands were formed between five and ten million years ago. The volcanic action still exists, particularly on the big island of Hawaii. Many of the present formations are rather recent entities. For example, the famous Diamond Head on Oahu is referred to as a "tuff cone," which exploded about 150,000 years ago when sea water came into contact with hot lava.

Due to the high levels of rainfall in the region, erosion of the volcanic islands occurred, creating majestic valleys and other spectacular land formations. In addition to the volcanic action and erosion, corals helped cement lava pebbles and other materials together forming coral platforms such as the Ewa Plain on the southwestern corner of Oahu.

It is believed that the first settlers on the eight Hawaiian islands were Polynesians who migrated from the South Seas to become the first group of "Native-Americans" residing in the present state of Hawaii. However, these Polynesian adventurers had no written language and so the early information is sketchy. The first known contact with Europeans occurred in 1778 when Captain James Cook became the first European to find these lands. The Spaniards came close during the 1600s on their way from Manila to Acapulco, but historians generally believe that they never really saw the islands. Cook named the new lands the Sandwich Islands, after his English friend, the Earl of Sandwich.

According to some historians, Cook's two ships were seen by two Kauai fishermen who believed the large vessels were actually floating islands which were described by a god named Lono. He had promised to return to the area on two floating islands. Cook recognized the people as appearing like the Tahitians he had encountered earlier.

On Cook's second visit, the Hawaiians finally decided that he was not a god when he went ashore in order to secure a longboat which had been taken by the Hawaiians. One of the warriors was protecting his chief and managed to strike Cook with a heavy blow. When Cook howled with pain, the Hawaiians decided that he was mortal and pelted him repeatedly, resulting in his death. In 1779 the Cook expedition left the islands.

Other expeditions from Europe occurred in 1786, when Britishers Portlock and Dixon visited the islands, as did a French captain, La Pérouse and his two French ships. The first American expedition did not occur until 1786 when Captain Robert Gray reached the Hawaiian islands with his ship *Columbia*. Many other Yankee expeditions soon followed.

At that time King Kamehameha I had become a prominent leader in the islands due to his success in uniting all of the eight islands in 1810. Originally a warrior chief, he founded the kingdom of Hawaii when he accepted the fealty of the chief of Kauai. He was able to establish political control over the archipelago. At the time of his death in 1819, Hawaii had established itself as a single political entity.

Beginning in 1820, Hawaii's early missionary period became established, largely through the efforts of the Reverend Hiram Bingham, a thirty-one year-old native of Vermont and a graduate of Middlebury College and Andover Theological Seminary. However, his first year in Honolulu was not too successful, as he attempted to inflict his puritanical beliefs on the port city of Honolulu. Regardless, the New England missionaries would have a profound effect on the island residents in the years to come.

The missionary rule greatly altered the life of the native Hawaiians. Not only did the missionaries impose their Puritanical beliefs on the people, but when the *U. S. S. Dolphin* became the first American ship to arrive in the port of Honolulu, the total population of the islands had dwindled dramatically due to epidemics which afflicted the native Hawaiians, who had no natural immunity against many diseases.

The missionary schools were coeducational and were eventually established on all eight islands. Eventually the missionaries were successful in originating an orthography for the Hawaiian language which had never been written down before the missionary period. However, the missionaries were unsuccessful in forcing Kamehameha III to make the Ten Commandments the primary law of his kingdom.

Another important part of the early Christian religious influence resulted through the efforts of a French attorney, Auguste de Morineau, who built a house and small chapel on the site of Our Lady of Peace Cathedral. The influence of Bingham and the other Puritan ministers began to decline and by 1837, just 1,300 Hawaiians had become church members during his time on the islands. However, in 1837 he was successful in persuading Kamehameha III to abolish the teaching of Catholicism.

Other Americans became successful in establishing businesses in Hawaii. One of the most significant early businesses was the development of the Ladd Company, which started the first sugar plantation on Kauai in 1835. But due to the declining birth rate of native Hawaiians, cheap labor sources were sought and in 1851 the first group of Chinese indentured servants were brought to the islands to work the plantations for a salary of three dollars a month and their room and board. In 1868 the first Japanese indentured servants arrived. This group of 149 (including six women and two small boys) departed just one day before Japan's Tokugawa government lost its power to the Mikado. Later, in 1885, a larger group of Japanese people, numbering 943, landed in Honolulu. They were mostly Japanese farmers who fled economic and social upheaval, along with the civil wars which occurred during the Meiji era. Also, in the last half of the 19th century, Hawaii commenced to acquire an even more multicultural flavor when German entrepreneurs arrived in the area in the 1860s, establishing operations in Honolulu as well as plantations on Kauai.

After the death of Kamehameha V in 1872, it was necessary to appoint a successor. William Charles Lunalilo, a relative of the Kamehameha family, was elected but unfortunately his term was abbreviated by his untimely death in 1874. He was replaced by Colonel David Kalakaua who became the first Hawaiian leader to visit the United States, which had growing influences on the islands by this time. He was accompanied by Henry Pierce, the American minister to the islands. In 1884 he appointed Robert Walker Irwin, a great-grandson of Benjamin Franklin, to be Hawaii's consul general in Tokyo. During Kalakaua's reign, 38,695 Japanese people migrated to Hawaii during the final days of the Hawaiian kingdom.

The immigrations continued and by the end of the century, with this influx of Chinese, Japanese, Germans, Americans, Norwegians, and others, Native-Hawaiians became a minority group. After Kalakaua's death in 1890, his successor was Queen Liliuokalani.

Hawaii became annexed to the United States in 1898 and became designated as a legal United States Territory in 1900 because of the Organic Act. The first territorial governor was Sanford B. Dole. For the Japanese and other contract laborers, territoriality meant that their labor contracts were null and void, and they suddenly were free to enter other occupational pursuits. However, many of them were still forced to endure the harsh realities of plantation labor.

Entrepreneurship proliferated during this period of Hawaii's history and pineapple became the number two crop in the early 1900s. One of the larger pineapple plantations was located next to the United States Army's Schofield barracks. The plantation was started by Jim Dole, a cousin of Sanford B. Dole.

The multicultural expansion continued during the early part of the twentieth century. Many of the new residents migrated from the more troubled parts of the world. Between 1903 and 1905, five thousand Puerto Ricans arrived, along with Filipinos, and Okinawans who came in 1906. However, during the first three decades of the twentieth century, the plantation life was still extremely difficult and many people left that line of work after the granting of territorial status. Among those who vacated their plantation jobs were several hundred African-Americans from Tennessee, along with about eight thousand Spanish workers.

Hawaii strongly supported the U.S. involvement during World War I. German-Hawaiians were often persecuted and the United States government was forced to intervene on their behalf. Captain Kenichi Sakai, a *nisei* from Kohala, became the first Japanese-American to become a commissioned officer in the United States Army. In 1919 the first bill for Hawaiian statehood was introduced into the United States Congress.

The first half of the twentieth century also marked the rise of organized labor on the islands. In 1917, the Plantation Laborers Wage Increase Investigative Association organized five locals on the Big Island. And the Japanese Federation of Labor joined with the Filipino Labor Union, whose membership consisted of Puerto Rican workers. Jointly, they created a list of demands against the Hawaii Sugar Planters Association. The first major strike occurred in 1920 and was supported by one mainland union, the IWW (Wobblies). Other strikes occurred at the Oahu Railway Company, Mutual Telephone (Maui), and other Oahu firms such as Honolulu Iron Works, California Feed, Libby Cannery, HC & C, and the Inter-Island Steamer Company.

With the bombing of Pearl Harbor in 1941, the face of Hawaii would change forever. The attack intensified the push for statehood, since Hawaii was now a part of the allied war efforts in the Pacific Theater. Of course, Japanese-Hawaiians suffered the most with many of their numbers being questioned and interned. In addition to the Japanese-Hawaiians who were arrested, German-Hawaiians, Austrian-Hawaiians, and Italian-Hawaiians were taken to Sand Island near Pearl Harbor. Prejudices were intensified and countless instances of propaganda abounded. And in spite of the efforts of right-wing senators Strom Thurmond of Georgia and Mississippi's James Eastland, Hawaii finally was granted statehood in 1959 during the presidency of Dwight Eisenhower. Because of its location and history, it became one of the most pluralistic states in the Union.

THE EDUCATIONAL SYSTEM

Formal education in Hawaii began with the missionary schools which were coeducational in nature. The main pieces of literature in the schools were the reading primers and the bibles. Because of their creation of a written alphabet, Hawaii was nearly completely literate by the middle 1800s. During the summer and fall of 1843, the Hawaii legislature passed a number of reforms, including the establishment of a Department of Education through the passage of Hawaii's first Organic Act. William Richards became the first Minister of Education.

While the first Hawaiian schools made use of the native language of the people, Lot Kamehameha (Kamehameha V) directed the Board of Education to order the islands' schools to change their instructional language from Hawaiian to English. He believed this was necessary in order for native Hawaiians to compete with the English-speaking newcomers to the islands. Abraham Fornander became the first inspector-general of the schools. He specifically was responsible for revising the curriculum so that it was compatible with the subject areas being developed in the western countries, particularly the United States.

Hawaii's schools have been and still are functioning as one centrally-controlled school district. This makes the schools in the state of Hawaii unique. They operate under the ministry model utilized by a majority of the world's nations. Gradually, Hawaii created a curriculum which utilized the same principles and ideals found in U.S. schools. This became a goal for all ethnic groups, particularly the Japanese-Hawaiians. The Reverend Takie Okumura started an educational campaign in 1921 which argued that Japanese school children should incorporate characteristics of the American lifestyle which existed in Hawaii. He was rebuked for this practice by many Japanese-Hawaiians, who believed that he was doing violence to many of Japan's basic traditions.

Throughout the history of Japanese involvement in Hawaii, Japanese language schools were quite abundant in the islands. However, these schools, coupled with the Japanese affiliation with the Buddhist religion, had created an uneasy attitude among some Christian factions. Gradually, attendance in these schools waned and many Japanese-Hawaiian students commenced matriculating in Hawaii's public schools.

As the history of Hawaii moved rapidly toward the twentyfirst century, the Hawaiian public school system has remained strong. The superintendent of schools is appointed by the Board of Education in Hawaii's state-wide school district and has the responsibility for directing the educational program in the entire state.

Physical punishment is not allowed in Hawaii's schools. However, teachers are able to use reasonable force in order to restrain students from hurting themselves or other persons or property. There are no statutory provisions regarding the use of prayer in the schools.

In order for Hawaii's prospective teachers to receive certification, they must pass a basic skills test or the National Teachers Examination (NTE). Final certification also requires successful in-class observations. For 28.7 percent of the population, the high school diploma is the highest level of education attained, compared with the national average of 30 percent. Compared to the national average of 13.1 percent, 15.8 percent of Hawaiians receive the bachelor of arts degree as their highest level of educational attainment. The per capita level of expenditures for elementary and secondary education is $711.69, compared with the national average of $931.76. Compulsory attendance ages are from six to eighteen and special education services are provided from ages three to twenty. The state has a number of "year-round" programs.

MULTICULTURAL EDUCATION EFFORTS

Responses to the authors' 1998 multicultural education survey indicated that Hawaii does not have a planned multicultural education program. However, multicultural concepts are integrated across the curriculum, especially in language arts and social studies. Nobody in the state office is specifically responsible for multicultural education efforts and there is no state funding for such ventures. Moreover, the state does not offer leadership to the schools for multicultural education.

Due to the extensive pluralism in Hawaii, it is best to characterize the state's schools as being extremely pluralistic with the primary microcultures consisting of European-Americans, Japanese-Americans, Filipino-Americans, Samoan-Americans, Chinese-Americans, Korean-Americans, and native Hawaiians.

Hawaii has no specific certification requirements such as coursework and/or other multicultural experiences. Courses dealing with such topics are electives and are not required. Cultural pluralism as a philosophy is stressed in the curriculum and instruction, and the state has extensive programs in bilingual education, ESL programs, and Hawaiian immersion for meeting the language needs of students.

Questionnaire responses stipulated that it is unknown whether racist incidents have increased or decreased in Hawaii's schools during the past few years. However, according to the respondent, there were few incidents cited by the media. The history of Native-Hawaiians is included in the state's regular curriculum as part of the social studies curriculum.

The state's Office of Education evaluates curriculum materials, library materials, and textbooks for any possible racist/sexist content. The questionnaire responses indicated that the biggest problem facing Hawaii's educational programs was that there were no specific multicultural programs in place. Integration of multicultural education concepts may or may not happen and no mandate or policy exists. The biggest need is the establishment of a policy on multicultural education.

Poverty among youth under the age of seventeen years is not a major problem compared to the national average. According to 1995 statistics, the state has 14.2 percent of its under-seventeen population in poverty compared to the national average of 19 percent. During the same year the median household income was $42,851 compared to a national median household income of $36,075.

REFERENCES

Ajlouny, Joe, *The Hawaiian Islands: A Colorful and Concise History.* New York: JSA Publishers, 1989.

Crlquist, Carl, *Hawaii: A Natural History.* New York: The Natural History Press, 1970.

Fuchs, Lawrence H., *Hawaii Pono: A Social History.* New York: Harcourt, 1984.

Gray, Francine Du Plessix, *Hawaii: The Sugar-Coated Fortress.* New York: Random House, 1971.

Kuykendall, Ralph S., *The Hawaiian Kingdom.* Three volumes. Honolulu: University of Hawaii Press, 1967.

Leiter, Richard A., (ed.), *National Survey of State Laws.* First edition. Detroit: Gale Research, 1997.

Morgan, Joseph R., *Hawaii.* New York: Westview Press, 1983.

Ogawa, Dennis M. Kodomo, *No Tame Ni (For the Sake of the Children): The Japanese-American Experience in Hawaii.* Honolulu: The University of Hawaii Press, 1978.

Council of State School Officers, *The Council.* Washington D.C.: Council of Chief State School Officers, 1998.

Sahlins, Marshall, *Islands of History.* Chicago: University of Chicago Press, 1985.

Tabrah, Ruth M., *Hawaii: A History.* New York: W. W. Norton, 1980.

United States Department of Education, *Digest of Educational Statistics,* Washington D.C.: United States Department of Education, 1997.

IDAHO

STATE HISTORY

The name for this state is not derived from the language of Native Americans. Originally, it was proposed as a name for the state of Colorado, but since that did not materialize, it became the name for the next region of the United States. Prior to the arrival of the Europeans, the area was populated with indigenous persons, particularly members of the Nez Perce and Shoshone tribes.

The Nez Perce, members of the plateau region and the Sahaptin language group, were located within a substantial portion of Idaho's present-day boundaries. Originally, they resided on the banks of the Snake River and its tributaries in central western Idaho, as well as southeastern Washington and northwestern Oregon.

The Shoshone were part of the Great Basin culture group, belonging to the Uto-Aztecan language faction. They were located in Death Valley (California), Nevada, northwestern Idaho, Utah, western Wyoming, and southern Idaho. Not a great deal is known about the time in history when these two Native-American tribes migrated to the present boundaries of Idaho. It is believed that they have resided in the region for well over 10,000 years.

Remains of the early Native-American cultures of Idaho have been found in numerous locations and many present- day names have Native-American origins. In addition to the Nez Perce and Shoshone tribes, the Coeur d'Alenes, Pend Orielles, Kutenais, Paiutes, and Bannocks also resided in Idaho.

The first known encroachments by European-Americans were carried out by the Lewis and Clark expedition in 1805. They were assisted by the Nez Perce and Shoshone, who helped them construct canoes which would carry them down the Clearwater and Snake rivers on to the Columbia as they made their way west to present-day Astoria, Oregon. And while the European immigrants were viewed rather kindly in the early days of European interaction, all that would change with the more aggressive incursions which took place over the years.

In 1809, the next major European interaction occurred when David Thompson built Idaho's first fur trading post by constructing Kullyspell House on the eastern shore of Lake Pend Orielle. Part of the North West Company, he previously arrived in Bonner's Ferry, in the Idaho panhandle, to create a trading house among the Kootenais. British trappers were also active in the region.

By 1834, Fort Boise and Fort Hall were established in order to aid the European settlers who were coming through the region on the Oregon Trail. Hudson's Bay Company established Fort Boise while Fort Hall was created by Nathaniel Wyath, who was interested in establishing a fur-trading enterprise in the lower-Columbia River region.

Similar to the occurrences in other parts of the United States, the discoveries of gold would change the fortunes of Native-Americans forever. By 1860, European-American immigration throughout the Pacific Northwest and Idaho was increasing.   Gold was discovered at Orofino Creek and the European incursions into Native-American lands increased in their intensity. Also, by this time, eastern Idaho experienced the immigration of numerous Mormons from Salt Lake City, who were interested in farming and converting Native-Americans to Mormonism.   The Mormons believed that the Native-Americans were members of the lost tribes of Israel.

As the encroachments continued, a number of ugly hostilities broke out between the European settlers and the Native-Americans who owned the eastern lands of Idaho. Originally, these European groups showed little interest in the lands occupied by the Shoshones, but with the discovery of gold, all of that changed.

The Nez Perce were known for their talents in breeding horses to improve the stock. After their positive relations with the Lewis and Clark expedition, they became involved in fur trading.   But their contact with European immigrants resulted in serious epidemics which substantially diminished their numbers.   By 1855, the Nez Perce and other members of the Sahaptin group were pressured into signing a treaty which entitled them to certain portions of their ancestral lands. However, these lands were arbitrarily reduced by 75 percent through actions of the United States government as a result of the gold strikes in the region. This led to the famous Nez Perce War of 1877.

This action took place throughout the present boundaries of Idaho. Due to the increasing friction between the adventurous Europeans and the Nez Perce, a bloody battle ensued at Whitebird Canyon, Idaho, north of the Salmon River. In that confrontation, the United States Army lost thirty-four men and numerous horses, while the Nez Perce had just four of its seventy braves wounded. While eluding the U.S. forces for nearly four months, Chief Joseph finally surrendered to General Howard, after achieving another enormous victory against Colonel Miles who lost fifty-three men against just eight losses by Chief Joseph's forces. In this surrender, Chief Joseph ended a short speech by saying, "I will fight no more forever."

The action between Chief Joseph's forces and the United States government occurred before Idaho achieved territorial status.   When Idaho finally achieved territorial status in 1863, the territorial boundaries included present-day Idaho, Montana, and most of Wyoming. Lewiston was the capital.   Statehood was granted in 1890 during the administration of Benjamin Harrison. At the time, the Republican-controlled Congress was searching for more congressional votes, and Idaho was admitted, since the perception was that it would probably become a strong Republican state...which it did. Its constitution contained a rather strong anti-Mormon clause. In the first state elections in 1890, the Idaho state legislature would not allow Mormons to vote. In that same year, polygamy was outlawed in the Mormon church.

During the latter quarter of the nineteenth century, Idaho grew in population with the lead/silver discoveries in the "Panhandle" region, and the construction of several railway systems. In the last decade of the nineteenth century, ugly confrontations occurred between the miners of the Coeur d'Alene region and mine owners. And by the early 1900s, irrigation projects in south Idaho dramatically increased the agricultural yield. During World War I a substantial increase in Idaho's agricultural industry occurred due to the immense need for food.

Prior to the onset of World War II, Idaho's population had shifted from an almost completely rural population to the point where about half of the state's citizens resided in the cities. Boise became one of the more rapidly growing areas in the United States because of water availability and the excellent climate for growing crops.

However, during World War II, Idaho also became known for housing one of the relocation centers for Japanese citizens. Located new Twin Falls, Camp Minidoka received Japanese-American citizens who were incarcerated in the camp until the end of the war.

While the racist relocation centers were ordered by the federal government during President Franklin Roosevelt's administration, recent events in northern Idaho have also plagued the state, creating the atmosphere which concerns people connected with the tourist industry. The "Reverend" Richard Butler established the Aryan Nations "Church" during the 1970s. Committed to the creation of a "whites only" subnation, the Aryans have caused great problems for Idaho residents because of their belief in the supremacy of European-Americans and their interests in "ethnic cleansing."

Adopting some of the philosophical ideas of Adolf Hitler, the Aryans have marched in parades, preaching their ideas of Aryan supremacy. In addition, some of their members have been arrested for participating in a variety of illegal activities. In addition to this group, Randy Weaver gained national notoriety for his anti-governmental actions at Ruby Ridge in the northern portion of the Idaho panhandle. In the confrontations with the Federal Bureau of Investigation, Weaver refused to comply with a federal arrest warrant. Weaver, wanted for illegal firearms activities, eventually sued the U.S. government, receiving a substantial settlement. The incident, along with the practices of the Aryan Nations organization, had the effect of portraying the state as a haven for antigovernment factions and racists. Organizations in Idaho have been working hard to dispel that image.

THE EDUCATIONAL SYSTEM

Early schools in Idaho were operated by missionaries for the training of Native-American children. According to early records, the first one was established in 1836 for Nez Perce youth near Lewiston. After this time, more European-American immigrants arrived in the area, precipitating discussions on the nature of their schooling. Also moving into southeastern Idaho were Mormon immigrants from the Salt Lake City region to farm and convert Native-Americans to Mormonism.

Public schools in Idaho originated soon after Mormons started the first non-Native-American school in 1860. A public school system was formally established in 1864 in the new territory. The following year, the first territorial superintendent of public instruction reported that the Idaho Territory had an enrollment of 1,239 children. The first high school was established in Boise in 1882.

From the outset, Idaho's public school system has struggled financially. Based on 1992–93 school-year statistics, the per-capita expenditures for elementary and secondary education on a per-pupil basis is $761.93. Only Alabama, Arkansas, Hawaii, Kentucky, Mississippi and Tennessee have a lower level of funding. During the 1990–1991 school year the average teacher's salary was just $25,500, about 75 percent of the national average.

Idaho's chief school officer is elected by popular vote. In order for Idaho teachers to become initially certified, they must acquire satisfactory scores on the National Teacher Examination and perform successfully during in-class observations. Compared to national percentages of teachers who have had over 20 years teaching experience, just 20 percent of Idaho's teachers have taught that long, compared to nearly 30 percent nationally.

Children in Idaho are required by law to attend school between the ages of seven and sixteen unless the child is otherwise comparably instructed or has a physical, mental, or emotional condition that does not permit attendance. Compulsory special education services are provided for children between the ages of three and twenty. The state has year-round schools with a written policy pertaining to their operation. Idaho's school districts are not required to operate kindergarten programs.

Census figures from 1990 revealed that Idaho residents were below the national averages in college degrees earned. Of Idahoans, 12.4 percent completed their bachelor's degrees, compared to the national average of 13.1 percent. Graduate or professional degrees were completed by 5.3 percent, compared to the national average of 7.2 percent.

Idaho has no statutory provisions pertaining to the use of corporal punishment or prayer in the schools. However, individual school districts have drawn up their own procedures which govern these two issues.

MULTICULTURAL EDUCATION EFFORTS

Responses to Idaho's questionnaire on multicultural education issues revealed that there is no planned multicultural education program in the state, and nobody at the state level is responsible for such efforts. Moreover, no state funds are set aside for multicultural education. However, the respondent indicated that the state department of education offered annual training for providing equitable education programs for English as a Second Language (ESL) students. Recently, the efforts have gone toward the preparation of advocates as change agents for ESL students.

Idaho requires no special coursework or other multicultural experiences in the teacher certification process. The respondent felt that the state's curriculum tended to emphasize an assimilationist approach (into the dominant European-American culture) as opposed to a strategy which tends to stress a more pluralistic notion about the curriculum.

Idaho's Department of Education does not sponsor special programs which attempt to provide instruction in the student's native language when needed. However, some school districts have established their own procedures for providing such instructional approaches when the need arises. Since the state has a dominant European-American English-speaking population, this need has been relatively minimal.

Because of this ethnic composition in Idaho, the state has had relatively few problems related to the need for school desegregation. However, in order to prevent racially-segregated schools from developing, attendance boundaries are drawn up in order to ensure that no racial segregation occurs.

It was felt that racist incidents had not increased in recent years. They have remained about the same. However, the respondent went on to point out that racism is more covert than overt. Some examples of covert racism are the denial of a challenging curriculum and a general tendency not to enroll migrant farmworkers' children in school when they arrive late in the semester. Other examples of covert racism included the practices of not providing native language literacy and the testing of some children in a language which is their second language of use. It was also felt that Idaho history was not taught as accurately as it should be.

Idaho's Office of Education does evaluate curriculum materials, library materials, and textbooks for racist and sexist content.

Finally, the respondent indicated that one of the biggest problems facing multicultural education in the state was that many people still believe it is better to just say we are all the same, thus negating any need for multicultural education programs. It was felt that the biggest improvement in the state's multicultural education program would be the recognition of the student's native language and to provide literacy instruction in that language. The biggest need was felt to be Spanish for Spanish speakers.

REFERENCES

Adkinson, Norman B., *Indian Braves and Battles with More Nez Perce Lore,* Grangeville: Idaho County Free Press, 1967.

Beale, Merrill D. and Wells, Merle W., *History of Idaho.* (Three volumes). New York: Lewis Historical Publishing Company, 1959.

Brown, Mark H., *The Flight of the Nez Perce.* Lincoln: University of Nebraska Press, 1959.

Chalmers, Harvey II, *The Last Stand of the Nez Perce,* New York: Twayne, 1962.

Colson, Dennis C., *Idaho's Constitution: The Tie That Binds.* Moscow: University of Idaho Press, 1991.

Council of Chief State School Officers, *The Council,* Washington D.C.: Council of Chief State School Officers, 1998.

Johnson, Claudius, O. *Borah of Idaho.* Seattle: University of Washington Press, 1967.

Josephy, Alvin M., *The Nez Perce Indians and the Opening of the Northwest.* New Haven: Yale University Press, 1965.

Leiter, Richard, A. (ed.), *National Survey of State Laws.* First edition. Detroit: Gale Research, 1997.

Limbaugh, Ronald H., *Rocky Mountain Carpetbaggers: Idaho's Territorial Governors, 1863–1890.* Moscow: University of Idaho Press, 1982.

Madsen, Brigham, *The Bannock of Idaho.* Caldwell: Caxton Press, 1958.

Peterson, Frank Ross, *Idaho.* New York: W. W. Norton, 1976.

Schwantes, Carlos A., *In Mountain Shadows: A History of Idaho.* Lincoln: University of Nebraska Press, 1991.

United States Department of Education, *Digest of Educational Statistics.* Washington D.C.: U.S. Department of Education, 1997.

Walker, Deward E. Jr., *American Indians and Idaho.* Moscow: University of Idaho Press, 1971.

ILLINOIS

STATE HISTORY

At one time Illinois was geologically located beneath a tropical sea that stretched throughout the center of North America. After this prehistoric body disappeared, its limestone deposits were responsible for creating the bedrock which provides a foundation for the city of Chicago and a large portion of the entire state, which is located on the American prairie. One of the favorite sons was none other than President Abraham Lincoln, but its history also includes the exploits of Al Capone, one of the nation's most famous mobsters.

The first residents were members of the Illinois, Iroquois, Chippewa, Ottawa, Potawatomi, Sauk (later known as Sac), Fox, Kickapoo, Mascouten, Plankashaw, and Shawnee tribal groups. Many of the tribes, such as the Iroquois, came from other regions. The Illinois, previously residing in the present boundaries of Michigan, populated present-day Illinois and first encountered Europeans during the 1670s. The tribe relied on agriculture, hunting, and gathering.

The Illinois were involved with intertribal confrontations on a rather regular basis. Several skirmishes took place with the Iroquois, which resulted in the tribe moving west of the Mississippi River. In 1673 they came into contact with the French who recruited them to become an ally. As a result of this action, they became more dependent on the French and as a result, lost many of their tribal traditions. They gradually became more involved in battles with pro-British and pro-Spanish tribes. In addition to their losses in these battles, the Illinois were losing the battle with the various diseases they contracted through their involvement with the Europeans. Moreover, since they were converted to Christianity, they rejected their polygamous practices which resulted in a declining birthrate. By 1800 their tribal numbers were estimated at just 500.

A treaty was signed by the Illinois and the United States government in 1832. They gave up all of their tribal lands in Illinois and eventually were relocated to lands in Indian Territory which would eventually become their reservation in 1867. They acquired a new name, the Peorias. On the reservation they intermarried with other tribal groups, particularly the Sauk, Fox, and Kickapoo. Eventually the tribe was legally terminated in 1959 but their tribal status was restored in 1978.

Some historians believe the Fox tribe migrated to Illinois from southern Michigan. Closely related to the Sauk, Kickapoo, and Mascouten, they belong to the Algonquian family. Their western migration was precipitated by pressures from the Chippewas. Eventually they ended up in southern Wisconsin and northern Illinois. This western Treat Lakes tribe became known as "People in the Calumet" because of the manner in which they employed pipes in some of their sacred ceremonies. Unlike the Illinois, the Fox aggressively opposed the French and attempted to charge French fur traders a toll for using the Fox River in Wisconsin. For years a series of wars occurred between the Fox and the French. The Fox were fierce warriors, but they were hopelessly outmanned. Finally, in 1837 the hostilities ended when the French granted a pardon to the Fox forces.

The Fox were closely allied with the Sauk, but the two tribes were regarded as a single entity by many European groups. The Fox and Sauk resisted the increasing numbers of Europeans who were storming into their areas. The two groups were involved in Little Turtle's War from 1790 to 1794 and also in the Tecumseh Rebellion from 1809 to 1811. However, in 1804 they ceded the Fox territories which were located east of the Mississippi in return for federal annuities which they received annually.

The religious life of the Fox was centered around a deep respect for the powers of nature. They believed that the universe was divided into the sky section and the earth portion. The sky part was referred to as the "Great Manitou", while the earth was referred to as the "Lower Region" and was ruled by lesser spirits. Upon the death of tribal members, gifts were buried with them in order to facilitate their lives after death.

It is believed that the first Europeans to enter the Illinois area were Father Jacques Marquette and Louis Joliet in 1673. They traveled south on the western boundary of the state and up the Illinois River northward. Twenty-six years later the first permanent settlement was established by French priests who were involved in the fur trading enterprises. For one hundred years the Roman Catholic Church was the only non-Native-American religious organization in the Illinois region.

By 1717 Illinois had become part of the Louisiana colony controlled by the French. However, after a series of battles, the British defeated the French, causing them to give up their lands in 1763. However, the British were unsuccessful in making amends to the French settlers in Illinois who moved west across the Mississippi. During the Revolutionary War, the European-American population of Illinois was believed to be about two thousand people. Many of them were missionaries, French and British settlers, and British troops.

George Rogers Clark and a group of frontiersmen known as the "Big Knives" were successful in wresting some of the region from English control, and it became a county of Virginia until the land was given to the national government in 1784. The Illinois territory was created in 1809 and in 1818 Illinois became the twenty-first state. Its boundaries were the Mississippi on the west, the Ohio on the south, the Wabash and a line extending northward to Lake Michigan on the east, and an east-west line north of the tip of Lake Michigan, a boundary stipulated in the Northwest Ordinance.

The state did not experience particularly rapid growth until after 1820, reaching a population of 157,455 in 1930 and 476,183 in 1840. When Chicago received its city charter in 1837, it had achieved a population of 4,000 residents. During the early growth stages of the nineteenth century, battles with the Native-Americans occurred because of the increasing number of European-Americans who occupied their lands. After the passage of the Removal Act of 1830, the federal government commenced moving many Native-Americans west of the Mississippi. In 1832 the U. S. Army and Illinois militia personnel defeated the Sauk and Fox tribes in the Black Hawk War.

Rapid population increases occurred during the 1830s and 1840s. In 1848 the Illinois and Michigan Canal was completed, which allowed farmers in the Illinois and Mississippi River valleys to ship grain and other products through the Great Lakes to the lucrative eastern markets. During the middle of the century new rail lines were constructed for the same purpose.

The state of Illinois attracted national attention in 1858 with the famous Lincoln-Douglas debates prior to the start of the Civil War. After Lincoln's subsequent election to the presidency, six states immediately seceded from the Union. After the war, Illinois continued its rapid growth, attracting numerous European immigrants to the Chicago area to work in the burgeoning number of new industries. Rapid growth also occurred in Joliet and Rockford.

In 1889 Illinois commenced attracting national attention for the work of Jane Addams and her establishment of Hull House, which became a center for social reform. Housing children from the culture of poverty, Hull House attempted to offer a comprehensive program of civic, cultural, recreational, and educational activities. Hull House started with the original intent of improving the immediate neighborhood. However, the mission acquired more comprehensive purposes, which were to champion state-wide campaigns for better housing, improvements in public welfare, stricter child-labor laws, and the protection of working women.

Addams also became involved in the peace movement, and in 1915 she founded the Women's International League for Peace and Freedom. Her pacifist views gained her strong supporters and enemies alike. However, she was regarded as the greatest woman of her generation, and in 1931 she shared the Nobel Peace Prize with Nicholas Murray Butler.

The multicultural composition of the state occurred because of the European immigrants, the Native-Americans who remained in the area, and a burgeoning number of African-Americans who left the South after the end of slavery. During the prohibition years of 1920–1933, Al Capone became the leader of the bootlegging movement in Chicago, precipitating an enormous increase in the city's crime rate. Also during this period of time, Chicago became known as a primary location of American jazz as a result of the closure of Storyville, New Orleans, where jazz was born. This caused an influx of African-American musicians, along with native Chicagoans, such as Benny Goodman, who helped develop this new multicultural American art form.

The rest of the 1900s saw the development of the atomic bomb during World War II, partly as a result of the instrumental work of Enrico Fermi and others at the University of Chicago. The industrial development continued, which increased the multicultural flavor of the state's largest city, Chicago. But the industrial growth also produced great pollution problems which have led to some creative solutions which have been copied by other states.

THE EDUCATIONAL SYSTEM

Public education in Illinois started with the creation of a free school system in 1825, seven years after statehood. The first school in Chicago was the Dearborn School on the north side. It was erected through the efforts of Ira Miltmore in

1845. Since that time, public schooling throughout the state has reached a position of leadership in the United States.

In addition to the K–12 program, higher education in Illinois has also led the way. The University of Illinois has long been considered one of the elite state universities in the land. And the private University of Chicago has produced numerous internationally renowned scholars in all disciplines. Its laboratory school for high school students produced some of the classic research findings in the area of creative thinking development under the leadership of professors Jacob Getzels and Phil Jackson during the 1960s and 1970s. Their avant-garde laboratory school became a model for educators all over the country.

Throughout its earlier history, Illinois had a large number of small school districts. However, after World War II, the number of districts in the state was reduced from 12,000 to 1,340. By 1969 the state became a national leader in teacher's salaries, jumping to a negotiated starting salary of $8,400. The state superintendent of schools is appointed by the State Board of Education.

The Civil Rights era of the 1960s had a profound effect on the schools in Illinois, particularly in Chicago. During this period of time the city was beleaguered with school boycotts over the city's refusal to integrate its schools. After numerous marches and protest, Chicago's schools were finally integrated.

The city of Chicago has sought ways of dealing with a burgeoning poverty problem in the past few decades. In an attempt to address these issues adequately, the city embarked on a program which became a national model. Entitled the "Adopt a School Program," the goal was to encourage local businesses and industries to select a school and provide extra resources designed to improve the performance of the students. It was a pioneering effort. Prior to that time the support of public school systems in America had relied primarily on state support provided through public funds. However, this program utilized private funding sources to improve the educational offerings in the schools. The concept was adopted by other school districts around the nation.

Also noteworthy has been the work of Marva Collins in her attempts to provide a better education for children from the culture of poverty. Her successes have inspired other educators to copy many of her ideas in the nation's attempt to deal with poverty problems which have constituted an enormous barrier to the successful school performance of poor children throughout the land.

In 1988, Illinois commenced requiring teachers to pass the National Teachers Examination in order to achieve certification for teaching in the schools. More then 46 percent of Illinois' teachers have completed the masters degree compared to the national percentage of 46. Just .05 percent of the state's teachers have completed a doctorate, slightly below the national average of .07 percent.

The compulsory attendance ages for Illinois school-age children are from seven to sixteen. Exceptions to this provision include children attending private or parochial schools; children who are mentally or physically unable to attend public school; children who are excused by the county superintendent of schools; children between twelve and fourteen who are attending confirmation classes; pregnant females with pregnancy complications; children who are necessarily and legally employed; and children who are excused by a teacher or principal. State law requires that educational services be provided free to special education children between the ages of three and twenty.

Illinois has no statutory provisions related to corporal punishment in the schools. State law provides for a one-minute period of silence which can be used for prayer or silent reflection. However, it is stipulated that the time period may not be used for a religious exercise conducted by teachers.

Compared to a national average of 13.1 percent, 13.6 percent of Illinois residents have received a bachelor's degree from college. On a per capita basis, the state spent $875.70 for elementary and secondary education, compared to the national average of $931.76.

MULTICULTURAL EDUCATION EFFORTS

According to Illinois' responses to the authors' 1998 multicultural education survey, Illinois does not have a multicultural education program and does not have anyone in the State Office of Instruction who is responsible for such enterprises. No funds are budgeted by the state for multicultural education, but the state does provide leadership to school districts in specific kinds of multicultural education programs. This assistance comes through the development and dissemination of resource materials, teacher training, and consultant services to local school districts.

As part of their certification requirements, Illinois teachers must take at least one three-semester hour course in non-western cultures from either the humanities or the social sciences. However, there are no requirements for teacher trainees work with students from microcultures which are different from their own.

The leadership from the state encourages local school districts to stress the value of appreciating cultural pluralism, as opposed to adhering to the practice of cultural assimilation. How this is carried out varies a great deal from district to district.

Illinois has special programs designed to teach school children in their native language when necessary. They are transitional in nature, the ultimate goal being to educate students who are bilingual by the time they graduate. Several hundred school districts have such programs.

In order to comply with the *Brown v. Board of Education* Supreme Court decision, Illinois school districts employ a number of strategies in order to be in compliance with this court ruling. Strategies include: boundary changes, grade reorganization, school closings and consolidations, magnet school programs and student reassignments.

While Illinois keeps no exact records of racial violence incidents in the state's schools, the respondent believed that the general impression among the parents and educators is that such actions have increased in the schools during the past five years.

Illinois has no official state curriculum, therefore it is difficult to tell the extent of student exposure to the history of Native-Americans in the state. However, the Illinois School Code requires that the teaching of U.S. history includes the roles and contributions of the states' various racial and ethnic groups. The questionnaire responses indicated that there was no procedure in the state's Office of Education for the evaluation of textbooks or curriculum and library materials for racist and sexist content.

According to the respondent, Illinois' biggest problem facing multicultural education programs in the state was the lack of adequate teacher preparation in multicultural education. The state needs to move curriculum and instruction beyond the role and contributions of the states' microcultures to an emphasis on looking at the world from multiple perspectives. Further, there was a need to include critical thinking and comparative approaches in the study of social sciences and humanities. It was also felt that there needed to be an improvement in the quality of social interaction within schools which have diverse populations. It was felt that this could be accomplished through improved teacher preparation and support for local school districts to address these problems.

Like most large American cities, Illinois is struggling with an increasing poverty population which impacts a variety of multicultural education issues, particularly in the area of overall school performance. Slightly more than 20 percent of the state's children between the ages of five and seventeen are below the poverty level. This is one percentage point above the national percentage of 19.

REFERENCES

Bray, Robert C., *Rediscovery: Literature and Places in Illinois.* Champaign: University of Illinois Press, 1982.

Cohen, Lizabeth, *Making a New Deal: Industrial Workers in Chicago, 1919–1939.* Cambridge: Harvard University Press, 1990.

Cronon, William, *Nature's Metropolis: Chicago and the Great West.* New York: W. W. Norton, 1991.

Dedmon, Emmett, *Fabulous Chicago.* New Haven: Yale University Press, 1983.

Gearing, Frederick O., *The Face of the Fox.* Chicago: Aldine, 1970.

Hagan, William T., *The Sac and Fox Indians.* Norman: University of Oklahoma Press, 1958.

Hoffman, John, (ed.), *A Guide to the History of Illinois.* Westport, CT: Greenwood Press, 1990.

Josephy, Alvin M. Jr., *Five Hundred Nations.* New York: Alfred Knopf, 1994.

Leiter, Richard M., (ed.), *National Survey of State Laws.* First edition. Detroit: Gale Research, 1997.

Markowitz, Harvey, (ed.), *American Indians,* Volume II. Pasadena, CA: Salem Press, 1995.

McTaggart, Fed, *The Wolf That I Am: In Search of the Red Earth People.* Boston: Houghton Mifflin, 1976.

Nardulli, Peter F., (ed.), *Diversity, Conflict, and State Politics.* Champaign: University of Illinois Press, 1989.

Stout, David, et al., *Indians of Eastern Missouri, Western Illinois, and Southern Wisconsin, from the Proto-Historic Period to 1804.* New York: Garland, 1974.

Tingley, Donald F., *The Structuring of a State: The History of Illinois, 1899–1928.* Champaign: University of Illinois Press, 1980.

Travis, Dempsey J., *An Autobiography of Black Politics,* Chicago: Urban Press, 1987.

United States Department of Education, *Digest of Educational Statistics,* Washington D.C.:   U.S. Department of Education, 1997.

INDIANA

STATE HISTORY

Indiana is often referred to as the "Hoosier State" and its residents as "hoosiers." Interestingly, the origin of the name "Hoosier' is still hotly debated. There are several explanations which still exist. The first theory is that the word "Hoosier" comes from an old greeting from its early day. It is postulated that people knocking at a cabin door were greeted with "Who's yere" or "who is yer" (Who's here?). A second possibility is that the word originated as a result of a group of "husars" who were considered to be rowdy drunks, crossing the Ohio River from Kentucky into Indiana. A third notion is that the term came from a contractor on the Ohio Falls Canal from Louisville named Samuel Hoosier, who preferred to hire Indiana men as laborers on his project.

Ironically, the three theories for the nickname have little to do with the real pioneers of the state who were the original residents of the area. Prominent in the region were the mound builders from the Miami, Delaware (Lenni Lanapes) and Potawatomi tribes. Other groups included the Plankashaw, Kickapoo, Wea (also known as the Quiatenon), and Shawnee.

Originally occupying the Green Bay, Wisconsin areas during the seventeenth century, the Miami migrated to the southern end of Lake Michigan. The name "Miami" is thought to have originated from the Ojibwa word *oumamik,* meaning "people of the peninsula." During the eighteenth century the Wea and Plankashaw entities of the Miami tribe moved to the Wabash region of Indiana and fought a courageous battle to save their lands from the European-American advances.

In 1791, Little Turtle, a Miami, led a coalition of Miami, Shawnee, Potawatomi, and others in one of the worst defeats suffered by the United States Army against the native residents of the new republic. The American forces suffered losses of 647 killed and 217 wounded in the battle. However, the ultimate power of the United States won out and Little Turtle was eventually defeated at the Battle of Fallen Timbers three years later. Through the Treaty of Greenville in 1795, most of Ohio and part of Indiana were ceded to the United States. Between 1832 and 1840 the Miami moved to Kansas, where they were given reservations. Many of the Miami tribe avoided relocation and remained in the Peru, Indiana region. Most of the descendants of the original tribal residents are now of mixed ancestry.

The Lenni Lenapes and Poatawatomi tribes originally resided in the eastern portion of the United States. They were pushed westward by the new European residents who demanded their lands for themselves. Some of their numbers eventually ended up in present-day Indiana. However, as a result of the Removal Act of 1830, most of them relocated to Indian Territory in present-day Indiana. However, as a result of the Removal Act of 1830, most of them relocated to Indian Territory in Oklahoma, where they lived on designated reservations.

One of the first Europeans to enter present-day Indiana was the French fur trader and explorer, Rene-Robert Cavelier, Sieur de La Salle, who explored the present South Bend area in 1679. He traveled along the St. Joseph River, portaged to the Kankakee River, and traversed westward to the Illinois River. During this period of time and on into the first half of the eighteenth century, the French attempted to protect their lucrative fur trading interests in the inland midwest regions. In 1732 the French governor of Louisiana, believing that his jurisdiction extended northward into Indiana, was interested in establishing a fort along the Wabash River. Eventually forts were established at Fort Miami (now Fort Wayne), Fort Quiatenon, near Lafayette, and Fort Vincennes.

The defeat of the French in the so-called French and Indian War, resulted in the French ceding Canada and the eastern half of the Mississippi Valley to England. However, the Native-Americans, who had either remained neutral or sided with the French during the conflict, did not take kindly to the British occupation and for two years after the termination of the French and Indian War, the Native-American tribes attacked the British forts. However, the uprising eventually failed.

The Proclamation of 1763 resulted in the English setting aside lands west of the Appalachian Mountains for Native-Americans. Eleven years later the Quebec Act guaranteed religious freedom for Indiana's French settlers, and, at the end of the American Revolution, Indiana was included as part of the territory ceded to the new nation by the British. The state then became part of the Northwest Territory because of the Ordinance of 1787. By 1800, when Ohio was about to become a state, the remainder of the Northwest Territory became the Indiana Territory, and William Henry Harrison became the first territorial governor.

After the end of the American Revolution, Native-Americans became increasingly disgruntled over the increase in European-American settlement. After suffering a number of major defeats, the American forces prevailed in the 1794 Battle of Fallen Timbers. Many large tracts of land were ceded to the Americans under the terms of a treaty. However, under Chief Tecumseh, the stiff Native-American resistance repeated itself during the first decade of the 1800s. However, by 1815, Native-American opposition to European-American settlement waned.

The growth continued and four years after the War of 1812 Indiana became the nineteenth state of the new Union. This action motivated numerous immigrants to become new residents as people from Virginia, North Carolina, and Kentucky moved across the Ohio to join other immigrants from Pennsylvania, New Jersey, and New York, who floated down the river from Pittsburgh. Tom Lincoln moved from Kentucky, purchasing 1,670 acres for a farm on Little Pigeon Creek near the Ohio. His two children, Abe and Sarah, had already learned how to read and write in Kentucky, since they went to school there. However, since Indiana had no schools in the area, the two children were schooled by their mother, Nancy, prior to her untimely death in 1818.

Indiana has had a long history of higher education. Even though the state had been a strong agricultural area, education became a strong issue early in its history. Asbury (DePauw) College was one of the first, followed by Notre Dame University in 1842. Caleb Mills, president of Wabash College, became one of the nation's most important educators. He was instrumental in establishing the state's elementary and secondary education program, relying heavily on the support of Robert Dale Owen. A New Englander, Mills was able to arouse an interest in education through his eloquent oratory. His efforts paid dividends because in the 1851 constitution the state accepted responsibility for free public schools.

Hoosiers were loyal to the Union during the Civil War and with the fall of Fort Sumter, both Democrats and Republicans stepped forward to support the Union cause. The Hoosier volunteers were not prepared when war broke out in 1861. Nonetheless, the common belief was that the war would be over in just a few months.

During the last half of the nineteenth century, the proliferation of east-west rail lines spurred the industrial development of the state. And by 1910, Gary, Indiana, had come into existence when United States Steel bought land on the southern tip of Lake Michigan in order to take advantage of the Great Lakes shipping potential. The city became quite multicultural, with African-Americans and European-Americans from a multitude of ethnic backgrounds moving to this new planned city to secure employment.

One of Indiana's more controversial sons, Eugene Debs, was a native of Terre Haute. He was extremely concerned about people from the culture of poverty and became the leader of the Socialist Party, running for the presidency five times. He opposed America's entrance into World War I, but was eventually sentenced to ten years of prison for violating the Espionage Act. While in prison, he polled 901,062 votes in 1920.

But World War II affected the state of Indiana much more that the First World War. Camp Atterbury was an enormous facility which trained entire divisions. Also included in the complex was Wakeman Hospital for the war wounded and a stockade which housed 12,000 prisoners of war. But equally important to Indiana's contributions to the war effort was the industrial potential in the northern part of the state. General Electric and International Harvester of Fort Wayne and Indianapolis, as well as Studebacker and Bendix Corporation of Indianapolis, became defense contractors. Servel Refrigerators of Evansville made wings for fighter planes, along with cartridge cases and land mines. Shipbuilders along the Ohio and Allison and Curtis-Wright of Indianapolis made aircraft engines and propellers.

After the war, Indiana's enterprises continued to grow for a short period of time. However, by 1976, the population of Gary had declined from a peak of 180,000 in the mid-1960s to 161,000. Indiana experienced a decline in the work force as 60,000 young men were involved in the Vietnam War during that period of time. In 1976 Indiana's largest employer was General Motors with more than 50,000 employees. However, in spite of some losses, Indiana's industrial strength has still remained strong, particularly in the northern part of the state. It has consistently been ranked among the top ten industrialized states in the nation, while its agricultural ventures are also powerful, particularly in the southern part of the state.

Like other states, Indiana has been blessed with a number of key events and prominent figures throughout its history. Legislation was enacted in 1949 which required the desegregation of all Indiana's schools, five years before the *Brown v. Board of Education* Supreme Court decision. In 1967 Richard Hatcher was elected major of Gary, becoming Indiana's first elected African-American mayor.

Indiana's rich history has also relied on the escapades of many key figures who have contributed substantially to the welfare of the state. In addition to outstanding governors such as Evan Bayh, Henry F. Schricker, and Paul V. McNutt, senator Birch Bayh became a powerful congressional leader. But in addition to these and other well-known politicians, the state has produced a who's who list of outstanding writers such as Theodore Dreiser, Booth Tarkington, Kurt Vonnegut, James Whitcomb Riley, and Jessamyn West.

THE EDUCATIONAL SYSTEM

In the early days, Indiana's free schools were regarded as pauper schools, a common practice in many parts of the United States. Indiana's second constitutional convention decided to require the state to provide for a free common school system which would be open to all. Moreover, at this time the office of the Superintendent of Public Instruction was created. This was and is an elected office which originally was not politicized. William C. Larrabee, a professor of mathematics at Indiana Asbury University, was the state's first superintendent. However, due to a state supreme court decision, funding for Indiana's free public school system was not available until the end of the Civil War.

Indiana's State Department of Public Instruction supervises public elementary and secondary schools, teacher training, and licensing. In addition, it is responsible for licensing, school health and attendance, and a number of other duties. The state's city school systems are administered by local superintendents and school boards, as are rural districts.

Prospective teachers must score successfully on the National Teachers Examination, which measures basic skills, professional skills, and appropriate content knowledge. Indiana State University, Terre Haute, is the state's first teacher preparation institution.

On a per-capita basis, Indiana spends about $70 less than the national average for the education of its elementary and secondary school children. Compared to the national average of 42 percent, nearly 73 percent of Indiana's teachers have completed the master's degree.

Indiana's compulsory attendance ages for students are from seven to eighteen. Exceptions to this policy include students who attend another school taught in the English language; children who are provided instruction equivalent to public education; and children who are physically or mentally unfit for attendance. Special education programs must be provided to all children between the ages of three and twenty-one years of age. The state has no written policy on year-round schools, even though a number of school districts have such programs. All school districts are required to offer half-day kindergarten programs.

Indiana has no statutory provisions regarding corporal punishment in the schools and state statutes provide for a brief period of silent prayer or meditation. Indiana has a high school graduation rate which is above the national average but is below the national average in the percentages of school graduates who achieve the bachelor's degree and professional or graduate degrees.

MULTICULTURAL EDUCATION EFFORTS

According to the authors' survey, responses provided by the Indiana Department of Education, the state has no planned program for multicultural education and nobody in the state office is responsible for such efforts. No funding exists for such ventures, and the state provides no leadership to school districts in specific kinds of multicultural education programs. Indiana requires no special coursework and/or other multicultural experiences for teacher certification.

The respondent felt that the state of Indiana stressed cultural pluralism as opposed to an emphasis on assimiliationist philosophy in its approaches to the curriculum content and instructional practices. Also, Indiana makes use of English as a Second Language (ESL) programs in the state's schools.

Seven Indiana School districts are under court-ordered desegregation. Other districts request technical assistance in race, gender, and national origin issues from Indiana's Title IV funded state office. Due to the elimination of Title IV funds for state agencies, Indiana's Title IV office is staffed by only two persons, a coordinator and a secretary. This makes it virtually impossible to meet the needs of the state's school districts.

The history of Native-American involvement is included in the state's regular curriculum in the fourth, fifth, and eighth grade social studies curriculum. It is also included in various high school subjects. All curriculum materials, library materials, and textbooks are evaluated by the state's Office of Education for racist and sexist content.

Indiana's respondent indicated that the biggest problems facing multicultural education programs in Indiana were the lack of resources and the long standing opposition of conservative groups to the concept of multicultural education. The respondent felt that the biggest improvements in multicultural education programs would be to get them incorporated into the state board policies and guidelines, which should be developed. Multicultural education programs should be incorporated into the curriculum of every school district in Indiana.

Compared to the national average of 19 percent, Indiana has just 14.5 percent of its children between the ages of five to seventeen who are below the poverty level.

REFERENCES

Buley, R. Carlyle, *The Old Northwest, 1815–1840.* Bloomington: University of Indiana Press, 1962.

Carmoy, Donald F., (ed.), *Indiana: A Self Appraisal.* Bloomington: Indiana University Press, 1966.

Dillon, Lowell I. and Lyon, Edward E., *Indiana: Crossroads of America.* Dubuque: Kendall/Hunt, 1978.

Ginger, Ray, *The Bending Cross: A Biography of Eugene Victor Debs.* New Brunswick,NJ: Rutgers University Press, 1949.

Hojnacki, William P., *Politics and Public Policy in Indiana.* Dubúque: Kendall/Hunt, 1983.

Josephy, Alvin Jr., *Five Hundred Nations.* New York: Alfred Knopf, 1994.

Kraft, Herbert C., *The Lenape: Archaeology, History, and Ethnography.* Newark: New Jersey Historical Society, 1986.

Leibowitz, *My Indiana, a History.* Englewood Cliffs, NJ: Prentice Hall, 1964.

Leiter, Richard A., (ed.), *National Survey of State Laws.* First edition. Detroit: Gale Research, 1997.

Madison, James H., *Indiana Through Tradition and Change.* Indianapolis: Indiana Historical Society, 1982.

Peckham, Howard H., *Indiana: A History.* New York: W. W. Norton, 1978.

United States Department of Education, *Digest of Educational Statistics.* Washington D.C., United States Department of Education, 1997.

Wilson, William E., *Indiana: A History.* Bloomington: Indiana University Press, 1966.

IOWA

STATE HISTORY

According to the best estimates of anthropologists, Native-Americans have inhabited the present boundaries of Iowa for approximately 12,000 years. These paleo-Indians migrated to the area in order to hunt buffalo and woolly mammoth for food. Their dead were buried with shell necklaces and weapons, which were intended to defend themselves from whatever dangers they might encounter in the next world.

Among the more recently-arriving tribes of Native-Americans are the Iowa, Algonkian (Algonquian), Hopewell, Oneota, Mill Creek, and Glenwood. Actually, the Algonquian was a language group which consisted of a large number of tribes which all spoke the Algonquian language. The Oneota are believed to have resided originally in Minnesota, Wisconsin, and Illinois. However, they also lived in Iowa.

The effigy mounds are masses of earth which were shaped to look like animals and geometric forms. Found in Iowa, and other nearly states, anthropologists believe that they were constructed for religious purposes, but the vast majority seem to have been build for burial sites. They were created in the states of Illinois, Ohio, Michigan, and Wisconsin, in addition to the present-day boundaries of Iowa. Some of the mound areas have been transformed into parks.

It is believed that the first European to have set foot in the present boundaries of Iowa may have been Louis Joliet. Accompanied by a priest, Jacques Marquette, and five voyageurs in 1673, he traveled down the Wisconsin River to its junction with the Mississippi, Iowa's eastern boundary. Interestingly, the formal cession of Iowa's land occurred in Paris in 1803 when Napoleon signed over the Louisiana Territory to Jefferson's representatives.

The state was named after the French word, "Aiaouez" ("Ioway"). The name for the Iowa tribe in its native Chiwere language (part of the Siouan language group) was "Pahoja" which means "gray snow." The reason for the name has never been clearly determined.

Originally residing in the upper Great Lakes region, the Iowa followed the Mississippi River south and west to the present boundaries of the state sometime in the early seventeenth century. The women cultivated such crops as corn, beans, and squash, while the male tribal members hunted raccoon, deer, buffalo, and otter. The tribe was also known for its artistic pursuits, crafting catlinite pipes (calumets).

The Iowas had a patrilineal clan system with strict rules against marrying outside the clan. Chiefs and religious leaders arrived at their positions according to their clan membership. The Medicine Dance was the primary religious ceremony. Because of this practice, they functioned similarly to the tribes which resided in the great lakes areas.

The Dakota Sioux were the primary warring foes of the Iowa tribe. They also suffered through a number of hostile actions with the Sauk and Mesquakie (Fox) but eventually the groups made peace with each other, and they developed a close association. In fact, they lived together on a reservation which was located along the present Kansas-Nebraska border. After the federal government attempted to move the Iowas to Oklahoma (Indian Territory), many of them remained behind, eventually blending into the burgeoning farm economy. By 1851, the Native-American tribes had ceded all of their land to the United States.

In 1804, the United States Congress provided a government for the latest acquisition known as the Louisiana Purchase by dividing the region into the Territory of Orleans and the District of Louisiana. Iowa was included in the District of Louisiana. After Missouri joined the Union in 1821, Iowa was left in limbo until it became the twenty-ninth state in 1846. Just one year later, the University of Iowa received its charter.

During 1805, Zebulon Pike was commissioned to determine whether the source of the Mississippi River was within the American boundaries. In carrying out his mission, he traveled north on the Des Moines River. In addition to the various tribes and bands of Native-Americans, he also encountered fairly large numbers of European-Americans who were on their way to Saint Louis.

The 1830s was a decade which saw Iowa experiencing tremendous growth of new European-American residents. In 1838 a land office was established in Dubuque. The purpose of the office was to promote the sale of new lands acquired in the Black Hawk Purchase. During the previous five years an estimated 38,000 European-Americans had moved into the region.

When Robert Lucas, Iowa's first territorial governor, arrived in the area, he was chagrined to discover that there were no public schools for children. However, in spite of his lobbying efforts, he was unsuccessful in convincing Iowa's legislature that such facilities were badly needed to ensure that Iowa had an educated populace. In fact, public schools in Iowa did not become established until the 1850s when Governor Grimes persuaded Massachusetts' distinguished educator Horace Mann to lead a commission which would study the educational needs of this new region.

During 1857, the second state constitution was approved by the Iowa Legislature, and the state capital was moved to Des Moines, where it still remains. During the Civil War, Iowa contributed about 80,000 young men to the armed forces of the Union. This new constitution also required the development of a public system of education for the state's children. And just three years after the termination of the World II horrors, grand trunk rail lines were constructed across the state. During this same year, the Republican Party dominated Iowa politics for a century afterward.

After the completion of these east-west trunk lines, agriculture commenced to dominate the agricultural scene in Iowa. The first farm organization, known as the Grange, became supportive of the Anti-Monopoly Party, gaining control of Iowa's General Assembly in 1873. By 1880, Iowa's economy shifted from an emphasis on wheat production to the production of hogs and corn. The emphasis on corn production has persisted throughout the years and Iowa is still one of the leading corn-producing states in the Union.

After World War I, many young Iowans commenced moving from the state to other parts of the country in search of new occupations. Many young veterans moved to places such as southern California in order to take advantage of the citrus industry which thrived in a warmer climate. These citrus groves offered the opportunity to remain in agricultural pursuits in warm climates which were closer to the oceans and mountains. Southern California cities such as Long Beach experiences huge influxes of Iowa immigrants. For many years the "Iowa Picnic" in Long Beach was one of that community's major events.

However, not until after World War II did political leaders in Iowa begin to argue for a movement in the direction of more industry, in an attempt to balance the state's economy more successfully. Consequently, Iowa started to develop an industrial economy in the midst of some of the nation's most productive farmlands.

The state's system of higher education has become viewed as one of the national leaders. The University of Iowa, first established in 1847 by Iowa's first General Assembly, started as an institution of higher education in 1855 as the State University of Iowa. In 1962 it changed its name to the University of Iowa. Among its many achievements has been its willingness to admit men and women on an equal basis, the first state university to do so. It established the first law school west of the Mississippi, and it also has the distinction of creating the nation's first school of religion in a state university.

The University was also instrumental in pioneering some of the early tests used in elementary and secondary schools throughout the nation. The *Iowa Basic Skills Test* is used in many school districts to assess the educational levels of children in reading, language arts, math, science, and social studies.

More than most states, Iowa is recognized for pioneering an interest in gender and racial equity in its educational programs shortly after the termination of the Civil War. In addition to the distinguished contributions of the state university, other institutions of higher education in Iowa have also made noteworthy achievements. For example, Samson College admitted George Washington Carver, a former slave, who went on to become a famous botanist, particularly noted for his pioneering research on the peanut. Starting his education at Samson College on the Indianola campus, he completed his work at Iowa State University at Ames. In addition, Alexander Clarke of Muscatine, Iowa began his law studies at the University of Iowa becoming the first African-American to argue cases before the Iowa Supreme Court. Finally, Arabella Babb Mansfield, an Iowa Wesleyan graduate, became the first American woman to be admitted to the bar.

These noteworthy achievements in higher education were accomplished during a period of time when the state was predominantly Republican in its political persuasion. It was in this climate that the state produced the thirty-first president of the United States, Herbert Clark Hoover, who served from 1928 to 1932.

THE EDUCATIONAL SYSTEM

It is believed that the first school established by European-American immigrants was a private school for settler's children which opened its doors in 1830.

Moreover, the other early schools of this type were also private. One of them opened in Fort Madison in 1834. Because of the rural nature of Iowa, the early public school system tended to include a large number of one-room schools which only operated about two months during the year. These schools had very small numbers of students, and it was not until 1902 that the state finally made attendance compulsory between the ages of seven and sixteen.

The first consolidated township school in Iowa originated in Buffalo township in Winnebago County in 1897. Rural schools were closed, and the children were sent to a new central school in horse-drawn wagons. However, this practice was slow to catch on until the state eventually provided funding for transportation costs connected with transporting students to the consolidated schools. By 1921 there were 439 consolidated schools in the state, but due to the depression and the war, the number stayed almost the same for twenty-one years.

However, many of the financial problems for public education were solved in 1945 when the state passed the Community School District Act, which shifted the funding burden from rural farmers to the state. Thus, the rural schools became a thing of the past as students were bused to the consolidated state-funded schools, sometimes at great distances. Indeed, many Iowans were amused when Alabama governor George Wallace talked about the "poor little children" who had to be bused to school in order to achieve desegregated schools.

Iowa's director of eucation for the state's schools is appointed by the governor. Children are required to attend school between the ages of six and sixteen years. Exceptions to this requirement include: students who attend accredited private schools or have access to competent private instruction, students who receive a GED or complete their graduation requirements, students who attend religious services or receive religious instruction, and students who have physical or mental conditions which do not permit school attendance. Students can be home schooled as long as the curriculum includes competent private instruction, including basic arithmetic, reading, writing, grammar, spelling, U.S. history, history of Iowa, and American government for at least 140 days. Parents can be prosecuted for noncompliance. Fines for a first offense are $100 and escalate to a thirty-day jail sentence and $1,000 fine for the third offense.

Iowa has no statutory provisions regarding the use of corporal punishment in the schools. That is left up to local school districts. Likewise, no statutory provisions exist regarding the use of prayer in schools. Interestingly, Iowa is one of eight states which require no testing for the initial certification of teachers. The approvement process relies on in-class observations instead.

Per capita expenditures for public education are slightly above the national average, and the state is well above the national average as far as high school graduates are concerned. While 67 percent of Iowa's teachers have the bachelor's degree, just 31 percent hold the master's degree, compared to the national average of 42 percent (based on 1994 statistics).

Iowa students are entitled to special education programs between the ages of birth to twenty years. Only four other states provide such educational services from birth. There is no policy for year-around schools, and Iowa is one of thirteen states which does not require school districts to offer kindergarten programs.

MULTICULTURAL EDUCATION EFFORTS

Responses to the authors' survey instrument revealed that Iowa does have a planned multicultural education program. Chapter 256.11 of the Iowa Code reads that: *The State Board shall promulgate rules to require that a multicultural, nonsexist approach is used by schools and school districts. The education program shall be taught from a multicultural, nonsexist approach.* The Iowa Code also requires that each school district create a written plan which must be evaluated and updated every five years.

These written plans must include processes which foster knowledge of, respect and appreciation for the contemporary contributions of diverse cultural groups to society. Special emphasis must be placed on Asian-Americans, African-Americans, Latinos, Native-Americans, and the handicapped. Also required is the inclusion of nonsexist in-service training activities for all staff members. The person in charge of multicultural education programs is the educational equity team leader. However, no specific funds from the state have been designated for multicultural education programs.

The state office provides school districts with special conferences and workshops, publications, and monitoring services in order to ensure that appropriate multicultural education efforts are being carried out at the local level. The predominant microcultures, in addition to European-Americans, are African-Americans and Latinos.

In order to become certificated, teachers must take a human relations class that focuses on multicultural education issues. The curriculum approaches must stress cultural pluralism as opposed to a more assimilationist approach. However, the respondent observed that there is always a gap between theory, legislation, and actual classroom practice.

Iowa has rather sophisticated programs for teaching children in their native languages when necessary. The state funding formula provides a weighted dollar factor based on the number of students who have a native language other than English. The special programs used for such students include both bilingual education and English as a Second Language (ESL). The respondent stated that the majority of the assistance programs are ESL.

Iowa's school standards require that schools take the necessary steps to prevent racially segregated schools from developing. Strategies employed throughout the state include the use of magnet schools, voluntary transfers, school pairings, and boundary changes.

Like many other states, Iowa does not have an adequate system for keeping track of the numbers of racial confrontations in the schools. However, the respondent went on to say that the general feeling among educators tended to be that some increase in such confrontations had occurred in recent years.

Since Iowa does not have state adoptions for textbooks, library holdings, and curriculum materials, they do not screen for racist and sexist content at that level. This is all carried out at the local school district where all of the decisions are made in regard to the use of such materials.

In response to the final two questionnaire items, the respondent felt that Iowa's two greatest problems were the lack of racial and ethnic diversity among professional educators around the state and a lack of cross-cultural experiences among most of the state's educators. Iowa's biggest needs were expressed as the need for an adequate multicultural Education budget in order to implement the sophisticated legislation and rules pertaining to multicultural education efforts.

As noted by the respondent, Iowa's students tend to come from a huge majority of European-American backgrounds. Thus, the "minority" population is rather small. Also, the state has just 15.5 percent of its students from the age five to seventeen group who are from poverty circumstances. This compares favorably with a national average of 19 percent.

REFERENCES

Alex, Lyn M., *Exploring Iowa's Past*. Iowa City: University of Iowa Press, 1980.

Bureau of School Administration and Accreditation, *Multicultural, Non-Sexist Education: The Legal Authority*. Des Moines: Iowa Department of Education, 1994.

Bureau of Administration and School Improvement Services, *Guidelines for the Development of Multicultural, Non-Sexist Education Plans*. Des Moines: Iowa Department of Education, 1998.

Friedberger, Mark, *Shake Out: Iowa Farm Families in the 1980s*. Lexington: University of Kentucky Press, 1980.

Gue, Benjamin F., *History of Iowa*. New York: Century History Company, 1903.

Hake, Herbert V., *Iowa Inside Out*. Ames: Iowa State University Press, 1968.

Hasrick, Royal B., *The Sioux: Life and Customs of a Warrior Society*. Norman: University of Oklahoma Press, 1964.

Larew, James, *A Party Reborn: The Democrats of Iowa*. Des Moines: State Historical Society of Iowa, 1989.

Leiter, Richard A., (ed.), *National Survey of State Laws*. First edition. Detroit: Gale Research, 1997.

Markowitz, Harvey, (ed.), *American Indians* Volumes 1, 2, and 3. Pasadena, CA: Salem Press, 1997.

Rood, David S., "Siouan." In *The Languages of Native America: Historical and Comparative Assessment*, edited by Lyle, Campbell, and Narianne, Mithun, Austin. University of Texas Press, 1979.

Sage, Leland, *A History of Iowa*. Ames: Iowa State University Press, 1974.

United States Department of Education, *Digest of Educational Statistics*. Washington D.C.: United States Department of Education, 1997.

Wall, Joseph Frazier, *Iowa: A History*. New York: W. W. Norton, 1978.

KANSAS

STATE HISTORY

During the decade prior to the Civil War, the nation was embroiled in controversies pertaining to the issue of slavery. The Kansas-Nebraska Act of 1854 resulted in the creation of two new territories, and slavery was no longer illegal north of the Missouri Compromise border. In fact, the new territories had the right to choose whether or not they would have slavery. Ugly battles ensued between the antislavery and pro-slavery factions. As a result, the area was known as "bleeding Kansas." However, when Kansas finally became a state in 1861, it adopted a constitution which outlawed slavery. However, the history of Kansas began hundreds of years before this period of time.

The state has had several main tribes of Native-Americans residing within its present boundaries. The name "Kansas" was derived from the Kansa tribe, also known as the Kaw. The Dhegiha branch of the Siouan language group includes the Kansa, Osage, Quapaw, Omaha, and Ponca. While the population was estimated at approximately 1,500 in 1700, the numbers had dwindled to only about 200 by 1905, due to the usual ravages of disease and warfare.

The Kansa tribe referred to themselves as "Hutanga" which meant "by the edge of the shore." Some anthropologists believe this meant that originally they had probably resided somewhere near the shores of the Atlantic Ocean sometime before 1600. After migrating westward, the Kansa settled near the confluence of the Kansas and Missouri Rivers.

Part of the Siouan language group, the Osage tribe included two divisions (moieties): the Tzisho or Sky People and the Hunkah or Land People. The name itself (Osage) is a corruption of the tribal name, Wa-sha 'zhe. Like the Kansa, archaeological evidence and tribal legends suggest that at one time the Osage resided somewhere between the Mississippi River and the Atlantic Ocean. Religious leadership was provided by tribal shamans, and both men and women belonged to religious societies.

Geographically, the Osage were located in present-day Oklahoma, Arkansas, and Missouri, in addition to Kansas. However, by 1808 they ceded northern Arkansas and most of Missouri to the United States government. By 1825, a number of Osage-U.S. treaties resulted in the designation of their reservation in southern Kansas. In the 1990 census, their population was listed at 9,257.

At one time, the Comanche lands included much of the present boundaries of Texas, New Mexico, Oklahoma, Colorado, and Kansas. Numbering 11,322 in the 1990 census, the Comanches were nomadic and dominated large portions of the southwestern United States because of their excellent riding skills. They relied on the buffalo, which roamed the grassy plains areas until the late 1800s. Noted for their horsemanship, the Comanches would often venture clear to Mexico in order to replenish their stock.

Comanche men usually did not marry until after they were successful warriors. They could marry as many women as they could support, and they were able to acquire divorces in a simple manner. Wives who committed adultery were often beaten or given nose clippings. Due to their nomadic status, Comanches often dwelled in fancy tipis, which were made by the women. After the Medicine Lodge Treaty and the Battle of the Washita, a large number of Comanche bands moved to reservations.

Native-Americans in present-day Kansas were thought to have first encountered Europeans in 1541 when Francisco Coronado and a party of Spanish explorers entered present-day Kansas in search of gold. Leaving the Mexican province of Nuevo Galicia with a band of about 300 Spanish soldiers, they were in search of the "Seven Cities of Cibola." After being thwarted in their quest when they traveled through the southwestern portion of the United States, they received another tip and proceeded to the northeast, traversing various portions of modern-day Kansas's boundaries. And even though Coronado's party left the region, Frey Juan de Padillo returned to the area, only to meet his death at the hands of some of the native residents.

In spite of Coronado's failure to find riches in his quest, another expedition led by Juan de Oñate in 1601 sought to confirm Coronado's claim that this portion of the new land had enormous value to Spain. These Spanish expeditions resulted in the introduction of horses in the region, which greatly facilitated the hunting and warring exploits of the Native-American groups in the area.

For about 200 years, only a handful of Europeans entered the regions which comprise the present boundaries of the state of Kansas. During the first half of the nineteenth century, Fort Scott, Fort Leavenworth, and Fort Riley were constructed to provide a level of safety for the Europeans who were coming into the territories. However, the population figures of 1850 revealed that only about 1,500 European-Americans resided in present-day Kansas. Most of them were missionaries and their families, along with military personnel. Approximately 34,000 Native-Americans resided in the area at that time.

During the 1850s, a large number of New Englanders moved into the region. They tended to be strongly opposed to slavery and highly supportive of measures which promoted human freedom. In addition to this group, people moved into the area from eastern Missouri, the original Northwest, and the upper Mississippi River valley. While their primary motivation for emigration was the betterment of their economic circumstances, many of them tended to be quite passionate about their moral and religious beliefs.

The 1850s in Kansas might be best characterized as the period of turbulence leading to the start of the Civil War. In 1856, antislavery forces under the leadership of John Brown attacked proslavery factions at Pottawatomie Creek, resulting in the death of five proslavery men. This battle was typical of the numerous hostile confrontations which occurred during the 1850s and up to the end of the American Civil War in 1865.

During the war, Kansas fought on the Union side and contributed an enormous number of fighting personnel to the Union cause. However, it also suffered one of the highest proportion of casualty rates of any of the participating states. Actually, Kansas/Nebraska territories were considered to be detrimental to the cause of slavery because of the subhumid and semiarid climate which would not support a cotton economy, thus negating the need for a large cheap labor force.

After the war, the state saw a large number of its towns becoming railheads for the big cattle drives which would become a trademark of the state's history. In fact, for two decades after the war, Dodge City, Wyatt Earp, the Long Branch Saloon, and Bat Masterson became prime focal points for many Hollywood "westerns." The Long Branch saloon became a choice Hollywood site for quick-draw contests and the other western antics, which typified the events in Hollywood westerns.

One of the greatest periods of growth in Kansas's history occurred during the twenty-five years following the termination of the Civil War. The Homestead Act of 1862 allowed many immigrants from the eastern portion of the United States to acquire fertile lands for farming. Very few immigrants from other countries settled in the region, and to this day African-Americans comprise only about 5 percent of the population. Many of them are the descendants of freed slaves who were falsely promised "40 acres and a mule."

After an unusually severe winter in 1865–1866, a permanent structure was created on the original site of Fort Dodge, named after General Grenville Dodge. Originally, the fort was erected in order to keep the peace between the European immigrants who were streaming into the lands and Native-Americans who were struggling to retain their homelands as well as their way of life. A rail line finally reached the new community, originally named Buffalo City, in order to transport buffalo hides to eastern markets. As the great buffalo herds became depleted, Native-Americans were motivated to reside on the reservations in Indian Territory and the confrontations between the Native-Americans and the European-American immigrants diminished. The name "Buffalo City" was changed to "Dodge City."

However, Dodge City soon became famous for becoming a shipping terminal for Texas cattle. After the mid-1870s, cowboys commenced arriving as a result of the cattle drives. They had money to spend and the city soon became known as a wide-open western town.

An example of one of the early Kansas schools was the first school in Dodge City, which was opened in September of 1880, for elementary and secondary students. State law provided for the establishment of county schools which were funded with property taxes. The facilities in the school were meager, and there weren't enough textbooks for all the students. However, state funding made it possible to secure more books, and eventually night classes were offered to adults who wished to improve their writing and penmanship skills.

Kansas is also known for Carrie Nation and her saloon-smashing exploits around the turn of the century and for the election of President Dwight D. Eisenhower, who spent his boyhood in Abilene, Kansas. It was Eisenhower who appointed Earl Warren to be the Chief Justice of the United States Supreme Court. The famous Warren Court presided in the landmark 9-0 decision in *Brown v. Board of Education* case which ruled on a Topeka practice of maintaining racially-segregated schools. The decision made it illegal for states and/or school districts to segregate students by race.

This United States Supreme Court decision is probably the primary factor for the motivation of the American Civil Rights era, which attracted attention to the issues of inequality in educational opportunities for minorities and women, eventually leading to the establishment of Affirmative Action programs all over the land.

THE EDUCATIONAL SYSTEM

The state superintendent of schools in Kansas is appointed by the Board of Trustees. The compulsory attendance age is from six to seventeen years, although compulsory special education services are provided to children from age three to twenty. Exceptional children may have different requirements. In lieu of public school attendance, Kansas children are allowed to participate in private, denominational, or parochial schools. However, Kansas courts have determined that "home schools do not meet the requirements of the state's compulsory attendance law" (*State v. Garber*, 197 K. 567-569, 419 P.2d 896). In another case (*State v. Lowry*, 191K. 701-704; 383 P.2d962) home schooling was not deemed to be the equivalent of private, denominational, or parochial schools.

As of the 1995–96 school year, there was no policy on year-around schools and no Kansas school districts had them. The state had no requirements for the maintenance of kindergarten programs, either on a half-day or full-day basis.

In order to teach in Kansas schools, teachers must demonstrate a basic knowledge of basic skills and be observed in successful in-class teaching performances. The state spends about $945 per capita for the education of elementary and secondary students on an annual basis. This amount compares with the national average of $932 per child. Kansas teachers are exactly at the national average in terms of the 42 percent of teachers who have finished their master's degree.

Kansas state law does provide for a brief period of silence to be used as an opportunity for silent prayer or for silent reflection. However, students cannot be directed by school personnel in their silent use of this time. Records of students and the privacy of Kansas students' school records is governed by the Family Educational Records Protection Act.

MULTICULTURAL EDUCATION EFFORTS

According to the respondent in the authors' national 1998 study of multicultural education, Kansas does not have a planned program in multicultural education and there is no funding specifically earmarked for multicultural education programs. However, it was reported that better than 4 million dollars was budgeted for ESOL/Bilingual education during the 1995–1996 school year. The state of Kansas offers leadership to school districts for training school district personnel in specific kinds of multicultural education program.

The predominant microcultures in Kansas consist of Native-Americans, Mexican-Americans, and Southeast Asian-Americans. The respondent indicated that the state requires one multicultural education course in order to receive an ESOL endorsement on the teaching certificate. Kansas does not evaluate curriculum materials, library materials, and textbooks for racist and sexist statements. This is carried out at the local level.

Kansas has a relatively low rate of children under the age of seventeen who are from poverty circumstances. Compared to the national poverty rate of 19 percent, only 10.7 percent of Kansas children between the ages of five and seventeen find themselves in such circumstances. Only seven other states have a smaller percentage.

REFERENCES

Baird, W. David, *The Osage People*. Phoenix: Indian Tribal Series, 1972.

Council of the State School Officers, *The Council*. Washington D.C.: Council of State School Officers, 1998.

Davis, Kenneth S., *Kansas: A Bicentennial History*. New York: W. W. Norton, 1976.

Faulk, Odie B., *Dodge City: The Most Western Town of All*. New York: Oxford University Press, 1977.

Hagan, William T., *United States-Comanche Relations: The Reservation Years*. New Haven: Yale University Press, 1976.

Johnson, Samuel A., *The Battle Cry of Freedom*. Westport, CT: Greenwood Press, 1977.

Leiter, Richard A., (ed.), *National Survey of State Laws*. First edition. Detroit: Gale Research, 1997.

McNall, Scott, *The Road to Rebellion: Class Formation and Kansas Populism, 1865–1900*. Chicago: University of Chicago Press, 1988.

Miller, Nyle H., *Kansas and the West*. Topeka: Kansas State Historical Society, 1976.

Miner, Craig, and Unrau, William E., *The End of Indian Kansas: A Study of Cultural Revolution, 1854–1871*. Lawrence: Regents Press of Kansas, 1978.

United States Department of Education, *Digest of Educational Statistics*. Washington D.C., United States Department of Education, 1997.

Unrau, William E., *The Kansa Indians: A History of the Wind People, 1673–1873*. Norman: University of Oklahoma Press, 1971.

Wallace, Ernest and Adamson, E. Hoebel, *The Comanches: Lords of the South Plains*. Norman: University of Oklahoma Press, 1952.

Wilson, Terry P., *The Osage*. New York: Chelsea House, 1988.

KENTUCKY

STATE HISTORY

Early Kentucky history is known for the exploits of Daniel Boone, who was instrumental in creating the "Wilderness Road" through the Cumberland Gap across the Appalachians prior to the outset of the American Revolution. However, the Europeans who entered the area, which would later become the state of Kentucky, intruded on the intertribal hunting grounds of the Shawnee, Iroquois, Delaware, and Cherokee tribes which led to severe friction between these Native-Americans and the European immigrants.

The large number of burial fields, mounds, and cave shelters lead archaeologists to believe that many Native-Americans resided in Kentucky long before the arrival of the Europeans. The eastern mound area covers much of Kentucky's bluegrass region and other aboriginal remains have been found in every one of Kentucky's counties. The Native-American tribes in the area were eventually overcome by the Europeans who poured into the area after Dr. Thomas Walker led the first known group of European immigrants through the Cumberland Gap in 1750.

However, the battles between the various groups and the European-Americans were relatively short-lived but extremely violent. The Iroquois Confederacy was powerful but headquartered a great distance from the bluegrass areas of Kentucky. One reason for the lack of permanent residency in the area has been attributed to a possible bone disease which afflicted Native-Americans who might have resided in the area. They may have blamed the problem on the environment.

The newly-discovered lands were fertile, and the first permanent European settlement was established by James Herrod in 1775 at present-day Harrodsburg, Kentucky. During this year the first known school for European-Americans was created there. Boonesborough, established by Daniel Boone, joined forces with Harrodsburg in an attempt to drive the Native-Americans away for good. This was finally accomplished in 1782 at Blue Licks when the Native-Americans were forced to retreat to the west side of the Ohio River.

Before the establishment of these permanent settlements, several explorations into the region occurred. In 1669 a German explorer named John Lederer made three trips into the Blue Ridge area, and two years later an English group entered the Ohio valley. While originally they were not greatly impressed with what they found, their interest was rekindled when the French claimed all of the territories of the Mississippi River and its tributaries.

Kentucky became the first state west of the Appalachian range to become admitted to the Union. This occurred in 1792 when Kentucky became the fifteenth member of the new Union. It was admitted as a slave state, even though the populace was quite divided over the issue.

Daniel Boone is certainly one of the most important figures in Kentucky's colorful history. However, history has recorded mixed signals about this complicated frontiersman. On one hand he was viewed as a woodsman, frontiersman, and an Indian fighter. However, according to some sources, Boone rejected these characterizations. Instead, he liked to think of himself as a devoted family man and a devout Quaker. Many of his critics suspected his loyalty, feeling he was beholden to the Crown.

However, regardless of the controversy, Boone is still known as one of the key, exciting figures during the nation's pioneer days. The fact that he surveyed and helped to construct the Wilderness road motivated many people to leave the eastern seaboard and move westward.

Another famous Kentucky figure was Abraham Lincoln, born in 1809 in Hardin County, Kentucky (now Larue County). Although its authenticity is disputed, the original residence of Tom and Nancy Hanks Lincoln and their famous son Abraham is now on display.

By 1800 a number of private academies had been established in Kentucky. One of these institutions was Transylvania Seminary, now named Transylvania University. It was actually founded in 1780 in Danville and was moved to Lexington in 1788. Historians believe it was the first school of higher education west of the Alleghenies. Founded by the state, the school was dominated by Presbyterians who moved into the area with interest in doing missionary work among the newly arriving European-Americans. At the time, there was a feeling in the south that public funding for schools should be relegated to higher education institutions.

Between 1818 and 1827, Transylvania College became known as an excellent liberal arts institution under the leadership of President Horace Holley, a well-educated Yale graduate. However, pressure by right-wing Presbyterians eventually forced Holley to leave and the institution declined in stature.

The Kentucky legislature passed the first public school law in 1838, even though there was little progress until 1847. However, by 1853, all of Kentucky's counties had public schools, even though they were quite poorly funded. These schools were racially segregated and the educational opportunities for African-American children were practically nonexistent. Many southern slave owners did not want to educate African-American children at all, and they went to great lengths to ensure that they would not learn to read. Any education that did exist below the Mason-Dixon line was generally provided by the plantation owners. Thus, by the end of the Civil War, most African-Americans were illiterate. Interestingly, records show that about one half of the European-American men in the south were also illiterate at this time.

Through the influence of the Freedmen's Bureau, a bill passed the Kentucky legislature in 1866, appropriating a miniscule amount of funds from the taxation of African-American property and dog taxes on African-American canines for the support of schools for African-American children. However, these funds were also provided for poverty programs which created substantial financial shortages for funding such schools.

While both elementary-secondary schools and colleges and universities were segregated in Kentucky, Berea College was an exception. Founded in 1853 by John G. Fee, Cassius M. Clay, and John A. R. Rogers, the school admitted students of all races at a time when schools were segregated in the South. The landmark 1903 *Berea v. Kentucky* Supreme Court decision ruled that "separate but equal" segregation applied to the private as well as the public sector.

On May 20, 1961, Kentucky proclaimed its neutrality over the Civil War and thousands of young men fought for the Confederacy and the Union. The last Civil War battle was fought in Perryville in 1862. As a result of this battle, the Confederacy abandoned all attempts to persuade Kentucky to join them in the war effort against the Union forces.

By 1884, the Kentucky public schools had lagged behind those of the other states, even though they were rather successful compared to the other southern states. However, legislation for school funding pertained to the local communities' abilities to raise the appropriate funds, causing large disparities in the quality of education statewide. It seemed that the first educational priorities were centered around the public colleges and universities, particularly the University of Kentucky at Lexington.

However, during the first quarter of the twentieth century, the Kentucky Education Association became actively involved in urging the citizens to support school reform. By 1933 this organization was successful in securing generous support of the state's school's public schools and the consolidation of many confusing school laws.

While Kentucky always experienced problems with race relations throughout its history, African-Americans were not turned away from the polls, as was the case with other southern states to the south. Governors Stanley and Morrow personally intervened to prevent lynchings and prohibit racist mobs from rioting. Stanley was a Democrat, while Morrow was a Republican. Many historians have opined that Kentucky was the southern leader in complying with *the Brown v. Board of Education* Supreme Court decision which terminated racial segregation. And by 1966 a Civil Rights Act was adopted with support form Governor Edward Breathitt.

Kentucky, like other southern states, has been plagued by European-American poverty, particularly in the eastern portions of the state. VISTA and University Year for Action volunteers were recruited to address the needs of poverty encountered by people who resided in the Appalachians and the rest of the nation. Most of these programs were designed to help such persons become upwardly mobile. The University of Kentucky was one of the first nine universities in the nation to receive grants for such undertakings. Sister institutions involved in these programs included the University of Nebraska, Kent State University, Eastern Washington University and Western Washington University. However, in spite of these programs and other poverty efforts initiated during the Johnson administration, poverty continues to be a major problem in Kentucky.

THE EDUCATIONAL SYSTEM

Kentucky's state commissioner of education is appointed by the state board. Children are required to attend school between the ages of six and sixteen. The exceptions include graduation from an approved four-year school or enrollment in a private, parochial, or church school. Children under the age of seven can also attend private kindergarten/nursery schools. Children under seven are not required to attend school if their physical/mental condition prevents it. Also, children in this age bracket are allowed to attend special state-supported schools for exceptional children.

Compulsory programs in special education are offered for children in need between the ages of three and twenty. While there is no policy on year-round schools, some school districts are involved in such educational efforts. School districts are not required by Kentucky law to offer kindergarten programs, but some of them do. There are no written procedures available for Kentucky residents who wish to home school their children. Parents who fail to comply with the attendance requirements are fined $100 for a first offense and $150 for a second offense. Subsequent offenses may result in Class B misdemeanor charges being filed.

Kentucky allows time for the recitation of the Lord's Prayer to teach the history of the United States. Verbal interactions between school counselors and Kentucky students are considered to be privileged communication and postsecondary school records are considered to be confidential.

Teacher certification in Kentucky requires candidates to perform successfully on the National Teachers Examination (NTE), as well as demonstrating successful teaching skills through in-class observations. Basic skills acquisition is certified through successful performance on the NTE. Of Kentucky's population, 31.8 percent are high school graduates, while another 27 percent have gone on to college. Eight percent of the population hold the bachelor's degree, compared to 13 percent nationally. The state spends just under $685 per capita for elementary and secondary education, compared to a national outlay of $931.76 per child. Only Alabama, Mississippi, and Tennessee spend less.

MULTICULTURAL EDUCATION EFFORTS

Kentucky is one of the few states which has a planned program in multicultural education. These district-wide programs are regulated by Kentucky's State Multicultural Guidelines of 1992. The primary goal of these guidelines is to "move the multicultural agenda forward and, in so doing, create a positive school climate for all students." In addition, the guidelines were written to bring about self-awareness of one's own cultural background.

The state's program guidelines state that "multicultural education is a process, not a product, and must be infused throughout the entire educational structure, including curriculum design; in-school and extracurricular activities; school-based decision-making councils; textbook and curricula materials review and selection; and recruitment and retention of minority students and staff."

Kentucky was one of but a handful of states which has a person in the State Office of Instruction who is responsible for multicultural education. While no special funds are earmarked for such efforts in Kentucky, Title IV monies are used for such purposes. Through these and other funding sources, Kentucky provides training modules and workshops which are offered for professional development.

At the present time, teacher certification does not involve special coursework or other multicultural experiences. The state is involved in a reform process and is transforming the curriculum with specific realignment directions which require attention to cultural pluralism. Also, there are special programs such as English as a Second Language (ESL) and Limited English Proficiency (LEP). These efforts are designed to meet the needs of students who do not speak English as their primary language.

In an effort to comply with the mandates inherent in the *Brown v. Board of Education* Supreme Court decision, Kentucky districts are in the process of redistricting the larger school districts in order to ensure that schools are not racially segregated. Such practices are being carried out in Louisville, Lexington, Paducah, Covington, and several other large school districts. Louisville has a magnet school program to alleviate possible segregated schools and other strategies, such as Renaissance, are designed to do the same.

The history of Native-Americans of the Kentucky region is included in the state's curriculum and the state's Office of Education evaluates curriculum materials, library materials, and textbooks for the inclusion of racist/sexist content.

Kentucky's respondent to the questionnaire items felt that the biggest problem facing multicultural education programs in the state was a lack of awareness regarding the manner in which the contents of the programs and various materials should be utilized. Another problem articulated was the focus on holidays, celebrations and single group studies, as opposed to full infusion. It was felt that this could have been due to the relatively short period of time that multicultural education programs had been functioning in Kentucky.

The biggest improvements in Kentucky's multicultural education program, according to the respondent, would be for educators to realize that the curriculum is not representative of the state's students and cultures. Also, it is important for educators to realize that nonrecognition, violence, racism, and sexism are perpetuated through a reluctance to address diversity issues. In addition, the respondent felt that the state needed to focus on other diversity problems, rather than exclusively adhering to black-white issues.

Poverty still causes problems throughout the state. More than 19 percent of the state's children between the ages of five to seventeen are below the poverty level. While this is just slightly above the national percentage, it still creates a major problem for Kentucky educators who must meet the needs of all of the state's microcultural populations.

REFERENCES

Carr, Audrey T., *Program Guidelines for Multicultural Education.* Lexington: Kentucky Department of Education, 1992.

Channing, Steven A., *Kentucky: A History.* New York: W. W. Norton, 1977.

Clark, Thomas D., *A History of Kentucky.* New York: Prentice-Hall, 1937.

Faragher, John Mack, *Daniel Boone: The Life and Legend of an American Pioneer.* New York: Henry Holt and Company, 1992.

Federal Writers Project of the Kentucky Works Projects Administration, *Kentucky: A Guide to the Bluegrass State.* New York: Hastings House, 1954.

Giles, J. H., *The Kentuckians.* Lexington: The University of Kentucky Press, 1988.

Leiter, Richard A., *National Survey of State Laws.* First edition. Detroit: Gale Research, 1997.

McCague, James, *The Cumberland.* New York: Holt, Rinehart, and Winston, 1973.

United States Department of Education, *Digest of Educational Statistics,* Washington D.C.: United States Department of Education, 1997.

LOUISIANA

STATE HISTORY

Historians have argued that Louisiana is unique in terms of its diversity, the colorful history, and the various problems which have been addressed throughout the years. Located close to the Gulf of Mexico, adjacent to one of the most shallow large lakes in the nation, it is steeped in the lore of the Mississippi and blessed with a multicultural population which has accentuated its rich appeal nationally and internationally.

While Hernando de Soto became one of the first Europeans to arrive in present-day Louisiana, Native-Americans are believed to have resided in the area some 10,000 years before that time. Long before the civilizations of Athens and Rome, the Caddo of northwest Louisiana were building enormous mounds. Archaeologists have uncovered a mound in West Carroll Parish which is more than two football fields long and 70 feet high. The Caddo, members of the Caddoan language group, resided in northwest Louisiana and hunted deer and bear. In addition, they cultivated the rich lands of northwest Louisiana, southwest Arkansas, and southeastern Oklahoma. They are known to have grown corn, beans, and pumpkins and knew how to preserve food through drying. The first written information about the tribe was recorded by de Soto in his 1542 visit.

In addition to the Caddo, the Choctaw tribe played an important role in the development of the area. Part of the Muskogean language group, the Choctaw tribe is presently the fifth largest in the United States. In addition to Louisiana, they originally resided in Mississippi, Alabama, and Oklahoma. In pre-Columbian history they were excellent farmers and had an abundance of corn, beans, melons, and sunflowers, in addition to tobacco. Their hunting exploits made it possible for them to exploit their love for bear ribs, turkey, and venison. While the Removal Act of 1830 resulted in their relocation to present-day Oklahoma, many members of the Apache, Jena, and Clifton bands of Choctaw still reside in Louisiana.

Prior to the arrival of de Soto, two other adventurers may have spotted the Mississippi's mouth before 1542. Alfonso Alvarez de Pimeda reportedly came upon the mouth of a great river in 1519. However, it could have been the Mississippi or perhaps the Mobile bay. Then in 1528, Alvar Nunez Cabeza de Vaca and other survivors of a Spanish expedition known as Panfilo de Narvaez also came across an extremely sizable river in their search for present-day Mexico.

Much later, during the reign of Louis XIV, René-Robert Cavelier, Sieur de La Salle claimed the lands along the Mississippi for France and Louis XIV. In 1682 his party reached the mouth of the river, and the countryside, seas, harbors, ports, bays, adjacent straits and all the people, provinces, cities, towns, villages, minerals, fisheries, steams and rivers comprised the areas to be known as

"Louisiana." La Salle was then successful in persuading the French king to launch a venture which would establish a French colony in the New World. While Louis XIV was slow to respond to the idea, he moved quickly twelve years later when he discovered that the English and Spanish were planning colonies in the same region. Then in 1698 a French Canadian, Pierre Le Moyne, Sieur d' lberville, attempted to colonize the territory along with his brother Jeanne Baptiste Le Moyne, Sieur de Bienville.

However, in 1762 the French territories were transferred to the Spanish in a secret treaty. The area prospered under Spanish rule and by 1770 Louisiana's estimated population was about 13,500. The population of New Orleans had climbed to about 3,500.

The Acadians, who were expelled from the British in Nova Scotia, were welcomed in the Louisiana region. Settling in the bayou areas and rural lands of southern Louisiana, subsequent generations became known as Cajuns. They carried on their French language and maintained many of their original ethnic traditions. With an estimated population of some one million people, they are the largest French-speaking microculture in the United States.

During the Revolutionary War, the Louisianians sided with the American colonists, and the Spanish never attempted to colonize the region. Louisiana was a lucrative economic resource, and the Spanish were happy with the profits they derived. However, in 1800, Spain ceded Louisiana back to the French, and it became part of the United States as a result of the Louisiana Purchase in 1803.

One year later the portion of the Louisiana Purchase which lay south of 33 degrees north latitude was designated as the Territory of Orleans. The United States Congress allowed the new region to draw up a constitution, but by 1812 the new area was admitted to the Union as Louisiana, the new nation's eighteenth state. That same year, the first steamboat navigated the river, arriving in New Orleans. Interestingly, no plans for the creation of a public school system accompanied Louisiana's membership into the Union.

The so-called War of 1812 actually began along the Canadian border, and Louisiana did not become directly involved until the famous Battle of New Orleans in 1815. By that time, Andrew Jackson had assumed the leadership of the Southwest from General Wilkinson, who by that time had proved to relatively ineffectual. Jackson had little military training, but he made up for it with intelligence and tenacity. A British army was assembled in Jamaica and ordered to take New Orleans. However, the British were unable to penetrate Jackson's earthworks prior to the major battle which was fought on the morning of January 8, 1815.

British forces suffered enormous losses, some 2,000, including General Packenham, while Jackson's losses were minimal, including just six or seven fatalities. This battle helped to solidify the new nation, and the Louisianians developed a spirit of belonging to the new nation. The fact that both freedmen and slaves fought with European-Americans and Choctaw warriors, also helped to kindle the multicultural spirit for which New Orleans became famous.

Between the Louisiana Purchase in 1803 and the eve of the Civil War in 1860, the state's population had grown from about 50,000 to more than 700,000. New Orleans became the largest city in the South, and the system of slavery grew as the plantation system eventually dominated the agricultural industry. In 1838 the first Mardis Gras occurred in Louisiana, the result of the Catholic influences of the Spanish and French during its earlier days. Finally, by 1845, the Louisiana constitution authorized the development of a public school system, and by 1848 there were 646 schools in the state. However, their terms were only for six months each year.

In 1861 Louisiana seceded from the Union and joined the Confederacy in March of that year. While two of the South's full generals (P. G. T. Bueauregard and Braxton Bragg) hailed from Louisiana, more than 24,000 African-Americans served in the Union army. And while the Union goal in the east was to capture Richmond, the capital of the Confederacy, the Union goal in the west was to establish control of the Mississippi River which occurred in April of 1862, when Farragut took New Orleans after a major victory over the River Defense Fleet of the Confederacy. In July of 1863, the Confederacy suffered another major loss when Port Hudson, north of Baton Rouge, fell.

During Reconstruction, Louisiana was forced to deal with a struggling economy and the enormous social changes that occurred in the "Old South." African-Americans had been emancipated and had nowhere to go. Most of them had been forced into illiteracy by their owners, and so, lacking an education, many of them tended to remain in their previous occupations, although they were not "owned" anymore. However, the primary goal of Louisiana's European-Americans was to maintain the supremacy they had enjoyed throughout history. The various "Jim Crow" laws which had developed set the stage for one of the nation's historic Supreme Court decisions, which occurred in 1896.

In 1890 the Louisiana legislature had passed ACT 111, which decreed that railroads were forced to require African-American passengers to ride in separate cars from the European-American passengers. Interestingly, railroads opposed this action because of the added expense. In 1896 Homer Adolph Pleassy climbed on board an east-bound train, sitting in the "Whites only" car. He was arrested and his case reached the U.S. Supreme Court which ruled in favor of Louisiana's ACT 111, ruling that "separate but equal" facilities were constitutionally acceptable. However, one Justice, John Harlan, a former Kentucky slaveowner, ruled against the other justices, arguing that the Constitution was colorblind and knew no racial distinctions. Thus, the concept of "separate but equal" was used to defend racial segregation until 1954.

By 1898 the state constitution mandated the levying of taxes to support public education. At this time there were 2,221 schools for European-American children and 982 schools for African-American youth. The average annual wage for the teachers of European-American children was $240.43 per term compared to $139.55 for African-American children.

In the arts, Louisiana is undoubtedly best known for the development of jazz and blues in and around New Orleans. The Mississippi had a way of transporting music from virtually all parts of the world to New Orleans, which led to the development of jazz. The melodic classical music from Europe combined with the rich African influences, as well as music from the minstrel shows, led to the creation of jazz around the turn of the century. This music flourished in Storyville, a notorious red-light district in New Orleans. Pioneers such as Buddy Bolden, King Oliver, Bunk Johnson, and Jelly Roll Morton helped it become the musical art form which began in the United States and occurred because of the pluralistic contributions of musicians in the area. While Louis Armstrong was not even born during the earliest stages of development, he became the most famous practitioner of traditional New Orleans jazz.

But while jazz was born in the city, the blues was more of a country phenomenon pioneered by such stalwarts as Huddie "Leadbelly" Ledbetter, who learned his craft from Blind Lemon Jefferson. Eventually, the blues became part of jazz, as singers such as Ma Rainey and Bessie Smith provided the blues vocals for the early jazz groups.

One of the education contributions attributable to Governor Huey P. Long was his promise of free textbooks for school children. Since that time the state has provided learning materials to all students. And by 1948, under the leadership of Governor Earl K. Long, the Louisiana legislature approved a state-supported free lunch program, which started on a partial basis during the 1938–1939 school year.

The 1954 *Brown v. Board of Education* Supreme Court decision had a dramatic effect on Louisiana and the rest of the south. In 1958 segregated seating on streetcars ended, and two years later desegregated schools in New Orleans became a reality, even though there was a great deal of resistance to this major change in that old southern tradition.

Following the Vietnam War, a number of Southeast Asian refugees settled in southern Louisiana. Some became shrimpers, in keeping with their Southeast Asian traditions. The result was a great deal of friction with the existing European-American shrimpers. However, this new influx of people increased the diversity of the area to an even greater extent.

THE EDUCATIONAL SYSTEM

During the first quarter of the twentieth century, education in Louisiana commended to experience some major changes. Funding levels improved and under the leadership of governor John Parker, a 2 percent tax was initiated which vastly improved the funding levels for the state's schools. Presently the state superintendent of schools is appointed by the State Board of Education. The compulsory attendance ages are from seven to seventeen and special education students are entitled to school services between the ages of three and twenty-one years of age. However, there is no policy on year-round schools and the school districts are not required to offer kindergarten programs.

In order to home school children, parents must apply to the local Board of Education in order to secure approval. Approval may be granted for a one-year period and parents must reapply in order to continue such ventures. Parents must agree to maintain a curriculum that is equal in quality to that provided by the public schools. Upon parental request, the schools may be called on to test their children.

Louisiana law provides for a brief period of time for student meditation or prayer. Parents, both custodial and noncustodial, have a right to inspect the records of their children. Louisiana spends $785.06 per capita for elementary and secondary education of students. This compares with the national average of $931.76 per capita.

To become a certificated teacher in Louisiana it is necessary for prospective educators to perform successfully on the National Teachers Examination. In addition, some teachers must pass tests in specialty areas for certification. As of 1996 the state had no in-class observation requirements for becoming certified. Thirty-one percent of the state's teachers have received a master's degree, compared with the national average of 42 percent.

MULTICULTURAL EDUCATION EFFORTS

Responses to the authors' survey indicated that Louisiana does have a multicultural education program. Responsibility for such efforts rests in the Bilingual Education/ESOL section. However, no specific state funding has been designated for such undertakings. Louisiana's state education office provides leadership in multicultural education programs through regional workshops and conferences offered by groups such as the Louisiana Teachers of English to speakers of Other Languages (LaTESOl).

Questionnaire responses stated that the predominant microcultures in the state were African-American, Hispanic, Asian, and Eastern Europeans. However, as earlier noted, there is also a large Cajun population, as well as a small Southeast Asian group.

Louisiana does not require special coursework and/or other multicultural experiences for teacher certification and the state's curriculum tends to stress cultural assimilation as opposed to cultural pluralism. The state offers special programs to teach children in their native languages when necessary. They consist of transitional bilingual programs and immersion bilingual programs.

Forty-two Louisiana school districts have been under recent court orders to become racially desegregated. The East Baton Rouge Parish's recent desegregation plan relied on the continued use of school buses. Schools on the city's primarily European-American western side of the parish were paired with the predominantly African-American schools along the Airline Highway corridor. A variation of the "pairing" plan, students in both attendance zones spend some grades with one school and some grades at the other. Another part of the desegregation strategy is the use of magnet schools which are designed to lure students to specific areas within the total school community.

The 1998 survey respondent replied that racist incidents in Louisiana's schools seem to have declined during the past five years. It was also indicated that the state's Office of Education evaluated curriculum materials, library materials, and textbooks for racist and sexist content. The history of Native-Americans is also included in the state's regular curriculum.

When asked about the major problems facing multicultural education in Louisiana, the respondent thought there was a faulty perception as to the meaning of the term. The respondent argued that many people seem to think it only related to African-American persons rather than all of the nation's other racial and ethnic microcultures. It was felt that this type of multicultural inclusion would strengthen such efforts in the state of Louisiana.

In addition to these survey responses, it should be noted that another of Louisiana's problems has to do with problems of poverty within the state. Recent poverty studies have revealed that 24.4 percent of Louisiana's children under the age of seventeen are in poverty status. The national average is 19 percent and only Mississippi, New Mexico, South Carolina, and West Virginia have a higher poverty rate.

REFERENCES

Debo, Angie, *The Rise and Fall of the Choctaw Republic.* Norman: University of Oklahoma Press, 1934.

Giraud, Marcel, *A History of French Louisiana.* Volume 1. Baton Rouge: Louisiana State University Press, 1974.

Gregory, H. F. (ed.), *The Southern Caddo: An Anthology.* New York: Garland, 1986.

Hansen, Harry, (ed.), *Louisiana: A Guide to the State.* New York: Hastings House, 1941.

John, Elizabeth A., *Storms Brewed in Other Men's Worlds: The Confrontation of the Indians, Spanish, and French in the Southwest, 1540–1795.* College Station: Texas A & M University, 1975.

Leiter, Richard A., (ed.), *National Survey of State Laws.* First edition. Detroit: Gale Research, 1997.

Perttula, Timothy K., *The Caddo Nation: Archaeological and Ethnohistoric Perspectives.* Austin: University of Texas, 1992.

Roberts, W. Adolphe, *Lake Pontchartrain.* New York: Bobbs Merrill, 1946.

Taylor, Joe, *Louisiana: A Bicentennial History.* New York: Norton, 1976.

United States Department of Education, *Digest of Educational Statistics.* Washington D.C., United States Department of Education, 1997.

Usner, Daniel H., Jr., *Indians, Settlers, & Slaves in a Frontier Exchange Economy: The Lower Mississippi Valley Before 1783.* Chapel Hill: The University of North Carolina Press, 1990.

Wilds, John, Dufour, Charles L., and Cowan, Walter G., *Louisiana Yesterday and Today: A Historical Guide to the State.* Baton Rouge: Louisiana State University Press, 1966.

MAINE

STATE HISTORY

In order to understand Maine's history, it is necessary to discuss the first known residents, the Native-Americans. Two of the tribes which were prominent in the state's early years were the Passamaquoddy and the Abenaki. The Passamaquoddy practiced a number of traditions carried on by the Abenaki tribes which were located in southern Quebec, Maine, New Hampshire, and Vermont. In addition to their summer fishing villages, they also hunted during the fall and winter.

Although it is thought that Leif Ericsson visited Maine as early as 1000 AD, the first verified contacts with the Europeans occurred during the late 1400s when Spanish, French, Scandinavian, and Englishmen fishermen encountered them as they all fished for cod along the coast of Maine. The first written descriptions of the tribe were recorded in 1524 by Giovanni de Verranza. Contacts with the Europeans resulted in major health problems due to the smallpox epidemics which the Europeans brought with them.

Fur trading changed a number of Passamaquoddy mores due to the introduction of guns and alcohol and new religious influences. Many of the native Passamaquoddy people converted to Catholicism and were sympathetic to the French. Most of them supported the colonists during the American Revolution. The tribe was not formally recognized by the federal government until well over 300 years later, when it became involved in the Maine Indian Claims Settlement Act of 1980. Funding in the act helped the Tribe repurchase some of their lands, which were previously ceded to Massachusetts.

The Abenaki tribe is part of the Algonquian language group and inhabited New England and Quebec during pre-Columbian times. There are three reservation-based bands, one of which (Penobscot) is located in the state of Maine. Anthropologists believe that the Payatan people moved to Maine and other parts of the Northeast about 3,000 years ago.

The Abenaki people banded together in groups of up to 300 people, utilizing wigwams for housing. A band chief ("sakom") was elected to lead them. After the introduction of horticulture, Abenaki women raised corn, squash, and beets in the fields, which were cleared by the men. Hunting, fishing, and gathering was important and the Abenaki constructed forts to protect them from potential raiders.

Trade with the Europeans began early in the 1600s. At the time of first encounters, the Abenaki population was estimated at about 25,000. However, after the first 100 years of interaction with the Europeans, the tribal population had diminished to only about 2,500 as a result of smallpox and other epidemics. From 1675 the Abenakis continually fought against the British in King Philip's War, King William's War, Queen Ann's War, Governor Dummer's War, King George's War, and the French and Indian War.

When France surrendered Canada to the British, many European-American immigrants commenced moving into the Abenaki lands, causing them innumerable new problems. Like the Passamaquoddy, they too were involved in the Maine Indian Settlement Claims Act of 1980. These funds allowed them to acquire some of their lands which were taken by the encroaching Europeans.

One of the first known encounters with the state by Europeans occurred in 1614 when Captain John Smith charted the Maine coast. However, much earlier, John Cabot came upon a land mass that may have been Newfoundland. But, like Columbus a few years earlier, he thought that he had come to the Orient. One other European group, led by the Verrazzano brothers, were perhaps the first to acquire a good perception of the Native-Americans encountered in the areas which they explored. But while the brothers apparently liked the Wampanoags of Narragansett Bay, they had less positive things to say about the Abenaki population, who evidently had experienced problems with other Europeans who came before that time. The brothers' writings show that they fell in love with the Maine coast.

By 1662 Massachusetts began extending its jurisdiction over the new settlements in the present state of Maine. However, Cotton Mather, the indomitable Boston religious figure, had a rather negative view of the lands to the northeast of Boston. In particular, he viewed Maine as a sort of desert. But in spite of Mather's view, the Maine coast became famous for its cod banks, and the fishing industry became an important part of its economy for years to come. By 1691 Massachusetts extended its jurisdiction over Maine, as stipulated in a new charter, which was granted to Massachusetts during that year.

Colonial Maine, unlike Massachusetts, offered but meager educational opportunities for children. The early teachers were mostly parents and ministers who were lacking in pedagogical background. It is believed that the first Maine school may have been a mission school for Native-American children, which was started by a Catholic priest in 1696. The first known school for European-American children opened its doors in York in 1701. Berwick was the site of the first known school construction. This occurred in 1719. Finally, in 1828 (eight years after statehood) a school fund was provided by the legislature. However, it was not until 1868 that Maine's schools derived their funding through the levy of taxes.

The period between Anne's War (1702) and King George's War (1844) were excellent expansion years for Maine. Since it was a time of relative calm, more settlers moved into Maine and land companies experienced substantial growth spurts. The abundance of timber lands, fishing banks, and fine harbors made it quite attractive for European-American entrepreneurs.

William Pepperell of Maine led his forces in the ultimate capture of the French fortress of Louisbourg in Nova Scotia, leading to the 1763 Treaty which terminated all of the French claims to Maine and most of the other North American lands.

As a result of many British laws which the New Englanders perceived to be tyrannical, the American Revolution commenced in 1775. Beginning in Lexington and Concord, Massachusetts, the war resulted in major problems for the towns in Maine. Perhaps the most severe encounter was the British assault on Falmouth (present-day Portland) which resulted in the British purchase of the town in order to atone for the people's opposition to British policies.

After the war was over, Maine's population increased dramatically. Participation forces were rewarded greatly for their efforts. Many of Maine's soldiers were given gifts of land. By 1785, due to the increased population and a growing attraction to this region of New England, the movement for Maine's separation from Massachusetts and admission to the Union began. In 1819 the people voted in favor of separation, and one year later (1820) Maine was admitted to the Union as the twenty-third state. As part of the Missouri Compromise Agreement, Maine was admitted as a free (antislavery) state. Only twenty-six years after its admission to the Union, Maine became the first state to prohibit the manufacture and sale of alcoholic beverages, although the new law did not provide for adequate law enforcement. Nonetheless, Maine remained a dry state until 1934.

During the early 1830s, antislavery sentiment became quite strong. Baptists, Methodists, and Congregationalists opposed the practice vigorously, resulting in Maine being a strong foe of the southern Confederacy. About 72,000 men fought with the Union forces and an ex-Maine Senator/Governor Hannibal Hamblin served with Abraham Lincoln as the vice-president during the war.

After the Civil War the state of Maine experienced substantial industrial development, particularly among the textile and leather businesses. During the last half of the nineteenth century, the state also experienced a decline in the rural populations as people commenced moving to the cities in order to take advantage of new industrial occupations.

Toward the end of the 19th century Maine began the development of hydroelectric sites along its rivers. But by 1909 the state legislature outlawed the sale of hydroelectric power outside of the state in order to keep the existing power in Maine to attract new industries. During this time period, the number of small farms in the state continued to decline. Larger farms were developed in the first quarter of the twentieth century. These agricultural enterprises specialized in potato growing along with dairy and poultry products.

One of Maine's favorite daughters was Margaret Chase Smith, who became the first woman to be elected to both branches of the United States Congress. A Republican, she served in the House of Representatives from 1940 to 1949. Her four terms in the Senate spanned the years 1949 to 1973.

THE EDUCATIONAL SYSTEM

Maine's governor appoints the commissioner of education along with a nine-member board of education. All such appointments are subject to the approval of the state legislature. Board members serve five-year terms, while the commissioner's term of office is for a period of four years.

Maine children are required to attend school between the ages of seven and seventeen. Exceptions to these compulsory attendance ages are early graduations; completion of the ninth grade or fifteen years of age; parental permission; principal approval of a suitable program of work and study; habitual truancy; permission from the school board and written agreement that parent(s) and board will meet annually to review educational needs; full-time student in a degree-granting college or university; and equivalent instruction from a private school. School districts are required by law to provide special education programs for children who are between the ages of three and nineteen.

Maine does have provisions for home schooling. They consist of any approved "equivalent education." Approval is granted by the state's commissioner of education. Local school boards are not required to play any role in the application, review and approval or supervision of such programs. Likewise, there is no state policy on year-round schools nor any requirement for the provision of kindergartens.

Students are allowed a period of silence during the school day. This time can be used for reflection or meditation. The records of students in Maine schools are subject to the privacy requirements, as stipulated in the Family Educational Records Protection Act.

In order for teachers to become certificated, they must perform successfully on the National Teachers Examination. Minimum score levels are: 656 in communication skills, 649 in general knowledge, and 648 in professional knowledge. Compared to the national average of 42 percent, 28.4 percent of Maine's teachers hold a master's degree. The state spends an average of $957.67 per capita on education, compared to the national average of $931.76 per capita.

MULTICULTURAL EDUCATION EFFORTS

Responses to the authors' multicultural education study revealed that Maine has no multicultural education program, nor is there anyone in Maine's state education office who is responsible for multicultural education programs. In addition, Maine has no funding for multicultural education, and the state provides no leadership to local school districts for various types of multicultural education efforts.

The respondent failed to respond to the question about the various microcultures in the state. However, despite a small Native-American population, Maine's population consists mostly of persons with English, French, Irish, French-Canadian, and German ancestry. Migrants from Canada were also largely European-Canadians.

Maine does not require a culture course of any type for teacher certification except for persons who wish to acquire the endorsement in English as a Second Language and/or Bilingual Education. The state's curriculum offerings tend to stress a philosophy of cultural pluralism rather than cultural assimilation. Special programs to teach children in their native language include two-way bilingual French/English programs in grades kindergarten to eight, and a reservation program which teaches children their native Passamaquoddy tongue. Maine also carries on a Lau Development Plan for Equity Access to Limited English Proficient Children.

The state does have an endorsement in English as a Second Language. Persons wishing to become certified in this specialty must complete a number of requirements in order to teach English as a Second Language in kindergarten through grade twelve. These requirements include: graduation from an accredited baccalaureate of master's degree program approved for the education of English as a Second Language education with a formal recommendation from the preparing institution. A second part of the requirement stipulates that candidates must complete fifteen semester hours from five different cluster groups. At least three years of successful teaching experience is also required.

School systems are also required to identify all students whose primary language is other than English; those students who cannot learn or achieve on parity with their English-dominant peers; or other students who have or may have difficulty performing ordinary class work in English.

The respondent believes that racist incidents have increased in the state's schools during the past five years and there is a major concern in Maine's Attorney General's office over the high incidence of hate crimes.

Native-American history is dealt with in Maine's regular curriculum through the state's Maine Studies program. However, the state office of education does not evaluate curriculum materials, library materials, or textbooks for racist and sexist content.

The Maine respondent felt that the biggest problems facing multicultural education in Maine were policy-level adoption. His final response to the question about the biggest problems facing multicultural education programs in the state was that the "question assumes existence." This response seems to verify the lack of any centralized efforts in Maine.

One fortunate set of circumstances for Maine is its relatively low level of poverty compared to other states. The poverty status of children between the ages of five and seventeen is just 14.3 percent, compared to the national average of nineteen percent. Only sixteen other states have a smaller percentage.

REFERENCES

Banks, Ronald F., (ed.), *A History of Maine: A Collection of Readings on the History of Maine, 1600–1970.* Dubuque: Kendall/Hunt, 1969.

Chadbourne, Ava Herriett, *The Beginnings of Education in Maine.* New York: Bureau of Publications, Teacher's College, Columbia University, 1928.

Clark, C. E., *Maine: A History.* New York: W. W. Norton, 1985.

Gould, John, *There Goes Maine.* New York: W. W. Norton, 1990.

Leiter, Richard A., (ed.), *National Survey of State Laws.* First edition. Detroit: Gale Research, 1997.

Maine Department of Education, *Administrative Letter Number Five; Administrative Policy Code: IHBEA.* Augusta, Maine: Department of Education, 1996.

Markowitiz, Harvey, (ed.), *American Indians.* Pasadena, CA: Salem Press, 1995.

Morrison, Kenneth, M., *The Embattled Northeast: The Elusive Ideal of Alliance in Abenaki-Euramerican Relations.* Berkeley: University of California Press, 1984.

Snow, Dean, "Eastern Abenaki," in *Northeast,* edited by William Sturtevant. Washington D.C.: Smithsonian Institution Press, 1978.

United States Department of Education, *Digest of Educational Statistics.* Washington D.C.: United States Department of Education, 1997.

MARYLAND

STATE HISTORY

The state of Maryland has been known historically as a border state, sometimes thought of as "American Miniature." When the first United States census was taken in 1790, the center of population was discovered to be in Maryland. One of the thirteen original states in the Union, the first European settlements occurred in 1634, primarily developed by Roman Catholics who became financially secure through growing tobacco and selling it to England. However, the original residents, the Susquehannock and Nanticoke, along with other tribes of Native-Americans, did not fare nearly as well after the Europeans invaded their lands.

The Susquehannocks, members of the Iroquoian language group, resided in northern Maryland, as well as southeastern Pennsylvania. During the early seventeenth century, the Susquehannock people served as go-betweens, negotiating disputes between the European immigrants and other Native-American tribes in the area. After the arrival of the Europeans, the tribe's numbers were reduced from approximately 5,000 in 1600 to only about twenty people in 1763, as a result of diseases incurred by the encroaching Europeans and losses suffered in battles against them.

Practicing matrilineal kinship, the Susquehannocks were wild animal hunters and also raised corn and other agricultural products. Their pottery was well known through the use of the paddle-and-anvil technique, rather than the coil method. Their dead were buried outside their villages in specially-dug graves and pottery and personal belongings were buried with them.

The Nanticoke resided in Delaware and New Jersey, in addition to Maryland. Originally, they lived around the Chesapeake Bay, along Maryland's Nanticoke River. They were well known for their processing of shell beads to make wampum and for their processing of furs. Like their Susquehannock neighbors, they also suffered greatly from the European settlers due to deaths from European diseases and from constant pressures from the European-Americans who were interested in wresting their lands away from them.

By the mid-1770s many Nanticoke migrated to Pennsylvania, settling in Iroquois Territory. After the American Revolution, they moved west to Oklahoma, finally becoming part of the Delaware (Lenni Lenape) tribe. Those who remained in Maryland abandoned their land and settled on Indian River Hundred near Millsboro, Delaware. The state finally recognized them as Nanticoke Native-Americans in 1903.

Among the early European adventurers in Maryland were John Smith and William Claiborne. Smith explored the Chesapeake Bay region in 1608 and Claiborne established a trading post on Kent Island, just east of the Chesapeake Bay shores. Charles I of England granted a charter to George Calvert for the founding of a colony for Roman Catholics. His son carried out the plan after his father died in 1632.   This land grant included parts of Delaware and Pennsylvania, in addition to the present state of Maryland.

While the colony was founded primarily for Catholics, Calvert welcomed non-Catholics as well. And in 1649 Maryland passed a religious measure which granted freedom of worship to all Christians, the first of its kind in America. However, conflicts ensued with Puritans from Virginia colony who settled at present-day Annapolis. Ultimately, Maryland became a royal colony in 1692, with the Church of England becoming the official religion. At this time taxes were levied to support the colony. Just three years later, the government was moved to Annapolis, which ultimately became the capital of the state.

During the first half of the eighteenth century, Maryland's tobacco crop flourished. It led to a single-crop economy and in order to make the greatest profits, cheap labor was necessary. Consequently, Maryland utilized the services of African slaves and indentured Europeans in order to create an economic equation which yielded the greatest profits.

After the American Revolution, Maryland became the seventh state to ratify the Federal Constitution. The 1790 census recorded a population of 209,000 Europeans, 103,000 African-American slaves, and 8,000 free African-Americans. By 1810 the state's population had experienced a greater than ten percent increase.

While the Revolutionary War had left Maryland relatively unscathed, the War of 1812 more than made up for it. In February 1813, a fleet of twelve ships led by George Cockburn entered Chesapeake Bay, setting up a blockade of the Bay and Baltimore. This continued for a year and a half. In addition, British Marines invaded the areas surrounding Baltimore and Annapolis, pillaging and plundering homes and utilizing their rockets. After suffering huge losses in their advance on Washington D.C., it was decided that Baltimore must be obliterated.

However, enormous new defenses on Hamstead Hill near Baltimore caused the British to retreat and instead attack Fort McHenry.   Despite a heavy bombardment by the British fleet of sixteen warships, Fort McHenry did not surrender, and the British backed off. This 1814 battle inspired Francis Scott Key to write the verses which ultimately became *The Star Spangled Banner,* the nation's national anthem.

During the Civil War, Maryland was divided in its sympathies for the Confederacy and the Union forces.   After Lincoln's election, the city of Baltimore refused to provide him with the usual welcome when his train proceeded through the city on his way to Washington D.C. for his inauguration. The history of slavery and the ill-fated attempts to rewrite the United States Constitution to allow such practices, coupled with the new loyalties to the fledgling Union, created huge chasms.

And during the conflicts, one enormous battle was fought on Maryland soil. The battle of Antietam took place only twelve miles from the juncture of the Shenandoah and Potomac rivers.   But even though the Confederate forces occupied Frederick, they were defeated in the Battle of South Mountain and Antietam in 1862. Historians claim that this was one of the bloodiest battles during the Civil War. Finally, in 1864 a new state constitution was adopted in which the provisions disallowed the time-honored practice of slavery. Just three years later a revised state Constitution was drawn up.

Slavery in Maryland was terminated at the end of the Civil War. While they were in servitude, one of the slaves' jobs was to pick off the tobacco worms which sometimes attacked the tobacco plants. On some plantations, if the slaves missed these two-inch long worms, they were forced to eat them as punishment. Some of the women were allowed four weeks off during childbirth. After that time the baby was cared for by an older child. However, if this was impossible, the mother was forced to take her infant to the fields, where she cared for the child while doing her work.

While some planters permitted their slaves to become educated, even those attempts were meager and little learning took place beyond the acquisition of basic reading and writing skills. Consequently, many of Maryland's African-Americans were illiterate at the end of the Civil War.

Following the Civil War, Maryland experienced a gradual transition from a state which was primarily agricultural in nature to a state with a growing industrial base. The tobacco economy never really recovered, even though some freed slaves stayed to work. Also, the Maryland soil couldn't compete with the rich loams in the Midwest. In 1876 the Johns Hopkins University opened in Baltimore, and in 1904 the great Baltimore fire occurred.

Prohibition came to Maryland in 1928 when Maryland's general assembly ratified the eighteenth amendment to the Constitution. Just one year later, in 1919, it was adopted nationally. It was repealed in 1933, during the Roosevelt administration, much to the delight of H. L. Mencken, one of Maryland's most intellectual journalists and writers.

Among Maryland's more famous citizens was Eubie Blake, one of the early African-American pioneers of ragtime piano. Born in Baltimore in 1883, he was still performing professionally in his nineties. He was the author of *Charleston Rag* and other well-known jazz numbers.

One of the nation's more interesting United States Supreme Court decisions occurred in Maryland in 1967. *Whitehill v. Elkins* (389 U.S., 54, 1967) dealt with loyalty oaths. A University of Maryland professor refused to take a loyalty oath. The Court found that the Due Process Clause of the Fourteenth Amendment prohibits such infringement and the Maryland requirement was held to be unconstitutional.

THE EDUCATIONAL SYSTEM

The Maryland constitution of 1851 had no provisions for a state school system, which left that responsibility to the individual counties. In 1864 the adoption of the new constitution included a provision that created a uniform system of public schools in Maryland. However, schools for African-American children were not developed until later. In fact, the educational provisions for such children were at best piecemeal clear through 1916, when there were still no high schools for African-American children in the counties.

The Flexner Report of 1916 and the University of Columbia's Teachers College Report of 1920 criticized Maryland for its poor educational efforts. In 1921 the Baltimore School Board revised the curricula, established new instructional methodology, improved vocational training, raised teachers salaries, improved supervisory personnel and upgraded school buildings. Education for

African-American children in segregated schools was also improved, even though it was still dramatically inferior.

Presently, Maryland's state superintendent of schools is appointed by the State Board of Education. Children are required to attend school between the ages of five and sixteen years of age. Exceptions to this requirement include children who are receiving other regular, thorough instruction in studies usually taught in public schools to children of the same age group and children with mental/emotional/physical conditions which make their instruction detrimental to this progress or whose presence presents a danger of serious harm to others. Home school provisions can be provided though regular instruction in studies usually taught in the public schools to children of the same age group.

Maryland has a provision for allowing students to meditate silently for about one minute. Students or teachers may read the holy scriptures or pray. The latter part of this provision is thought to be unconstitutional by some. "Persons of interest" may inspect student records, but the observations of teachers, counselors, or principals during consultations may not be used as evidence against the student. Such data are not admissible.

The National Teacher Examination is used in Maryland for certification purposes. In-class observations are not required. Maryland's per-capita educational expenses for elementary and secondary education are only slightly below the national average. Nearly 50 percent of Maryland's teachers have a master's degree. This is slightly above the national average. Compulsory education ages for special education children extend from birth to twenty years.

Maryland started on a school reform program in 1977 in preparation for the year 2000. The primary purpose of this twenty-year venture was to identify minimum skills which all children should master for graduation and to create a "Beyond the Basics" movement. In order to succeed in this reform effort, a "Blueprint for Change" was created.

This blueprint was designed for constructing a statewide school improvement framework with accountability as the cornerstone. The responsibility for implementation was shared by each school, the local school district, and the State Department of Education.

Another element of the plan was the state's "Schools for Success" component. In order to accomplish this, the Maryland School Performance Program (MSPP) would provide information about school progress; expectations for what students should know and be able to do; and authentic assessments of these student expectations. MSSP assesses student achievement.

Another ingredient is "Ensuring Quality Teaching." This is accomplished by passing a competency test and creating higher standards for teaching certification.

MULTICULTURAL EDUCATION EFFORTS

Questionnaire responses from Maryland reported that the state does have a planned multicultural education program and a person in the State Office of Instruction is responsible for such efforts, even though no specific funding is available. The state does provide leadership to school districts in the form of a statewide multicultural advisory board, along with training and networking. A new Maryland regulation requires education that is multicultural. The underlying notion is that excellence in education is equity in education and multicultural education is education for social justice.

All of Maryland's educational activities, including assessments and curricular frameworks, shall contain a multicultural focus. Seven pages in Maryland's education code relate to the State Board of Education requirement that education in Maryland must be multicultural. That is, all educational efforts shall be multicultural in nature in order to prepare students to live, learn, interact, and work creatively in an interdependent global society.

The respondent indicated that while there is no special coursework requirement for teacher certification, several school systems require the completion of a three-credit course. The state's curriculum stresses pluralism, which is a legal requirement in Maryland. However, in actual practice, cultural assimilation appears to be the norm in Maryland and other states as well. While there are some minimal bilingual education efforts, in general there are no special state programs to teach children in their native language.

Two strategies are currently being employed in Maryland's school districts in order to comply with the *Brown v. Board of Education* Supreme Court decision. The first is a change in feeder patterns for schools, and second is the use of magnet schools. However, the respondent articulated a number of concerns connected with desegregation patterns, including: "in-school segregation" through gifted/talented programs, tracking, and special education; self-segregation of students in extracurricular activities and sports; and housing patterns which are greatly segregated.

According to the questionnaire responses, racist incidents have increased in Maryland's schools during the past five years. This has prompted the creation of a Statewide Coalition Opposed to Violence and Extremism. Composed of law enforcement personnel and human relations professionals, this group provides support and information on the topic.

The history of Native-Americans is included in the state's regular curriculum. For example, fourth graders are exposed to a social studies unit which focuses on the state's Native residents. And while Maryland does not screen textbooks, curriculum materials, and library holdings for racist and sexist content, the state education office provides training to local school systems to evaluate such materials for racist/sexist content.

Finally, the respondent felt that the biggest problem facing multicultural education programs in Maryland was a lack of understanding and fear of radical right opposition which seems to keep state leaders from moving ahead. And the biggest improvements in such ventures would be a greater accountability to the law.

REFERENCES

Bode, Carl, *Maryland: A Bicentennial History.* New York: W. W. Norton, 1978.

Land, Aubrey, C., *Colonial Maryland: A History.* White Plains, NY: KTO Press, 1988.

Leiter, Richard A., (ed.), *American Indians.* Pasadena, CA: Salem Press, 1995.

Maryland State Department of Education, *Education Reform in Maryland: 1977–1996.* Baltimore: Maryland State Department of Education, 1996.

Rollo. V. F., *Your Maryland.* Baltimore: Maryland Historical Society.

Schaun, George, and Schaun, Virginia, *Everyday Life in Colonial Maryland.* Baltimore: Maryland Historical Press, 1982.

United States Department of Education, *Digest of Educational Statistics.* Washington, D.C.: United States Department of Education, 1997.

Walsh, Richard and Fox, William Lloyd, *Maryland: A History, 1632–1974.* Baltimore: Maryland Historical Society, 1974.

Wilson, Richard, and Bridner, E. L., Jr., *Maryland: Its Past and Present.* Baltimore: Maryland Historical Press, 1987.

MASSACHUSETTS

STATE HISTORY

Some historians believe that Norse explorers were the first Europeans to set foot on Cape Cod more than 1,000 years ago. If this is true, they would have encountered Eastern Woodland Indians of the Algonquian group. Three of the many important tribes residing on and around the eastern seaboard, were the Nauset on Cape Cod, the Massachusett, and the Wampanoag.

The Nauset were part of the Algonquian language group, but they were also known as Cape Indians. It is believed that they inhabited the Cape Cod area thousands of years before the arrival of either the Norse explorers or other groups of Europeans who came to North America. Seven Nauset were taken prisoner by English Captain Thomas Hunt in a kidnapping escapade in 1614. Earlier during that century they were also visited by Samuel de Champlain, the French explorer.

In general, the Nauset were rather friendly with the European adventurers who came into contact with them. Some adopted Christianity, and many were loyal to the English settlers during King Philip's War. In 1622 the Nauset shared their food with colonists from Plymouth who were in danger of starvation. Because of their friendly demeanor, many of the Nauset tribal members adopted a number of the new Christian beliefs.

While the Nauset were able to avoid the diseases encountered by other tribes, they lost many people to the diseases that the new settlers brought from Europe. Because of this problem, the tribe suffered numerous fatalities. By the early 1700s, their numbers had dwindled to only a very small handful.

The Massachusett tribe was also a member of the Algonquian language group. The tribal name (Massachusett) means *"at the great hill"* in the Algonquian language. Obviously, one of the tribe's contributions was the name of the tribe itself, which became the name of this eastern state. However, this was far from the most significant accomplishment of this colorful eastern group of Native-Americans. Their first encounter with Europeans occurred in 1614 when Captain John Smith reported that the tribe had thirty villages.

Since their first encounter with the Europeans, the Massachusett tribe suffered continually due to the diseases brought by the European settlers. By 1674 the Massachusett population dipped to only one tenth of what it was before their tragic encounters with the European-born diseases. The survivors tended to cohabit with other tribes and by the nineteenth century, the Massachusett no longer existed as a separate tribe.

Perhaps the most well-known of these three Massachusetts tribes were the Wampanoags. Also known as the Pokanoket, these Native-Americans had a population of 2,175, according to the 1990 census. Anthropologists and archaeologists have determined that this tribe lived in present-day Massachusetts for approximately twelve thousand years. They became well known in history books because of their involvement with the "Pilgrims," the English immigrants who came to the area in 1620. Their supreme sachem, Massasoit, along with other sachems in the Massachusetts area, signed a number of treaties with the Wampanoags and other local tribes. The Wampanoags participated with the Pilgrims in what is presently known as the First Thanksgiving. However, by the end of the seventeenth century, the tribe ended up fighting with these English settlers. These conflicts eventually resulted in the famous King Philip's War, which occurred as a result of Wampanoag sachem King Philip's attempt to confederate the tribes in the area in hopes of driving out the colonists in order to recapture their native lands.

Prior to these hostilities, the Wampanoag people taught the European colonists a great deal about life in New England. For example, they taught the colonists that the deer was not only good for its meat, but the hide could be processed and used for clothing and the organs could be made into pouches. Of course, the European-initiated diseases ravaged the Wampanoags, as well, and during the eighteenth and nineteenth centuries the survivors tended to live in small European-American communities in Cape Cod and other southeastern Massachusetts hamlets.

The English Puritans were among the first European groups to populate the present-day state of Massachusetts. Throughout its history Massachusetts became a haven for European immigrants due to its location. Presently, the largest groups of non-Native-Americans are from Canada, Portugal, Italy, Ireland, the United Kingdom and Africa. It ranks eleventh in population but only forty-fifth in land space.

The first immigrants came from England and settled at Plymouth in 1620. Known as *"Pilgrims"*, these English-Americans came to this land in search of religious freedom. Coming over on the *"Mayflower"*, this group of about 100 immigrants signed the *Mayflower* Compact, establishing the first self-governing group of European-Americans. They had also broken away from the Church of England, and their primary purpose for coming to Massachusetts was to acquire the freedom to worship as they chose.

Nine years later, John Winthrop became the first governor of the Massachusetts Bay Colony. He and his followers established a colony under a charter from King Charles I. During the second quarter of the seventeenth century, Massachusetts launched its industrial history with shipbuilding, fishing, and the manufacture of shoes, ropemaking, and printing.

The Puritans believed in a strict interpretation of the Bible and felt that the Christian Bible contained a number of laws which required compliance. While many of these "laws" applied to the church, others dealt with family affairs, the regulation of business, and even clothes. Those who objected to the laws or were out of compliance, were dealt with harshly. Moreover, Calvinist theology was paramount in the lives of these New England Puritans. In their view, "man" was basically a sinner in a world of evil and temptations.

Some persons who were not in agreement with the conservative views of the Puritans moved elsewhere. For example, Roger Williams was ousted from Massachusetts and moved to Providence, now known as the state of Rhode Island. Anne Hutchinson also moved there after she was exiled from

Massachusetts. Eventually, Massachusetts Bay, Plymouth, and Maine became the royal colony of Massachusetts.

In actuality, the Puritans had an enormous influence on American history compared to their small numbers. Their notions of Christianity and their aggressive influences on the religious life of the fledgling colonies, far exceeded their actual numbers. Calvinist theology dominated their thoughts and actions and the adherents of the religion believed that people were sinners and the world provided constant temptations of evil. To the Calvinist, earthly pleasure was unimportant. The welfare of the soul was what mattered.

Interestingly, no "system" of public schools was ever envisioned by the early residents of Massachusetts, even though that state pioneered the development of such entities. The family was important, and the father ruled the family. Women were in a role of subservience. Consequently, in the early days of education, only boys were believed to be in need of an education. The *New England Primer* became one of the first important textbooks in the early days of Massachusetts education. In addition to the alphabet, it contained numerous religious references.

A large number of the incidents that motivated the American Revolution occurred in Massachusetts. Objections to the various British taxes and a boycott of English goods led to the Boston Massacre of 1770. And the Boston Tea Party of 1773 constituted another major protest against English taxes. Minutemen trained in the Massachusetts colony, and in 1775 the hostilities began with the Battles of Lexington and Concord. After the Revolution, Massachusetts became the sixth state to ratify the Federal Constitution.

By the time of the War of 1812, Massachusetts had vigorously opposed the election of Thomas Jefferson and also was strongly opposed to the embargo acts. The state was against any involvement in the War of 1812 and refused to let its militia leave the state. By 1814 there was even a discussion about the possibility of Massachusetts seceding from the Union. However, both the Embargo Act and the War of 1812 helped in the development of numerous Massachusetts industries. Water power and steam power led to the creation of many factories and the Elias Howe invention of the sewing-machine helped foster the creation of Massachusetts' textile and shoe industries.

Among the noteworthy Massachusetts politicians are John Adams, John Quincy Adams, Calvin Coolidge, and John F. Kennedy, all elected to the presidency. Edward W. Brooke became the first African-American elected to the United States Senate by popular vote.

One of Massachusetts' most noteworthy pieces of legislation related to health insurance. In 1988 Governor Michael Dukakis signed a bill guaranteeing health insurance to all of the state's residents. However, he was later unsuccessful in his bid for the presidency.

Like most other states, Massachusetts history is not without its racist overtones. In 1974 a Boston plan, designed to achieve Constitutionally-required racial integration, erupted in boycotts by European-Americans, along with violent demonstrations.

THE EDUCATIONAL SYSTEM

Massachusetts can truly be viewed as one of the main leaders in the development of free education in America, a basic principle which is essential to the very fiber of the United States. The very first school law in all of North America was passed in Massachusetts in 1647. In towns which had at least fifty families, the teaching of reading and writing was required. Towns of 100 or more families were required to establish secondary schools. America's system of private academies began in Massachusetts when the Boston Latin School opened its doors in 1635. Moreover, the first college in the United States was established in 1636 in present-day Cambridge when Harvard University started educating students. Charles W. Eliot became one of its most famous presidents.

One of Massachusetts' famous educational leaders was James G. Carter, a graduate of Harvard College in 1820. Carter believed strongly in the importance of the common schools and wrote a number of newspaper pieces in which he deplored the present state of affairs. He attacked the lack of professionally-prepared teachers, short school terms, and irregular attendance. After being elected to the state legislature, he was successful in goading that body into creating the first state board of education in the United States.

But perhaps the most famous Massachusetts legislator was Horace Mann, who became the first secretary of education in Massachusetts. However, his reform efforts extended far beyond the state of Massachusetts and through his dedication, Mann was able to convince the rest of the young nation that free tax-supported schools were not only necessary but mandatory in order for a democratic society to be truly functional.

Massachusetts has had one of the more advanced systems of public elementary and secondary education in the United States. While some of the newer states were slow to adopt the notion of the importance of public education in a free society, Massachusetts was one of the national leaders. In fact, many of the states coming into the new Union turned to Massachusetts for assistance in their own fledgling educational programs.

At the present time, Massachusetts requires school attendance between the ages of six and sixteen years of age. However, children can be excused from this requirement if they are between fourteen and sixteen years of age, provided that they have finished the sixth grade. This may be allowable if they have employment in domestic service or on farms, provided they have written permission from the school superintendent. A final reason for being excused from school attendance is if there are physical/mental conditions which preclude the possibility of attendance. The state also has provisions for home schooling; however, the approval requires the establishment of standards that are consistent with those of private schools.

In order to become certificated as teachers in Massachusetts, it is necessary to perform successfully on an examination which measures basic skills. Candidates must also perform successfully through in-class observations.

Massachusetts has identified a number of competencies which prospective teachers must master in order to achieve certification. These competency areas include subject matter knowledge, communication skills, instructional practice, evaluation, equity, and professionalism. These competency requirements differ somewhat for the provisional and standard teaching certificates.

Massachusetts expenditures for elementary and secondary education are below the national average of $931.76 per capita. Massachusetts spends $827 per capita each year. The state ranks third in the percentage of teachers who have more than twenty years of teaching experience. Their 41 percent compares to the national average of 29.8 percent. Massachusetts also ranks fifth in the percentage of teachers who hold a master's degree. They have 54.8 percent of their teachers holding a master's, compared with the national average of 42 percent.

Massachusetts offers special education services for children from the ages of three to twenty-one. School districts are required to offer half-day kindergarten programs, but there is no written state policy on year-round schools.

The state allows one minute for a period of silence which can be used for personal thoughts. Voluntary prayer participation requires the approval of the student's parent(s). School records may be inspected by the parent(s), guardians, or students over 18 years of age.

MULTICULTURAL EDUCATION EFFORTS

Massachusetts' multicultural education efforts are articulated in the strong equity program which is required for teacher certification. The competency requirement for teacher certification states that: "The effective teacher deals equitably and responsibly with all learners and understands the impact of western and non-western civilizations on contemporary American culture and uses this knowledge to develop appropriate strategies."

Moreover, certification for school administrators requires that the candidate "understands the importance of education in a democratic society, including the need to provide equal educational opportunities; and accepts and respects individual and group differences with regard to gender, language, race, sexual orientation, religion, socioeconomic background, and values."

In addition, administrative certification requires that candidates "Understand and address the historical and political backgrounds of the major gender, racial, ethnic, and cultural groups in the school district." The requirements also stipulate that school administrators recognize and address bias in teaching materials, assessment instruments,among others, and utilize an understanding of intercultural relations and communication in order to meet the needs of students in a diverse society.

While poverty problems are acute in some states, this is not the case in Massachusetts compared with the rest of the nation. Compared to the national average of 19 percent, Massachusetts has 16.85 of its children who find themselves below the poverty level. But while this percentage is below the national average, it still creates a problem for Massachusetts schools due to the learning difficulties encountered by children from poverty backgrounds.

REFERENCES

Brown, R. D., *Massachusetts: A Bicentennial History.* New York: Norton, 1978.
Daugherty, James, *The Landing of the Pilgrims.* New York: Random House, 1987.

Heryman, C. L., *Commerce and Culture: The Maritime Communities of Colonial Massachusetts, 1690–1750.* New York: W. W. Norton, 1986.

Leiter, Richard A., (ed.), *National Survey of State Laws.* First edition. Detroit: Gale Research, 1997.

Massachusetts Department of Education, *Regulations for the Educational Personnel in Massachusetts.* Malden, MA: Massachusetts Department of Education, 1995.

Peters, Russell M., *The Wampanoags of Mashpee.* Mashpee, MA: Indian Spiritual and Cultural Training Council, 1987.

Rippa, Alexander, *Education in a Free Society: An American History.* New York: Longman, 1992.

Sewell, Marcia, *The Pilgrims of Plimoth.* New York: Macmillan, 1986.

United States Department of Education, *Digest of Educational Statistics.* Washington D.C.: United States Department of Education, 1997.

Weinstein, Laurie. "We're Still Living on our Traditional Homeland: The Wampanoag Legacy in New England" in *Strategies for Survival,* edited by Frank W. Porter III. Westport: Greenwood Press, 1987.

Weinstein-Farson, Laurie, *The Wampanog.* New York: Chelsea-House, 1989.

MICHIGAN

STATE HISTORY

Michigan's recorded history commences with the activities involving a number of Native-American groups, most of them being connected with the Algonquian and Iroquoian tribes. One of the larger U.S. tribes, the Ojibwas, resided in present-day Michigan, as well as Wisconsin, Ontario, Canada, Minnesota, and the upper Great Lakes areas. They are actually the ancestors of the Chippewa.

The Ojibwa's early encounters with Europeans occurred in the early 1600s when they had contacts with Etienne Brule (sent by Samuel de Champlain), Jesuit missionaries, and French trappers (*coureurs du bois*). The trappers were a mobile group, moving about the area in order to be involved in their hunting, fishing, and trading activities.

However, after 1650 the Ojibwa encountered difficulties with Iroquois raiders and their population declined substantially. During the late 1670s they began to cede their lands to the British and later to the Americans. Eventually they were confined to a small reservation. During the first half of the nineteenth century many tribal members turned to farming, raising Indian corn, potatoes, peas, oats, wheat, and hay.

In order to acquire a high level of prestige in the Ojibwa society, tribal members sought positions as warriors, civil leaders, or shamans. Marriages were monogamous, although polygamy was acceptable. Children were born into their father's clan and were not allowed to marry within a clan. During the twentieth century, many Ojibwa commenced moving to urban centers. In fact, Michigan is one of nineteen states which have no reservations.

As was typical among most United States tribes, the Ojibwa suffered the usual misfortunes after the Europeans commenced to take over their lands by virtue of their notion of manifest destiny. During the 1960s and 1970s, many Ojibwas became involved in a number of Indian-activism enterprises, particularly those connected with the acquisition of federal recognition for the unfulfilled promises from the federal government, and the usual broken treaties.

Jean Nicolet, a Frenchman, was sent by Samuel de Champlain to explore some of the Great Lakes areas. In 1634 he visited the straits of Mackinac and also explored the southern shores of Michigan's upper-peninsula regions. The first permanent settlement was established in 1668 by Father Jacques Marquette at Sault Ste. Marie. Three years later a permanent mission was erected at St. Ignace.

During the French and Indian War, Pontiac, chief of the Ottawa Tribe, joined forces with the French during the French and Indian War. He was an imposing figure and visualized a pan-Indian confederation which would be able to drive the British from Native-American lands. However, toward the end of the conflicts, after he embarked on a massive offensive to drive out the British, the British marshaled substantial armies in the area and were finally successful in defeating Pontiac's coalition. The pan-Indian forces were composed of Delawares, Hurons, Illinois, Kickapoos, Miamis, Mingoes, Potawatomis, Senecas, and Shawnees. One reason for their failure was the lack of French support. Finally, a treaty was signed at Oswego in 1769. However, Pontiac had been successful in discouraging some British encroachments in the Great Lakes region.

Later, large numbers of New Englanders migrated westward to Michigan and other Great Lakes states. Immigrants came from Germany, Poland, Ireland, Finland, and Scandinavia. Many New Yorkers and New Englanders also migrated west to Michigan and other states in the Great Lakes region. They followed the Canadian fur traders and trappers who were some of the earliest European residents of present-day Michigan. Following World War I, increased numbers of African-Americans migrated to Detroit and other manufacturing centers in southern Michigan. The burgeoning industries, particularly the automotive plants, were in need of laborers. So at this time the state began to acquire a more pluralistic population.

Still more African-Americans came north to Michigan as the automobile industry rejuvenated itself after of World War II. More recently, Latinos, Asians, and middle-eastern emigrants have helped Michigan maintain the racial and ethnic diversity which it enjoys.

After of the American Revolution in 1783, the British were not willing to leave Detroit. In fact, they behaved as if what had happened in the East made no difference to their western holdings. The British were successful in recruiting some of the Native-Americans in the region. However, in 1794, Anthony Wayne led a force of well-trained soldiers through western Ohio and into Michigan. The Native-Americans soon realized the futility of their position, as did the British a bit later. Finally the United States flag flew over Detroit, and the region was secured for the new nation.

Michigan Territory was then created by the United States Congress in 1805 and statehood was finally achieved in 1837, the same year in which the Erie and Kalamazoo Railroad completed its rail line which extended to Adrian. Michigan's first rail line was thirty miles long, and, even though it was quite primitive by modern standards, it was viewed as an important step in the state's passionate interest in transportation.

When the Civil War broke out, there was never a question in Michigan as to what form of action should be taken. The state refused to send delegates to the peace conference, which futilely sought to create some sort of a compromise. Michigan felt that the secessionist states had committed acts of open rebellion against the United States and thus were traitors to the nation. The state sent about 87,000 men to join the Union efforts and 14,700 of them were killed in action.

Soon after of the Civil War, the automobile pioneers in America commenced their work on the creation of an internal combustion engine. Some of these efforts were motivated by urban growth, which led to increased pollution because of horse droppings in the growing eastern cities. During the last quarter of the nineteenth century, mechanics from all over the country were attempting to create a workable internal combustion engine. Finally, by 1901, automobile production began in Michigan when Ransom E. Olds' fledgling company built over 400 cars. By 1904 his Lansing plant turned out more than 5,000 automobiles each year.

Henry Ford was one of the pioneers in the creation of automotive assembly lines. His Model T made Ford wealthy, even though he stubbornly refused to produce it in any color except black for many years. These early pioneers helped Michigan become the leading producer of automotive products in the United States. This led to a state economy which derives about 36 percent of its total funding from manufacturing.

One of the earliest educational efforts in the state was the founding of a school system which was founded for both Native-American and European-American children. This was made possible through the combined efforts of the Reverend Gabriel Richard and the territorial legislature in 1835. However, the state's present system of elementary and secondary schools began in 1835 and included a state superintendent of schools.

THE EDUCATIONAL SYSTEM

Michigan's state superintendent of public instruction is appointed by the State Board of Education. In addition to the usual course work and internship experiences, prospective teachers must pass a basic skills test and perform successfully in actual instructional situations. Some teacher education institutions, such as Central Michigan University at Mount Pleasant, require their students to complete a second student teaching experience in an environment different from the one in which they grew up. Some of these sites are located in other countries, while domestic placement opportunities can be secured in inner cities, barrios, or Indian reservations. In the 1970s at least one prospective teacher did a quarter of student teaching as far away as the Colville Reservation in the state of Washington.

Nearly 11 percent of Michigan residents have completed their bachelor's degree, while 6.4 percent of the state's population have graduate or professional degrees. Thirty-two percent of the state's population have high school diplomas representing their highest level of educational attainment. More than 23% have not graduated from high school.

Michigan spent $1,081.91 per capita on elementary and secondary education during the 1992–93 school year compared to the national average of $931.76. These figures were prepared in May 1997 by the United States Department of Commerce, Bureau of the Census. Michigan ranked eighth nationally in per-capita expenditures. The state spent $44.34 per capita for higher education during the same time period. This ranked 11th nationally.

When turning to the issue of teacher preparation, 48.1 percent of all the state's teachers earned a master's degree compared to a national average of 42 percent. Michigan children are required to attend school between the ages of six to sixteen. Exceptions to this requirement include children who are enrolled in approved non-public schools which teach subjects that are comparable to those in the state's public schools. The subjects must include reading, mathematics, and writing. Other exceptions to the required attendance regulations include children who are regularly employed as a page or messenger; children under nine years of age who live more than 2.5 miles from a school in which no transportation is provided; and children between the ages of twelve and fourteen who are in attendance in confirmation classes.

Michigan's *Hanson v. Chusman* decision (490 F. Supp. 109) resulted in a subsequent state ruling which prevents parents from home schooling their children unless a certificated teacher is present to provide instruction which is comparable to the public school offerings.

While corporal punishment or threats of such practices are not allowed in Michigan, "reasonable physical force" may be used in self defense, in defense of others, to obtain possession of weapons and other dangerous objects, or to protect property. Michigan's "prayer" policy allows schools to grant time for silent meditation.

Michigan's policies, regarding the privacy of school records, allow their use in legal proceedings, but counselors, teachers, and school employees are not allowed to disclose any information which they have received in confidence unless formal consent is given.

MULTICULTURAL EDUCATION EFFORTS

The Michigan respondent to the authors' 1998 multicultural survey instrument stated that Michigan had a planned multicultural education program, although it never received state board approval. However, the state has nobody in charge of such educational efforts, no funding, and the respondent also indicated that no leadership in multicultural education is offered by the State Department of Education to the various school districts.

In addition to the European-American population, the predominant microcultures in Michigan are Latinos, Arab-Americans, Asian-Americans, and African-Americans. Also, in regard to teacher certification, no special multicultural coursework is required, although as previously mentioned, at least one university requires students to student teach in an environment which is different from the one in which they lived through most of their childhood and early adulthood.

Michigan does have special programs to instruct students in their native languages. These bilingual programs were described by the respondent as "immersion programs" in bilingual education/English as a Second Language (ESL).

The Michigan respondent replied that racist incidents have increased during the past five years. The respondent to this question went on to state that schools reflect the community and whatever happens in the cities eventually happens in the schools. One survey response stated that the history of Native-Americans was not included in its curriculum. Michigan does evaluate curriculum materials, textbooks, and library materials for racist and sexist statements.

The respondent opined that the biggest problems facing multicultural education were that the leadership in the state government, the legislature, the governor's office and the State Board of Education was controlled by the Republican party. Finally, it was felt that the biggest improvements which could be made in Michigan's multicultural education program would be to get state board approval of the current program proposal which was recently developed. While multicultural language is used in Michigan's current school code, it is not a mandatory program but merely a recommendation without funds or budgets.

REFERENCES

Clifton, James A., *People of the Three Fires: The Ottawa, Potawatomi, and Ojibwa of Michigan.* Grand Rapids: Grand Rapids Inter-Tribal Council, 1986.

Council of State School Officers, *The Council* Washington D.C.: Council of State School Officers, 1998.

Fuller, George, (ed.), *Historic Michigan.* 3 volumes. Lansing: The National Historical Society, 1924.

Leeckham, Howard H., *Pontiac and the Indian Uprising.* Princeton, NJ: Princeton University Press, 1947.

Leiter, Richard A., (ed.), *National Survey of State Laws.* First edition. Detroit: Gale Research, 1997.

McKee, Russell, *Great Lakes Country.* New York: Thomas Y. Crowell, 1966.

Peckham, Howard, *Pontiac and the Indian Uprising.* New York: Russell & Russell, 1970.

Schmalz, Peter S., *The Ojibwa of Southern Ontario.* Toronto: University of Toronto Press, 1991.

United States Department of Education, *Digest of Educational Statistics.* Washington D.C.: United States Department of Education, 1997.

Warner, Robert, and Vanderhill, C., (eds.), *A Michigan Reader, 1865 to the Present.* Grand Rapids: William B. Eerdmans Publishing Co., 1974.

MINNESOTA

STATE HISTORY

Archaeologists and anthropologists have traced Minnesota's history to approximately 20,000 years ago when people roamed about the area. In 1931, at Pelican Rapids, a skeleton was discovered, leading to the term "Minnesota Man." Some time later, there is evidence of Native-American life by virtue of the mounds and abandoned village sites. And one of the major historical arguments centers around a purported visit by Vikings in 1362. This hypothesis was put forth as a result of the discovery of the Kensington Rune Stone in 1898. This supposedly documented the Vikings' visit. However, this theory has been denounced by a number of scholars.

Two of the more influential Native-American tribes in present-day Minnesota were the Sioux and the Chippewa. One of the largest tribes in the United States, the Sioux, populated the Minnesota prairies. In addition to Minnesota, they also resided in the present-day Dakotas, Montana, Nebraska, and parts of Canada. The name "Sioux" did not denote a single tribe but rather a number of bands who spoke a dialect of Dakota.

The core of traditional Sioux society was the extended family, which was the smallest unit. The Sioux nation was beleaguered by hordes of European-American settlers who streamed into the region during the 1840s and 1850s. Known for their ferocity, the Sioux responded to these encroachments on their lands with hostility and defiance. In 1851 the Treaty of Fort Laramie was signed between the Northern Plains tribes and the United States. However, the Sioux were still reluctant to allow the new settlers to pass through their region and the hostilities continued.

Perhaps the most famous Sioux leader was Sitting Bull, who was affiliated with the Hunkpapa Lakota Sioux. A proven warrior, he had a vision of soldiers being killed and, in June 1876, he orchestrated the famous victory over General Custer at the Little Bighorn.

The Minnesota Sioux were involved in confrontations which were also quite violent. After European-Americans had poured into Minnesota and tried to pressure the Sioux into farming, chief Little Crow and the Sioux warriors attacked the European settlers. Eight hundred settlers lost their life in the skirmishes. However, by 1889 the Sioux were in poor health and bitter over the loss of their land. The Ghost Dance revitalization led to a spirited renewal of the tribe and the federal government saw this as an act of hostility. In a retaliatory action in the Battle of Wounded Knee in 1890, more than 300 Sioux men, women, and children were killed.

Hostilities between the federal government and the Sioux nation have always existed. In modern times the population of the Sioux continues to rise. In addition to the residents on the reservations, sizable numbers of Sioux also reside in urban areas such as Denver, Los Angeles, and the San Francisco Bay area.

The Chippewa (sometimes called the Ojibwa, who actually were their ancestors), resided in Wisconsin, Michigan, and the Upper Great Lakes area, in addition to Minnesota. In addition to the information about them in the Michigan entry, it should be noted that the Hiawatha lore was based on that tribe. Lake "Kitchi Gamma" was the Chippewa name for Lake Superior, meaning "great water" in the Chippewa tongue. Henry Wadsworth Longfellow dubbed it "Shining Big-Sea Water" in the *Song of Hiawatha.*

Minnesota was first claimed by the French when they claimed the St. Lawrence River regions in 1536. However, expensive wars prevented them from exploiting the river and so they turned their interests to fishing, particularly along the Grand Banks of Newfoundland. Important European participants in the early development of Minnesota were René-Robert Cavelier Sieur de La Salle, Samuel de Champlain, Jacques Marquette, Daniel Greysolon and many others. But in the Treaty of Paris, enacted in 1763, the Union flag replaced the French flag. Two years after Minnesota became part of the United States by virtue of the Louisiana Purchase in 1803, Zebulon Pike led an expedition up the Mississippi River in the Minnesota region to enforce U.S. claims against a number of British fur traders.

Aiding the involvement of the new European immigrants in the fledgling nation was the construction of Fort Anthony in 1819–1820 at the meeting of the Minnesota and Mississippi River. And in 1837, the United States government purchased a triangle of land between the St. Croix and Mississippi Rivers. After this, land became available for settling, a huge influx of lumbermen, farmers, artisans, storekeepers, doctors, and teachers moved into the area.

Eventually, the United States Congress organized the Minnesota Territory in 1849. The federal government took over these lands from the Native-Americans and the influx of European immigrants was even greater than before. Finally, Minnesota became the thirty-second state of the Union in 1858, just before the outbreak of the Civil War.

Occurring just two years after statehood, Minnesota became the first state to provide troops for the Union cause. The state provided 22,000 soldiers for the Union cause during the Civil War. Minnesota volunteers played a major role in a huge Union victory over the Rebels.

Immigration continued through the 1980s and 1990s. The new arrivals had an intense desire to reject their past and start anew. Consequently Minnesota was blessed with the vigor of the new residents. The state's population had reached 439,000 by 1870 and tripled during the next two decades. After the passage of the Homestead Act of 1862, Minnesota's good farmland commenced disappearing. By the mid-1880s many immigrants were forced to travel farther west into North Dakota to find decent land.

In addition to its German-American population, Minnesota's Scandinavian tradition developed throughout the years because of its large number of Danes, Norwegians, and Swedes. The Danish population in the 1890 census was about 14,000. The total numbers of these Scandinavian groups was greater than the German population.

Toward the end of the nineteenth century, Minnesota showed signs of adding to its rich agricultural heritage. In Rochester, the Mayo Clinic was founded and became one of the truly outstanding health-care institutions in the United States. And in 1890 substantial iron-ore deposits were discovered in the Mesabi Range. This discovery created a need for thousands of new unskilled workers. Finns, Ukrainians, Yugoslavs, Ruthenians, Italians, Bulgarians, Hungarians, and numerous others ended up working at the range, expanding the pluralistic population of Minnesota to even greater proportions.

Today, the European-American population of Minnesota consists of approximately 98 percent of the state's peoples. The remaining two percent are mostly African-Americans, Latinos, and Native-Americans. Most of the African-American population is located in Duluth and the Twin Cities. In addition to the African-Americans who came to the area as steamboat laborers and fur traders, other large numbers came to Minnesota after World War I in part of the same northward movement which saw many African-Americans moving to Chicago and Detroit.

Minnesota is also noted for its diverse celebrities and their contributions nationally. Sinclair Lewis was noted for authoring such books as *Babbitt* and *Main Street,* while F. Scott Fitzgerald was much admired by fellow authors such as Ernest Hemingway for his classical works like *The Great Gatsby.* And arguably, the nation's best storyteller is Garrison Keillor. His classical tales of mythical Lake Wobegon can be looked upon as a kind of oral history relating to the state's diverse ethnicity.

Outstanding politicians such as Walter Mondale, Hubert H. Humphrey, and Eugene McCarthy have contributed much of value to the state's history, as have Supreme Court Justices Harry A. Blackmun and Warren Burger. In industry, probably no name stands out more than Jean Paul Getty, who became one of the richest Americans in history through his involvement in the petroleum industry. His two museums in Malibu and its newer counterpart in West Los Angeles are among the finest in the nation.

In the entertainment world, Bob Dylan is known for his music of protest which was so popular during the 1960s. Another Minnesotan, Judy Garland, captured the world's imagination with her performances in the movie industry. Her acting in *The Wizard of Oz* is still considered to be one of the all-time performances of the cinema industry.

THE EDUCATIONAL SYSTEM

Minnesota's common schools were originally established in 1849 through an act of the territorial legislature. Today, Minnesota's elementary and high school systems is coordinated by the state's Department of Education and functions through actions of the local school board. Most rural one-room school houses have disappeared and students from rural areas are bused into consolidated centers. More than 605 of the operational costs for Minnesota's elementary and secondary schools are paid for by the state. The state also has an equalizational funding formula which provides more money for school districts with inadequate tax bases. The state also has a system of tax credits for parents who send their children to private schools.

Minnesota's required attendance ages are between seven and sixteen. Education services are provided for special education students between the ages of three and twenty. Children can be excused from the seven through sixteen attendance requirement for "good cause." Such determinations are made by the local school board. Grounds for "good cause" are developmental immaturity of the child; significant family stress; physical/mental conditions which would make school attendance inappropriate; and the early completion of graduation requirements.

Parents are allowed to home school their children and superintendents can make on-site visitations to determine if the instruction is being carried out in the required manner. Writing, reading, literature, math, science, social studies (including history, geography, and government), physical education, and health must be included in the curricular offerings. All textbooks and teaching materials must be written in English.

Minnesota has no provisions for school prayer and students' school records are kept private except for directory information and can be released only through court order. Minors may request that information be withheld from a parent or guardian. The state superintendent of education is appointed by the governor.

In order to become a certificated teacher in Minnesota, it is necessary to pass a basic skills test and successfully perform during in-class observation periods. About one-third of Minnesota's citizens have a high school diploma as their highest level of educational attainment. This compares with the national average of 30 percent. Of the state's population, 15.6 percent have received a bachelor's degree, compared with 13.1 percent of the nation.

Minnesota does have a policy for year-around schools and a number of them exist in the state. All Minnesota school districts are required to maintain half-day kindergarten programs. Minnesota spends $1,121.22 per child for elementary and secondary education. This compares favorably with the national average of $931.76 education than Minnesota.

MULTICULTURAL EDUCATION EFFORTS

While the Minnesota respondent stated that there was no planned multicultural education program in the state, there is a diversity education officer who attends to such matters. While the respondent indicated that this was the equivalent of a multicultural education program, it was specified that the state spends no money on such enterprises. The predominant microcultures in the state were listed as Scandinavian-Americans, Native-Americans, African-Americans, and Asian-Americans.

The respondent replied that Minnesota did not have special programs to teach children in their native language when necessary. The "programs" indicated were charter schools, English as a Second Language, and home schools.

Desegregation strategies in Minnesota have been going through major revision in order to meet recent changes in demographics and meet the requirements of the *Brown v. Board of Education* Supreme Court decision of 1954.

The respondent replied that there is no state-adopted curriculum for all the school districts so no state-level procedure exists for evaluating curriculum materials, library materials, and textbooks for racist/sexist content. Whatever is done in this regard is carried out at the local level. Finally, the respondent indicated that the state's largest problem facing multicultural education was the new state board rules in diversity education.

Compared to the national average of 19 percent, 10.4 percent of Minnesota's children under the age of seventeen are in poverty status. Only four, Alaska, Missouri, New Jersey and Utah, have a lower rate.

REFERENCES

Blegen, Theodore, C., *Minnesota: A History of the State.* Minneapolis: University of Minnesota Press, 1975.

Broker, Ignatia, *Night Flying Woman: An Ojibwa Narrative.* St. Paul: Minnesota Historical Society Press, 1983.

Carley, Kenneth, *The Sioux Uprising of 1862.* St. Paul: Minnesota Historical Society, 1976.

Christianson, Theodore, *Minnesota: The Land of Sky-Tinted Waters.* Chicago: American Historical Society, 1935.

Council of Chief State School Officers, *The Council.* Washington D.C.: Council of Chief State School Officers.

Hassrick, Royal B., *The Sioux: Life and Customs of a Warrior Society.* Norman: University of Oklahoma Press, 1964.

Hyde, George E., *A Sioux Chronicle.* Norman: University of Oklahoma Press, 1956.

Lass, William E., *Minnesota; A History.* New York: W. W. Norton, 1977.

Leiter, Richard A., (ed.), *National Survey of State Laws.* First edition. Detroit: Gale Research, 1997.

United States Department of Education, *Digest of Educational Statistics.* Washington D.C.: United States Department of Education, 1997.

Winchell, Newton H., *The Aborigines of Minnesota.* Minnesota Historical Society, 1911.

MISSISSIPPI

STATE HISTORY

Mississippi, one of the deep-south states which historically has relied on the Mississippi River and all it has offered, has sometimes been called the land of the Choctaws and the Chickasaws. Part of the Muskogean language group, the Choctaws inhabited Mississippi, Oklahoma, Louisiana and Alabama. They were part of the "Five Civilized Tribes." One of their primary residential sites was near the confluence of the Alabama and Tombigbee Rivers. As a result of the Removal Act of 1830, they were required to cede their land and relocate west of the Mississippi River in Oklahoma. However, before that occurred they had a comparatively easy time interacting with the new European microcultures which were moving into the areas.

They were well known for their agricultural prowess, cultivating beans, corn, melons, and even tobacco. They were also a weaving tribe, and, to this day, Choctaw women take great pride in their work, entering their baskets in county fairs. Interestingly, the Choctaws never fought against the United States.

The Treaty of Dancing Rabbit Creek resulted in the removal of the Choctaw. After the War of 1812 the Mississippi area experienced a large influx of European-Americans who commenced moving into the area. After Andrew Jackson was elected to the presidency in 1828, the pressure for Native-Americans to vacate their lands intensified. One of Jackson's campaign planks had been to force the removal of Native-Americans who resided east of the Mississippi.

Closely related to the Choctaws, the Chickasaws were members of the Muskogean language group. Their social structure was based on a clan system. A person's clan was derived from one's mother and marriage between clan members was not allowed. The "High Minko", or principal tribal chief, was selected by a council of clan elders. Among the neighboring tribes, the Chickasaws had achieved a reputation for being fierce warriors.

When the tribe was visited by Hernando de Soto in 1540, his expedition suffered enormous losses. Eventually, the Chickasaws sided with the British in the eighteenth century and the Chickasaws fought with them throughout the Revolutionary War. After the end of the Revolution, the Chickasaws signed the Treaty of Hopewell in 1786. This acknowledged that they were under American protection. However, like the Choctaws, they were pressured into selling the remainder of their lands by Andrew Jackson, who wanted all of the Native-Americans out of the area.

As a result of this action, they were forced to move to Indian Territory in Oklahoma where they settled on land purchased by the Choctaws. In 1837 the Choctaws and Chickasaws became tribal citizens as a result of the 1837 Treaty of Doaksville. The Chickasaws brought about 1,000 slaves with them when they moved west, and when the Civil War broke out they sided with the Confederacy. At the end of the war it was necessary for the tribe to make peace with the United States and in the process the Chickasaws lost a large tract of their land in southwestern Oklahoma and were forced to accept the termination of slavery.

A French Canadian, Pierre Le Moyne sieur d' Iberville, build a log palisade at Biloxi in 1699. They decided that the soil was less than fertile, so they moved on to Mobile Bay and later to New Orleans, which has a street named after this early European adventurer. However, other explorers acquired a differing notion about the Mississippi land. In December, 1697, the Sieur de Remonville, an erstwhile ally of La Salle, addressed a memoir to the Count de Pontchartrain on the importance of establishing a colony in the lower Mississippi valley. He found that the country abounded in all things required for living. He mentioned the variety of grapes for making wines, the pure air, the ability of the soil to produce crops of maize and/or Indian corn each year.

By 1716 Natchez, Mississippi was beginning to experience a rapid growth spurt. By 1723, at least 300 settlers and slaves lived by Fort Rosalie and just six years later the population had more than doubled. The new residents cleared the land and commenced to raise tobacco, wheat, indigo, silk, hogs, and timber. It was hoped that tobacco would find a more receptive growing region than that of Virginia. French involvement at this time was major.

However, by 1763 the British influences commenced to take precedence and by 1754 the struggle between Great Britain and France for control of the new colonial lands was in full force. But the American Revolution against British control of the colonies had a dramatic effect on other regions as well, and the conflict had little effect on the early beginnings of Mississippi.

The year 1800 saw the election of Thomas Jefferson to the presidency of the new nation and in 1800 the Congress of the United States ordered the election of a territorial assembly for the new Mississippi Territory. After the Creek War ended in 1815, the population of the Mississippi Territory grew dramatically, particularly in those regions east of the Pearl River. By 1820, in the first census after statehood, Mississippi's population had grown to 75,448.

By the end of the territorial period the state had started to acquire a sectionalism mentality. River counties were heavily dependent on slavery and were quite conservative politically. In fact, the slave population of the four oldest river counties was more than 50 percent. Fears of insurrections became a problem for European-American slaveowners. But eastern residents tended to rely more on herding and small farming. They had fewer slaves and seemed to have a more egalitarian perspective. They distrusted the elitist sophistication of Natchez.

Mississippi's slave laws were restrictive and pervasive. Education was denied to slaves as were weapons, liquor, private property, and trade. However, these restrictions were not always strictly enforced. The European-American Mississippians' attitudes toward slavery commenced experiencing a subtle change. Instead of Mississippians feeling that slavery was a "necessary evil," it became viewed as a "positive good."

By the beginning of the Civil War, white supremacy in Mississippi had become the only rational answer for a European-American population which was outnumbered by African-Americans, and Mississippi provided the Confederacy with an important line of defense in the lower South. However, in 1862,

Ulysses Grant captured Fort McHenry and disembarked his army near Shiloh Church at Pittsburg Landing. The war touched on the northern border of the state and later the Union gunboats controlled that portion of the river, allowing Grant to ferry his army across the Mississippi south of Vicksburg. Soon after, Grant had defeated the Confederate forces from Jackson and defeated them at Champion Hill.

Toward the end of the war slaves left their owners in droves and an estimated 17,000 African-Americans joined the Union army. And the state suffered enormous numbers of casualties in the various conflicts. The Civil War devastated Mississippi economically and spiritually. Its economic bases were virtually destroyed and poverty still afflicts its regions. The reconstruction period did new injustices to African-Americans who became sharecroppers instead of slaves, and the state's economic subservience for African-Americans continued on.

However, another severe poverty in Mississippi was white poverty. By the turn of the century nearly half of Mississippi's sharecroppers were European-Americans. But by that time Mississippi had developed a public school system for all children, even though they were forced to attend school in racially-segregated schools. This occurred in 1868 and even the skeptics had realized the necessity of providing a rudimentary education for former slaves.

In 1903, a Mississippi Supreme Court decision had a dramatic effect on education all over the nation. While the *Plessy v. Ferguson* case of 1896 related to the constitutionality of black-white racial segregation, *Gong Lum v. Rice* dealt with other types of racial segregation. The superintendent of Mississippi excluded a Chinese student from attending a white school on the grounds that she was not white. In a 9-0 decision the Supreme Court ruled that her constitutional rights were not violated and the separation of white and Asian students is constitutionally acceptable. It should be noted that this court had a similar philosophical orientation as the court which ruled in *Plessy v. Ferguson* seven years before.

The era of James K. Vardaman's period of service in the governor's mansion was interesting but turbulent. Elected in 1904, he served two terms before being elected to the senate in 1912. While governor, he was able to initiate a number of reforms, including the raising of teachers pay by 30 percent and the rate of school apportionment by 20 percent. He broke the monopoly of the American Textbook Company and pushed through legislation focused on insurance companies, railroads, utilities, and banks. He also believed in the rehabilitation of convicts and was able to overturn the practice of leasing African-American convicts to private citizens.

Since the end of slavery, the Ku Klux Klan (KKK) was active in Mississippi. Its views of white supremacy and a basic hatred of African-Americans and Jews became one of the primary issues of contention during the Civil Rights movement. During the early 1970s, an organization located in Montgomery, Alabama, worked with the federal Bureau of Investigation (FBI) to help target the activities of the KKK and militia groups. Led by attorney Morris Dees, the group won a number of lawsuits against the Klan, resulting in huge financial settlements against the Ku Klux Klan.

The era of the 1960s and the American Civil Rights movement was a period of turbulence for Mississippi. Its racially-segregated school system was under attack because of the *Brown v. Board of Education* system in 1954. Governor Ross Barnett, a genial person, resided in the state house when James Meredith, an African-American, decided he wanted to attend the University of Mississippi ("Old Miss"). He had been rebuffed because of the state's strong segregationist stance. Barnett had assured Mississippi's European-American residents that James Meredith would not be able to attend Old Miss as long as he was governor. However, in spite of vigorous actions on the part of the KKK and other segregationist/racist entities, Meredith ended up attending the university, thus breaking the long pattern of educational segregation which had persisted through the years.

No brief history of Mississippi would be complete without mentioning its musical heritage. Perhaps the state is best known for its influence on the creation of the blues. The early development of this art form occurred through the misery of slavery and the problems that human beings are forced to endure in their daily lives. For these reasons, it is not hard to understand why the banks of the Mississippi led to the creation of this music.

THE EDUCATIONAL SYSTEM

Mississippi's state superintendent of schools is appointed by the State Board of Education. Teachers are certified when they complete their university course requirements, pass the National Teachers Examination and successfully demonstrate the attainment of professional skills and content knowledge through in-class observations.

The state spends $681.73 per capita for elementary and secondary education. This compares with the national average of $931.76 per student. This places Mississippi last in the nation in terms of per capita schooling expenses. However, a word of caution is needed before rushing to judgment over Mississippi's interest in education. The rest of this equation rests in the statistic that Mississippi has more children in poverty than any other state. Thirty-six percent of Mississippi's children under seventeen years of age are below the poverty level. Compared to the national average of 19 percent, it is easy to see why poverty in Mississippi makes it difficult to properly fund the state's educational system.

Mississippi's teachers are slightly below the national average in terms of the percentages with master's degrees. Compared with the national average of 29.8 percent, 26.9 percent of Mississippi's teachers have taught for twenty years or more.

The compulsory attendance ages for Mississippi children are from six to seventeen, unless the children are physically, mentally, or emotionally incapable of functioning in a public school setting. Children can be home schooled as long as parents file an acceptable "certificate of enrollment." Special education services are offered for all children between the ages of three and twenty. There is no policy on year-around schools, but some Mississippi school districts have such programs in place.

Mississippi has no state requirements which address the issues of corporal punishment. Student-initiated voluntary prayer is acceptable in Mississippi schools. The school records of school children are not available to the public and are governed by Family Education Protection Act (FERPA) regulations.

MULTICULTURAL EDUCATION EFFORTS

While Mississippi's respondent stated that there was no multicultural education program, the respondent stipulated that there was a person who was responsible for such efforts. However, there is no funding for such a program and the state does not provide leadership to school districts in specific kinds of multicultural education programs.

Reportedly, the predominant microcultures in Mississippi are the Vietnamese, Choctaws, and African-Americans in addition to the European-American residents. The history of Native-Americans is being taught in Mississippi schools through social studies classes with a multicultural approach.

The State Office of Education evaluates curriculum materials, library materials, and textbooks for racist and sexist content, and the biggest problems facing multicultural education were reported to be the lack of state funding for such efforts.

In summary, it should be noted that when considering the history of pluralistic enterprises in Mississippi, any efforts which have been undertaken have been severely hampered by major funding problems. The state has been regarded as one of the most economically challenged entities in the land, and, consequently, it has been difficult to fund even the basic education programs.

The other primary issue besides poverty has been the state's history of slavery, and the strong support of that concept by its citizens for many years. The equation is further complicated by the historical notion that education for African-American children was not needed because slaves should not learn to read because it might lead to an understanding of their predicament which could result in insurrections. Consequently, at the end of slavery, Mississippi had a population of African-Americans who were mostly illiterate. However, what is not so readily addressed is the fact that many European-American males also suffered from the same problem.

Consequently, education in Mississippi has endured hard times, and it seems that it will require a substantial period of time before the problem can be solved on a satisfactory level.

REFERENCES

Council of Chief State School Officers, *The Council.* Washington D.C.: Council of State School Officers, 1998.

Debo, Angie, *The Rise and Fall of the Choctaw Republic.* Norman: University of Oklahoma Press, 1934.

DeRosier, Arthur H., Jr., *The Removal of the Choctaw Indians.* Knoxville: University Press of Tennessee, 1970.

Foreman, Grant, *The Five Civilized Tribes.* Norman: University of Oklahoma Press, 1934.

Gibson, Arrell M., *The Chickasaws.* Norman: University of Oklahoma Press, 1971.

Leiter, Richard A., (ed.), *National Survey of State Laws.* First edition. Detroit: Gale Research, 1997.

McLemore, Richard A., (ed.), *A History of Mississippi,* Hattiesburg: University and College Press of Mississippi, 1973.

Oliver, Paul, *The Story of the Blues.* New York: Chilton Book Company, 1969.

Skates, John Ray, *Mississippi: A History.* New York: W. W. Norton, 1976.

United States Department of Education, *Digest of Educational Statistics.* Washington D.C.: United States Department of Education, 1997.

Walton, Anthony, *Mississippi: An American Journey.* New York: Knopf, 1996.

Zirkel, Perry A., and Richardson, Sherry Nalbone, *A Digest of Supreme Court Decisions Affecting Education.* Bloomington: Phi Delta Kappa Foundation, 1988.

MISSOURI

STATE HISTORY

Missouri is a land of great diversity in its landscape, its people, and its economy. Part of its rich history is directly related to the Mississippi and Missouri Rivers and its lore, as well as the location of the state itself. It is well known in history because of its historical role as a starting point for many excursions to the western portions of the United States. Its limestone caves, the rivers, and the Lake of the Ozarks are prime tourist attractions.

The state is also the primary site of the mound builders, who consisted of numerous Native-American tribes, including the Missouri, Fox, Sauk and Osage. The largest tribe, the Osage, are members of the Siouan language group. Archaeological evidence seems to indicate that, originally, the Osage were located east of the Mississippi River.

Before the introduction of the horse, the Osage were held in high esteem by the neighboring tribes. They relied heavily on the buffalo for food, but they also farmed. Dogs were used as beasts of burden before the introduction of the horse. The tribe consisted of two moieties (divisions): the Tzisho ("sky people") and the Hunkah ("land people").

The first known contacts with European groups occurred in 1673 with French explorers, Marquette and Joliet. The French established a working relationship with the Osage who became a significant force among the plains tribes because of their new-found role as middlemen for the growing trade enterprises. They became known as the gatekeepers in the entrepreneurial trade activities in the region.

However, by 1825 they had ceded all their land to the United States government and were provided reservation lands in the southern Kansas area in Indian Territory. During the Civil War they were split in their loyalties with some tribal members supporting the Union cause while others were lured to the Confederacy. Following the termination of that conflict, the Osage suffered severe hardships due to poor medical aid and a scarcity of food and clothing. One of the biggest problems for the Osage was the depletion of the buffalo herds.

By 1700, French-Canadian villages had been established near the Mississippi in present-day Missouri, and the first permanent settlement was established at Ste. Genevieve. By 1762 the French had given up most of their territory west of the Mississippi River to Spain, who returned the land to France in 1800. It was included in the 1903 Louisiana Purchase agreement with France during the Jefferson administration.

Missouri was admitted as a slave state in 1821, being affected by the Missouri Compromise. The state underwent an enormous period of growth for the three decades after statehood, with European-American settlers moving into the region from the East, from Kentucky, and other regions as well.

Slightly more than three decades later, the United States Supreme Court spoke on the issue of congressional power over slavery within the territories. The key issue of contention centered around Dred Scott, a slave from the Missouri area, who was in search of his freedom. The court ruled that African-Americans were not and could not become citizens of the United States and that African slaves did not gain their freedom when they were able to escape to free territories in the United States. This ruling occurred in the city of Saint Louis. This decision motivated some African-American slaves to escape northward to Canada. During the Civil War, Missouri was presented with a dilemma. While the state's economic interests were northern, a great deal of southern sympathy existed because a number of factions were clearly prosouthern. During the war, the state remained loyal to the Union but a number of pro-Confederacy groups supported the southern war effort. Over one thousand battles and skirmishes were fought in Missouri. Only the conflicts in Virginia and Tennessee exceeded that number.

The end of the Civil War brought no immediate gains for the state's African-American population. The Ku Klux Klan (KKK) was determined that Missouri should be kept "white" and lynchings took place clear through the 1930s, as they did in other states as well. Racial segregation became the norm and state's schools were racially segregated until after the 1954 *Brown v. Board of Education* decision which determined that such practices were unconstitutional and, therefore, illegal. However, residential patterns have made it difficult to maintain racially-integrated schools.

Toward the end of the Civil War in 1864, George Washington Carver was born in Missouri and was later forced to leave the state in order to receive his education in nearby Kansas and Iowa. But the state also produced Harry Truman who became the first president to integrate the armed forces.

Around the turn of the century, Missouri-born Scott Joplin was one of the musical pioneers who became responsible for the creation of ragtime, which was one of the primary ingredients in the development of jazz. He was forced to practice his craft in Sedalia brothels since other establishments would not allow African-American performers during this period of time. The rest is history. Joplin went on to become one of the great ragtime piano players, and as a composer he is perhaps best known for writing *The Maple Leaf Rag*. His work has been used in the musical score of the famous movie, *The Sting*. Sedalia, Missouri still hosts an annual ragtime festival honoring Scott Joplin.

No brief history of Missouri would be complete without referring to the work of one of the state's favorite sons, Samuel Clemens (Mark Twain). During a time when Missouri and the rest of the United States were embarking on a period of industrial and financial capitalism, the tales of Huckleberry Finn and Tom Sawyer brought Americans back to the fanciful days in which the supposed traditional values of the country supposedly held forth. The exploits of Finn and Sawyer further accentuated the mystique which the Mississippi River provided the state of Missouri.

After 1920, Missouri embarked on an era which opened up the rural areas of the state because of the expanded highway system. The Great Depression provided the motivation for the state to pass a number of legislative actions which helped Missouri residents deal with the economic problems which had befallen them.

Manufacturing continued its expansion after World War II as the population grew and the cities of St. Louis and Kansas City continued their expansion. During this time period St. Louis became an area known for the expansion of various aircraft and missile enterprises. The agriculture industry continued to prosper as enormous quantities of soybeans, corn, livestock, wheat, and cotton were produced on Missouri farms. The state's iron-ore reserve were expanded with the discovery of extensive deposits in the counties southwest of St. Louis.

But despite its healthy economic position, Missouri wrestled with numerous fiscal problems in the 1970s but in 1970 the voters rejected a proposed increase in personal and corporate income taxes in an attempt to address these pressing problems. These funds were desperately needed to finance the increasing state budgets and to provide needed aid to the state's educational system.

THE EDUCATIONAL SYSTEM

After Missouri decided to truly integrate its schools following the 1954 *Brown v. Board of Education* Supreme Court decision, education in that state has been characterized as adhering to the rigid separation of church and state, unlike a number of other American states. In fact, Missouri's constitution has been interpreted by the courts to forbid public assistance of any sort for the financing of the numerous private schools in the state.

As in other states, a number of strategies have been attempted to loosen that rigid principle through publicly financed school busing or supplying textbooks. However, Missouri voters have consistently rejected such efforts because of their questionable legality because of the First Amendment to the United States Constitution. While fairly large numbers of urban children attend private schools, approximately 85 percent of all Missouri children attend public schools.

State financing for Missouri's public schools only covers about 35 percent of the operational costs. The public school system, established in 1839, functions by virtue of local boards of education. The State Board of Education appoints the State Commissioner of Education, who is in charge of Missouri's State Department of Education.

In many parts of the state, local boards of education are hard pressed to raise the necessary education budgets due to their need to raise about 65 percent of the operating costs of schools. Thus, poorer communities sometimes find it difficult to provide the kinds of educational services which are needed by the children. Moreover, many districts require a two-thirds majority for a tax increase, which is next to impossible to attain in many cases.

Compulsory education ages in Missouri are between the ages of seven and sixteen years of age. Special education services are available for children between the ages of three and twenty. While there is no state policy on year-round schools, some of them are presently operational in the state. School districts are required to provide half-day kindergartens, a practice which was initiated in St. Louis in 1873 under the leadership of superintendent William T. Harris of the St. Louis schools.

In order to become a certificated teacher in Missouri, teachers must be observed in their teaching performances and pass tests which measure basic skills and content knowledge. The state spends a little more than $784 per capita on education, substantially below the national average of over $931.76. Only seven other states allot less for the education of elementary and secondary children on a per capita basis.

Missouri still allows spanking as long as it is approved in a reasonable manner and is in keeping with local board rules and regulations. When unreasonableness is alleged, the investigation is carried on by the school. Voluntary school-initiated prayer is acceptable in Missouri's schools, and there are no specific provisions related to the privacy of school records.

MULTICULTURAL EDUCATION EFFORTS

Responses to the national survey on multicultural education revealed that Missouri had no planned multicultural education program, nor was there anyone responsible for such undertakings. Also, no state funding exists for any such operation. The respondent indicated that there are no special course work requirements in multicultural education for teacher certification and the curriculum tends to express a cultural assimilation philosophy.

The respondent indicated that there were special programs to teach children in their native languages when necessary, and they consisted of English as a Second Language (EEL) efforts. Another questionnaire response indicated that there are court-ordered desegregation requirements in St. Louis and Kansas City.

Survey responses stipulated that racist incidents had increased in Missouri during the past five years. Also, the questionnaire responses indicated that the history of Native-Americans was not included in the state's regular curriculum. The State Office of Education does evaluate curriculum materials and textbooks for racial and sexist content, but it does not do so for library materials.

Missouri has only 9.8 percent of its children under the age of seventeen who are below the poverty level. Only Alaska, New Hampshire, Utah, and New Jersey have a lower rate of youth in poverty.

REFERENCES

Baird, W. David, *The Osage People*. Phoenix: Indian Tribal Series, 1972.

Din, Gilbert C., and Nasatir, Abraham P., *The Imperial Osages: Spanish-Indian Diplomacy in the Mississippi Valley*. Norman: University of Oklahoma Press, 1983.

Foley, William E. *The Genesis of Missouri: From Wilderness Outpost to Statehood*. Columbia: University of Missouri Press, 1989.

Leiter, Richard A., (ed.), *National Survey of State Laws*. First edition. Detroit: Gale Research, 1997.

Nagel, Paul C., *Missouri: A History*. New York: W. W. Norton, 1977.

Rippa, Alexander S., *Education in a Free Society*. New York: Longman, 1992.

Troen, Selwyn K., *The Public and the Schools: Shaping the St. Louis System, 1838–1920*. Columbia: University of Missouri Press, 1975.

United States Department of Education, *Digest of Educational Statistics*. Washington D.C.: United States Department of Education, 1997.

Wilson, Terry P., *The Osage*. New York, Chelsea House, 1988.

MONTANA

STATE HISTORY

The present boundaries of Montana have been occupied for over 10,000 years by human beings according to anthropological and archaeological research data. These Native-American tribes consisted of the Blackfeet, Assinboine, Crow, Cheyenne, and Atsina (Gros Ventre), who lived in the plains regions east of the Rocky Mountains. Tribes residing west of that mountain range consisted of the Kutenai, Kalispell, and the Flatheads.

Members of the Siouian language group, the Crow called themselves *Absaroka* or *bird people*. They inhabited Montana and Wyoming and their name "Crow" was erroneously given by French explorers. Actually, their traditional name seems to have come from the sparrow hawk. After the introduction of the horse, the Crow became clever hunters and also evolved into an effective fighting force.

By 1851, European-American trading posts and forts had been constructed in Crow territory. Initially friendly to the European-Americans who moved into their territory, they became highly disillusioned as a result of a number of land treaties which were eventually broken by the U.S. government. These land transactions resulted in the Crows ultimately being able to keep about three million acres of their land.

The tribe was subdivided into thirteen clans, and the tribal members resided on lands which were suitable for farming. The 1990 Crow population was listed as 8,588, making them the second largest tribe in Montana. Many tribal members also reside in Canada.

But the largest tribe in Montana, according to the 1990 census, is the Confederated Blackfeet tribe. The Blackfeet population was more than 32,200 people. More than 11,000 Blackfeet reside in Canada. The Blackfeet Confederacy consisted of four primary tribes with Algonquian roots. These were the Siksika, Kainah, Northern Piegan, and the Southern Piegan. The term "Piegan" means "poorly dressed robes" and is used to describe the tribal members who live in the foothills of the Rocky Mountains.

A significant part of the Blackfeet religion was the Sun Dance. The ceremonies required a great deal of preparation time of about three days. The ceremonies consisted of dancing and a number of secret ceremonial rites. Sometimes these events were sponsored by a "vow woman.". These ceremonies were sometimes undertaken after some of the men had exhibited great bravery in the face of warfare.

Some of the most critical contacts between Blackfeet tribal members and European-Americans occurred in 1806 when Merriwether Lewis came through the region. However, more formal trade arrangements were consummated in the 1830s. In 1855 the tribe signed an agreement with the federal government which allowed for the construction of a railroad on tribal lands.

After World War II, reservation conditions became much improved for the Blackfeet. Part of the improved conditions occurred because of policy changes by the federal government which saw its original resettlement plans met with stern opposition by the Blackfeet people.

The area comprising modern-day boundaries of Montana was claimed by France in 1682 as part of "Louisiana" which was later included in the famous Louisiana Purchase of 1803. Ceded to Spain in 1762, it was later returned to France in 1800. Geographically, it included the northwest portion of the Louisiana territory. Prior to the explorations by the Lewis and Clark expedition, the first Europeans to enter the lands of the Native-American residents were thought to be fur trappers who came to these regions from Canada.

John Jacob Astor's American Fur Company came into prominence after 1828 when it build Fort Union at the confluence of the Yellowstone and Missouri Rivers. The organization dominated the Montana fur trade from that time on. Fur trading was quite active during the first half of the nineteenth century with other companies, such as the Hudson Bay Company coming into prominence in Montana. Explorations by David Thompson were responsible for the development of sophisticated maps of the Montana region.

While Montana's first gold strike occurred in 1852 at Gold Creek, it was not until 1862 that a larger strike at Grasshopper Creek ushered in the Montana gold rush. Thousands of experienced miners and "would-be" miners flocked to that part of the country. But the most lucrative strike of all occurred in 1853 at Placer Gulch, leading to the establishment of Virginia City, perhaps the most famous gold town in Montana.

As was the case in many other western regions, the influx of Europeans created enormous problems for the Native-Americans. They were pushed out of their native lands by aggressive European-American adventurers who slaughtered the buffalo herds and forced the native residents to move away from their lands. Moreover, most of the negotiated treaties were not honored seriously by the United States government.

Eventually, the Flatheads, Crow, and Blackfeet tribes went to their assigned reservations, but others, such as the Cheyenne and Sioux of the Montana-Dakota plains fought a number of battles, culminating with the huge defeat of General George Custer at the Little Bighorn River. The final confrontation occurred when Colonel Nelson Miles defeated the Nez Perce tribe which, under the leadership of Chief Joseph, successfully eluded the United States forces in their northward retreat through Montana. In addition to the gold seekers, the native Montanans were beleaguered by cattlemen who moved into central and eastern Montana, causing further removal of the Native-American groups.

Among the earliest formal education efforts in Montana were Catholic schools at Fort Owen and St. Ignatius Mission between 1862 and 1864, along with private schools in some of the mining towns, particularly Virginia City and Bannack. The state's territorial school system was established in 1865. After statehood, the legislature established a State Board of Education.

Territorial status occurred in 1864 when Montana Territory was sliced out of the enormous Idaho Territory. Twenty-five years later, Montana achieved statehood, along with Washington and the two Dakotas. The state capitol was located at Virginia City but was moved to Helena in 1875.

Wide-scale silver and copper mining evolved into lucrative economic ventures for the state. Marcus Daly's Anaconda Copper Company began to dominate the American copper industry by the mid-1990s. Also centered in Butte was Montana's large silver industry, pioneered by William A. Clark. Politically, these two tycoons waged a battle for political control of the state.

Homesteading did not reach Montana until the early part of the twentieth century. During this time, homesteaders poured into the state, creating a burgeoning population of European-American setters along with an extremely small proportion of persons of color. The state's agricultural industry experienced hard financial times due to droughts, poor crop prices, and bank failures. Despite a short improvement period during the mid-1920s , these problems persisted until World War II.

Throughout its history, Montana has tended to attract substantial numbers of European-Americans who mistrust the federal government and wish to reside in rural areas. The extent of this phenomenon can be seen in the 1870 census which revealed a population of just 183 African-Americans in the entire Montana Territory.

One religious group in Montana was led by Elizabeth Claire Prophet. Convinced that a nuclear attack by the Soviet Union was imminent, they took refuge in forty-five newly-constructed fallout shelters in 1990. Another similar group was the Freemen, who disavowed the authority of the United States government. Many of their activities were proven to be illegal in a court of law and its members received a number of prison sentences.

THE EDUCATIONAL SYSTEM

Since 1972 an elected board of trustees has been in charge of each county's educational program. The State Board of Education is comprised of seven members who are appointed by the governor. The state superintendent of schools is elected by the people and must be at least twenty-five years of age.

In order for teachers to become certified in Montana, they must first pass the National Teachers Examination which assesses their knowledge of basic skills. In addition, they must be observed in successful teaching experiences in the classroom. Compulsory attendance ages in the state are between seven and sixteen years of age or completion of the eighth grade, whichever comes latest.

Montana does have provisions for home schooling as long as notice is given to the county superintendent of schools. Parents must provide at least 180 days of instruction and the place of instruction must be in compliance with health and safety regulations. Penalties for parents who refuse to comply with the compulsory schooling requirements can result in fines or imprisonment for up to thirty days.

Corporal punishment in Montana is allowed if it is deemed necessary. However, it must be administered in front of a witness without undue anger. It cannot be administered as an undue or severe punishment and advance notice to parents is required except in cases where there is some sort of open and flagrant defiance of authority. If there is, corporal punishment can be administered by teachers or principals without notifying parents. Undue or severe punishment by teachers and principals is a misdemeanor.

Montana has a school prayer policy which allows any teacher, principal, or superintendent to open the school day with prayer. Some have argued that this practice is unconstitutional in light of the 1962 *Engel v. Vitale* Supreme Court decision which declared the recitation of prayer in the public school system to be unconstitutional.

Public school records in Montana are private unless the owner requests that they become public. Direct expenditures for elementary and secondary education in the state amount to $955 per capita, somewhat higher than the national average of $932 per capita.

Montana has no policy on year-round schools but school districts are required to offer half-day kindergartens. Fourteen percent of Montanans complete their bachelor's degrees, substantially higher than the national average of 13 percent. Compared to the national average of 42 percent, only 26 percent of Montana's teachers hold a master's degree. Just six other states have a smaller percentage.

MULTICULTURAL EDUCATION EFFORTS

Montana is the only state in the Union which has the same percentage of poverty children under the age of seventeen as the national average. Nineteen percent of the state's children find themselves in this predicament.

Montana's questionnaire responses to the authors' 1998 national survey of multicultural education revealed that the state had no multicultural education program and nobody has been given the responsibility for such educational efforts. In addition, no state funding had been set aside for such undertakings. However, the state does assist school districts through "soft money" funding in the area of teacher training.

Montana's non-European-American population consists almost exclusively of Native-Americans from the tribes which were mentioned previously. Considered to be a northwestern state, the Montana population patterns reflect the relative lack of racial and ethnic diversity of the Idaho Panhandle, Eastern Washington, and other western states. But the Montana constitution does recognize the distance and unique cultural heritage of the Native-Americans. Moreover, the state's educational goals convey a commitment to the preservation of their cultural integrity.

Presently, Montana has no multicultural education requirements in its teacher certification program but there is a movement to create changes in the state's curricular offerings to stress notions of cultural pluralism. The respondent indicated that there were some special programs to teach children in their native language when necessary, but they were "soft money" Title VII federal programs.

Other questionnaire responses indicated that Montana has experienced an increase in racist incidents during the past five years, although the respondent speculated that this could be partially due to the fact that such actions are now more highly publicized.

Instruction in the history of Native-Americans was reportedly not included in the state's regular curriculum. Instructional materials which related to the topic were said to be only in supplemental form.

According to the questionnaire responses, Montana's biggest problems facing multicultural education have been a lack of funding as well as a lack of support from the state governance boards. It was felt that the biggest improvement in Montana's multicultural education program efforts would be support from the Board of Public Education (K–12) and the Board of Regents (higher education).

REFERENCES

Howard, Joseph K., *Montana: High, Wide and Handsome.* Lincoln: University of Nebraska Press, 1983.

Keenan, Nancy, *School Laws of Montana.* Helena: Office of the Superintendent of Public Instruction, 1997.

Leiter, Richard A., (ed.), *National Survey of State Laws.* First edition. Detroit: Gale Research, 1997.

Lowie, Robert H., *The Crow Indians.* New York: Holt, Rinehart and Winston, 1958.

Malone, Michael P., et al., *Montana: A History of Two Centuries.* Seattle: University of Washington Press, 1991.

McFee, Malcolm, *Modern Blackfeet.* New York: Holt, Rinehart, and Winston, 1972.

Spence, Clark C., *Montana: A Bicentennial History.* New York: W. W. Norton, 1978.

Taylor, Quintard, *In Search of Racial Frontier.* New York: W. W. Norton, 1998.

United States Department of Education, *Digest of Educational Statistics.* Washington, D.C.: United States Department of Education, 1997.

Voget, Fred W., *The Shoshoni-Crow Sun Dance.* Norman: University of Oklahoma Press, 1984.

NEBRASKA

STATE HISTORY

Like more than half of the fifty states in the Unites States, Nebraska is an Indian name, meaning "flat water" in the Oto and Omaha languages. Nebraska and the surrounding regions have been populated for about 12,000 years according to archaeological research. The evidence seems to show that the state had numerous people living and wandering through the region during this long period of time.

Anthropologists believe that the earliest humans to reside in the present-day boundaries of Nebraska were persons associated with the Folsom culture, which was probably one of several Native-American groups residing in the plains areas some 8,000 years ago.

It has been posited that the Pawnee, a Caddoan group, are believed to have resided in the region for the longest period of time of any of the present-day groups of Native-Americans. They are thought to be the one Native-American group that is the most closely associated with the state of Nebraska. Anthropologists believe that they may have migrated to the Nebraska region as early as 1600 from the lower Mississippi valley. During the middle 1700s, the Pawnee became embroiled in controversies with the Sioux over their hunting grounds. Also, the Pawnees, along with the other plains tribes, were becoming overrun by European-American settlers. In 1825 they signed a treaty which guaranteed safety for the settlers in return for "benefits" and "acts of kindness" from the U.S. government. There were unspecified and actually were never received by the tribe.

Due to the Removal Act of 1830, relocated eastern tribes were moved into the parts of Nebraska and the other plains state regions in which the Pawnee resided. This caused a number of clashes between the Pawnees and the new Native-American groups over hunting grounds. In a treaty enacted in 1833, the Pawnees gave up all claims to lands south of the Platte River. In 1874 they were removed to a reservation west of the Arkansas River in an area which later became part of Oklahoma. However, it was not until 1957 that the Pawnees were able to use the lands on their reservations as they chose.

Until about 1500 the Omaha lived in the eastern woodlands. At that time they relocated in the present state of Nebraska where they continued to grow corn, beans, squash, and other vegetables. However, during the spring and autumn, they hunted buffalo in order to acquire meat for food; hides for tipis and clothing; and shoulder blades for hoes. During the hunting periods, they encountered Sioux and Pawnee hunting parties, often fighting over hunting privileges.

Never fighting with the United States, the Omaha agreed to a number of treaties and eventually were given reservation lands in Nebraska and Iowa. They too were plagued with the usual Native-American problems of poor education, poverty, and the danger of losing their native culture. However, in recent years the Omaha tribe has taken steps to ensure that their native tribal language is not lost.

The Oto, part of the Siouan language group, are believed to have once resided in the Great Lakes region. They commenced moving southwest of that area in the 1500s, eventually ending up at the confluence of the Mississippi and Iowa rivers. By 1829 the Otos had merged with the Missouris, both groups having been devastated by diseases brought from Europe.

While the Oto women cultivated corn, beans, squash, and melons along the rivers, the men were primarily hunters. In the spring and summer, their time was spent hunting buffalo, while turkeys, raccoons, deer, and rabbits were the game of choice during the rest of the year. Oto society was patrilineal but the household property and lodges were owned by the women.

The first Europeans who entered the region which today comprises the state of Nebraska were probably Spanish members of Coronado's expedition. Coronado was searching for the legendary Kingdom of Quivira, believed to be a wealthy area where even the poorest of the poor ate from bowls made of gold.

Somewhat later, during the eighteenth century, French fur traders traversed the area, and information pertaining to the character of these lands soon reached Europe as well as other parts of the United States. Also, the Lewis and Clark expedition provided excellent information about the early Nebraska residents after the lands comprising the present state were acquired in the 1803 Louisiana Purchase.

While Hall J. Kelley was not known as a Nebraskan, his writings helped the state to become an important player in the migration to the west. This young Boston school teacher aroused the interest of Easterners to head to Oregon and soon, the Platte Valley-South Pass Trail became the most popular route to Oregon, eventually being known as The Oregon Tail.

The enthusiasm of this latest westward migration of European-Americans, meant that many of these adventurers were passing through Nebraska on their way to the west coast. This 2,000 mile jaunt emanated from Independence, Missouri and went through Nebraska on the way to Oregon. The trail entered Nebraska between Gage and Jefferson counties and followed the Platte River Valley. Thousands of European-Americans went through the area on their way to Oregon. Many of them stayed.

In addition to persons passing through Nebraska on their way to Oregon were the Mormons who were forced out of Nauvoo, Illinois, because of their polygamous practices. They wintered in Montana and set out for the Salt Lake Valley in 1847. And just a short time later the California gold strike resulted in thousands of would-be prospectors traveling along the Platte River-South Pass route to the California gold fields near the American River in the Sacramento area.

In 1854, Nebraska became a United States Territory and Omaha and Bellevue were the leading candidates for becoming the capital. However, the first session of the new territorial legislature was convened at Omaha, and that city became the territorial capital. Moreover, Omaha became the largest city in the territory of Nebraska.

The Civil War was not particularly popular in Nebraska. The reduction in strength of the Fort Kearny garrison and other Union strongholds in the region, left the area open to attacks from various Native-American groups. During the conflict, Nebraska's First Cavalry, commanded by Brigadier General John M. Thayer, served at Fort Donelson and Shiloh. Nebraska supplied the Union armies with huge numbers of fighting personnel. Particularly noteworthy was the Second Nebraska Cavalry.

After the Civil War hostilities, the issue of statehood for Nebraska became a prime concern. Before the war even started, the *Omaha Times* had urged that the issue be presented to the people for their consideration. Statehood was finally granted in 1867 and the renamed city of Lincoln became the capital of the new state. Of course, one of the major issues surrounding possible statehood for new U.S. regions prior to the Civil War was related to the issue of slavery. Many southern states did not opt for including Nebraska because it would not be a slaveholding state.

Since the granting of territorial status, Nebraska has had rather strong backing for the concept of public education supported through tax dollars. In 1855, the Free Public School Act created the office of a territorial school superintendent who had the ultimate responsibility for maintaining schools. However, the popularity of this act waned in 1857 due to an economic panic which closed down many school buildings throughout the territory. In order to keep some of these educational programs afloat, churches and/or private teachers sometimes jumped in to keep the school programs alive.

The Kansas-Nebraska Act expanded the territorial development in the plains states regions, creating new hardships for Native-Americans. Numerous tribes ceded their lands during this period of time. This measure had the effect of terminating the notion of a Native-American country west of the Missouri. The tribes in eastern Nebraska were not particularly aggressive and were relatively quick to relinquish their lands to the European-Americans. However, some tribes, such as the Dakotas terrorized the travelers on the Platte Valley Trail, particularly due to the contemptuous actions of a twenty-one year old inexperienced lieutenant from Vermont, John Grattan, whose actions precipitated a series of hostilities at some nearby trading posts.

The latter portion of the nineteenth century was a difficult time for Nebraska. Suffering from drought, grasshopper plagues, and conflicts with the Native-Americans precipitated by ill-advised government policies, the state suffered major economic hardships. However, the depletion of the buffalo herds helped the cattle industry, and toward the end of the century the economy commenced to recover, largely because of the cattle industry.

By World War I, a number of social and economic changes occurred, particularly in the areas of women's suffrage and the prohibition of alcoholic beverages. And while electricity and the automobile helped to make life easier for Nebraskans, farmers did not generally share in the new-found prosperity. In fact, the economic depression of the 1930s was accompanied by more grasshopper plagues and droughts which made life more difficult for farmers. During the latter stages of the twentieth century the sizes of farms increased, and the rural populations decreased except for the counties located along the Platte River.

THE EDUCATIONAL SYSTEM

Nebraska's constitution of 1875 provided for a complete system of public education from the elementary level clear through the university. However, the funding for such enterprises was largely left up to the local levels. Compulsory school laws were not enacted until 1891. This legislation finally guaranteed the opportunity for a common school education to all Nebraska children.

Nebraska's state commissioner of education is appointed by the State Board of Education. All children between the ages of seven and sixteen years of age are required to attend school unless they reach the age of fourteen and are employed, because they have to support themselves or their dependents; if they have graduated from high school; or if the child is mentally or physically handicapped. Compulsory special education programs are provided to handicapped children between the ages of three and eighteen.

The state allows for home schooling as long as it complies with existing state regulations. Such efforts are subject to general school laws as they apply to grades, qualifications and certification of teachers and promotion of students, adequate supplies and equipment, etc. The course of study must be substantially the same as the one in the public school which the child should be attending.

Nebraska has no statutory provisions related to prayer in school and student records are withheld from the public unless they are disclosed in a court of law. The state has no statutory provisions related to the use of corporal punishment in the schools.

In order for prospective teachers to become certified in Nebraska they must pass the National Teachers Examination which measures knowledge of basic skills and subject matter competencies. In addition, they must be observed in successful teaching performances.

Nebraska spends $999 per capita on education. This is substantially higher than the national average of $932. The state has a policy governing year-round schools but there are no requirements for either half-day or full-day kindergartens. Thirty-six percent of Nebraska's teachers hold a master's degree compared with the national average of 42 percent.

MULTICULTURAL EDUCATION EFFORTS

Most Nebraskans had their roots in Europe, many migrating from Pennsylvania, Ohio, Illinois, Indiana, and Iowa. These Europeans came from the northern part of Europe and German-Americans comprise the largest group of European-Nebraskans. However, German-speaking Nebraskans also migrated to the United States from Russia, Austria-Hungary, and Switzerland. In addition to these Europeans, large numbers of Nebraska residents had their roots in England, Ireland, Sweden, Czechoslovakia, Poland, and Denmark. People from Mexico, Italy, and Greece also help to comprise Nebraska's pluralistic society.

African-Americans make up about 4 percent of the state's "minority" population and about 1 percent of Nebraska's people claim to be Native-Americans. About one-third of the Native-American population resides on reservations, while a substantial portion of the state's African-American population lives in Omaha.

Ethnically, Catholics still comprise Nebraska's largest religious group. However, large numbers of Nebraska's Protestant population are members of the Lutheran and other major Protestant denominations.

One problem that has plagued school districts in Nebraska and the rest of the country has been the difficulty in providing acceptable support levels in the low-income school districts of each state. In other words, many public school children in America suffer because the schools they attend are woefully underfunded. While Maryland, Nevada, and Delaware spend the same amount of money in all school districts on a per-capita basis, great discrepancies exist in some states. For example, in Texas and Ohio, some high-spending public school districts spend nearly three times as much money on public education for affluent regions as the low-income districts. In Nebraska, the ratio of spending between high and low spending districts is about 1.6 to 1. Thus, it can be seen that the culture of poverty has a dramatic effect in the spending levels for rich and poor students. Nebraska is not so badly affected as many states. However, the fact that there is a problem of unequal funding in Nebraska means that a number of poor children in the state may be "at risk."

Nebraska's African-American population, one of the largest "minority" groups in the state, commenced moving to the region after the Civil War ended. Many of them ended up in Omaha, becoming employed as custodians, maids, porters, railroad construction workers, stockyard employees, and workers in meat packing companies such as Swift and Cudahay. By 1910 the population of African-Americans in Omaha reached 4,426, making Omaha the third largest African-American population among large western cities.

Moses O. Ricketts became the first African-American to graduate from the University of Nebraska College of Medicine in 1884, a time in history when racial segregation still existed in the southern states and many others such as Texas, Missouri, and Oklahoma.

In recent years Nebraska has had a multicultural education program with a person in charge of such functions. Moreover, multicultural education requirements are built into the certification process, and there is a procedure for screening textbooks and curriculum materials for possible racist and sexist content. Nebraska has a policy statement which stipulates that multicultural education and cultural pluralism must be built into the curriculum in order for schools to pass the accreditation requirements. Nearly 12 percent of Nebraska's children under the age of seventeen are below the poverty level, a figure which is well below the national average of 19 percent.

REFERENCES

Alexander, Kern and Alexander, M. David, *The Laws of Schools, Students, and Teachers.* St. Paul: West Publishing Company, 1995.

Berliner, David C., and Biddle, Bruce, *The Manufactured Crisis: Myths, Fraud, and the Attack on America's Public Schools.* New York: Addison-Wesley, 1995.

Council of State School Officers, *The Council.* Washington D.C.: Council of State School Officers, 1998.

Creigh, Dorothy Weyer, *Nebraska: A Bicentennial History.* New York: W. W. Norton, 1977.

Meredith, Howard, *Southern Plains Alliances.* Lawrence: University Press of Kansas, 1994.

Miewald, Robert, (ed.), *Nebraska Government and Politics.* Lincoln: University of Nebraska Press, 1984.

Mitchell, Bruce and Salsbury, Robert, *Multicultural Education: An International Guide to Research, Policies, and Programs.* Westport, CT: Greenwood Press, 1996.

Olson, James, *History of Nebraska.* Lincoln: University of Nebraska Press, 1966.

Taylor, Quintard, *In Search of the Racial Frontier: African-Americans in the American West, 1528–1990.* New York: W. W. Norton, 1998.

NEVADA

STATE HISTORY

Early in its pre-Columbia history, the state of Nevada was populated by paleo-Indian mammoth hunters for some 12,000 years. More recently, the state has been inhabited by several Native-American groups, particularly those from the Northern and Southern Paiute tribes and some western Shoshones. At the time of the first interactions between the Europeans and the Native-Americans, the Shoshone resided in most of Nevada in addition to other western regions.

Some anthropologists believe that they arrived in the Nevada area from the south of the region approximately 2,000 years ago. They were part of the Uto-Aztecan language group considered to be a very versatile tribe which had the capacity to respond favorably to their environment. While they were primarily hunters, they also were able to rely on various plants for their sustenance when necessary. When gold was finally discovered in the Great Basin regions, the Europeans invaded their lands and the typical problems of disease and broken treaties ensued.

The Paiute group has been divided into northern and southern divisions by anthropologists. The Northern Paiute, part of the Uto-Aztecan language faction like their Shoshone neighbors, were considered to be one of the primary groups of Native-Americans residing in the Great Basin of Nevada. While the northern group dwelled in the areas around Reno and eastward to Winnemucka, Battle Mountain, Elko, and Wells, the southern Paiutes lived in southern Nevada, in addition to parts of Utah and Arizona.

Northern Paiutes lived in grass-covered structures in the winter and then moved outside in the warmer seasons, finding shaded areas which would protect them from the hot desert winds. They were primarily hunters, pursuing deer, antelope, and bighorn sheep. They first came into contact with the Europeans in 1804 when reportedly some of the tribal members encountered members of the Lewis and Clark expedition. The southern Paiutes were among the last Native-American tribal groups to come into contact with the European-American settlers.

One of the most famous Paiute women was Sarah Winnemucka. The town of Winnemucka, Nevada was named after her family. When the lands of the northern Paiutes were invaded by European-Americans, she became something of a linguist, having mastered several Native-American tongues, as well as Spanish and English. Consequently, she became an interpreter for the United States Army during the Bannock War. After Paiutes had been assigned to scattered reservations in Oregon, Nevada, and Washington, she pleaded her people's case to the public, lecturing throughout the nation, particularly in the Northeast and California. Although she was an eloquent spokeswoman for the Paiutes, she also spoke on behalf of Native-Americans throughout the land. Sadly, her efforts were not too successful.

It is believed that Franciscan missionaries may have been the first Europeans to enter the Paiute lands during one of their searches for a route between their holdings in New Mexico and California. However, it was not until 1820 that Peter S. Ogden traveled around the state's northern boundary in connection with his work with Hudson's Bay Company. In 1828 he became the first known European-American to encounter the Humbolt River where he trapped.

However, two years before that escapade, Jedediah Smith, European-American explorer, went through southern Nevada on a trip to California. And in 1833, Joseph Walker followed the Humbolt and Carson Rivers on the way to California with a party of trappers. Ten years later he led a group of immigrants across the Great Basin area on their way to California.

John C. Fremont led scientific expeditions across the Great Basin during the mid-1840s, but it was the California gold discovery and the Treaty of Guadalupe Hidalgo which changed the state forever. The 1848 Treaty of Guadalupe Hidalgo ended the Mexican War and granted the lands comprising the present Nevada boundaries to the United States. The discovery of gold at Sutter's Mill resulted in the migration of gold seekers to the West.

Nevada became included in the lands of the Utah Territory in 1850 when that region of the country became formally recognized as a United States Territory. During that period of time, the California gold rush motivated the same kinds of explorations in Nevada, particularly in the northern regions of the state in the Sierra Nevada regions. Near Carson Valley, Sun Mountain (also known as Mount Davidson) beckoned to gold seekers who would uncover the Comstock Lode, recognized as the world's largest deposit of silver and gold to be located in such a concentrated area. Discovered in 1859, it eventually yielded $300,000,000 in its first twenty years. Many experienced California miners came over the mountains to take advantage of this lucrative lode.

Virginia City was incorporated by territorial legislative action in 1862. This mining town was racially segregated. While the European-American miners resided in one large section, the mining superintendents and the town's leading merchants lived on the upper streets of the town. There was a racially-segregated Chinese section and some huts for Native-Americans.

One of the main problems connected with Nevada's mining boom was the intense heat which miners sometimes encountered. Temperatures reached more than 130 degrees fahrenheit, and buckets of ice were poured on the miners, who were only able to work short shifts. Consequently, production costs were sometimes quite high.

But it was not only mining that attracted the early European-Americans to the state of Nevada. After becoming a separate territory in 1861, Nevada achieved statehood in 1864, primarily because the Lincoln administration was anxious to have another anti-slavery state. About this time the mining industry was starting to drop off, but the agriculture/ranching business was beginning to flourish. By the turn of the century, Nevada was able to take advantage of the Reclamation Act of 1902 and transported water from the Truckee River to the Carson River in order to provide irrigation for the Fallon area, which became one of Nevada's most important agricultural centers.

The last two decades of the nineteenth century were difficult times for Nevada. The state lost about one third of its population. However, mining rebounded after the turn of the century when silver and gold were discovered in Tenopah and Goldfield. A copper strike occurred near Ely. However, by 1921 the mining industry again fell on hard times but a number of federal projects helped the state's economic circumstances. Because of its size and geographical position, Nevada benefited from road construction, largely due to the need for the creation of automobile routes across the northern and southern portions of the state. Also, construction on the Boulder Dam (later re-named the Hoover Dam) commenced in 1929, adding more income to the state's economy.

However, an action by the Nevada legislature in 1931 would change the state forever. Gambling was legalized, but due to the economic depression it was slow to grow until after World War II. Also, in an attempt to encourage more travel to the state, the time period for getting a divorce in Nevada was reduced to six weeks.

During and after World War II the state began to experience more rapid growth as a result of the construction of numerous new gambling casinos in Las Vegas, creating the famed "Strip." Legislation was enacted which made it possible for corporate-financed operations to be constructed. And, while there have been temporary periods of time where the growth of the gambling industry subsided, on the whole the growth has been quite dramatic, particularly in the 1990s with the construction of super casinos.

Military involvement continued after World War II. In 1951 the United States government commenced atomic testing at Yucca Flat, but after 1962 the testing was done underground. In addition to atomic testing, flight training has been carried on in Nevada by both the Air Force and the Navy. Also, gunnery and bombing test sites are located throughout the state.

In the late 1990s, Las Vegas experienced such dramatic growth that it became one of the fastest growing cities in the United States. While much of this growth can be attributed to the gambling industry, the state also experienced a much greater diversity in its industrial development. Growth in Las Vegas has been occurring so rapidly that it is very difficult to keep up with housing needs. Accommodating the educational demands of this enormous growth spurt has necessitated the hiring of hundreds of new teachers each year and the construction of many new schools.

THE EDUCATIONAL SYSTEM

Nevada school districts were first established in 1845. These early districts were supported by county taxes, although the state also provided minimal support. But while the public and private schools which were located in the larger towns fared fairly well, rural schools suffered, as was the case in virtually every state's educational history.

Education for Native-American children was also minimal throughout Nevada's history. Much of it consisted of federal day schools on the reservations. Located near Carson City, the Stewart Indian School was also established by the federal government in 1890, but it was closed down in 1980. During much of its operational history, Native-American children were denied admittance to public schools. The *Brown v. Board of Education* Supreme Court decision was instrumental in changing this practice.

Nevada's state school superintendent is appointed by the State Board of Education. Nevada's compulsory attendance requirements are between the ages of seven and seventeen years. However, children are not forced to attend the public schools if they are enrolled in a private school program or have a physical/mental condition which might prevent attendance. Other excuses for nonattendance include residing too far from school, receiving equivalent, appropriate instruction, or completing the twelfth grade prior to the age of seventeen years. Children can also be home schooled if their instruction is equivalent to the kind approved by the State Board of Education. Education for special education students is provided between the ages of three and twenty-one.

Teacher certification requires successful test performance on basic and professional skills, as well as successful in-class observations. Nearly 43 percent of Nevada's teachers have their master's degree compared to the national average of 42 percent.

The state spends about $857.19 per capita, compared to the national average of $931.76 per capita, and just 11.1 percent of the state's children under the age of seventeen are below the poverty level. Only eight other states have a smaller percentage.

Ten percent of Nevada's citizens have the bachelor's degree compared to the national average of 13 percent. While corporal punishment in Nevada is allowed, it is discouraged. Punishment may not be administered about the face or head and parents must be notified. Local school boards can adopt their own policies regarding corporal punishment. It can be used only when all other forms of discipline have proved to be ineffective.

Nevada has no mandatory kindergarten requirements, although kindergarten programs are available in the larger districts around the state. Nevada allows students to have a period of silence for meditation or prayer. Both custodial and non-custodial parents have access to children's school records, but communication between counselors-pupils and teachers-pupils is privileged.

MULTICULTURAL EDUCATION EFFORTS

Responses to the authors' 1998 multicultural education survey revealed that Nevada does not have a planned multicultural education program in the state, although there is a person in the State Office of Instruction who is responsible for such activities. That person is the gender equity consultant. However, there is not state funding for multicultural education programs. The state does offer assistance in the form of local, regional, and state workshops, and conferences in regard to gender, ethnicity, culture, and language.

In addition to the European-American groups, the predominant microcultures in Nevada are Latinos, Asian-Americans, African-Americans, and Native-Americans. No special coursework or other multicultural experiences are required for teacher certification in Nevada.

Since the state of Nevada leaves curriculum development to the local school districts, there are no state policies pertaining to the philosophical issue of cultural pluralism versus cultural assimilation. The respondent opined that most school districts harbored an assimilationist view.

It was reported that the issue of native language instruction was left up to the local district. Clark County has a number of bilingual education programs in existence. Since most of Nevada's school districts are quite small, the issue of school segregation has not been particularly difficult for Nevada to deal with. However, Clark County is the tenth largest school district in the United States and as previously stated, is growing rapidly. That school district has filed a desegregation plan with the United States Office of Civil Rights.

The curriculum in Nevada does address the history of Nevada's Native-Americans but with a European perspective. Also, the state's Office of Education evaluates library materials and textbooks for racist and sexist content.

Finally, the respondent felt that the biggest problems facing multicultural education programs in Nevada were the problems of raising awareness to counter myths and stereotypes about gender, race, class, age, religion, immigration status, and disability. Another problem is the lack of program funding. The biggest improvements in their state's multicultural education efforts would be to address these issues in a positive manner.

REFERENCES

Bunte, Pamela, A., and Franklin, Robert J., *From the Sands to the Mountain: Change andPersistence in a Southern Paiute Community.* Lincoln: University of Nebraska Press, 1987.

Elliott, Russell R., *History of Nevada.* Lincoln: University of Nebraska Press, 1984.

Euler, Robert C., *The Paiute People.* Phoenix: Indian Tribal Series, 1972.

Hopkins, Sarah Winnemucka, *Life Among the Paiutes: Their Wrongs and Claims.* New York: G. P. Putnam's Sons, 1883.

Hulse, James W., *The Silver State: Nevada's Heritage Reinterpreted* Reno: University of Nevada Press, 1991.

Leiter, Richard A., (ed.), *National Survey of State Laws* First edition. Detroit: Gale Research, 1997.

Ostrander, Gilman M., *Nevada: The Great Rotten Borough, 1859–1964.* New York: Alfred A. Knopf, 1966.

Rusco, Elmer R., *Good Time Coming? Black Nevadans in the Nineteenth Century.* Westport, CT: Greenwood Press, 1975.

Trimble, Stephen, *The Sagebrush Ocean, A Natural History of the Great Basin.* Reno: The University of Nevada Press, 1989.

United States Department of Education, *Digest of Educational Statistics.* Washington D.C.: United States Department of Education, 1997.

NEW HAMPSHIRE

STATE HISTORY

New Hampshire's primary Native-American tribes belonged to the Algonquian language group. The coastal bands who were the first native residents of New Hampshire, were overrun by British intruders who settled throughout the region. The English settlers used the names of the Native-American villages in the terms they used to designate the tribes. Consequently, the Native-Americans in present-day New Hampshire were referred to as Nashaway, Piscataqua, and Squamscot. However, anthropologists have referred to the New Hampshire tribes as the Abenaki and Pennacook, the two largest tribes in the New Hampshire region.

The Abenaki are thought to have arrived in the New Hampshire area some 3 thousand years ago. Because of the region's geographical characteristics, the Abenaki enjoyed a rich subsistence of fowl, fish, and game. Their hunting exploits netted deer, bear, moose, beaver, and seals. From the ocean they were provided with shellfish, eel, salmon, and sturgeon.

They selected a leader (*sakom*) and dwelled together in small groups of ten to fifty people in extended families. However, at times up to 300 would band together. The women raised corn, beans, and squash in the fields, which were prepared by the male members of the tribe.

The first tribal contacts with Europeans occurred during the early 1600s when they commenced to trade with the European settlers. Beaver pelts were bartered for copper, kettles, blankets, knives, axes, and alcohol. However, the contacts with Europeans caused the usual fatalities among the various Native-American groups for hunting grounds, resulted in a series of intertribal conflicts referred to as the Beaver Wars.

To make matters worse, when France surrendered Canada to the British, thousands of European-American settlers invaded the lands of the Abenaki, and finally, in 1796 a reservation was provided for everyone living in the Penobscot Valley. Many others commenced moving to cities and villages but since the 1960s the tribe has attempted to revitalize its cultural traditions.

The Pennacook are part of the western arm of the Abenaki, having resided in present-day New Hampshire. Wanalancet, the tribal chief in 1675, led the tribe into the woods in order to avoid involvement in King Philips's War. Kankamagus, the last of the Pennacook chiefs, led his people north to Canada, where a number of them joined French mission villages. Consequently, a large number of the tribal members lost most of their Pennacook tribal identity.

One point of contention between New Hampshire and the Pennacook/Abenaki people has to do with one of their religious customs of burying their dead in unmarked sites near their homes. Consequently, the Native-Americans consider all of these burial sites to be sacred burial grounds. The state has generally disagreed with this contention.

The earliest known European settlements in New Hampshire were established along the banks of the Piscataqua River at its mouth by David Thompson, an entrepreneur from Plymouth, England. A Londoner, David Hilton, established a second settlement about seven miles up the river. From that time on the growth in the area was rather steady, due to the exploits of other English settlers. A London-based organization known as the Council for New England made the major decisions which affected the new residents.

However, the settlement of New Hampshire proceeded rather slowly because of the threats of Native-American reactions against their land encroachments. Savage attacks were initiated by both the Europeans and Native-Americans during the last quarter of the seventeenth century and the first quarter of the eithteenth century. This condition changed when the Native-Americans withdrew to Maine and Quebec.

After the termination of the French and Indian Wars, things calmed down in the area, and, by 1775, the New Hampshire colony had a population of about 83,000,000 people. Approximately 650 of them were African-American or Native-American slaves.

New Hampshire was actually the first state to challenge Britain in a pre-Revolution arms confrontation. Led by a New Hampshire merchant, John Langdon, an estimated 400 armed colonists from New Hampshire prevailed in an attack on Fort William and Mary in Portsmouth Harbor. They were rewarded with 100 barrels of gunpowder which they captured from the British and used in subsequent conflicts. On June 15, 1776, the New Hampshire provincial congress voted in favor of independence from England and three New Hampshire regiments were organized to battle against the British. At that time, the 1776 legislature established a judicial system.

New Hampshire became the first state to adopt a revolutionary constitution and declare its independence from England in January, 1783. However, their constitution was not ratified until October, 1783. Finally, in 1788 New Hampshire became the ninth state to ratify the United States constitution. Concord became the state capital in 1808.

New Hampshire had a strong voice in the early days following the Revolution. In the War of 1812 the state drafted about 39,000 men to battle for the Union. The first president of the United States from New Hampshire was Franklin Pierce, who was elected to office in 1852.

While New Hampshire had slavery in its history, by 1820 the practice had ceased and population figures estimated that about 786 free persons of color resided in New Hampshire. Thus, in the years leading up to the Civil War, New Hampshire had become a rather solid opponent of the practice. In fact, the site legislature had ruled slavery to be morally wrong. Lincoln had given a presentation at Phenix Hall on a number of slavery issues.

After his election, New Hampshire sent the First New Hampshire Regiment of United States Volunteers to Washington, where they marched down Pennsylvania Avenue and passed in review before President Abraham Lincoln. At the final count, it was determined that the various New Hampshire military units had lost about half of their original numbers in killed, wounded, and missing military personnel. All told, about 36,000 New Hampshire men were members of various branches of military service.

By 1900 New Hampshire had shed its rural image and the state had become much more industrialized, more urban, and more ethnically diversified than ever before in its history. Transportation had improved, particularly in the number of rail miles and a plethora of waterpower facilities, factories, and textile mills had begun to replace the gristmills and sawmills which had become New Hampshire trademarks in years past.

After World War II, an estimated 100,000 New Hampshire men and women were returning home from their involvement in a number of military units. Politically, the state had become more independent and more parochial and conservative.

From that time onward, New Hampshire had been viewed as a fiscally conservative state. Both the Republican and Democratic parties have vigorously fought the creation of new taxes and consequently, the New Hampshire taxes have always been low. However, while this has created a conservative fiscal image, it has been a hardship for public schools which have sometimes been hard pressed to pay for their required services. This phenomenon has placed New Hampshire in the unenviable position of "bringing up the rear" as far as providing tax support for public schools is concerned.

Since its early beginnings, New Hampshire has always required its towns to hire a schoolmaster as soon as they had 50 householders. A grammar school was to be maintained after the number of householders increases from 50 to 100. For many years in New Hampshire, the elementary schools were of the red brick style and many were ungraded. While the state was settled by persons with English, Scottish, and Irish backgrounds, others of French ancestry moved into the region which required English/French bilingual education programs in the schools.

Dartmouth College is New Hampshire's best known college or university. Originally, it was a liberal arts institution for men under a charter granted by King George III. It is still known as one of the nation's most prestigious institutions of higher learning.

THE EDUCATIONAL SYSTEM

Since 1919 New Hampshire has had a State Board of Education, which had the responsibility of certifying teachers, enforcing attendance, and prescribing school standards of various types. Also, this body appoints the Commission of Education. While the state has been in charge of such functions, local school districts were given the responsibility for directing elementary and secondary education. Presently, the State Board of Education consists of six members who appoint the Commissioner of Education.

Certification for teachers in New Hampshire requires successful completion of the National Teachers Examination which measures basic skills. Also, prospective teachers must be observed in successful classroom experiences. Thirty-six percent of New Hampshire's teachers have completed the master's degree compared to the national average of 42 percent.

Compulsory attendance ages for New Hampshire children are between six and sixteen years of age. The exceptions to this requirement include: the welfare of the child; regular and lawful occupations; or physical/mental conditions which prevent attendance or make it undesirable. Home school provisions are allowed for planned supervised instructional and related educational activities, including curriculum and instruction in science, math, and language, government, history, health, reading, writing and spelling, United States and state history, New Hampshire constitution and exposure to and appreciation of art and music.

While New Hampshire has no statutory provisions regarding the use of corporal punishment in the schools, five minutes is allowed students for prayer in the schools but there can be no teacher supervision involved. Only 4.3 percent of New Hampshire's children are below the poverty level, the smallest percentage in the nation.

MULTICULTURAL EDUCATION EFFORTS

While New Hampshire has no special program for multicultural education, there is a person who is responsible for such undertakings in the Bureau for Equity. But there is no special funding for such programs. The state has a race consultant who responds to specific requests from school districts who need assistance in various sorts of multicultural education issues. The assistance often takes the form of workshops.

In addition to the predominant European-American culture, New Hampshire has a small population of Native-Americans, Asians, Latinos, and Eastern Europeans. There are no special multicultural education requirements in the form of special courses or experiences for teacher certification. There are some special programs to teach students in their native language when necessary. These efforts take the form of limited English Proficiency (LEP) programs. In the introduction to the state's compliance guide for LEP programs, it is stated that "it is a violation of the Civil Rights Law to have Limited English Proficiency Children sitting in classrooms where they do not understand the language of instruction."

Since the non-European-American population in New Hampshire is only about 3 percent, there have been no desegregation programs which are functioning. The respondent referred to New Hampshire's curriculum framework, which can be used if local districts so choose. Some references are made to the history of Native-American people. However, the state has no provisions for the evaluation of curriculum materials, library materials, and textbooks for racist or sexist statements.

The biggest problem facing multicultural education efforts in New Hampshire is the perception that since the state is comprised of primarily European-American persons, there is no need for such programs. New Hampshire's biggest challenge is convincing people that the need is just as real in that state as it is in more pluralistic populations.

REFERENCES

Calloway, Colin, G., *The Western Abenakis of Vermont, 1600–1800: War, Migration, and the Survival of an Indian People.* Norman: University of Oklahoma Press, 1990.

Clark, Charles E., *The Eastern Frontier: The Settlement of Northern New England, 1610–1763.* New York: Knopf, 1970.

Council of Chief State School Officers, *The Council.* Washington D.C.: Council of State School Officers, 1998.

Leiter, Richard A., (ed.), *National Survey of State Laws.* First edition. Detroit: Gale Research, 1997.

Morison, Elizabeth Forbes and Morison, Elting, *New Hampshire: A Bicentennial History,* New York: W. W. Norton, 1976.

Morrison, Kenneth M., *The Embattled Northeast:' The Elusive Ideal of Alliance in Abenaki-Euramerican Relations.* Berkeley: University of California Press, 1984.

New Hampshire Department of Education, *Equal Education Access for Students with Limited English Proficiency.* Concord: New Hampshire Department of Education, 1998.

Noon, Christine, (ESL Coordinator, NH Department of Education), *Memo Regarding National Study of Multicultural Education.* Concord: State of New Hampshire, Department of Education, 1998.

Speck, Frank G., *Penobscot Man: The Life History of a Forest Tribe in Maine.* Philadelphia: University of Pennsylvania Press, 1940.

United States Department of Education, *Digest of Educational Statistics.* Washington D.C.: United States Department of Education, 1997.

NEW JERSEY

STATE HISTORY

The original residents of New Jersey were the Leni Lenape Native-Americans who greeted the Europeans when they arrived in New Jersey, northern Delaware, and southeastern New York. The word "Lenape" means "Real People". They were part of the Algonquian language group, and it has been estimated that the tribal membership numbered approximately 10,000. However, these numbers dwindled due to the contraction of European diseases and alcoholism.

The Lenape resided in small groups or subtribes which were located along the major waterways of New Jersey, including the ocean shores. Each subtribe or band had distinct ethnic characteristics. They survived by hunting, primarily, relying on the rich supplies of fish, deer, elk, bear, beaver, and muskrat. In addition to the hunting exploits of the men, the women raised crops of corn, squash, beans, and tobacco. The small villages normally contained only about twenty-five or thirty persons.

While the European settlers tended to harbor Christian beliefs which attested to their superiority, the Lenape people thought they were an important cog in the natural world. They were a spiritualistic group who worshipped different gods. even though they believed in a supreme being. They believed they were an integral part of the natural world. Manito was their supreme being and was responsible for the creation of the earth.

The Lenape were one of the most influential East Coast tribal groups until about 1720. However, as European-American settlers moved into the region, the Lanape left. Many of them eventually moved west to Indian Territory (now Oklahoma). They dominated the eastern groups until about 1720. Some became members of the Cherokee tribe. Others relocated in upper New York, while still yet some went to the Lake Erie region.

It is believed that the first Europeans to arrive in the area were Spaniards who sailed with the explorer Giovanni da Verrazano in 1524. However, it is believed that no other Europeans may have reached the area until 1609 when Henry Hudson's explorations led to the establishment of a Dutch colony (New Netherlands) in 1626. In 1664, Colonel Richard Nichols led an English fleet to the New Jersey area. A few days after he arrived, Governor Peter Stuyvessant surrendered to the British. Actually, the Dutch were not particularly interested in establishing a colony in the area.

By 1676 West Jersey was essentially under the control of William Penn who helped the people acquire a document titled "Laws, Concessions, and Agreements" which promised complete freedom of conscience, a liberal land policy, and a representative government. At the time, the area was closely allied with Philadelphia as far as economic and religious issues were concerned.

However, East Jersey was led by a company of Quakers who were actually considered to be part of the economic province of New York City. The people lived on small farms which tended to be located near towns. Scottish Calvinists settled Perth Amboy and were considered to be an economic threat to the port of New York for a short period of time. Eventually, East and West Jersey were reunited after their proprietary interests agreed to come under control of the British Crown early in the eighteenth century.

One of America's premier institutions of higher education, Princeton University, was established in 1746. And by the year 1775, just one year before the beginning of the American Revolution, New Jersey carried out its own version of the Boston Tea Party when New Jerseyites dressed as Native-Americans and dumped British tea into the mouth of the Delaware River.

Due to New Jersey's location between New York and Washington D.C., over 100 battles and/or skirmishes were fought during the American Revolution. One of the most important conflicts was the Battle of Trenton in December of 1776. During the winters of 1776–77 and 1779–80, Washington located his winter headquarters at Morristown.

During the war in 1776, New Jersey became a state and adopted its constitution, which was in effect until 1844. The United States Constitution was ratified in 1787, making New Jersey the third state to do so. Trenton became the state capital in 1790. During the Constitutional Convention of 1787, New Jersey presented its New Jersey Plan, which called for the formation of a legislature of just one house which would have two representatives for each state on an equal basis. However, this proposal was defeated, even though the proposed enactment led to the formulation of the United States Senate.

Following the successful American Revolution, the New Jersey Plan was instrumental in motivating people to vote in favor of the plan to create a one-house legislature with an equal number of participants in each state, regardless of size.

During the first three decades after statehood, New Jersey became interested in its transportation system. John Fitch, along with Robert Fulton was one of the early pioneers in the creation of steamboat transportation. The Trenton to New Brunswick rail line was established in 1815 when a railroad charter was issued by the New Jersey legislature to John Stevens.

During the latter part of the eighteenth century, New Jersey's industrial development commenced to materialize when Alexander Hamilton selected the location of the Passaic River Falls as a workable site for the city of Paterson. Between the War of 1812 and the Civil War, the state's industrial growth was substantial in the cities of Newark, Jersey City, Camden, and Paterson. All of these cities experienced dramatic growth.

The Marquis de Lafayette visited Newark in 1824. Because of his participation in the American Revolution, Newark citizens conducted a parade which drew crowds of people who lined the streets to catch a glimpse of the popular Frenchman who was aging by this time.

The Morris Canal opened in 1831 and connected the newly-developed industrial regions of New Jersey with a number of lucrative mining locations. And the Camden and Amboy railroad became the only line which was commissioned to provide transportation between New York and Philadelphia. This phenomenon ushered in a long period during which the railroads exerted enormous economic influence on the state's political and economic fortunes.

Slavery was outlawed in 1846. Every slave was made an "apprentice for life." However, all of their children were granted complete freedom from that time onward. By 1850 there were about 235 African-Americans who were "apprentices for life," but this number had dwindled to eighteen just ten years later. Large numbers of escaped slaves traveled northward through New Jersey on the underground railway on their way to Canada. The Society of Friends were instrumental in these episodes.

During the Civil War, New Jersey was able to acquire enough volunteers so that a military draft was not necessary. Although New Jersey lost large numbers of young men during the ensuing conflicts, the state benefited economically from its participation in the war.

Politically, New Jersey was considered to be a democratic state during its earlier years. With the exception of its support of Ulysses S. Grant, it voted for democratic presidents from 1868 until it backed Republican William McKinley in 1896. Woodrow Wilson resigned his gubernatorial position to become a democratic president in 1912.

After World War I, New Jersey became a highly industrialized state. Five of its counties were included in the New York City area. During World War II, New Jersey's industrial might became an important element of the nation's war effort. Its coastal locations resulted in the establishment of elaborate defense systems and many young men were stationed at Fort Dix and Fort Kilmer on their way to Europe and North Africa.

Following World War II, New Jersey began to suffer many of the ills encountered by the nation's large urban area. The need for increased urban services initiated a need for higher taxes, which irritated some of the state's residents. Waste disposal became a major problem and the state's aging cities required much more attention in order to maintain and resurrect the infrastructure. Moreover, the new gambling industry became an open invitation for organized crime, which sometimes presented a problem.

THE EDUCATIONAL SYSTEM

Children in New Jersey are required to attend school between the ages of six and sixteen. Exceptions include children who have mental conditions which might prevent them from benefiting from educational programs in the schools. Other exceptions include physical problems which would not allow the children to benefit from school attendance or attendance in other day schools which offer instructional programs which are equivalent to that which is provided in the public school. Home schooling is also acceptable as long as it is equivalent to those programs offered in the public schools.

Corporal punishment is prohibited in the schools. However, reasonable force is allowed to quell a disturbance or to obtain possession of weapons which may be in the student's possession. Reasonable force is also allowed for self defense or for the protection of a person or property.

In order for prospective teachers to become certificated, they must pass the National Teachers Examination which assesses basic skills. In addition, teachers must perform successfully in actual in-class teaching performances. Thirty-seven percent of New Jersey's teachers have completed the master's degree, compared to the national average of about 42 percent.

New Jersey requires all schools to offer kindergarten programs on a minimal half-day basis. The average expenditure for the education of elementary and secondary children in New Jersey is $1,272 per capita. Only Alaska and New York spend more. New Jersey's Commissioner of Education, the chief school officer, is appointed by the governor.

MULTICULTURAL EDUCATION EFFORTS

New Jersey education has been affected by their *Guidelines for Education that is Multicultural (GEM)*. The foreword for their document describing this function quotes Marshall McLuhan, who has suggested the concept of a "global village" which connects the lives of all the people on the planet. The GEM goals are as follows:

1. To enable students and school staff to recognize and make appropriate responses about discrimination based on race, sex, national origin, sexual orientation, or disability, and strive for equity in a diverse society.
2. To provide students with multicultural experiences designed to enable them to interact more effectively in a pluralistic society and an interdependent world.
3. To transform curricular content areas to include ideas, perspectives, and experiences of women and men of diverse racial, cultural, and ethnic groups.
4. To create a school and classroom climate that enhances learning by recognizing the history and culture of all people.
5. To empower students and their families to become active participants in the process of learning.
6. To increase students' knowledge of diverse cultural attitudes, traditions, and values.
7. To assist students in developing a positive self-image.
8. To improve intergroup/interpersonal relations.
9. To provide a school atmosphere that fosters respect for all languages and dialects.
10. To develop students' ability to recognize, critically analyze, and make intelligent decisions about complex social problems and issues such as discrimination and   racism in contemporary society so that the students will act as agents of social change.

Responses to the authors' 1998 multicultural education survey revealed that New Jersey does have a multicultural education program. The program addresses such issues as bilingual education, gender equity, and equal educational opportunities. Such efforts are part of New Jersey's Office of Bilingual Education and Equity. Assistance to states is provided in the form of workshops, technical assistance teacher training, and assistance in the preparation of multi-year equity plans.

New Jersey is one of the few states which does provide funding specifically for multicultural education. In addition to the previously-mentioned functions, the State Office of Education sponsors excellent conferences in multicultural education, such as their December, 1995, Model Programs Conference. The theme of that event was *Pride In Who We Are*. The word *PRIDE* was an acronym for Peace (antiviolence, antibias, anticrime); Respect (issues such as Holocaust education); Inclusion (bilingual education and dual languages); Diversity (multicultural education); and Equity (particularly gender equity).

Another New Jersey program sponsored by the State Department of Education is the magnet school program which consists of a large number of magnet schools scattered throughout the state. These schools specialize in educational enterprises such as theatre arts, basic skills, fine arts, gifted and talented, foreign languages, bilingual education, math and science, family and the environment, intellectually gifted in music and art, finance, medical profession, cosmetology, legal profession, finance, computers, and world cultures. These magnet schools are used not only as a means of providing the best possible school programs for students, but as a strategy for ensuring that schools are racially integrated.

Another fine New Jersey program is their Integrated Quality Education Strategy (IQE). This program is used in school districts in which school integration is virtually impossible. This alternative strategy requires organizing students into instructional groups that reflect the district's makeup with regard to race and national origin. A pluralistic and enriched learning environment is created through the integration and inservice of staff, multicultural curricula, infusion, student training, parental involvement, and strategies to maximize interpersonal growth.

New Jersey is one of the nation's more multicultural states. The microcultures include Latinos, Portuguese-Americans, Korean-Americans, Polish-Americans, Haitian-Americans, Indian-Americans, Native-Americans, Japanese-Americans, Arabic-Americans, Vietnamese-Americans, and Chinese-Americans.

New Jersey's curriculum and instruction stresses the concept of cultural pluralism rather than an assimilationist approach. In fact, the New Jersey Administrative Code stipulates that children must be taught at an early age to live and work together in a multiracial/multicultural society. The state's content standards also stresses multiculturalism.

Unlike a few other states such as California, bilingual education programs are strong. They are mandated whenever a school district has twenty or more students with limited English proficiency.

In addition to the usual desegregation strategies used in school districts, New Jersey has Interdistrict Outreach Programs for helping students to increase their awareness of cultural and socioeconomic differences and to reduce racial isolation. These interdistrict desegregation programs integrate inner city school children with more affluent neighboring districts. The magnet school program, described earlier, is another unique strategy utilized in New Jersey.

The respondent replied that racist incidents had increased in the state's schools during the past five years. However, a recent bias incident report revealed that in 1994 there had been a 22 percent decrease in such incidents. African-Americans were affected by bias crime more than any other racial group. The Jewish religion was the target group for the largest number of bias crimes against a religious group; and Latinos were victimized by bias crime more than any other ethnic group.

New Jersey does not have a state-mandated curriculum, but school districts are urged to incorporate the history of Native-Americans into their local curriculum offerings. New Jersey school districts are required by law to screen curriculum materials, library materials, and textbooks for racist/sexist content.

New Jersey's biggest problems facing multicultural education are the general lack of awareness about the importance of such educational enterprises and the inability to provide ample resources and training sessions for all of the state's teachers and administrators.

The respondent felt that the biggest improvement in the state's multicultural education efforts would be the full implementation of the state's Multi-Year Equity plans in each of the more than 500 school districts in New Jersey.

REFERENCES

Cross, Dorothy, *New Jersey's Indians.* Trenton: New Jersey State Museum, 1976.

Council of Chief State School Officers, *The Council.* Washington D.C., Council of Chief State School Officers, 1998.

Dowd, Gregory Evans, *The Indians of New Jersey.* Trenton: New Jersey Historical Commission, 1992.

Fleming, Thomas J., *New Jersey: A Bicentennial History.* New York: W. W. Norton, 1977.

Huber, Richard and Wheaton, J., (eds.), *New Jersey Historical Series.* New York: Van Nostrand, 1960–1965.

Kraft, Herbert, C., *The Lenape; Archaeology, History, and Ethnography.* Newark: New Jersey Historical Society, 1986.

Leiter, Richard A., (ed.), *National Survey of State Laws.* First edition. Detroit: Gale Research, 1997.

New Jersey Department of Law and Public Safety, *Bias Incident Report* (1994). West Trenton: Department of Law and Public Safety, 1994.

New Jersey State Department of Education, *Guidelines for Education That Is Multicultural.* Trenton: Office of Educational Opportunity of the New Jersey State Department of Education, 1993.

United States Department of Education, *Digest of Educational Statistics.* Washington D.C.: United States Department of Education, 1997.

NEW MEXICO

STATE HISTORY

New Mexico's history dates back long before the arrival of the Europeans. Archaeologists have established that the earliest New Mexicans seem to have been Big Game Hunters in eastern New Mexico. According to the records, Clovis People and Folsom People were making stone spear points which have been dated back to about 9200 BC.

Unfortunately for these two groups, the climate heated up and became quite dry. Consequently, so-called desert dwellers replaced their former ancestors. These initial desert-dwellers were primarily hunters and gatherers. However, their replacements, residing in the area from approximately 5,000 to 2,000 years ago, became successful gardeners.

Following this era, the Mogollon dwelled in west-central New Mexico. Their neighbors, the famous Anasazi, lived to the north. They were the forerunners of the Navajo, Zuni, Hopi, and Pueblo cultures. Actually, the term "Anasazi" refers to "ancient ones." They resided in the so-called "four corners" region of the United States. They augmented their foodstuffs which were acquired by hunting and gathering through agricultural experimentations. They cultivated maize, squash, and beans.

Somewhere between 300 and 500 BC the Anasazi underwent a cultural revolution which had the effect of setting them apart from their neighbors. During this period, they commenced constructing sizable villages which relied on pit houses. They also constructed pottery and baskets which later became valued art objects.

During the next era, the pit houses gave way to majestic apartment-like structures which eventually became known as Chaco Canyon in New Mexico and Mesa Verde in Colorado. These dwellings were not exceeded in height until the late 1800s in New York City.

The final stage of Anasazi culture ended in the early 1600s. Many of the traditional towns were abandoned and the Spaniards under Coronado migrated to the Anasazi region in search of the Seven Cities of Cibola. A great deal of conflict marred the relationships between the Spaniards and the Anasazi during this period. The large apartment buildings were mysteriously abandoned.

By this time in history, the Spaniards' attempts to build an American empire has been unsuccessful, as were their attempts in locating the fabled Seven Cities of Cibola. Unsuccessful in their quest for riches, the Spaniards left the region. In 1609 the Spanish king claimed New Mexico to be a Spanish colony. Santa Fe was declared the new capital in 1610. Many of the Native-Americans were converted to the Catholic faith. However, a revolt by the Pueblo Native-Americans resulted in the Spaniards being ousted from New Mexico. By 1696 the Spaniards had regained control of the Rio Grande Pueblo Native-Americans.

However, in the 1700s, Spain's ambitions in the United States were becoming threatened by France. But New Mexico continued to be a Spanish possession until 1812 when it became part of Mexico, which had received its independence from Spain. At that time in history the Pueblo Native-Americans of New Mexico owed much of their ethnicity and cultural values to their ancestors, the Anasazi. To this day, a great deal of the architecture, art work, and music can be traced to the heavy influences of the Pueblos and their Anasazi ancestors.

New Mexico remained under the control of Mexico until 1849 and the Treaty of Guadalupe Hidalgo, which granted all of New Mexico to the United States. During this period of Mexican control, New Mexico became involved in outside trade. For example, in 1821, William Becknell, a Missouri trader, came to Santa Fe. And from that time on, United States goods made their way into New Mexico over the Santa Fe Trail.

As a result of the U. S. victory over Mexico in 1848, New Mexico became a territory. However, the southern boundaries were not clearly established until the Gadsden Purchase of 1853. Just seven years later, New Mexico became a major player in the Civil War. The territory had not become involved in the African slave trade because other sources of cheap labor were available. The landholding classes were able to acquire the services of Mexican peons and Native-American slaves. The Native-American slaves were captured in battles and sold as house servants. The few African-American slaves in the territory were freed when Congress banned slavery in the territories.

During the Civil War, two battles were fought in the state. Besides the battle at Valverde, located seven miles north of Fort Craig, probably the most famous one occurred at Glorieta Pass on the confederate's approach route to Fort Union, close to Las Vegas. Some historians have referred to this battle as the "Western Gettysburg." It was a highly significant confrontation, since the Union victory discouraged the Confederacy from its goals of controlling the West.

The general confusion in New Mexico during the Civil War emboldened the Native-Americans to become more aggressive in their attempts to oust the European-Americans from their lands. A number of settlements in New Mexico were attacked by groups of Apaches, Navajos, and Plains tribes. These conflicts finally ended in 1886 when all non-Pueblo Native-American groups had been taken to reservations.

Like other parts of the western regions at that time, law and order was slow to arrive in New Mexico. Consequently there were numerous conflicts between the newcomers and the old timers. One of the most famous confrontations was the so-called Lincoln County Range War of 1878–1881, involving Billy the Kid.

While New Mexico had been relatively isolated for many years, all that changed with the coming of the railroads in 1879. However, in spite of improving communication with the rest of the nation, several attempts at acquiring statehood failed. In fact, New Mexicans looked on the 1898 Spanish-American War as an opportunity for proving their loyalty to the United States. Many served with distinction but not until 1912 did New Mexico Territory become a state. The 1912 New Mexico Constitution still contains provisions that maintain a bilingual citizenry.

The First World War provided New Mexico with the opportunity to improve the state's agricultural and mining yields. After the war, 1924 was a good year for Native-Americans in New Mexico. In that year Congress finally passed legislation which recognized the Pueblo people's land rights. And in the same year, Congress finally gave citizenship to Native-Americans in the United States. However, both New Mexico and Arizona refused to allow Native-Americans to vote until 1947.

While the state prospered economically during the 1920s, New Mexico, like other states, suffered greatly during the economic depression of the 1930s, particularly the residents in the eastern "Dust Bowl" regions. This condition did not improve significantly until the beginning of World War II.

Of course, New Mexico was an active participant during that conflict and of the 1,800 New Mexican military personnel who were stationed in the Philippines, 900 perished in the Bataan Death March and subsequent imprisonment. Also, some of the Navajo "code talkers" were from New Mexico. They created a code based on the Navajo language which the Japanese were unable to decipher.

The atomic age had its origin in Los Alamos, New Mexico, as well as Richland, Washington. Testing for the first atomic bombs occurred at White Sands Proving Ground in New Mexico. After World War II hostilities much of the atomic research still occurred in New Mexico. The 1960s saw a number of civil rights issues unfold in New Mexico. Members of the Taos tribe were successful in demanding that the federal government return Blue Lake to them in keeping with a promise that the U.S. government had not yet fulfilled. Also, New Mexico's Latino villagers fought to regain the territories which had once been theirs. Reies Lopez Tijerina claimed that much of their land had been stolen from European-American ranchers and lawyers. After seizing the Echo Amphitheatre, which was located on national forest land, he was thwarted in his efforts to establish an independent nation. Although he was defeated in his effort, he was acquitted in the subsequent trial. Regardless, this and other similar actions undertaken by Tijerina and his followers served to illustrate the racial and ethnic problems of northern New Mexico.

THE EDUCATIONAL SYSTEM

It has been argued that New Mexico's education system began with the Furgusson Act passage in 1898. Up until that time, many politicians in other parts of the country were arguing that New Mexico would not be ready for statehood until it passed "English-only" laws. Prior to this time, public education seemed to take a back seat to other issues. One pronounced reason was that the New Mexico Territory was viewed by some as a tri-lingual community. The three prevailing languages were the Native-American tongues, Spanish, and English. Also, prior to the twentieth century, education in New Mexico was not viewed as being overly important in many quarters. Also contributing to the slow start of public education was the general poverty of the state.

At the present time, New Mexico provides free public education for all children between the ages of five and eighteen. Exceptions to this educational requirement include children who attend private school or those who are home schooled. Moreover, children who are sixteen years of age or older and are employed in a gainful trade or occupation or are engaged in an alternative form of education can be exempt from public school attendance as long as the education is commensurate to the child's needs and parental permission is acquired. Children can also be excluded from the public school attendance requirement if they are unable to benefit from schooling because of physical/mental/learning disabilities/or emotional conditions.

All Mexican children who are in need of special education are entitled to such services between the ages of three and twenty-one. Even though the state has year-round schools, there is no official policy. School districts are required to offer half-day kindergarten programs and attendance is required.

New Mexico's state superintendent of schools is appointed by the State Board of Education. There are no statutory provisions pertaining to prayer in schools or the use of corporal punishment in the state's schools. Both custodial and noncustodial parents have access to students' school records.

In order to teach in New Mexico it is first necessary to pass the National Teacher Examination (NTE), which measures basic and professional skills. It is also necessary to be observed in successful teaching performances.

Over 43 percent of New Mexico's teachers have achieved a Master's degree compared to a national average of 42 percent.

MULTICULTURAL EDUCATION EFFORTS

Survey responses revealed that New Mexico does have a planned multicultural education program which is headed by the director of the Bilingual Multicultural Education Program. According to the responses, 32 million dollars were budgeted for bilingual multicultural education during the 1995–96 school year. New Mexico offers leadership to school districts for various types of multicultural education programs. This assistance is often in the form of workshops, state institutes, research dissemination training institutes, school programs and teacher exchanges.

The predominant microcultures in New Mexico in addition to European-Americans are Latinos and Native-Americans, particularly Navajo, Apache, and seven Pueblo linguistic groups.

New Mexico does require special coursework in bilingual multicultural education in order to master the competencies which were approved by the State Board of Education and have been in effect since 1989. Most of these competencies deal with bilingual education issues.

The respondent to the authors' 1998 multicultural survey indicated that New Mexico stresses cultural pluralism in the curriculum as opposed to an assimilationist philosophy. Also, New Mexico has special programs in place for teaching children in their native languages when necessary. The state's commitment to bilingual multicultural instruction has existed since statehood. The state's 1912 constitution provided for the preparation of teachers in English and Spanish to properly teach children and facilitate the teaching of English.

The state's Constitution also protects the right of all New Mexican citizens to vote, hold office, or sit upon juries regardless of religion, race, language, or color, or the inability to speak, read, or write English or Spanish languages.

Other provisions of New Mexico's Constitution also prevent the segregation of "Spanish descent" children in the schools, and establishes that any amendments to the state's Constitution shall be published in both English and Spanish.

As the state's constitution implies, school segregation by race in New Mexico is illegal. Therefore, local districts are required to identify and assess all students with a native language other than English. School districts may select bilingual education as the best procedure for meeting the needs of Limited English Proficiency (LEP) students.

New Mexico schools are required to prepare an Educational Plan for Student Success (EPSS) which describes how schools will provide an equal education opportunity for all of its K-12 students. The plan must include a systematic process which provides programs and services in order to ensure individual student success. In addition, a description of how student assessment and screening will be used to meet the needs of individual students is also required.

The respondent stipulated that the quantity of racist incidents in New Mexico's schools had remained about the same during the past five years. In regard to the issue of the inclusion of Native-American history in the state's regular curriculum, it was stated that information about the state's indigenous populations is addressed within the topic of New Mexico history.

Attempts to screen curriculum materials, library materials, and textbooks for racist and sexist content is dealt with in New Mexico's materials adoption processes.

Finally, the respondent believed that the biggest problems facing multicultural education efforts in the state were ensuring the students' understanding of the deep meanings of culture and how such teachings could be incorporated into the K-12 curriculum.

REFERENCES

Ambler, J. Richard, *The Anasazi: Prehistoric People of the Four Corners Region*. Flagstaff: Museum of Northern Arizona, 1977.

Barry, Michael S., *Time, Space, and Transition in Anasazi Prehistory*. Salt Lake City: University of Utah Press, 1982.

Beck, Warren, *New Mexico: A History of Four Centuries*. Norman: University of Oklahoma Press, 1962.

Council of Chief State School Officers, *The Council*. Washington D.C., Council of Chief State School Officers, 1998.

Beck, Warren A., and Hasse, Ynez D., *Historical Atlas of New Mexico*. Norman: University of New Mexico Press, 1969.

Ellis, Richard N., (ed.), *New Mexico, Past and Present: A Historical Reader*. Albuquerque: University of New Mexico Press, 1971.

Fergusson, Erna, *New Mexico: A Pageant of Three Peoples*. New York: Alfred A. Knopf, 1964.

New Mexico State Department of Education, *Bilingual Multicultural Education: Guidelines for Compliance with Existing Federal and State Law.* Santa Fe: New Mexico State Department of Education, 1995.

New Mexico State Department of Education, *Procedures for Identification and Assessment of Limited English Proficiency (LEP) Students.* Santa Fe: State of New Mexico Department of Education, 1994.

Roberts, Calvin A. and Roberts, Susan A., *A History of New Mexico.* Albuquerque: University of New Mexico Press, 1991.

Simmons, Marc, *New Mexico: A History.* New York: W. W. Norton, 1977.

Taylor, Quintard, *In Search of the Racial Frontier.* New York: W. W. Norton, 1998.

NEW YORK

STATE HISTORY

New York, for much of the nation's history as the most populous state in the Union, has provided the United States with many of the most famous names in history. Most Americans are familiar with presidents such as Chester A. Arthur, Franklin Delano Roosevelt, Grover Cleveland, Millard Fillmore, Martin Van Buren, and Theodore Roosevelt. Other prominent New Yorkers throughout history include baseball players Lou Gehrig and Babe Ruth; publishers Horace Greeley and James Pulitzer; writers Washington Irving and Damon Runyon; musicians George Gershwin and Oscar Hammerstein; and artists like Grandma Moses. Obviously many other New Yorkers have shaped American history, but long before the exploits of these famous residents, an estimated 30,000 Native-Americans greeted the early European adventurers.

Before the arrival of the Europeans, the area was populated by the Mohegan (also known as Mohican), Lenni Lenape, and Mohawk. In addition to these three groups were the various members of the Iroquois League, which included the Cayuga, Mohawk, Oneida, Onondaga, Seneca, and in 1722, the Tuscarora. Dwelling in the New York State area which was mostly forested at the time, these tribal groups were hunters and gatherers and also engaged in some agriculture. Influential in the founding of the Iroquois League (or Iroquois Confederacy) was a Huron prophet named Deganawida who had a vision of a white pine which was so tall that it penetrated the heavens in order to communicate with the "Master of Life." An eagle functioned as a sentinel in the top of the tree, trying to keep the peace and watching for intruders. The tree's roots consisted of the five original tribes.

Historians believe that his organization was created some time between 1400 and 1600 in order to protect the five tribes from the attacks by other hostile tribes in the region. After the French and Indian War in 1760, new Europeans poured into the lands of the Iroquois people, causing the usual problems of the settlers' interest in taking away the lands of the native residents.

The strength of the Iroquois Confederacy remained intact until the beginning of the Revolutionary War. The various battles in their lands forced many tribal members to leave the region and numerous injuries and fatalities were suffered at the hands of the two warring factions.

Early Europeans in the region included Giovanni da Verrazano, Esteban Gomez, and Henry Hudson. Verrazano, a Florentine in France's service, sailed into present-day New York Bay. While he was supposedly searching for a northwest passage to the Orient in 1524, it has been argued that he was really on a mission for the purpose of claiming North America for France. However, he did very little exploring and left after a short period of time. Gomez, an African-Portuguese in the services of Spain, arrived in the New York area in the winter of 1525. However, when he journeyed up the Hudson River he encountered ice floes and turned back. Henry Hudson, the English navigator, under contract with the Dutch East India Company, sailed into the New York Harbor area in 1609 in search of the Northwest Passage and explored the Hudson River extensively. Returning to Holland on his ship, *The Half Moon,* the information about New York Harbor and the surrounding area spread rapidly throughout Europe. The Dutch later erected Fort Orange in 1624 near the present location of Albany. During the next two years, immigrants from the Netherlands arrived in Manhattan and in the Fort Orange region. New Amsterdam was then developed after Manhattan Island was purchased from a group of Algonquians who were passing through the area. The island was then named New Amsterdam.

Conflicts between the Dutch and the British were terminated in 1664 when Dutch Governor Peter Stuyvessant surrendered New Amsterdam to the English Fort Orange and then renamed Albany and New Amsterdam became New York. During that year, New Jersey was separated from New York. Connecticut followed suit in 1665.

The French and Indian War (1754–1763) resulted in a final defeat for the French. After a number of earlier losses, the British captured Montreal, essentially terminating any French control of North America and Canada.

The revolutionary period was an era of great turbulence for New York. In 1765 the Stamp Act Congress was convened in New York City and just ten years later the colonist forces captured the British garrison at Fort Ticonderoga. In 1776 New York ratified the Declaration of Independence in White Plains. But during the same year New York City was captured by the British. General George Washington led the unsuccessful resistance. New York City was abandoned in 1783.

After the Revolutionary War, a rift occurred over the issue of ratification of the new U.S. Constitution. Supporters of ratification, led by Alexander Hamilton, John Jay, and Robert Livingston, barely prevailed by just three votes in 1788. George Washington was inaugurated as the nation's first president in a New York City ceremony a year later. By 1797 the New York State capital was finally located in Albany after two temporary locations in Poughkeepsie and New York City.

During the War of 1812, many key battles were fought in New York State. New Yorkers, expecting a British invasion after the burning of Washington D.C., dug trenches in an attempt to fortify themselves. However, the invasions never materialized and in 1815 the Treaty of Ghent ended the conflict.

The problems encountered during the War of 1812 pointed to the need for alternative types of transportation. Robert Fulton had constructed his steamboat and water transportation had proved to be a reasonable alternative to land transportation. This condition helped motivate De Witt Clinton in his efforts to create a canal from Albany to Buffalo for transportation purposes. Thus, the Erie Canal provided New Yorkers with an alternative to land transportation to the western areas.

Eventually, New York's development was greatly enhanced by the construction of railroads. By 1842 a line from Albany to Buffalo had been constructed adjacent to the Erie Canal. And by 1851 a trunk line extended from Piermont on the Hudson River to Dunkirk on Lake Erie.

African slaves arrived in New York in 1626 to work on construction projects. However, the West India Company allowed slaves to earn their freedom and to have the same status in the New York court system as European-Americans. However, on the whole, slavery in New York was relatively minimal, and it was outlawed in 1827, nineteen years after the United States Congress abolished slave trade.

Volatile clashes took place in New York in regard to participation in the Civil War. Even though opposition to the war resulted in 1,200 deaths in the 1863 draft riots, New York provided nearly 500,000 troops for the Union cause. About 50,000 men died in the conflicts. During and after the war the state's economic development expanded rapidly as corporations became larger. This economic growth required new workers, and immigrants from Europe poured into New York City, expanding the state's pluralistic populations. By 1892 the entire processing of European immigrants had shifted from Castle Garden to Ellis Island. In addition to the earlier immigrants from north and western Europe, new immigrants arrived from Italy, Russia, Poland, Austria, Hungary, and the Balkans. Russian Jews comprised a substantial proportion of this new group.

In 1898, a city charter incorporated the present five boroughs which make up New York City: Brooklyn, Queens, the Bronx, Staten Island, and New York (Manhattan). However, Brooklyn passed the incorporation by a very narrow margin. The incorporation constituted an attempt to upgrade New York Harbor and all of the Boroughs were harbor ports. By 1900 the consolidation resulted in a census which revealed a population of 3,437,202 people, more people than all but six states and twice the size of Chicago. At that time, the pluralistic population of the state included people from virtually every corner of the earth.

Rearmament for the Second World War was an enormous economic aid to New York following the Great Depression. And after Congress terminated free immigration in the early 1920s, the new immigrants to the state included political refugees from Germany, particularly those fleeing Nazi Germany. Also, residents of the southern states who were in search of employment migrated to New York in substantial numbers.

However, during this period of time New York experienced three major problems. The city, historically, had provided social service benefits for its needy citizens which became increasingly costly. Moreover, the aging infrastructure of the city began causing enormous problems which exist to this day. Finally, New York has always prided itself on its public education system, and the state had always been a national leader in its high level of state aid for schools and children.

THE EDUCATIONAL SYSTEM

New York's attempt to establish a public school system occurred in 1812 when the state legislature agreed on a system for providing education funds for the towns which were located throughout the state. However, public schools charged tuition until 1867 when educational reformers were able to secure funding for the state's elementary schools. Secondary education followed suit after the Civil War.

New York spends about one-third of its annual budget on public education. State funding is provided to school districts on the basis of their need, which is determined by the economic status of the community. The state lottery revenues generate a great deal of the required annual funding. The State Education Department is the administrative arm of the University of the State of New York. It was created just one year after the end of the Revolutionary War. The state superintendent is appointed by the State Board of Education.

Compulsory attendance requirements in New York are from the ages of six to sixteen. However, in New York City and Buffalo, the required attendance ages are between six and seventeen. New York's policy on year-round schools enables the state to have a number of schools which operate on this basis. And while the state has no mandatory kindergarten requirements, most school districts offer such programs for children.

In order for teachers to become certified for teaching in New York, they must receive an acceptable score on the National Teachers Examination. They must also be observed in successful teaching performances within the public school setting.

Historically, New York teachers' salaries have been exceptional compared to the rest of the country. Slightly better than 66 percent of the nation's teachers hold the master's degree, second to Indiana's 73 percent. It also has the highest percentage of teachers holding a doctorate.

New York state is slightly below the national average of persons graduating from high school. While the national average is 30 percent, New York's is 29.5 percent. However, 13.2 percent have attained a bachelor's degree compared to the national average of 12.1 percent. However, one of New York's nagging problems is the percentage of poverty children between the ages of five and seventeen. More than 23 percent of New York's children find themselves in such circumstances. Only eight other states have a higher poverty percentage.

The state allows a brief moment of silence which can be used to think about religion or other personal silent reflections. New York's state policy on school records allows parents to apply for the records of a complying minor. The state has no statutory provisions pertaining to the use of corporal punishment in the schools.

MULTICULTURAL EDUCATION EFFORTS

New York does have a program of multicultural education but there is no specific funding for it. Bilingual education programs and special services for children with limited English proficiency are available in the state's school districts. They are mandated according to the number of students in need of them. Compensatory education programs are offered through federal, state, and local funds. Individual school districts or schools develop additional multicultural programs.

The State's Office of Intercultural Education reviews and approves the state grants for magnet schools. These are two of the main ways that New York deals with the issue of school desegregation.

New York's Office of Intercultural Education and the Office of Bilingual Education provide leadership to school districts in regard to the issue of multicultural education. Local school districts request their services in providing workshops and seminars.

Practically every microculture in the world is represented in New York schools. The respondent to the authors' 1998 multicultural survey stipulated that the predominant microcultures (in addition to European-Americans) are African-Americans, Latinos, and Asians.

Prospective teachers who are seeking certification must complete a program that ensures abilities to work with children from a variety of homes, including homes where the main language is something other than English. They must also demonstrate the capacity to work with handicapped children and with children who are talented and gifted. How this is carried out is up to the individual college or university.

New York's curriculum and instruction tends to stress cultural pluralism rather than an assimilationist philosophy. The state also has a strong program of bilingual education which is designed to provide the instruction in the child's native language when necessary. In order to comply with *the Brown v. Board of Education* school desegregation requirement, New York relies primarily on magnet schools for desegregation, as well as urban-suburban voluntary interdistrict transfer programs.

The history of Native-American people is included in the social studies curriculum. The state has been preparing new frameworks during the past few years. At the present time the New York State Department of Education does not evaluate curriculum materials, textbooks, and library materials for possible racist/sexist content.

The respondent felt that the biggest problem regarding multicultural education programs was the actual definition. However, it was pointed out by the respondent that New York does not have a multicultural education program. But a number of programs address various cultural needs and local school education agencies also develop multicultural programs and initiatives. The New York State Board of Regents has had a long history in support of understanding and appreciating cultural diversity.

REFERENCES

Bliven, Bruce, Jr., *New York: A Bicentennial History*. New York: W. W. Norton, 1981.

Henry, William R., *Wilderness Messiah: Hiawatha and the Iroquois*. New York: Bonanza Books, 1955.

Kammen, Michael G., *Colonial New York: A History*. New York: Scribner, 1975.

Leiter, Richard A., (ed.), *National Survey of State Laws*. First edition. Detroit: Gale Research, 1997.

Markowitz, Harvey, (ed.), *American Indians*, Volume II. Pasadena, CA: Salem Press, 1995.

Morgan, Lewis Henry, *League of the Ho-de-no-sau-nee or Iroquois*. Rochester: Sage and Brothers, 1851.

Taylor, Colin F., *The Native Americans: The Indigenous People of North America*. New York: Smithmark, 1991.

United State Office of Education, *Digest of Educational Statistics.* Washington D.C.: United States Department of Education, 1997.

Zimmerman, Joseph F., *The Government and Politics of New York State.* New York: New York University Press, 1981.

NORTH CAROLINA

STATE HISTORY

Like its neighbors to the north, North Carolina was the home of eight tribes of Native-Americans who greeted the Europeans. An estimated 30,000 Algonquian Native-Americans in North Carolina and elsewhere in the East included people from the Cape Fear tribe, Catawbas, a large population of Lumbees, a group of Ocaneeche, about 1,000 Pamlicos, the Tuscarora, and a small number of Tutelos had resided in North Carolina long before the Europeans came.

While it is believed that the Tuscarora originally resided in New York, they migrated to North Carolina some time after 500 BC. While these Iroquoian language group people were excellent horticulturists, they were also adept at hunting and gathering. The English colonization of North Carolina precipitated the Tuscarora War, which occurred between 1711 and 1713. An estimated 1,000 Tuscarora were killed in the battles with the British who recruited the Yamasee Tribe to help them inflict heavy losses on the Tuscarora Indians. After their defeat, the British set aside some lands for a reservation.

The Catawba were a small tribe which resided at the North Carolina/South Carolina border. They, too, were known for their horticultural prowess, growing corn, beans, and squash. In addition, they were quite adept at pottery making and basket weaving.

The Catawba were rather friendly to the English and even became their allies during the skirmishes with the Tuscarora. Eventually, they were awarded reservation lands in South Carolina. Since the mid- 1800s, they have been involved in legal battles to get their land back. The Lumbee tribe is one of the largest Native-American groups in the entire region, and very little is known about their origin.

In 1990 their population was listed as 48,444 residents. They were English speaking with Europeans moving into the area, leading anthropologists to believe that they may have descended from Native-Americans who had been survivors of Sir Walter Raleigh's "lost colony." Others argue that they may have been descendants of the Cheraw Native-Americans who inhabited the North Carolina area in the seventeenth and eighteenth century.

The first European to arrive in the area was thought to be Giovanni da Verrazano, who sighted Cape Fear in 1524. The next European in the region was probably Lucas Vázquez de Ayllón, who established a temporary colony at the mouth of the Cape Fear River. However, no permanent colonies were established until the British, led by Sir Walter Raleigh, established a colony at Roanoke.

After Charles I became the new king, Sir Robert Heath, his attorney general, appealed to Charles I for a grant to explore, exploit, and settle. In 1629 he became the proprietor of the southern half of North America. This area was called Carolina. Heath's charter also stipulated that people might be protected by law from the abuse of authority by the government, a rather new notion at the time. Obviously, this concept grew with intensity and provided the very foundation for the American Revolution nearly one and one half centuries later.

Over the years, the Carolinas became known as North and South Carolina and by the early 1650s colonists from Virginia commenced to relocate over the boundary line which would eventually separate North Carolina from Virginia. By 1663, King Charles II had regained the British throne and made a group of English lords proprietors of Carolina. By 1729, North Carolina became a royal province as a result of King George II purchasing the shares of the existing proprietors.

Between 1739 and 1776, approximately 20,000 highland Scots settled in the Cape Fear valley while about 60,000 Ulster Scots and some 25,000 Germans settled throughout the Piedmont. By the start of the Revolution, the entire colony of North Carolina had a population of some 300,000 European-Americans.

In 1776, North Carolina became the first colony to officially declare its independence from England. During its involvement in the American Revolution, North Carolina furnished thousands of militia and ten regiments of Continental forces, which did battle with the English. North Carolina's forces were sent to South Carolina, Virginia, and north to participate with George Washington's army. Its contingent at the Constitutional Convention lobbied for a Bill of Rights and a number of other amendments to the newly written Constitution. The Constitution was ratified in 1789 and North Carolina became the 12th state to do so. During that same year the University of North Carolina was created.

After the War of 1812, North Carolina fell on hard times. Political apathy, the one-party system and economic stagnation all contributed to the loss of many North Carolinians who were lured west. Moreover, the issues of slavery in the state caused great divisiveness. By 1845 approximately one fourth of the native North Carolinians left the area to live in other states.

However, the era of disappointment gave way to a more hopeful period which lasted until the start of the Civil War. During this time, North Carolina established a healthy two-party system (Whigs and Democrats), provided financial aid for the construction of roads and railroads, and commenced to provide support for public education efforts. Eventually, this era of hope was terminated by the Civil War, which started in 1861.

In 1861 North Carolina seceded from the Union and joined the Confederacy. It was the last state to do so. The war brought major political division to North Carolina. Moreover, an estimated 35,000 North Carolinians lost their lives in the conflicts. Approximately 11,000 men were killed in battle, while about 24,000 died of disease. North Carolina provided about 140,000 men to the Confederacy cause. Much of the state's wealth was destroyed and 350,000 African-American slaves were emancipated.

After federal troops were withdrawn from North Carolina in 1870, the Ku Klux Klan, organized in Tennessee, spread to North Carolina and became a powerful force in the state. At the time, the North Carolina Klan's primary purpose was to keep African-Americans from voting and "in their place," as well. The organization also persecuted European-Americans who were carpetbaggers or were perceived by the Klan to be guilty of crimes for which they were not prosecuted.

While North Carolina struggled for the first five years after the war, the economy began to pick up in the next two decades as a result of the growth of the cotton, tobacco, furniture, and other manufacturing industries. However, African-Americans were still mostly disenfranchised and the notorious Jim Crow laws prevailed.

European-Americans dominated the state for most of the 20th century, although educational opportunities for African-Americans improved as the popularity of the automobile led to better highways and the cities grew, which necessitated a more comprehensive work force. The agricultural industry flourished and state government became more responsive to the needs of the people.

Over 80,000 North Carolinians served during World War I and nearly 2,400 of their numbers died in battle. The Great Depression of the 1930s created such economic hardships that the state was forced to take over the schools. During World War II, an estimated 7,000 North Carolinians died in battle and more than 360,000 men and women served in the armed forces.

By the middle of the nineteenth century, North Carolina was still primarily an agricultural state, but the economy was becoming more diversified, which caused the creation of new community colleges, which were needed to provide the people with more diversified and more sophisticated work skills. It was called the most progressive southern state after World War II.

The *Brown v. Board of Education* Supreme Court decision of 1954 had a dramatic effect on the state's schools. North Carolina reluctantly agreed to desegregate. For example, the state legislature passed a measure which made it unconstitutional to use school buses for desegregation purposes. However, in a major Supreme Court decision, the North Carolina anti-busing law was declared unconstitutional in a 9-0 ruling (*North Carolina State Board of Education v. Swann*, 402 U. S. 43, 1971). After the ruling, North Carolina embarked on one of the nation's first large busing programs for the purpose of achieving racially-integrated schools.

THE EDUCATIONAL SYSTEM

Like other southern states, public schools were slow in arriving. However, in 1853 things improved. The first State Superintendent of Schools Calvin H. Wiley developed the state's system of public schools into one of the better systems in the country. However, the state's schools were racially segregated.

At the present time, North Carolina has a compulsory education requirement for children between the ages of seven and sixteen. Any exceptions require approval by the local school district. Home schooling is allowed as long as the program consists of the minimal curriculum standards which are required in the public schools. The course of instruction must run concurrently with that of the public schools and be at least as long. Moreover, home-school programs must be recognized by the Office of Non-Public Schools and meet the requirements of standardized testing, high school competency, and health/safety standards.

Corporal punishment can be used in the schools according to North Carolina law. Principals, teachers, and others may use reasonable force in exercising lawful authority to restrain or correct students and maintain order. Local school boards are not allowed to prohibit the use of such force, but they may adopt policies which govern its administration. The state has no statutory provisions for prayer in the schools.

Students' school records are not subject to public inspection. Minimum competency test scores of students are available consistent with the Family Education Records Protection Act (FERPA). Counselor communication is privileged.

Teacher certification in North Carolina requires successful performance on the National Teacher Examination. Teachers must also be observed in successful classroom performances. Thirty-five percent of the state's teachers hold a master's degree, substantially lower than the national average of 42 percent. North Carolina spends $774.92 per capita on elementary and secondary education. Only Idaho, Alabama, Arkansas, Kentucky, Hawaii, Tennessee, and Mississippi spend less.

North Carolina school districts are required to offer special education services to all children between the ages of three and twenty. The state has year-round schools and North Carolina has a policy regarding their structure and use. While school districts are not required by law to provide kindergartens, many of them do. The state superintendent of schools is elected by popular vote.

MULTICULTURAL EDUCATION EFFORTS

North Carolina's multicultural education program is supervised by the state's consultant in Equity and Workforce Development. However, the funding for this effort is meager and consists of only federal funds. Leadership to school districts for multicultural education is provided, according to the respondent of the authors' 1998 survey.

The predominant microcultures in the state are Asian, Native-American, Latinos, African-Americans, and European-Americans. The state is in the process of requiring coursework and/or other experiences in multicultural education in order for teacher candidates to become certified.

According to the respondent, the state has just one program which provides children with instruction in their native language. This was listed as "vocational/workforce development at the secondary level." When asked about desegregation strategies that are presently being used in North Carolina, the response was student assessment, student registration, student placement, and employee hiring.

Survey responses also revealed that racist incidents had been declining in North Carolina, and the history of Native-Americans is being included in the state's history curriculum.

North Carolina does have a procedure for screening textbooks and curriculum materials for racist and sexist content. The respondent was not sure if or how library materials were being subjected to the same kind of scrutiny.

Finally, the respondent felt that the biggest problems facing multicultural education programs in North Carolina were acceptance of the employee at the local level and the need for fair, unbiased student assessment and meeting student needs. The biggest improvements needed were more funding from the state level and teacher certification requirements in multicultural education.

REFERENCES

Council of State School Officers, *The Council.* Washington D.C.: Council of Chief State School Officers, 1998.

Lefler, Hugh T. and Newsome, Albert R., *North Carolina: The History of a Southern State.* Chapel Hill: University of North Carolina Press, 1973.

Leiter, Richard A., (ed.), *National Survey of State Laws.* First edition. Detroit: Gale Research, 1997.

Markowitz, Harvey, (ed.), *American Indians.* Pasadena, CA: Salem Press, 1995.

Powell, William S., *North Carolina: A History.* New York: W. W. Norton, 1977.

Powell, William S., *North Carolina Through Four Centuries.* Greensboro: University of North Carolina Press, 1990.

United States Department of Education, *Digest of Educational Statistics.* Washington D.C.: United States Department of Education, 1997.

Zirkel, Perry A. and Richardson, Sharon Nalbone, *A Digest of Supreme Court Decisions Affecting Education.* Bloomington, IN: Phi Delta Kappa Educational Foundation, 1988.

NORTH DAKOTA

STATE HISTORY

Perhaps the state of North Dakota can best be characterized as a land of hearty people who have become so because of a need to survive its bitter winter climate. Moreover, its isolation has created an aura of mystery. Indeed, there seems to be a general ignorance about the state which is shared by many Americans and the rest of the world as well. Indeed, North Dakota was one of the last remaining areas of the United States where homesteading lands were still available. If these European-Americans were unfortunate enough to reach the area in mid-winter, they were forced to construct temporary homes out of whatever materials were available in order to survive the bitter cold.

But prior to the arrival of these European immigrants, North Dakota was home to the Mandan tribe which settled along the Missouri River banks. Later, they were joined by the Hidatsu and Arikara, who were driven away from their original homelands. Other tribes, such as the Assinboin, Cheyenne, Cree, and Crow lived in the region for short periods of time.

It is believed that the Mandan, members of the Siouan language group, migrated to the area in the early 1400s, settling in the Big Bend area of the Missouri River. Originally, they resided on the banks of the Ohio River. They lived in permanent villages and were fine horticulturists, raising crops such as tobacco, beans, and squash. The men also hunted buffalo on occasion. Before the introduction of the horse in the 1700s, they drove the animals off cliffs. Their prey was used for food, clothing, and shelter.

The Mandan religion was based on the notion of a sun god and part of the Mandan religious ceremony was an annual sun dance. The young men who become warriors were subjected to various ritualistic acts, which included being tortured. The more pain the young warriors could endure, the higher their status as warriors became. In addition to achieving recognition through resistance to pain, Mandan braves also achieved status through being kind to old people, learning the language of the gods, and allowing older men to have sex with their wives in order for the old man's power to be transmitted to the younger man. This confused the European-Americans in North Dakota, who thought that the Mandans were shameless perverts.

After the European-Americans arrived in the area, the population of the tribe, believed to be about 9,000, diminished to about 200 because of the diseases the Europeans brought to the region. In 1874 most of the Mandans were moved to a reservation, and today there are only a handful of full-blooded Mandans living.

The Arikara, belonging to the Caddoan language group, lived along the lower Missouri River basin in North and South Dakota. They were fine horticulturists, raising corn and other crops. They were originally part of the Pawnee tribe, moving up the Missouri River to the Dakotas. During the winter, they hunted, sometimes moving as much as forty miles in search of game. They also played a role as "middleman" for distributing horses from the nomadic tribes located south and west of the Missouri to the tribes residing to the north and east.

The Arikara were also known as good swimmers and were accomplished fishermen as well. They were clever traders, swapping their agricultural products with the American Fur Company for knives, ammunition, beads, tobacco, and hoes. Trading enterprises by this peaceful tribe were also carried on with the Sioux.

European contacts in the present state of North Dakota occurred when the Sieur de La Verendrye, a French explorer, visited the Mandans in 1738. After that, consistent contact occurred because of the European interest in furs. By the time of the American Revolution, North Dakotan Native-Americans were trading with the Hudson's Bay Company. Other trading enterprises were taking place with French and Spanish traders who were headquartered in St. Louis.

Other trading enterprises occurred when a trading post was established at Pembina, making it the first European-American center. Trade in buffalo skins was carried on between the Canadian Metis and Europeans. The Metis are a mixed Native-Canadian/European ethnic group. The markets in this trading enterprise were as far away as St. Paul, Minnesota.

The North Dakota region became part of the United States as a result of the 1803 Louisiana Purchase from France. Lewis and Clark visited the area a year later, and other traders soon followed. They described the area as "one of the fairest portions of the globe, fertile, well watered, and intersected by such a number of navigable streams."

For over half a century, sporadic fighting occurred in the region, primarily between the Sioux and the European-American settlers. In 1876 the conflicts ceased when most of the Sioux bands were relocated to reservations.

By 1861 the region was organized into Dakota Territory, but rapid settlement did not occur because of the lack of transportation facilities and the bitter winter climate. However, in 1864 Congress passed legislation which authorized the construction of the Northern Pacific Railroad, which runs from Duluth to the Puget Sound. This made it possible for immigrants and others to travel to North Dakota in order to take advantage of the 1862 Homestead Act.

North Dakota began to experience significant growth after Oliver Dalrymple started a highly successful wheat farm near Fargo. The hard spring wheat was taken by train to Duluth or the Twin Cities where it was milled. Soon, North Dakota wheat acquired the reputation of being among the world's best. To the west, cattle ranchers moved in and Dickinson soon became known as a northern counterpart of the rowdy Dodge City. However, throughout the state's history, wheat has been the king in North Dakota.

The Dakota Territory was divided into two geographical sections and in 1889, North and South Dakota achieved statehood status, along with Washington and Montana. At the time there was not a great deal of interest in statehood generally and the new status was accomplished through the efforts of a few hundred highly energized North Dakotans. From that time on, North Dakota has often struggled economically because of its heavy reliance on wheat production. Another factor affecting the state's economy has been its general isolation and the distance from major markets. The bitter cold winters have made it difficult to attract new businesses and industries.

In addition to the Native-American population, North Dakota's European-American population is quite diversified, consisting of French and Scotch settlers, as well as Germans, German-Russians, Czechs, Poles, Finns, Icelanders, and Norwegians. As recently as 1970, nearly 40 percent of the state's population consisted of Lutherans. Compared to other states North Dakota has had a very small number of immigrants from Africa, Asia, South America, and the Caribbean area.

The Great Depression had a devastating effect on North Dakota. Because of its farm economy, foreclosures were common, and the state lost population. Coupled with the economic problems, the state suffered through a severe drought. Franklin Roosevelt's New Deal saved the state, and the state received more federal benefits than it paid in federal taxes. World War II finally turned things around economically and socially.

THE EDUCATIONAL SYSTEM

Statehood in North Dakota brought a system of public education to the area. A federal land grant provided support for public education and the state's constitution provided for a system of school governance by empowering local districts to levy taxes for its support. A state superintendent of public schools is elected by popular vote. District sizes were determined by the first state legislature, teacher licensing procedures were established, and compulsory attendance ages from eight to fourteen were established.

Because of the state's highly rural nature, by World War I there were almost 5,000 one-room elementary schools in the state. Most of these children were taught by teachers who had little training. However, after World War II, the state reformed its education system, and the state agreed to pay 67 percent of the costs for elementary and secondary education.

North Dakota requires school attendance of all children between the ages of seven and sixteen. Children must be enrolled in a public or private school. Attendance is not required of children who have completed high school, regardless of their age. Children can be excused from the compulsory attendance requirement if they are needed to support their family or if they have a handicap which makes school attendance impractical. Home schooling is allowed as long as the home instructor is certified.

Corporal punishment is still used in North Dakota schools as long as it does not create a substantial risk of death, bodily disfigurement, or gross degradation. State law allows a period of silent time of one minute, which can be used for meditation or prayer. Students' medical records are confidential and may not be released without written consent of the student. If the student is under fourteen years of age, written consent of the student's parent or guardian is required in order for records to be released.

Teacher certification in North Dakota requires evidence of basic skills achievement and candidates must be observed performing successfully in the classroom. However, there are no testing requirements at the present time. North Dakota's teachers have the distinction of having the highest percentage of teachers who have completed the master's degree. Compared to the national average of 52 percent, 79.3 percent of north dakota teachers have completed this advanced degree.

MULTICULTURAL EDUCATION EFFORTS

North Dakota does not have a planned program of multicultural education. However, there is an Office of Education Equity. In addition to this program, there are also persons in charge of the state's Office of Bilingual Education and Indian Education. On occasion, the respondent to the authors' multicultural education survey of 1998 said that North Dakota offers leadership to school districts in multicultural education. These efforts are designed to assist the districts in the use of multicultural teaching materials.

In addition to the powerful European-American group, the predominant microcultures in North Dakota are Native-Americans, a few Asians, African-Americans, Cuban refugees, Bosnian refugees, and Russian-speaking refugees. The state requires no special coursework or other multicultural experiences in order to teach prospective teachers about multicultural education.

The respondent indicated that North Dakota was a strong "local control" state. Therefore, it was not known whether cultural pluralism (as opposed to a more assimilationist philosophy) was the major emphasis in the curriculum of the state.

North Dakota does have a number of bilingual education programs which are designed to instruct students in their native language. Racial segregation in the schools has not been a large factor in the state, due to the great lack of citizens who are from non-European-American backgrounds. Consequently, virtually no school integration programs have been in effect.

North Dakota schools may request assistance from the state's Department of Education for assistance in the evaluation of curriculum materials, library materials, and textbooks for racist/sexist content. However, this is only carried out when requested at the local level.

The biggest problem facing North Dakota's multicultural education programs is a lack of local level acceptance that the state is "not all white." The respondent felt that North Dakota needed to develop a general acceptance of this phenomenon by the general populace.

REFERENCES

Bowers, Alfred, W., *Mandan Social and Ceremonial Organization.*   Chicago: University of Chicago Press, 1950.

Council of Chief State School Officers, *The Council.* Washington D.C.: Council of Chief State School Officers, 1998.

Howard, Thomas W., (ed.), *The North Dakota Political Tradition.* Ames: Iowa State University Press, 1981.

Jackson, Donald D., (ed.), *Letters of the Lewis and Clark Expedition,* Urbana: University of Illinois Press, 1962.

Lamar, Howard, *Dakota Territory: A Study of Dakota Politics.* New Haven: Yale University Press, 1956.

Leiter, Richard A., (ed.), *National Survey of State Laws.* First edition. Detroit: Gale Research, 1997.

Markowitz, Harvey, (ed.), *American Indians.* Pasadena, CA: Salem Press, 1995.

Robinson, Elwin B., *History of North Dakota.* Lincoln: University of Nebraska Press, 1966.

United State Department of Education, *Digest of Educational Statistics.* Washington D.C.: United States Department of Education, 1997.

Wilkins, Robert P. and Wilkins, Wynona H., *North Dakota: A History.* New York: W. W. Norton, 1977.

OHIO

STATE HISTORY

Ohio is a state which has numerous people who have been prominent throughout American history. In addition to seven presidents, a few of the famous Ohioans include Thomas A. Edison, John Glenn, Annie Oakley, Eddie Rickenbacker, William Tecumseh, Sherman, James Thurber, and the Wright Brothers. However, long before the ancestors of these and other prominent European-Ohioans came to the country, the state was home of the famous mound builders who created enormous burial and effigy mounds. One of the most famous mounds is the "Serpent Mound" in Adams County.

These early residents included the Eries, Iroquois, Miamis, Shawnees, Wyandots, and Delawares. The Erie tribe occupied the regions south of Lake Erie, extending south to the Ohio River early in the seventeenth century. Members of the Iroquoian language group, they were closely related to the Hurons. It is thought that at their peak, their tribe numbered about 14,000 people. The Erie were known for their excellent diet. The women were fine horticulturalists, raising squash, corn, beans, and sunflowers, while the men supplemented these vegetables with fish and game.

They were considered to be skilled warriors and often skirmished with the Iroquois over hunting territories. In fact, the Iroquois were their undoing when in 1651, they attacked the Erie people, and essentially destroyed the entire tribe by either killing them or adopting them into the Iroquois tribe. The reason for this enormous victory was due to the fact that by this time the Iroquois had acquired firearms from the Dutch, while the Erie had no access to such weaponry. As a result of the victory the Erie language and culture disappeared, since the remaining tribal members adapted the Iroquoian traditions.

The Miami were originally residents of the Green Bay, Wisconsin region, but ended up migrating to Ohio during the eighteenth century, when they made a new home at the headwaters of Ohio's Maumee River. Members of the Algonquian language group, they consisted of six separate bands and had a relatively advanced political system based on a clan structure. It is believed that the name "Miami" probably came from an Ojibwa word *oumamik,* meaning "people of the peninsula." After the Removal Act of 1830, the Miami moved to Kansas, where they were given reservation status. Some tribal members managed to stay in Ohio, and a substantial number reside near Peru, Ohio.

Another Iroquoian tribe, the Hurons resided originally in their homeland which was located near Lake Simcoe, east of Lake Huron in south central Ontario. It has been estimated that their population was about 30,000 during the early 1600s. However, they were forced to disperse as a result of a two-year war with the Iroquois from 1649–1651. Consequently, one group, the Wyandot, settled in the Ohio valley and throughout the present region of Sandusky, Ohio. This name originally was "Wendat" which meant "peninsula dwellers" in the original Huron language. They took the name when they finally were relocated in Oklahoma.

The Wyandot were great story tellers and delighted in relating tales of mythology, some of which were quite frightening. One such story was called "The Hoostradoo," which was a yarn about a spirit who spent his time terrorizing the Wyandot people.

The first Europeans to view Lake Erie were probably the French. Louis Joliet, the fur trader, explored the lake's north shore in 1669 and René-Robert Cavelier de Sieur La Salle is thought to have located the Ohio River about the same time. Historians believe that La Salle may have explored the Ohio as far south as Louisville. Records also show that in 1685 English fur traders from New York traveled to the Macinac area through the Lake Erie route. Early in the eighteenth century, Europeans from Carolina, Virginia, and Pennsylvania were also in the Ohio area.

British and French animosities precipitated the first armed conflicts in the French and Indian War of 1754. Seven years before that time, a provisional grant was awarded to the Ohio Company, which was formed in Virginia. The geographical areas affected by the grant were located around the upper-Ohio region. After the first battles of the French and Indian War, the French were able to dominate the Ohio Valley, but eventually they were forced to cede the entire Northwest to the British. However, British policies prevented the settlement of the Ohio Valley.

During the American Revolution, the Native-Americans in the Ohio area were relatively uninvolved. However, hostilities between European-Americans and Native-Americans erupted in 1777. Most of the disputes were between Tories and Canadians, who used Native-American warriors from the Detroit area and European-American frontiersmen. The Treaty of Paris in 1783 terminated the Revolutionary hostilities and Britain lost control of the lands constituting the Ohio area as a result.

In 1788 European-American settlers had come to the region and by the middle of 1788 a territorial government was created. Cincinnati, originally named Fort Washington (after George Washington who visited the Ohio Valley before the Revolution), became the territorial capital. Chillicothe and Cleveland were founded in 1796.

The area grew rapidly because of the lure of the Ohio River Valley and the excellent soil throughout the region. By 1802 the issue of statehood for Ohio was presented in Congress and by November 1, 1802, statehood for Ohio was accepted. A constitution was drawn up and accepted by Congress and Ohio entered the Union as a free state. Chillicothe was the state capital until 1816 when the permanent capital was relocated to Columbia.

Ohio became a strong supporter of the War of 1812 and crucial battles were fought which ended the British threat to the new state. The first two victories were achieved by General William Henry Harrison, who repulsed two British attacks on Fort Meigs. A third victory occurred through the leadership of Captain Oliver H. Perry, who won a major naval victory on Lake Erie, enabling Harrison to cross into Canada, where he defeated the British during the Battle of the Themes in October of 1813. In 1815 it has been reported that the city of Cincinnati even had a Lancastrian school which was based on the work of Joe

Lancaster. The concept created large classes with the older students serving as teacher assistants.

The end of the War of 1812 started an era of rapid growth for Ohio. Trade, industry, and agricultural ventures expanded greatly, and the Ohio and Erie Canal connected Cleveland and Portsmouth when it was completed in 1832. In addition to the burgeoning canal system in the state, toll roads were constructed and in 1836 the Erie and Kalamazoo railroad was completed.

Ohio provided the third greatest number of troops for the Union cause during the Civil War. Its 300,000-men force was twice their assigned quota. Although Cincinnati was threatened in 1862, no important battles were waged in the state. Because of his fame which was acquired during the war, Ulysses S. Grant became the first Ohioan to be elected to the presidency.

Growth continued throughout the remainder of the nineteenth century and during the last two decades, the moneyed interests of the state became involved in politics when Henry Payne and Calvin Bryce became elected to the United States Senate. While these two senators were democrats, wealthy republicans such as Joseph Foraker and Marcus Hanna battled over control of the Republican party. However, discontent among the "have-nots" also surfaced, resulting in a devastating and cantankerous railroad strike in 1877.

Eventually, Ohioans commenced seeking a more progressive approach to government and by 1812, forty-one amendments were submitted to the public for approval. These included women's suffrage and the abolition of capital punishment, which were both rejected by the voters. Compulsory workmen's compensation, initiative, and referendum, and the regulation of workers' wages, hours, and working conditions were approved.

During World War I more than a quarter of a million Ohioans served in the armed forces. And while the state enjoyed good economic times in the 1920s, it was crushed by the stock market crash of 1929. The resulting economic depression was a most difficult time for the state. Federally-funded projects were the salvation of Ohio.

Ohio supplied 840,000 troops to the allied causes during World War II. Because of its existing infrastructure and geographical location, Ohio emerged from the conflict as one of the nation's leading industrial states. The war also saw a large influx of African-Americans who moved from the southern states in order to become employed in the various industrial enterprises. The state has the great distinction of seeing Carl Stokes become the first African-American to be elected mayor of a major American city. He was elected in 1967 and was a major force in developing a cleanup program for the Cuyahoga River, which became one of the most badly polluted rivers in the United States.

THE EDUCATIONAL SYSTEM

Education was private in Ohio until 1825 when taxes were finally levied for the funding of public education. However, it was not until 1847 when Ohio enacted special legislation which authorized the state's cities to create their own local school districts. During 1853, the system of state education commissioners was established for overseeing the operation of the common schools. The decade of the 1950s saw the establishment of a solid public high school system emerge which gradually replaced the private academies. By the mid-1950s most of the one-room schools in Ohio had ceased to exist.

At the present time, Ohio's state superintendent of schools is appointed by the Board of Education. School attendance is required of all children between the ages of six and eighteen, or until graduation. Children are also exempt from school if they are lawfully employed or if they are not physically or medically able to attend. Ohio has home schooling provisions which require approval by the school superintendent, and instructors must be qualified. In the case of religions challenges, the state applies a three-way test: (1) Are the religious beliefs sincere? (2) Will the application of the compulsory attendance law infringe on the right of individuals to exercise their free exercise of religion? and (3) Does the state have an overriding interest?

Ohio allows corporal punishment in the schools as long as it is reasonable and necessary in order to maintain discipline. Local school boards are not allowed to prohibit the use of force in order to curb any disturbance which might result in physical violence. The state allows reasonable periods of time for meditation upon a moral, philosophical, or patriotic theme. If students are under eighteen years of age, their school records can be released if the consent of the parent(s) is given. While directory information can be released, the rights of the school district to renew or select student records is restricted. Children over the age of eighteen must approve the release of any records. Ohio's per capita education expenses are $887.37 per child is somewhat below the national average of $931.76. The state allows for year-round schools, and school districts are required to provide half-day kindergartens.

In order for teachers to become certified to teach in Ohio, they must perform successfully on the National Teachers Examination, exhibit basic skills mastery, and be observed in successful teaching performances in the classroom. Of Ohio's teachers, 48.2 percent hold a master's degree, compared with the national average of 42 per cent.

MULTICULTURAL EDUCATION EFFORTS

Responses from the authors' 1998 multicultural education survey revealed that Ohio had no multicultural education program. There was nobody responsible for such undertakings, no money budgeted, and the state provides no multicultural education leadership.

In addition to the western European microcultures in Ohio, the state's predominant microcultures were listed as African-American, Latinos, Southeast Asians, and Russian-Americans. However, Ohio does require prospective teachers to understand how students differ in their approaches to learning. Moreover, they are expected to create instructional opportunities that are equitable and adaptable to diverse learners. These requirements came about in a 1994 presentation to the Ohio State Board of Education.

Ohio's educational curriculum stresses cultural pluralism as opposed to an assimilationist philosophy. The state also has special programs designed to teach children in their native language when necessary. Bilingual education is part of the curriculum in Cleveland and Lorain, while transitional bilingual education is utilized in other districts. Ohio has a Lau Resource Center which attempts to provide training and technical assistance to school districts enrolling Limited English Proficiency (LEP) students.   The Center provides teacher training, publishes a newsletter, has various publications available for use, has a resource library, provides technical assistance, and even helps in the development of multicultural programs that promote the recognition and appreciation of the diverse cultural backgrounds represented in the school and community.

The history of Native-Americans is included in the state's regular social studies curriculum, and Ohio evaluates curriculum materials, library materials, and textbooks for the inclusion of racist or sexist statements.

The respondent felt that the biggest problem facing multicultural education programs in Ohio was the lack of funding.   The biggest improvement would be to acquire a State Board of Education definition and more leadership.

REFERENCES

Collins, William R., *Ohio: Buckeye State.* New York: Prentice-Hall, 1974.

Council of Chief State School Officers, *The Council.* Washington D.C.: Council of Chief State School Officers, 1998.

Havighurst, Walter, *Ohio: A Bicentennial History.* New York: W. W. Norton, 1976.

Leiter, Richard A., (ed.), *National Survey of State Laws.* First edition. Detroit: Gale Research, 1997.

Markowitz, Harvey, (ed.), *American Indians.* Pasadena, CA: Salem Press, 1995.

Ohio Department of Education, *Final Recommendations of the Standards Revision Committee for Teacher Education and Certification.* Columbus: Ohio Department of Education, 1994.

Roseboom, Eugene H., and Weisenburger, Francis P., *A History of Ohio.* Columbus: Ohio State University Press, 1998.

Tanner, Helen Hornbeck, et al., *Atlas of Great Lakes Indian History.* Norman: University of Oklahoma Press, 1986.

OKLAHOMA

STATE HISTORY

The name "Oklahoma" first appeared in the records of the early Spanish explorers who were traveling with Hernando de Soto and Francisco Vázquez de Coronado throughout the Southwestern regions of the current United States boundaries. Leaving their new conquests in Mexico, they were searching for riches in the form of gold. After enduring the French and Spanish claims, the region became part of the United States as a result of the Louisiana Purchase in 1803. However, as was the case with most other regions of the United States, various groups of Native-Americans dwelled in the area prior to the arrival of these Europeans.

One of the tribes which greeted Coronado and other Spanish explorers were the Wichitas. Members of the Caddoan language group, the Wichita people were actually a kind of confederacy consisting of the Tayovaya, Yscani, Tawakoni, Waco, and Kichai sub-tribes. All of these subgroups except for the Kichai spoke similar dialects of the Caddoan tongue.

It is believed that their original homeland may have been located in south central Kansas along the great bend of the Arkansas River. Between the seventeenth and nineteenth centuries, the Wichitas resided in a number of villages located on river banks. Married couples lived with the wife's family, whose family head was a grandmother or great-grandmother. The women farmed corn, squash, beans, pumpkins, and tobacco, while the men hunted buffalo, bear, deer, and antelope. Their population dwindled to just 340 members by 1902. However, eighty-eight years later, in the 1990 census, the population had grown back to 1,275, still a far cry from their estimated 15,000 at the time of Coronado.

Horses entered the lives of the Wichita tribe by about 1700, which made them more effective buffalo hunters and much better warriors. Nonetheless, the Wichita were always considered to be a peaceful tribe, only going to battle when they were attacked in some manner. After the Removal Act of 1830, other tribes of Native-Americans commenced moving into the area, causing more intertribal conflicts. During the Civil War, the Wichita moved to Kansas but returned to Oklahoma after it was over. They were given reservation lands in Caddo County, Oklahoma.

Present-day Oklahoma became part of the United States as a result of the Louisiana Purchase of 1803. By 1817, the United States government had commenced moving Native-Americans into present-day Oklahoma. The first group to be forcefully moved were members of the Cherokee tribe. The Removal Act of 1830 was negotiated with the idea that Native-Americans could be relocated to Oklahoma Territory, which was not actually created until 1890. In fact, those lands were often referred to as "Indian Territory".

The Civil War proved to be catastrophic for Native-Americans, as well as the European-Americans and others who fought in it.   Native-Americans in Oklahoma actually fought on both sides.   After the war, the United States used the fact that some Native-American groups fought against the Union to extract even more land concessions from them.   New treaties were signed with the Five Civilized Tribes (Cherokee, Chickasaw, Choctaw, Creek, and Seminole) who ceded more of their lands to the United States and granted the government the right to construct railroads across their territory.

The Oklahoma lands, which were designated as "Indian Territory" were off limits for European-American settlement.   However, by 1889 President Benjamin Harrison was authorized to open the area for European-American immigrants.   Thus, homesteading in the region became possible in April of that year.   In 1890 Oklahoma Territory was formally established.

Interestingly, the new Oklahoma Territory was viewed by some African-Americans as a desirable location for homesteading opportunities.   By April of 1890 approximately seventeen hundred African-Americans had left Atlanta for resettlement in Oklahoma Territory.   Langston City became a predominantly African-American community, which had a population of about 200 people, including a teacher, minister, and doctor.

By the turn of the century, residents of Oklahoma Territory commenced petitioning for statehood.   Two factions wished to establish separate states.   The Native-American residents of Indian Territory lobbied for the creation of a state called Sequoyah. However, Congress decided otherwise and in 1907, Oklahoma became a state during the administration of Theodore Roosevelt.   Oklahoma City became the capital.

As was true in the other states, Oklahoma was heavily involved in World War I, with more than 90,000 Oklahomans serving in the armed forces.   During the 1920s, the Ku Klux Klan became strong, and, before its actions were dealt with adequately, the vicious actions of this hate group resulted in many unfortunate casualties.

The 1930s were devastating to Oklahoma.   Perhaps John Steinbeck's novel *Grapes of Wrath* described the dilemma best.   Thousands of farmers were forced to leave their lands because of the drought, which compounded the problems which occurred because of the Great Economic Depression.   Farmers migrated westward to California, and to the cities.   The situation did not improve until World War II in which more than 100,000 Oklahomans participated in military service. After the war, a new state school code was enacted in 1949 and in 1953 the state's mental health laws were revised.   The state's economy, which was formerly based on agriculture and farm product processing, became more diversified.

THE EDUCATIONAL SYSTEM

Prior to statehood, Oklahoma residents had organized school systems.   The Five Civilized Tribes had schools in Indian Territory and a number of Oklahoma Territory communities had school districts as early as 1890.   Enabling legislation passed in 1906 set aside land in each township for the development of common schools.

Oklahoma's schools are under the direction of the State Department of Education, headed by a state superintendent of public instruction who is elected by the people. School attendance is required for all children between the ages of five and eighteen, except for youngsters whose physical or mental disability prevents their attendance. Children who are sixteen years of age can also be exempted if they have the permission of their school and parents. Home schooling is allowed if it is carried out in good faith and is equivalent to that provided by the state.

Oklahoma is one of the few states which allows students and teachers to participate in voluntary prayer. The school records of children are confidential except for directory information. Teachers may not reveal student-obtained information unless it is part of a contractual requirement, or it is released to a parent or guardian on request.

In order for prospective teachers to become certificated in Oklahoma, they must pass a state competency test which measures basic skills. Other specialty area exams are required and candidates must perform successfully on these. In addition, all teacher candidates must be observed in successful teaching performances.

Per capita educational expenses for elementary and secondary education in Oklahoma are $842.09, compared with the national average of $931.76. Thirty-nine percent of Oklahoma's teachers hold a master's degree, compared with the national average 42 percent. There is a state policy on year-round schools and a number of districts in Oklahoma have such programs in existence. School districts are required to provide half-day kindergarten programs. Slightly more than 24 percent of Oklahoma's children between the ages of five and seventeen are below the poverty level. This compares with the national average of 19 percent.

MULTICULTURAL EDUCATION EFFORTS

The 1998 questionnaire responses stipulated that the state of Oklahoma did not have a multicultural education program but then indicated that there was a person in charge of such undertakings. However, there is no budget for multicultural education. It was reported that these leadership efforts came about through inservice training and technical assistance.

Besides the majority European-American macroculture, the predominant Oklahoma microcultures were reported to be Native-Americans, African-Americans, Latinos, and a few Asian-Americans.

While the respondent reported that the state requires no special course work and/or multicultural experiences for certification, it was indicated that some universities require their students to carry out their teaching practicum in a diverse setting.

It was reported that Oklahoma's school curriculum tends to stress the philosophy of cultural pluralism as opposed to cultural assimilation. It was also reported that the State Department of Education in Oklahoma does have bilingual education programs, and the state office provides special assistance to local school districts in that regard.

The respondent replied that racist incidents have increased during the past five years. Another response stipulated that educators were not taking the opportunity to instruct students about the establishment of positive cross-cultural relations.

Oklahoma's state textbook adoption committee evaluates all curriculum materials, library materials, and textbooks for racist and sexist content. The state education agency will assist local school districts in such matters on request.

Finally, the respondent felt that the biggest problem facing multicultural education programs in Oklahoma was that the topic is not promoted or encouraged on the national level. It was felt that this must occur in order for the states to take the matter seriously. It was also stated that the biggest improvement in multicultural education efforts would be for Oklahoma's local school boards to consciously seek textbooks and curriculum materials which have a multicultural perspective. Moreover, it was felt that state textbook committees should be composed of persons from diverse cultural backgrounds. These committees should ensure that any adopted materials would reflect the diverse nature of American society.

REFERENCES

Council of Chief State School Officers, *The Council.* Washington D.C.: Council of State School Officers, 1998.

Dorsey, George, *Traditions of the Caddo.* Washington D.C.: Carnegie Institution of Washington, 1905.

Gibson, Arrel, M., *Oklahoma: A History of Four Centuries, Guide to the Sooner State.* Norman: University of Oklahoma Press, 1988.

Leiter, Richard A., (ed.), *National Survey of State Laws.* First edition. Detroit: Gale Research, 1997.

Meredith, Howard, *Southern Plains Alliances.* Lawrence: University of Kansas Press, 1994.

Morgan, David R., et al., *Oklahoma Politics and Policies: Governing the Sooner State.* Lincoln: University of Nebraska Press, 1991.

Morgan, H. Wayne and Morgan, Anne H., *Oklahoma: A History.* New York: W. W. Norton, 1984.

Newkumet, Vynola Beaver and Meredith, Howard L., *Hasinai: A Traditional History of the Caddo Confederacy.* College Station: Texas A & M University Press, 1988.

Scales, James R., and Goble, Danny, *Oklahoma Politics: A History.* Norman: University of Oklahoma Press, 1982

Stein, Howard E. and Hill, Robert F., *The Culture of Oklahoma.* Norman: University of Oklahoma Press, 1993.

Taylor, Quintard, *In Search of the Racial Frontier: African-Americans in the American West, 1528–1990.* New York: W. W. Norton, 1998.

United States Department of Education, *Digest of Educational Statistics.* Washington D.C.: United States Department of Education, 1997.

OREGON

STATE HISTORY

Early Oregon history begins with an account of the key tribes of Native-Americans who resided in the area. Due to the geographic nature of the state, a variety of different cultures lived in the area long before the arrival of any European groups. In addition to tribal groups, such as the Umatillas in eastern Oregon, were many coastal tribes, such as the Tillamooks and Umpquas. The Klamath resided throughout a large south-central Oregon area.

Located near the "Big Bend" region of the Columbia River, the Umatilla tribe was part of the Sahaptian language group. Shortly before 1800 their population was estimated to be about 2,000. Anthropologists believe that they resided in the region for approximately 10,000 years prior to the arrival of European groups. They subsisted on a fine diet of Columbia River salmon and also gathered fruits and berries.

The Umatilla were relatively unaffected by European-Americans until 1840 when settlers commenced to arrive in that general region. They were located close to the Oregon Trail and were also near Walla Walla, site of the so-called Whitman Massacre of 1848. It is believed that some tribal members participated in the Cayuse War, which occurred after the Whitman incident.

Under the leadership of territorial governor Isaac Stevens, the Umatilla were given reservation lands in return for their original territory. The Umatilla reservation is also home to the Walla Wallas and the Cayuse.

The Umpqua tribe in southwestern Oregon, provides an example of the many coastal tribes in present-day Washington and Oregon. They resided near the shores of the Umpqua River which flows from the Cascade range to the Pacific Ocean. Anthropologists generally identify two sub-groups of Umpqua people. One group resided close to the Cascade range, while the other lived closer to the ocean.

After the incursions of European-Americans, the Umpqua lost much of their original land and were finally placed on the Silez reservation during the mid-1850s. At the present time a confederation consisting of the Coos, lower Umpqua, and Siuslaw constitute an officially-recognized Indian nation.

The Klamath resided in an area which extended to the Great Basin to the east, the Cascades to the west, north to the Central Plateau, and south to the California-Oregon border regions. They are thought to have lived in the area for approximately 10,000 years. Their staple diet was fish, with an abundant supply of salmon and trout available. They also gathered fruits and berries.

Due to the nature of their living territories, they were relatively isolated and tended not to be subjected to much of the same problems which were encountered by other Native-American groups. However, by the middle of the nineteenth century, European-Americans commenced intruding into Klamath lands on their way to the northern California gold fields. In comparison to other tribes, the

Klamath tried to maintain peaceful relations with the European-Americans and on occasion there are instances where the tribe punished their own people for committing acts of aggression against them. In 1864 they were given a reservation in south central Oregon in return for their original lands. By 1954 the tribe decided to terminate the reservation and each enrolled tribal member received a settlement of $43,000 from the federal government. Since that time, many Klamaths have expressed regret over the decision.

The Tillamook tribe resided on the coasts of present-day Oregon and Washington. They were considered to be one of the strongest Native-American groups, living along the coastal regions from Seaside, Oregon, to the Siletz River in Lincoln County. During the earlier parts of the nineteenth century, their population was estimated to be about two thousand.

Members of the Salishan language group, the Tillamook migrated north to the Columbia River areas and were believed to have been involved in trading enterprises with the residents of the western Columbia River areas. Baskets, canoes, and hides were often involved in various sorts of transactions.

Chiefs presided over the Tillamook villages. They seemed to have acquired these positions according to their wealth and the supernatural powers which they were thought to possess. According to the best available anthropological records, this group of Native-Americans flourished. The elite members of the Tillamook tribes were shaman and warriors. These elite groups were polygamous and represented the upper classes of the village.

Anthropologists believe that the tribal members worshipped no deities. They believed in the great power of the earth and thought it had the capacity to judge the behavior of the people. The tribe suffered from major epidemics in the 1830s and the population declined from more than 2,000 to only about 65 members during the census of 1910.

Early European involvement occurred in 1774 when Spanish explorer, Juan Pérez, was searching for the Northwest Passage. One of the first Europeans to see the Columbia river was Bruno Heceta, who did not actually sail east on the river in 1775. Other early explorers included James Cook, John Kendrick, and Robert Gray. The British naval officer George Vancouver explored the northwestern Oregon area between 1792 and 1795. About this time, the Spanish terminated their interest in the region, leaving the northwest Oregon regions open to British. However, after the 1803 Lewis and Clark expeditions, Oregon became the province of the United States. John Jacob Astor's Pacific Fur Company was based in Astoria between 1811 and 1813.

The coming of the missionaries between 1834 and 1842 heightened American interest in the Oregon regions, and by 1842 organized migrations over the Oregon Trail commenced. These new immigrants, retired fur trappers, and missionaries created the Oregon Provisional Government in the Willamette Valley. By 1848 Oregon became a territory and statehood was achieved in 1859. When territorial status was achieved, lands were set aside in each township to finance public schools. Free public elementary schools were opened in 1854 in the population centers, including Portland and Oregon City. The first compulsory attendance law was passed in 1889 and free public secondary schools were created in 1901.

These nineteenth century pioneers found good markets for their products in gold fields, which were located in British Columbia, Idaho, Montana, and Washington. Portland became a supply center for these ventures and the Northern Pacific Railway, stretching to Portland in 1883, allowed Oregon's products to be shipped to eastern markets.

During this period of time, the issue of African slavery invaded Oregon politics. Originally, the language of the Northwest Ordinance was used in prohibiting slavery in Oregon. However, quasislavery practices were carried on in Oregon between 1840 and 1860. In 1860 the African-American population in Oregon was reported as 128 out of a total population of 52,465.

After World War I, the key Oregon political issues were taxation and race. In 1920 one of the key factions of Oregon's political right was the Ku Klux Klan. By this time a larger number of its residents had come from the Bible belt. In 1923 the state passed legislation which prohibited Japanese-Americans and Chinese-Americans from owning land if they were ineligible for citizenship. But then the economic depression created a need for federal involvement. Franklin Roosevelt carried the state in 1932, 1936, and 1940. Bonneville Dam was finished in 1938.

After World War II, agriculture expanded and the Columbia River changed dramatically with the creation of the McNary, Dalles, and John Day Dams. Also, during this era, Oregon became known as one of the most environmentally friendly states with the so-called "Bottle Bill" legislation and other similar actions.

THE EDUCATIONAL SYSTEM

School attendance in Oregon is required between the ages of seven and eighteen or until the student has completed the twelfth grade. Exceptions to this requirement are children attending private schools; those with proof of equivalent knowledge of subjects through the twelfth grade; children who are sixteen or older and lawfully employed; and children who are home schooled. In order to be home schooled, it is necessary for parents to notify the superintendent, who must approve the application. Children are required to take annual examinations, and, if scores are insufficient, they can be required to attend public schools.

During the twentieth century, the number of school districts in Oregon decreased from a high of some 2,000 around the turn of the century to just over 300 in 1998. The public schools are supervised by a state superintendent of schools, who is elected by the people. The state has about 480,000 students attending about 1,250 elementary and secondary schools.

Teacher certification in Oregon requires candidates to perform successfully on the California Basic Education Skills Test (CBEST) and on other specialty-area examinations. Successful in-class observations are also required. The state spends $1,021.77 per capita on elementary and secondary education, better than the national average of $931.76. Compared to the national average of 19 percent, only 16.2 percent of the state's children under the age of seventeen are below the poverty level.

Oregon has no statutory provisions regarding the use of corporal punishment and there are no such provisions regarding prayer in schools. The state's regulations regarding the privacy of school records are consistent with state and federal law regarding record custody and disclosure. Oregon school districts are required by state law to offer half-day kindergarten programs and school districts must provide programs for special education students who are between the ages of three and twenty-one years of age. The state also has school districts with year-round schools.

Compared to the national average of 42 percent, 43.1 percent of Oregon's teachers hold a master's degree. Of Oregon's K–12 teachers, 0.8 percent hold a doctor's degree, compared to the national average of .07 percent. Twenty-six percent of Oregon's teachers have had more than twenty years teaching experience, compared to the national average of 29.8 percent.

MULTICULTURAL EDUCATION EFFORTS

Oregon's responses to the authors' multicultural education survey were unique because they were composite answers from three different persons. One of the respondent was directly involved in the state's IA Indian-Education program; a second respondent was directly connected with a Title IA Bilingual Migrant program; while the third person was involved in a Drug-Alcohol/Civil Rights program.

It was reported that Oregon had no multicultural education program and nobody was in charge of such undertakings. However, there is a state director for compensatory education programs. And while the state has no specific funds budgeted for multicultural education, the Oregon Department of Education does provide services to school districts in the form of equity issues such as bilingual, ESL, race, and gender. However, with the limitations on civil rights funding, this has been limited.

The state's predominant microcultures were listed as Hispanic indigenous cultures rooted in Mexico, the U.S. Southwest and Central America; Southeast Asians; Russian Old Believers; Pentecostal immigrants; and Native-Americans. There is also a large population of African-Americans, particularly in Portland. Between 1960 and 1970, the state's African-American population grew more than 30 percent.

For teacher certification, Oregon requires that prospective teachers take a course which reviews civil rights regulations. The respondents stated that Oregon utilized a cultural assimilation philosophy, as opposed to cultural pluralism.

Oregon does have special programs to teach students in their native language, when necessary. Warm Springs and Pendleton have charter school grants for creating language restoration in their schools. Some school districts offer Spanish immersion programs. While native language instruction is not mandated, an increasing number of schools are providing it, including Phoenix Elementary, Grant School (Salem), Alder School (Reynolds School District), Portland Public Schools, and the Woodburn Public Schools.

While the history of Native-Americans is not included in Oregon's regular curriculum, the Oregon Department of Education produced a supplement to the fourth grade curriculum entitled *Indians in Oregon Today*. It was disseminated to the schools in 1992.

Oregon's Office of Education does not evaluate curriculum materials, library materials, or textbooks for the inclusion of racist or sexist content.

The three respondents felt that the biggest problem facing multicultural education programs in Oregon was the lack of state support for providing leadership or funding for this endeavor. Also, it is not perceived as a critical need and there is no staff. Only superficial attention has been devoted to the topic, and it is always vulnerable to budget cuts. The biggest improvements in the state's multicultural education efforts would be the creation of state guidelines and common curriculum goals on multicultural education. A mandate is needed in order to provide multicultural education programs with common curriculum goals and standards.

REFERENCES

Abbott, Carl, *The Great Extravaganza: Portland and the Lewis and Clark Exposition.* Portland: Oregon Historical Society, 1981.

Clark, Malcolm, Jr., *Eden Seekers: The Settlement of Oregon, 1818–1862.* New York: Houghton, 1981.

Council of Chief State School Officers, *The Council.* Washington D.C.: Council of Chief State School Officers, 1998.

Dodds, Gordon B., *Oregon: A Bicentennial History.* New York: W. W. Norton, 1977.

Drucker, Philip, *Cultures of the North Pacific Coast.* San Francisco: Chandler, 1965.

Leiter, Richard A. (ed.), *National Survey of State Laws* First edition. Detroit: Gale Research, 1997.

Markowitz, Harvey, *American Indians.* Pasadena, CA: Salem Press, 1995.

Ruby, Robert H. and Brown, John A., *Indians of the Pacific Northwest: A History.* Norman: University of Oklahoma Press, 1981.

Schwantes, Carlos A., *The Pacific Northwest: An Interpretive History.* Lincoln: University of Nebraska Press, 1989.

Stern, Theodore, *The Klamath Tribe: A People and Their Reservation.* Seattle: University of Washington Press, 1966.

Taylor, Quintard, *In Search of the Racial Frontier: African-Americans in the American West, 1528–1990.* New York: W. W. Norton, 1998.

United States Department of Education: *Digest of Educational Statistics.* Washington D.C.: United States Department of Education, 1971.

PENNSYLVANIA

STATE HISTORY

The history of Pennsylvania has been enriched because of the involvement of diverse peoples from all over the world. While most have become part of the American macroculture, many ethnic and racial groups are still shaping the future direction of this large Eastern state. But the first Americans were the Native-Americans, particularly the Shawnees and Susquehannocks.

The Shawnee were thought to have migrated from the Susquehanna River from Tennessee. Their ancestors are believed to have descended from Asia and settled on United States soil. They were one of the prominent Algonquian-speaking groups of the Atlantic Northeast. They were divided into the following main divisions: Chillikothe, Kispokotha, Piqua, Hathawekela, and Spitotha.

The primary Shawnee residence was the *wegiwa* ("wigwam") and the authority was vested in the hereditary clan and division chiefs. During the American Revolution, the tribe found itself siding with the English. After being defeated at the Battle of Fallen Timbers after the American Revolution, the tribe was forced to relinquish its land to the European-Americans.

One of the most famous Native-Americans was a Shawnee chief Tecumseh. He encouraged abstinence from alcohol and argued against the sale of Native-American lands to European-Americans. He fought on the side of the British during the War of 1812 and died in battle. Eventually the Shawnee split into several groups. One group ended up on a reservation in Kansas, while another faction became part of the Cherokee tribe. A third group of Shawnee people finally settled in Shawnee County, Oklahoma.

Another group of Native-Americans residing in present-day Pennsylvania were the Susquehannock tribe, which was part of the Iroquoian language group. Archaeologists and anthropologists believe that they first resided on the north branch of the Susquehanna River near Binghampton. Their first encounter with Europeans seems to have occurred through interactions with Captain John Smith in 1608.

Their traditional nemesis was the Iroquois tribe, with whom they quarreled over hunting and trading issues. They were defeated by the Iroquois in 1676 and consequently relocated in New York. After their return to Pennsylvania some time later, they became known as the Conestogas. But warfare and disease brought by the Europeans resulted in their numbers dwindling to twenty from an estimated population of 5,000 in 1600. The 1990 census listed their population at just 125 tribal members.

The first Europeans to arrive in the present-day Pennsylvania area are thought to have been English, Dutch, and Swedish explorers who were investigating the possibility of securing trade options with other nations. One of the first Europeans to come to the present site of Philadelphia was Cornelius Hendricksen, a Dutch explorer who sailed up the Delaware River to the city's current location. It was estimated that about 15,000 Native-Americans resided in the region at that time.

Pennsylvania's first European-built settlement occurred in 1643, when Governor Johan Printz constructed it on an island near present-day Philadelphia. Named New Sweden, it was later captured by the Dutch under the leadership of Peter Suyvessant. At that time it became part of New Netherland until the English captured it in 1664.

Pennsylvania became an English colony when William Penn, a Quaker, persuaded King Charles to grant him land in the Pennsylvania regions in return for 16,000 pounds, a debt that his father had incurred some years earlier. The king agreed and Penn's colony became a haven for those who professed a belief in God. The colony was advertised as a place where "religious freedom" existed. Two other attractions were liberal government and inexpensive land. Penn recruited immigrants, particularly those of Scotch-Presbyterian and German-Protestant backgrounds. He was also interested in establishing friendly relations with the Native-Americans and was willing to pay them for lands, unlike many other Europeans, who opted for a "manifest destiny" philosophy.

In 1692 Penn was deposed as the colony's governing agent, due to his involvement with King James II. But his colony continued to sustain a steady growth, and by 1700 its population had numbered about 30,000 persons. By 1776 it had become one of the largest colonies, with a population of some 300,000. During his second visit, following the change of leadership in Pennsylvania, he drew up a constitution dubbed "The Charger of Liberties," which remained in effect until 1776.

Pennsylvania's early history was heavily influenced by the Quakers' attitude of pacifism. This philosophy had an effect on the French and Indian War, when the Quaker-dominated Pennsylvania Assembly refused to act in the face of hostile actions by the French and Indians, who had mounted an attack on the colony as a result of Pennsylvania's westward expansion. However, the 1863 Treaty of Paris ended the war and the French were driven from the continent.

The problems created by the French and Indian War resulted in a mounting British debt, which precipitated a rising level of taxation against the Pennsylvania colonists. Protest committees were organized by Pennsylvania merchants and the antagonisms against the British intensified. Eventually, the radical factions in the Pennsylvania assembly instructed Pennsylvania's congressional delegates to support the Declaration of Independence.

One of Philadelphia's most influential citizens was Benjamin Franklin, who founded the famous Franklin Academy, which ultimately became the University of Pennsylvania. While his intention was to keep the school's secular philosophy intact, he lost control to an Anglican provost William Smith, who was successful in turning it into a religious-oriented institution. In addition to his interests in education, his writings, scientific inventions, and political involvement, are well known.

During the Revolution, a number of important campaigns occurred in the colony. During the summer of 1777, British troops invaded Pennsylvania, defeating Washington's troops at Brandywine. This action paved the way for British occupation. The Continental Army spent the bitter winter of 1777–1778 at Valley Forge. But during the summer of 1778, the British withdrew from Pennsylvania.

During Pennsylvania's early days of statehood, a strong religious coalition of Quakers (Friends), German Mennonites, Amish, and Brethren were neutral in regard to the American Revolution. Nevertheless, Pennsylvania became the second state to ratify the United States Constitution. Benjamin Franklin was one of the key figures in the negotiations. Philadelphia became the United States capital until the permanent capital was established in Washington D.C.

After the election of Thomas Jefferson to the presidency in 1800, Philadelphia became a more stable state. While it took General Washington to quell the Whiskey Rebellion of 1794, many of the federalist taxes were repealed, which calmed down the residents. Harrisburg became the capital in 1812. During this era, cities began to grow because of the increase in manufacturing.

While some slavery did exist in Pennsylvania, it was quite fragmented and was totally gone by the start of the Civil War. In fact, Pennsylvania's willingness to assist runaway slaves became an enormous source of irritation to the southern states. Chester, York, Columbia, Gettysburg, and Chambersburg became key stations on the Underground Railway. The state provided strong support for the Union causes during the coming hostilities. When Union and Confederate forces met at Gettysburg in 1863, the Union prevailed in a brutal, bloody battle. Pennsylvania provided several Union generals and approximately 400,000 troops for the Union cause.

Pennsylvania politics were controlled by the Republican party until after World War I. The state's manufacturing industries grew rapidly, attracting a labor force of African-Americans from the South. This caused Pennsylvania to gradually become a more multicultural state. Andrew Carnegie expanded the state's steel production and John D. Rockefeller's Standard Oil Company became a major player in the state's economic structure. During this time, Pennsylvania was beset with numerous labor strikes in connection with the burgeoning coal industry.

Throughout Pennsylvania's history, one of the interesting European-American ethnic groups has been the Amish. Even though this religious body has settlements located in about twenty states, as well as Ontario, Canada, Lancaster County, Pennsylvania, is one of the oldest settlements. The Amish people reject many of the modern inventions, instead preferring to cling to the old ways. They reject telephones and even though they use automobiles, they are forbidden to own them. They have also spurned electricity and higher education. In general, this religious body has resisted modern inventions. Interactions with non-Amish people are discouraged and Pennsylvania German is viewed as the native language.

During the mid-twentieth century, Amish parents were sometimes imprisoned for refusing to send their children to school. However, in 1972, a Supreme Court decision (*Wisconsin v. Yoder*) made it possible for Amish people to establish their own school system in lieu of sending their children to public schools, as required by law.

Pennsylvania coal miners were one of the early American labor groups to organize into unions when the Workingmen's Benevolent Association was created in 1868. Another early union which was created in Pennsylvania was the

Trainmen's Union, as well as a number of craft unions which formed the Amalgamated Association of Iron, Steel, and Tin Workers. Numerous clashes occurred as the industrialists attempted to suppress their efforts. Finally, the unions prevailed when President Theodore Roosevelt forced the mine owners to enter into negotiations with the striking mine workers.

While World War I provided an economic stimulus to Pennsylvania's economy, it began to wear off and not even World War II caused the economy to enjoy the robust state it had acquired before. Natural resources were no longer available in such quantities, and many textile mills commenced moving to the South in order to find cheaper labor.

Pennsylvania's Bureau of Minority Development helped to revive the state's sagging economy by assisting urban persons of color in founding their own businesses. During the mid 1960s, nearly 2,500 new plants were built and the state's unemployment rate fell below the national average.

THE EDUCATIONAL SYSTEM

Pennsylvania was one of the first colonies to conceive of the notion that education for all children was important. As early as 1682, William Penn's Frame of Government provided for all children in the province. Even so, education was primarily a function of the various religious groups. But the 1790 constitution provided for free books for school children. Free public education was provided for all children by 1834, and a compulsory education requirement was instituted in 1895.

At the present time, Pennsylvania children are required to attend school between the ages of eight and seventeen. Exceptions include children who have graduated from high school; children enrolled in private schools or who are being home schooled; and children with physical or mental defects which render education impracticable. There are no statutory requirements pertaining to the use of corporal punishment and students are allowed a brief period of silent prayer or meditation, as long as it is not a religious exercise. Parents have access to school records.

Pennsylvania's state school superintendent is appointed by the governor. In order for prospective teachers to become certified, they must pass a test which measures basic skills. Compared to the national average of 19 percent, just 16.5 percent of Pennsylvania's children under the age of seventeen come from poverty circumstances. One thousand dollars per capita is spent on elementary and secondary education, compared to the national average of $931.76.

While 42 percent of the nation's teachers as a whole have achieved a master's degree, 45.6 percent of Pennsylvania's teachers have reached this level. Special education services are provided for children between the ages of three and twenty, and school districts are required to offer half-day kindergartens. There is no policy on year-round schools.

MULTICULTURAL EDUCATION EFFORTS

Unfortunately, Pennsylvania has no multicultural education program in the state and the Office of School Equity has been abolished. During its years of operation, it had the responsibility for providing technical assistance to schools in the development of programs which were multicultural and cross-cultural.

The predominant microcultures in the state were listed as African-American, Native-American/Alaskan-Native, Latinos, and Asian/Pacific Islanders. The respondent indicated that Pennsylvania had no special coursework and/or other multicultural experiences for certification requirements. The issue of cultural pluralism or cultural assimilation as a curriculum and instruction philosophy varies from district to district.

Pennsylvania employs a bilingual education advisor, who provides assistance to school districts in order to help them establish appropriate procedures for children with limited English proficiency. Local school districts can call on the services of regional desegregation centers in order to acquire assistance in the development of appropriate strategies to provide racially-integrated schools.

Based on data provided by the state, a dramatic request for assistance in hate crimes and racial violence has occurred during recent years. When the Office of School Equity existed, it increased its programming in relation to teaching practices and intergroup relationships.

The state does evaluate curriculum materials, library materials, and textbooks for racist and sexist statements. During the tenure of the Office of School Equity, workshops were conducted and materials were disseminated which taught educators how to evaluate such materials in an appropriate manner.

It was felt that the biggest problems facing multicultural education was the lack of any organized provision for education that is multicultural. Other problems include "barriers in opportunity structure"; cultural inequities; language inequities; assessment/evaluation inequities; and "denial of true assimilation."

Finally, the respondent felt that the biggest improvements in the state's multicultural education program would be the creation of a state-wide unit whose focus is the operation/maintenance of multicultural/multiethnic programs. Also needed is a commitment to such a program on the historical dimension and its interconnectedness. Multicultural education in practice would target teachers, school personnel, and students. Emphases would continue to be on changing teacher attitudes and practice; incorporated, infused curriculum, and teaching processes; and in raising ethnic/racial identity awareness and cultural pride. Optimally, the Pennsylvania Department of Education would be able to incorporate Ogbu's theory on educational responses to cultural diversity by moving from a core curriculum which focuses on assimilation to include cross-cultural understanding.

REFERENCES

Beard, Charles A., Mary R., and William, *New Basic History of the United States.* New York: Doubleday, 1968.

Hanna, William S., *Benjamin Franklin and Pennsylvania Politics.* Palo Alto: Stanford University Press, 1964.

Hoerr, John P., *And the Wolf Finally Came: The Decline of the American Steel Industry.* Pittsburgh: University of Pittsburgh Press, 1988.

Klein, Philip S., and Hoogenboom, Ari, *A History of Pennsylvania.* University Park: Penn State University Press, 1980.

Kraybill, Donald B., *The Puzzles of Amish Life.* Intercourse, PA: Good Books, 1990.

Leiter, Richard A., (ed.), *National Survey of State Laws.* First edition. Detroit: Gale Research, 1997.

Markowitz, Harvey, *American Indians.* Pasadena, CA: Salem Press, 1995.

United States Department of Education, *Digest of Educational Statistics.* Washington D.C.: United States Department of Education, 1997.

Zirkel, Parry A., and Richardson, Sharon Nalbone, *A Digest of Supreme Court Decisions Affecting Education.* Bloomington, IN: Phi Delta Kappa Foundation, 1988.

RHODE ISLAND

STATE HISTORY

Rhode Island was originally inhabited by the Narragansett tribe of Native-Americans who resided along the bay named after them. The Wampanoags inhabited the eastern shore areas, while the Nipmucks, a smaller group, lived in the inland regions north and west of present-day Providence. Also, Niantics lived in the coastal areas around the present-day towns of Charlestown and Westerly.

Anthropologists estimate that around 1600 there may have been approximately 16,000 Narrangansetts residing within the present-day boundaries of Rhode Island. They are part of the Algonquian language group. While they relied primarily on agricultural products such as beans, squash, corn and sunflowers, they were also adept trappers and hunters. Their typical residence was the wigwam.

The first European contacts were probably with Giovanni da Verrazano in 1524, even though permanent European settlers did not arrive until nearly a century later. At that time a smallpox epidemic ravaged some of the neighboring tribes, but somehow the Narragansett survived. However, in 1633 the plague struck the Narragansett tribe, which suffered an estimated 700 casualties.

Although the tribe remained neutral during King Philip's War, the English assembled a massive army and attacked the Narragansett, who were thought to be harboring members of the Wampanoag tribe. The massive British army killed at least 600 Narragansett and another 300 were taken prisoner. Many of the casualties were women and children in this massacre known as the Swamp Fight.

The remaining tribal members were provided a reservation, but the tribe became assimilated into the dominant European-American macroculture during the eighteenth and nineteenth centuries. However, in spite of the predicament, the culture did not completely die, and activists, such as Ella Thomas Sekatau and Eric Thomas Sekatau were successful in securing federal recognition of the tribe in 1983. About 1,800 acres of the original tribal lands were given to the Narragansett tribe.

The Niantic tribe, a much smaller group, resided on the coasts of Connecticut and Rhode Island. They were also part of the Algonquian language group. Anthropologists believe they resided in that region for thousands of years before the Europeans came. Their location provided them with a rich diet of choice seafoods, as well as beans, pumpkins, and maize. A series of Pequot raids divided them into an eastern and western faction.

Eventually, European incursions, disease, and the Pequot war had the effect of practically decimating the group. The small number of survivors became assimilated into the Mohegan tribe which made them subjects. By the nineteenth century, nobody claimed to be of western Niantic ancestry. The eastern group became assimilated into the Narragansett tribe during the latter part of the eighteenth century.

The name "Rhode Island" was provided by Verrazano, who compared Rhode Island's Block Island with the Island of Rhodes in the Mediterranean Sea. However, despite his long-reaching influence, the first permanent settlement occurred when Roger Williams, an English clergyman, left the Massachusetts Bay colony in search of a site where he could secure freedom of worship. He was given land for a village site by the Narragansetts.

Williams was also successful in recruiting other members of the Massachusetts Bay colony who were dissatisfied with the religious climate. Anne and William Hutchinson followed him, as well as William Coddington, who eventually founded Portsmouth in 1638. Later, Williams was successful in persuading the English Parliament to grant him a parliamentary packet, which united these and other Rhode Island-area towns into a single colony.

The new colony had complete religious freedom, and it became self-governing with a strong local autonomy. It was the most liberal charter of any of the English colonies. The religious freedom made it an attractive location for a number of religious sects which were experiencing difficulties in other regions. For example, the first American Baptist Church was founded in Providence in 1639. Quakers soon became a strong religious body in Rhode Island; a Jewish congregation was formed in Newport in 1658; and French Huguenots settled in East Greenwich in 1686.

During this colonial period, Rhode Islanders shied away from the provision of public schools which would have been supported by tax dollars. Consequently, the education that was available during this era could only be enjoyed by the children of wealthy parents. And when a free school act was passed in 1800, it was quickly repealed just three years later.

During the first two decades of the eighteenth century, Rhode Island established closer ties with Great Britain as a result of the leadership of Governor Samuel Cranston. Newport was becoming a prosperous port, and Providence began challenging that city for political dominance. By 1774 the colony of Rhode Island had over 59,000 people who resided in 29 municipalities.

England's decision to increase the supervision and control of its colonies had a profound effect on Rhode Island because of its high level of self-governance. Moreover, the colony had managed to skirt the Navigation Acts, which were not strongly enforced, and smuggling was a common practice as a result. Britain's Sugar Act of 1764 affected Rhode Island because of the manner in which it restricted the molasses trade. In an act of defiance, Rhode Islanders burned up a British revenue schooner. In another bold action, Rhode Island became the first colony to denounce King George III.

With the outbreak of hostilities, Rhode Island played a major role in the provision of troops and supplies. Nathanael Greene became chief of the Continental Army in the southern region, and was second in command to George Washington. Rhode Island supplied its share of volunteers, including a rather significant number of African-American and Native-American slaves, who became a detachment of the First Rhode Island Regiment. Esek Hopkins became Commander-in-Chief of the Continental Navy.

The British occupied Newport in 1776 and withdrew voluntarily in 1779. Throughout the conflicts, the Rhode Island colony participated in a number of skirmishes against the British, with the help of their French allies. The Battle of Rhodes, in August of 1779, was one of the first times in history when the colonists teamed up with the French in doing battle against the British forces.

One important change in Rhode Island's political structure after the Revolution was the decision to gradually abolish slavery, and a second law made it illegal to participate in the slave trade. Rhode Island was quick to ratify the Articles of Confederation which called for a weak central government. However, the state's history of rugged individualism created an unwillingness to back a movement to strengthen that government. Consequently, it was the last of the original thirteen colonies to ratify the new constitution, which it did in 1790.

During the nineteenth century, Rhode Island became more industrialized, immigration increased, and the new state became increasingly urbanized. By the 1840s, this combination of factors helped lead to an incident known as Door's Rebellion, which dealt with the state's constitutional government. Rhode Island's royal charter was still in effect, and it provided disproportionate powers to the rural areas, which had been declining in numbers. Also, at this time, only a small proportion of the population was franchised.

Dorr was an attorney who led a rebellion against the existing state legislature, and, between 1840 and 1843, he and the other reformers convened a People's Convention, bypassing the state legislature. A new constitution was finally in effect during 1843.

Rhode Island's Henry Barnard became one of the most influential American educators during the middle of the nineteenth century. He became Rhode Island's first commissioner of education in 1845. By this time the state had established a fund for the support of public schools, and under Barnard's leadership the notion of free tax-supported public schools became an important Rhode Island concept. He was instrumental in creating a highly respected system of public education. By 1882, all towns were required to establish public schools, and compulsory attendance was required in 1883.

Immigration to Rhode Island intensified during the second half of the nineteenth century. Increasing numbers of Irish-Catholics, as well as immigrants from France, Canada, Britain, and Sweden, moved into Rhode Island. Ethnoreligious factors became politically influential.

While conservative Republican business interests and rural factions controlled Rhode Island politics during the first part of the twentieth century, the decades of the 1920s and 1930s saw a gradual shift toward Democratic control. The Irish-led Democratic party took advantage of organized labor and the increasing tendency of the immigrants to back the more liberal political philosophy of the Democratic party.

THE EDUCATIONAL SYSTEM

Rhode Island's state school superintendent is appointed by a fifteen-member Board of Regents, which is appointed by the governor, with senate consent. In order to become certified to teach in Rhode Island, it is necessary to pass the National Teachers Examination for evidence of basic skills mastery. In addition, all prospective candidates must be observed in successful cadet teaching performances.

Rhode Island children are required to attend school between the ages of six and sixteen. However, services for special education children are provided between the ages of three and twenty. School districts are required to provide half-day kindergartens. The per capita amount of money spent on elementary and secondary education in Rhode Island is $928.98, slightly below the national average. Over 53 percent of the state's teachers hold a master's degree, one of the highest percentages in the nation. Just 16.4 percent of the state's children are below the poverty level, somewhat lower than the national average of 19 percent.

While the state has no statutory provisions regarding the use of corporal punishment in the schools, there is a statewide policy pertaining to the issue of prayer in school. Rhode Island allows children a period of time for meditation. This time shall not exceed one minute.

MULTICULTURAL EDUCATION EFFORTS

According to the 1998 questionnaire responses, Rhode Island has no multicultural education program. However, even though there is no formal program, education that is multicultural is supported. Unfortunately, nobody is in charge of such efforts, no funding is provided, and the state offers no leadership to school districts in specific kinds of multicultural education.

Rhode Island has always enjoyed a highly pluralistic population. The questionnaire responses stipulated that the predominant microcultures were Latino (particularly Puerto Rican, Colombian, and Dominican), Portuguese, Cambodian, Laotian, Cape Verdean, African-American, and Nigerian.

No special coursework and/or other multicultural experiences are required for teacher certification, and the state stresses a cultural pluralism approach to curriculum and instruction.

While there are no provisions for utilizing bilingual education programs with students for whom English is their second language, some school districts do not use such approaches. They offer the English as a second language portion and the instructional components are usually in English-only.

Since the 1954 *Brown v. Board of Education* Supreme Court decision, racial segregation in America's schools has been declared to be unconstitutional. Rhode Island's schools use controlled choice procedures and magnet schools also deal with the problem. School busing is another technique employed to ensure that the state's schools are racially integrated in order to be in compliance with *Brown v. Board of Education.*

While Rhode Island has no "state curriculum" per se, the respondent stipulated that the history of the region's Native-Americans was incorporated into the curriculum content throughout the school districts of Rhode Island. Rhode Island's State Office of Education has no procedure for evaluating curriculum materials, library holdings, and textbooks for racist and sexist content.

In response to the question pertaining to problems facing multicultural education and the state's primary needs in such programs, it was argued that there was no political support for even engaging in public discussion about this issue. The biggest multicultural education needs were perceived to be minimal inclusion of multicultural education in preservice teacher education. Also, it was believed that multicultural education concepts must be included in the history and social studies curricula.

REFERENCES

Conley, Patrick and Smith, Matthew J., *Catholicism in Rhode Island.* Providence: Diocese of Providence, 1976.

Council of Chief State School Officers, *The Council.* Washington D.C., Council of Chief State School Officers.

James, Sydney V., *Colonial Rhode Island.* New York: Scribner, 1975.

Leiter, Richard A., (ed.), *National Survey of State Laws.* First edition. Detroit: Gale Research, 1997.

Markowitz, Harvey, (ed.), *American Indians,* Pasadena, CA: Salem Press, 1995.

McLoughlin, William G.: *Rhode Island: A History.* New York: W. W. Norton, 1977.

United States Department of Education, *Digest of Educational Statistics.* Washington D.C.: United States Department of Education, 1997.

SOUTH CAROLINA

STATE HISTORY

When the first European-Americans arrived in present-day South Carolina, they encountered the original residents, who represented at least three main language groups. The Iroquois, Cherokees, Catawbans, and the Muskhogean were the primary groups.

As described in the entry on multicultural education programs in Georgia, the Cherokees first encountered Europeans who were members of Hernando de Soto's entourage in 1540. At that time they moved into the Georgia and South Carolina regions. By 1759, relations between the European settlers and the original Cherokee residents of the area had deteriorated to the extent that Governor Henry Lyttleton of South Carolina marched into the Native-American portion of the state in order to retaliate for a Cherokee act of revenge against frontier farmers, who had killed about 30 Cherokee warriors.

In 1760, a new governor, William Bull, sent the South Carolina militia and royal troops into Cherokee territory, destroying towns and agricultural fields, and defeating the Cherokees. One year later a peace accord with the Cherokees was agreed upon, but further hostilities broke out in 1776. A year later, the Cherokees surrendered and all of their lands east of the Blue Ridge Mountains were given to the European settlers.

The Catawbans, sometimes referred to as *Katapu,* grew squash, beans, and corn, and were adept in arts and crafts endeavors such as basket weaving and pottery making. After first encountering Spanish explorers, they established cordial relations with English immigrants and even sided with them against other Native-American Tribes.

The tribe was often involved in various encounters with the Iroquois, Cherokee, and Shawnee. Unfortunately, the tribe encountered problems with smallpox for about forty years during the mid-1700s, and their former prominence was never regained. After they were duped into giving their South Carolina land away, they were provided with reservation lands in York County, South Carolina.

Among the early Europeans in the South Carolina areas were the French and Spanish, who both established short-lived settlements on Parris Island in the last half of the sixteenth century. However, neither nation took advantage of these early inroads, leaving the area open to the English. Charles I granted Carolina lands to Charles Heath, whose unsuccessful attempts to colonize resulted in the ultimate withdrawal of the lands by the English king.

However, Charles II followed up on this notion, granting Carolina lands to eight proprietors, who commenced colonizing the areas comprising the present-day states of North Carolina, South Carolina, and Georgia. Carolina's original constitution was drafted by England's John Locke. However, it proved to be impractical and was abandoned about 1690.

During the late 1600s, two permanent colonies had been established in what is now South Carolina. One was located at Albemarle Point on the Ashley River, while another was located between the Cooper and Ashley Rivers. The possibility of acquiring land grants and the promise of religious freedom were attractive to Europeans from England and France. Henry Woodward and others were instrumental in initiating the South Carolina rice-growing industry, and by the beginning of the eighteenth century, African slaves were brought to South Carolina to provide growers with a cheap labor source. The English colonists felt that Gambian slaves were best suited to that particular area and consequently, many of the African slaves were brought from that country.

The colony of South Carolina prospered when the new rice culture was in full swing. However, problems created by pirate raids and Native-American conflicts eventually led to the creation of a formal English colony in 1729. After this time, new colonists arrived in large numbers. This colonization process occurred about the same time that Georgia, the next-door neighbor, also became a colony under the leadership of James Oglethorpe. New immigrants from Germany and Switzerland came to South Carolina. By the 1750s, Scotch-Irish Europeans came to settle in the Piedmont region of South Carolina.

Originally, South Carolinians paid little attention to the problems the northern colonies experienced in their relationships with England. Eventually, however, the thinking in South Carolina tended to support the northern colonies because of a fear that what was happening up north could easily occur in South Carolina before long. Thus, South Carolina supported the Declaration of Independence, even though the acceptance tended to be somewhat reluctant. The colony's first encounter with the British occurred in 1776, when the British attempted to capture Charles Town.

After this battle, South Carolina had little contact with the British until the British were defeated by the colonists at Camden, thus allowing them to attain control of the interior. However, rural colonists in the southeastern areas rallied and administered sound defeats to the British at King's Mountain, Cowpens, and Eutaw Springs. In effect, these Continental victories ruined British plans for acquiring control of the South.

Statehood for the state was achieved in 1788, when South Carolina became the eighth state in the new nation.

As was the case in the rest of the South, early education in South Carolina was considered to be a private and individual matter. There was virtually no Jeffersonian philosophy which argued the need for public education in a democratic society. And since the people from the southern colonies tended to subscribe to the tenets of the Anglican church, education was thought to be the responsibility of each family. Moreover, wealthy planters often tended to think that education was important for their own children, but there was no need to create a public education system for all youth.

That concept would not take hold until much later in South Carolina's history, when the state's legislature passed a law which provided for a state educational system in 1811. However, the schools that were created were woefully inadequate, and the established schools received insufficient financial support.

Some historians have described the Civil War as South Carolina's greatest tragedy. By the time of the hostilities in 1865, cotton production had established itself as the second great industry besides the cultivation of rice. Consequently, the notion of slavery had become a primary underpinning of the state's economy and its social structure as well. In 1861, the war actually started with the firing on Fort Sumter in Charleston Harbor, after the state had the dubious distinction of being the first to secede from the Union. The state contributed a total of 63,000 men to the Confederate cause and over 20 percent of them died when Sherman cut his swath across the state of Georgia and on through South Carolina. The capital of Columbia was consumed in flames.

The Reconstruction period following the Civil War was perhaps the most difficult time in South Carolina's history. Approximately 400,000 African-American slaves were suddenly free persons who were enfranchised citizens able to hold office. Indeed, some of South Carolina's freed slaves did hold government positions immediately after the war. But perhaps the biggest problem for South Carolina was the exposure of its weaknesses in its social and economic systems.

A new state constitution was initiated in 1868. It granted equal rights for African-Americans and finally established a free public education system. However, the schools were racially segregated and the school system for African-American children was decidedly inferior to the schools for European-Americans.

During Reconstruction, the textile industry experienced rapid growth because of the ever-present supply of cheap labor. Agriculture went into a slow but steady decline as the South Carolina towns gradually grew into cities. During the 1920s the cotton crop was devastated because of the boll weevil infestations, and many African-Americans commenced moving North in order to take advantage of a more lucrative job market. The policies of Franklin Roosevelt in the 1930s aided South Carolina farmers during the Great Depression. During this era, the state embarked in a new road building venture and after World War II South Carolina's economy commenced to prosper because of a more diversified industrial base.

However, it was not until nearly a decade after the *Brown v. Board of Education* antisegregation Supreme Court decision that South Carolina's schools started to become desegregated racially.

THE EDUCATIONAL SYSTEM

One of the major problems experienced in South Carolina and many other Southern states has been the enormous public education responsibilities in the face of major problems in raising adequate funds to create a viable public system of education. Compared to the wealthier states, Southern states such as South Carolina must designate a much higher percentage of their state budgets in order to fund public education programs.

South Carolina has about ninety public school districts, counting the county systems. Each district is governed by a board of trustees and basic education requirements are developed by South Carolina's State Board of Education. A state superintendent of schools is elected by popular vote and the compulsory attendance ages are between five and seventeen. Special education programs are provided for all children between three and twenty-one years of age.

Exceptions to South Carolina's compulsory education requirements include children who are enrolled in private, parochial, or other approved programs; children who have graduated; children with physical or mental disabilities; children who have completed the eighth grade and are lawfully employed; pregnant children who are either married or unmarried; children who are ten years or older who have been out of school for more than three years; and children attending vocational schools.

Home school provisions require that the instruction must be approved. Parents must have at least a high school diploma and a passing score on a basic skills examination. Evidence of the student's progress must be provided and children must have access to library facilities. Home-schooled children must participate in basic skills assessment programs.

Before the 1954 *Brown v. Board of Education* Supreme Court decision, elementary and secondary education programs in South Carolina were racially segregated. But even though the state balked at this landmark decision, their schools were desegregated by 1971, earlier than many states.

In order to become certified to teach in South Carolina, prospective candidates must first perform successfully on the National Teachers Examination and also on a state examination. Basic skills must be mastered, along with successful in-class student teaching performances, in order to become licensed in South Carolina.

South Carolina school boards may authorize corporal punishment for any student, as long as the local board deems it to be just and proper. There are no statutory provisions pertaining to prayer in schools. The per capita expenditures for elementary and secondary education programs in South Carolina are among the nation's lowest. Only nine other states spend less. However, it must be remembered that this is primarily due to the fact that South Carolina is one of the less wealthy states.

South Carolina school districts are required to offer half-day kindergarten programs in the state's school districts. Also, the state has a number of school districts which offer year-round school programs.

MULTICULTURAL EDUCATION EFFORTS

Repeated requests to complete the authors' multicultural education 1998 surveys were unsuccessful in securing valuable information about any multicultural education efforts in the state. However, statistics reveal that poverty is one of the main problems with which the state has been forced to contend. Nearly 32 percent of the state's children between the ages of five and seventeen are below the poverty level. Only Mississippi has a higher rate. This compares with the national average of 19 percent.

REFERENCES

Council of Chief State School Officers, *The Council.* Washington D.C., Council of Chief State School Officers, 1998.

Jones, Lewis P., *South Carolina: A Synoptic History for Laymen.* Columbia: University of South Carolina Press, 1971.

Kran, David H., *The Cherokee Frontier: Conflict and Survival, 1740–62.* Norman: University of Oklahoma Press, 1962.

Landers, Ernest M., *A History of South Carolina, 1865–1960.* Columbia: University of South Carolina Press, 1970.

Leiter, Richard A. (ed.), *National Survey of State Laws.* First edition. Detroit: Gale Research, 1997.

Littlefield, Daniel C., *Rice and Slaves: Ethnicity and the Slave Trade in Colonial South Carolina.* Baton Rouge: Louisiana Press, 1981.

Malone, Henry, *Cherokees of the Old South.* Athens: University of Georgia Press, 1956.

Sirmans, M. Eugene, *Colonial South Carolina: A Political History, 1663–1763.* Chapel Hill: University of North Carolina Press, 1966.

United States Department of Education, *Digest of Educational Statistics.* Washington D.C.: United States Department of Education, 1997.

SOUTH DAKOTA

While South Dakota has had a huge percentage of European-Americans populating the state, it also has one of the highest percentages of Native-Americans living within its boundaries. The two largest groups of Native-American residents are the Sioux (actually an Ojibwa word meaning "enemy"). In addition to South Dakota, the Sioux also lived in Montana, North Dakota, Minnesota, Nebraska, Manitoba, and Saskatchewan. The term "Sioux" actually refers to a number of bands which lived in the prairie and plains regions of the United States and Canada.

The core of the Sioux society was the extended family in which the family members resided together in a cooperative unit. At the next level were the lodge groups, which were often referred to as "bands." They were ruled by an elder and the members of the bands were usually related. The elders were known as "itancans." They were selected on the basis of their bravery, wisdom, generosity, and fortitude.

During the first quarter of the nineteenth century, the Sioux had been pushed out of their earlier homelands, which were located in Minnesota. The largest group ended up settling in the present-day state of South Dakota, in the Black Hills region. It is believed that gold might have been discovered in that area as early as the Lewis and Clark expedition. It has been argued that the gold discoveries in the Black Hills were suppressed by the United States military in order to forestall a rush of European-American adventurers, which might have upset the delicate balance between Native-Americans and European-Americans during the first part of the nineteenth century.

The Sioux roamed freely throughout this area and after the Civil War, more European-American settlers were moving into the region in search of gold. The United States government had attempted to acquire the lands of the Sioux, but to no avail. President Ulysses Grant was searching for a way to justify military action against the Sioux and other allied tribes in the region in order to open up these areas of South Dakota for settlement and prospecting. Enormous numbers of European-Americans were poised to enter these lands. However, the Sioux refused all of the government offers to acquire their land and force them to relocate into other regions.

The situation culminated in the famous Battle of the Little Bighorn of 1876, in which General George Armstrong Custer's forces were annihilated, with 263 killed and another 59 wounded. However, the victory for the Sioux and their allies was short lived. While chief Sitting Bull became famous because of this enormous victory over government forces, which were far superior in terms of their numbers and arms, the Sioux were finally forced to reside on reservations by the end of the 1870s.

The first known Europeans to enter present-day South Dakota were thought to be French fur trappers, who descended into the region during the last half of the eighteenth century. Traders and trappers from France, England, and Spain mingled with the Sioux and from that time on, the Sioux became at least somewhat dependent on these new residents.

In addition to such historical figures as Sitting Bull, Crazy Horse, Buffalo Bill, and Calamity Jane, early South Dakota was also the home of famous western celebrities such as Wild Bill Hickok and other "gunslingers" who became famous because of their exploits (some real and many others imagined) in Deadwood. Wild Bill Hickok was born in Illinois and was the son of parents who operated a station on the famous Underground Railroad, helping African-American slaves to seek their freedom. During the Civil War he became a scout and sharpshooter in the Union Army. By the time he came to the Black Hills in 1875, it was reported that he had already killed thirty-six men in gunfights.

South Dakota became part of the United States as a result of the 1803 Louisiana Purchase from France. Louis and Clark followed the Missouri River across the present state of South Dakota on their trek to the Pacific in 1804. By the mid-nineteenth century, United States forces established Fort Pierre in South Dakota, which constituted part of a plan to appease the European-Americans who wanted to settle in the lands of the Sioux. Indeed, the lush prairie lands contained some of the finest farmlands in the United States.

The Dakota Territory was created in 1861, and by 1873 a railroad connected Sioux City and Yankton. The Dakota Territory actually included the present states of North Dakota, South Dakota, and portions of Montana and Wyoming. In 1889 South Dakota achieved statehood, along with North Dakota, Washington, and Montana.

One year later, the infamous Wounded Knee Massacre occurred in South Dakota. The Sioux had fought gallantly for their lands, but had ended up on several South Dakota reservations by this time. The Sioux had adopted the Ghost Dance, created by Wokova, a Paiute, as a rallying cry against the encroachments of the European-Americans who took over their lands. The United States Army slaughtered 230 women and children and about 120 warriors. Most of the Sioux were unarmed. This ended the major conflicts between the Sioux and the European-Americans. By the time of the Great Depression of 1929, a number of socialistic reforms had been in vogue as a result of the efforts of Governor Peter Norbeck who helped the state to acquire forward-looking programs in workers' compensation, child labor, and hail insurance. However, after the Great Depression, the state returned to its conservative political posture and the Republican party returned to a high level of influence.

Public school districts in South Dakota were originally created in 1865. Their financial support was derived from the sale of public lands. However, public education in the state has been funded primarily from personal property and real estate taxes. Persons in each school district are taxed on the basis of their income, and the assessed valuation of their personal and real property.

Prior to the 1900s, South Dakota's schools were largely rural. However, in 1967, the South Dakota legislature passed a law which required the reorganization of school districts into entities which could offer twelve years of schooling to their children.

THE EDUCATIONAL SYSTEM

South Dakota's state school superintendent is appointed by the governor. In order to become certified, teachers must be observed in successful teaching performances. Candidates must complete an approved teacher education program and pass courses in human relations and South Dakota Indian studies. At least half of the required six semester hours of credit for the renewal of teaching certificates must be completed at a college or university.

The National Council for Accreditation of Teacher Education (NCATE) reviews South Dakota's teacher education programs every five years. The course in South Dakota Indian studies has four course strands, including culture dynamics, history, educational theory and background, and implementation and strategies. The human relations course strands deal with the awareness and understanding of the values, lifestyles, contributions, and history of a pluralistic society; recognizing and dealing with dehumanizing biases, such as racism, sexism, prejudice, and discrimination, and having an awareness of the impact such biases have on interpersonal relations; translating knowledge of human relations and attitudes, skills, and techniques resulting in favorable experiences for students; recognizing the ways in which dehumanizing biases may be reflected in instructional materials; respecting human dignity and individual rights; and relating effectively to other individuals and to groups in a pluralistic society, other than the teacher's own. Both in-state teaching candidates and out-of-state candidates must complete the Indian studies and human relations courses.

On a per capita basis, South Dakota spends $857 for elementary and secondary education, compared to the national average of $931.76 per capita. Compulsory attendance ages are from six to sixteen years of age and compulsory special education services are available for students between the ages of three and twenty-one years of age. Exceptions to the compulsory attendance requirements include children who have finished the eighth grade and are granted a religious exemption and children who receive competent instruction from another source. Home schooling is allowed and parents do not need to be certified. The state's Department of Education must ensure that the instruction is provided by a competent person. Such instructors are not allowed to work with more than twenty-two people.

South Dakota has a policy on year-round schools and school districts are required to offer kindergarten programs. The state has no statutory provisions related to prayer in the schools or the use of corporal punishment. Compared to the national average of 42 percent, just 23.2 percent of South Dakota's teachers hold a master's degree, one of the nation's lowest percentages.

MULTICULTURAL EDUCATION EFFORTS

South Dakota's responses to the 1998 questionnaire items acknowledged that the state had no program in multicultural education per se. No person was responsible for such efforts and no multicultural education funds are budgeted. However, the state does offer leadership to its school districts in specific kinds of multicultural programs. It should be noted that South Dakota's courses in Indian studies and human relations contain many of the instructional elements comprising multicultural education classes.

The predominant microcultures in South Dakota were listed as Native-Americans (Lakota), Hutterites (German-Russian-Americans who live in colonies), and Scandinavians. As indicated earlier, special coursework in multicultural education is required for teacher certification. The issue of curriculum and instruction stressing cultural pluralism or cultural assimilation depends on the philosophy of each school district.

Native language instruction is provided in South Dakota schools under Title VII funds. With the exception of the reservation schools, racial segregation has never been a problem in South Dakota because of the small non-European-American population. The respondent stipulated that racist incidents had increased in South Dakota schools during the past five years.

There is no statewide curriculum requirement for teaching the history of Native-Americans in the state's schools, but most school districts do so through local curriculum requirements. Likewise, the South Dakota Office of Education does not evaluate textbooks, curriculum materials, and library holdings for possible inclusion of racist and sexist content. That is left up to the local school districts.

Finally, it was felt that the biggest problem facing multicultural education programs in South Dakota was the attitude that since there was such a small non-European-American population, there was no need for such enterprises. The biggest need in South Dakota's multicultural education program would be to have more schools incorporate this function in the curriculum.

REFERENCES

Axelrod, Alan, *Chronicle of the Indian Wars: From Colonial Times to Wounded Knee.* New York: Prentice Hall, 1993.

Council of Chief State School Officers, *The Council.* Washington D.C.: Council of Chief State School Officers, 1998.

Hassrick, Royal B., *The Sioux: Life and Customs of a Warrior Society.* Norman; University of Oklahoma Press, 1964.

Hyde, George E., *A Sioux Chronicle.* Norman: University of Oklahoma Press, 1956.

Lamar, Howard R., *Dakota Territory, 1861–1889: A Study of Frontier Politics.* New Haven; Yale University Press, 1956.

Leiter, Richard A., (ed.), *National Survey of State Laws.* First edition. Detroit: Gale Research, 1997.

Milton, John R., *South Dakota: A History.* New York: W. W. Norton, 1977.

Rosenberg, Bruce A., *Custer and the Epic of Defeat.* University Park: Pennsylvania State University Press, 1974.

Schell, Herbert S., *History of South Dakota.* Lincoln: University of Nebraska Press, 1975.

United States Department of Education, *Digest of Educational Statistics.* Washington, D.C.: United States Department of Education, 1997.

TENNESSEE

STATE HISTORY

The earliest residents of Tennessee were probably attracted to the region because of the major rivers which provided an abundant supply of water, as well as excellent transportation routes. The Mississippi and its tributaries drain the western side of the state, while the Tennessee and Cumberland drain most of the remaining regions. Arrowheads found in the state trace the early residents back at least 5,000 BC Some of the early mound builders were also located in Tennessee. Two of the main Tennessee tribes were the Cherokee and the Chicakasaw.

Located in eastern Tennessee, Kentucky, and parts of Mississippi and Alabama, the Chickasaws were part of the Muskogean language group. It is believed that the first contact with Europeans occurred in 1540, when Hernando de Soto traveled through the area. After achieving a major victory against these Spaniards some time later, the Chickasaws became involved in a number of battles with the French and their Indian allies during the seventeenth century. During the same century, they became allied with the British and remained loyal to them during the American Revolution.

After the American Revolution in 1786, the Chickasaws signed the Treaty of Hopewell with the new nation. The stipulations of the agreement acknowledged that they were under the protection of the United States. By 1818 President Andrew Jackson persuaded the tribe to sell all their lands in Tennessee and Kentucky. After they sold the remainder of their lands in 1832, they moved to Indian Territory in Oklahoma.

When they moved West, the tribe brought about 1,000 of their slaves with them and consequently, they sided with the Confederacy when the Civil War broke out. After the war was over, they accepted the fact that their slavery practices had to end and they also lost a great deal of their land in southwestern Oklahoma.

Other Spanish adventurers followed de Soto into the present Tennessee area, but it was not until 1673 that French and English explorers came into present-day Tennessee. Other explorers during the latter part of the seventeenth century included Father Jacques Marquette, fur trader Louis Joliet, and the famous French explorer René-Robert Cavelier. Fort Prudhomme was constructed near the mouth of the Natchez River and Fort Loudoun was erected during the French and Indian War. The Cherokee eventually became allied with the French.

By 1769, the first permanent settlement in Tennessee was established by William Beam. Located near the Watagua River, Beam brought people to Virginia. During the 1700s, the British had banned the settlement of that region, but by the start of the American Revolution, there were at least four such settlements in what is presently the northeast corner of Tennessee.

Although the present areas of Tennessee were only sparsely populated with European-Americans at the outset of the American Revolution, they supported the colonists' cause. However, in 1776, faced with the prospects of an attack by Native-Americans, they appealed to North Carolina to be annexed in order to acquire protection. The following year, North Carolina created Washington County, which included most of the present boundaries of Tennessee. In 1784, North Carolina ceded its Tennessee lands to the new United States. During that same year, Congress passed a law which authorized the formation of new states in the federal territories. Statehood was finally achieved in 1796.

Tennesseeans eagerly supported the War of 1812 and sent large numbers of volunteers into combat. Likewise, many Tennessee volunteers saw service in the Mexican War, which helped the state to acquire the nickname, "Volunteer State". The University of Tennessee uses this name for their athletic teams.

During the early stages of the Civil War, Tennessee did not call a convention to discuss secession. This did not happen until the governor refused to respond to President Lincoln's call for troops. However, the east side of the state, which had only small numbers of slaves, was generally opposed to this action. Nonetheless, after secession, Tennessee became one of the leading battlegrounds during the war. Interestingly, 30,000 of Tennessee's 145,000 troops fought for the Union cause. Most of them were from the eastern side of the state. In 1865 the state constitution was amended to prohibit slavery.

Prior to the Civil War, educational opportunities in elementary and secondary schools were mostly limited to affluent children who could afford to attend private schools or academies. The public school system which existed was free to students whose parents could not pay, but there was a stigma attached to this practice. Tennessee' s present educational system was first established in 1873. Funding was then provided for the education of both European-American and African-American children. These schools were racially segregated.

Reconstruction affected Tennessee severely, like the other southern states. Not only did Tennessee incur a large debt, but it also had to contend with the Ku Klux Klan, which was active in the state. In 1874, African-Americans conducted state conventions in which complaints were raised about unchecked Klan violence. Other problems suffered by African-Americans included systematic discrimination by the state government, segregation in the public sector, poll taxes for African-American males (no women of any race could vote until the Harding election), and racism in the courts and juries.

Also, the economic distress experienced by the state's farmers led to the formation of Granges and Farmers' Alliances. The so-called Coal Miners' War erupted toward the end of the century, when convicts were used as strikers.

The 1925 Scopes "monkey trial" attracted much national attention in 1925 when John T. Scopes, a high school teacher in the state, refused to stop teaching about evolution, even though the state had passed a law outlawing this topic in the curriculum. The trial resulted in a confrontation between lawyers William Jennings Bryan and Clarence Darrow. While Scopes was convicted in this Dayton, Tennessee case, he only was required to pay a small fine and the state's antievolution law was eventually overturned in 1967, a resounding defeat for the "religious right."

Tennessee's farmers suffered again during the Great Depression. However, the Roosevelt administration's Tennessee Valley Authority (TVA) dramatically helped the state's economy to turn around. Also instrumental in this economic recovery was the increase in industrial growth during the decades following World War II. Finally the assassination of Dr. Martin Luther King in Memphis during 1968 led to new racial disorders, which began in Chattanooga and Nashville.

THE EDUCATIONAL SYSTEM

The *Brown v. Board of Education* system, in 1954, signaled a major change in Tennessee' elementary and secondary education programs. Nashville utilized a "grade-a-year program", which initiated a gradual desegregation plan. By the late 1960s, Tennessee's schools were mostly integrated racially. Other Tennessee school districts also adopted the concept of a "a grade a year."

Tennessee's state commissioner of schools is appointed by the governor. Teachers achieve certification through the usual coursework and by successful performance on the National Teachers' Examination. They must also be observed in satisfactory classroom teaching performances.

Compulsory school attendance is required of all students between the ages of seven and seventeen. Exceptions include children who have graduated from high school or achieved the GED; children who are physically and/or mentally incapacitated; and children whose conduct is detrimental to good order and the benefit of other children. Also excluded from the compulsory attendance requirement are children who have homebound instruction. Such home-schooling instruction must be approved by the local education agency. Parents who provide the instruction must have at least a GED for teaching at the K-8 level. Parents or guardians must have at least a baccalaureate degree for teaching at the grade nine through twelve level. Also, records must be kept and standardized tests taken.

Corporal punishment is allowed in Tennessee's schools, as long as it is administered in a reasonable manner. A Tennessee statute mandates a one-minute period of silence during each school day. Students are able to reflect on anything they wish, prayers included.

Sixteen percent of Tennessee's adult population over the age of twenty-five has less than a ninth grade education. This compares with the national average of 10.4 percent. The percentage of Tennessee residents who hold the bachelor's degree or a graduate/professional degree, is also below the national average.

An examination of the general per capita expenditures for elementary and secondary education revealed that Tennessee spends $622.02 per capita. This compares with the national average of $931.76, which places the state last in the nation. However, it must be remembered that no federal funds are spent for basic education budgets in the states, and Tennessee is one of the nation's poorest states financially.

Tennessee has some school districts with year-round schools, although there is no specific state policy on their operation or existence. The state requires school districts to operate half-day kindergartens.

MULTICULTURAL EDUCATION EFFORTS

Responses to the authors' 1998 multicultural education survey revealed that Tennessee does not have a planned multicultural education program in the state. But the respondent did say that they attempt to "weave the idea of diversity" through the curriculum frameworks and teacher training competencies. There is nobody who is responsible for multicultural education programs, and no special funding for this effort exists. Even so, the responses indicated that the state director of equity and excellence provides a variety of multicultural education programs through her office.

Tennessee's Office of Professional Development provides training in cultural diversity. This unit offers conferences and workshops in multicultural education. The director also counsels superintendents and other school personnel about diversity issues.

The predominant microcultures in the state besides European-Americans are African-Americans (23 percent), and Latinos and Asians (about 1 percent each). No mention was made of the Native-American populations.

Tennessee does have special multicultural education competencies which teachers must demonstrate in order to become certified. They must be able to adapt instructional techniques to students of diverse cultural and language backgrounds. They must also demonstrate an understanding of how cultural and gender differences can affect communication in the classroom.

While the respondent objected to the terms "cultural pluralism" and "cultural assimilation," she indicated that Tennessee stresses an "acculturation" approach, which the authors interpret as meaning "cultural pluralism." The reason for this interpretation is that the respondent felt Tennessee's approach to the curriculum stresses a respect for all cultures and their contributions. Also, the social science framework includes the contributions of Native-Americans.

Tennessee has no special programs for teaching children in their native languages when necessary.

The state still has school districts which are operating under court-ordered desegregation. Most are using busing in order to achieve desegregation. However, in Memphis, Nashville, Chattanooga, and Jackson, magnet programs are also used.

Tennessee's state Office of Education evaluates textbooks for racist or sexist statements. However, the same does not hold true for curriculum and library materials. Any evaluation for these items occurs at the local school district level.

The respondee felt that the greatest problems facing multicultural education efforts in Tennessee was the increasing cultural diversity of the students and the large numbers of Tennessee educators who have not had much training in diverse populations. The biggest improvement in this area would be the training of teachers in regard to the educational needs of students by race, ethnicity, and gender. Also needed is appropriate technical assistance from the State Department of Education on how to address issues of disparity among children from the various microcultures.

Tennessee is now addressing this issue, as the state was the first to pass Title VI of the Civil Rights Act. The Tennessee State Legislature passed T. C. A. 4-21-901, which requires the State Department of Education to assume much more leadership and responsibility in multicultural education issues. Because of this, intensive training in Title VI issues has occurred in recent years. Also, the Tennessee state office has been working with the regional branch of the Office of Civil Rights to examine a number of Title VI issues.

REFERENCES

Abernathy, Thomas P., *From Frontier to Plantation in Tennessee.* Westport: Greenwood Press, 1979.

Alexander, Kern and Alexander, M. David, *The Law of Schools, Students, and Teachers.* St. Paul: West Publishing Company, 1995.

Bergeron, Paul H., *Paths of the Past: Tennessee 1770–1970.* Knoxville: The University of Tennessee Press, 1979.

Cartwright, Joseph H., *The Triumph of Jim Crow.* Knoxville: The University of Tennessee Press, 1984.

Council of Chief State School Officers, *The Council.* Washington D.C., Council of Chief State School Officers.

Gibson, Arrell M., *The Chickasaws.* Norman: University of Oklahoma Press, 1971.

Leiter, Richard A., (ed.), *National Survey of State Laws.* First edition. Detroit: Gale Research, 1997.

Perdue, Theda, (ed.), *Nations Remembered: An Oral History of the Cherokees, Chickasaws, Choctaws, Creeks, and Seminoles, 1865–1907.* Norman: University of Oklahoma Press, 1993.

United States Department of Education, *Digest of Educational Statistics.* Washington D.C., United States Department of Education, 1997.

TEXAS

STATE HISTORY

Before the Europeans arrived in the region, Texas was inhabited by several tribes of Native-Americans. In the western part of the state were the Apaches and Comanches. The Tonkawa lived in the central regions of present-day Texas, the Karankawa resided along the gulf areas, and throughout the eastern region were the Caddo, Cherokee, Alabama, and the Conshatta.

The Caddo tribe of east Texas and other surrounding regions historically included the Hasinai, Kadohadacho, and Natchitoche alliances of Native-Americans. They hunted deer, bear, and other small game in east Texas. In addition, they made visits to the Gulf Coast, where they enjoyed dining on turtles and sea bird eggs. Also, expeditions to the southern plains produced supplies of buffalo meat. Another part of the Caddoan diet were the vegetable and fruit crops which were cultivated.

Like many other Native-American groups, the Caddoans made good use of the drum in the tribal dance and ceremonial functions. One example is the Turkey Dance. The drum is placed in the midst of the dancing area and the men singers are placed around the drum. The women dancers dance in a circle, moving on the balls of their feet in a clockwise direction.

The European immigrants to the region recognized the Caddoans as the dominant tribe in the region between the Mississippi and Rio Grande Rivers. Also, they got along well with the other Native-American tribes nearby. Eventually the tribe was removed to Oklahoma.

When the Pilgrims first landed at Plymouth Rock, Texas had already encountered Europeans and Africans for close to one century. First were the Spaniards who claimed much of the present state boundaries for Spain. However, discouraging reports from Hernando de Soto and Francisco Vásquez de Coronado tended to minimize much of the interest in Texas. The French moved into the area and René-Robert Cavelier, Sieur de La Salle claimed the Texas area for France in 1682. Fort Saint Louis was established in 1685. At that time the Spanish became motivated to take possession of their Texas province.

During much of the eighteenth century, Spanish activities in Texas fluctuated, depending on what was happening between Spain and France. By the end of this century, San Antonio, Goliad, and Nacogdoches were the only permanent Spanish settlements in present-day Texas. And by 1800, France had gained control of the area, only to sell it to the United States as part of the Louisiana Purchase agreement. However, the United States had a shaky claim on the territory because the southern boundaries were so vaguely defined.

In 1810, the Mexican Revolution era began when Father Miguel Hidalgo y Costilla sounded a battle cry known as "El Grito de Dolores." Finally, by 1821 the Mexicans were successful in acquiring their independence from Spain. During the following era, Moses Austin of Connecticut was given a grant by the

Mexican-Texans to settle 300 European-American families in the area. His son, Stephen F. Austin, continued the colonization effort and by 1835, approximately 20,000 European-American settlers and some 4,000 slaves had moved into the area. This influx of European-American interests convinced Mexican authorities that the United States had designs on conquering the Mexican Texan regions.

After the European-American settlers captured the Mexican stronghold at San Antonio, they were later annihilated in the famous "Battle of the Alamo," which occurred in 1836. However, this victory was short-lived, as General Sam Houston and his troops prevailed in a European-American victory at San Jacinto, a short time later. Texas declared itself to be an independent nation called the Lone Star Republic. This was the status of Texas until 1845, when it became part of the United States. The ensuing Mexican War ended in 1848, with the Treaty of Guadalupe Hidalgo. At that time, the Rio Grande River became the boundary between the two nations.

By the late 1850s, Texas wrestled with the slavery issues, along with the rest of the nation. Sam Houston, twice president of the Lone Star Republic and a Texas senator between 1846 and 1859, sided with the Union. His election to the governorship in 1859 became unpopular and the secessionists were successful in defeating his attempts to stay with the Union. He was deposed in 1861, after Texas seceded from the Union.

During the war, Texas supplied troops to the Confederate cause, but there was almost no fighting on Texas soil. Union sympathizers were persecuted and run out of the state and in some cases, Texas troops even invaded Arizona and New Mexico, but were driven off. Texas ports were blockaded by Union troops, but interestingly, the last battle of the war resulted in a Confederate victory near Brownsville. Shortly after, Lee surrendered at Appomatox.

Following the end of hostilities, Texas was occupied by Union troops and attempts by the state's strong right-wing faction to hold freed slaves in bondage was thwarted by Congress. Finally, Texas was readmitted to the Union in 1870. But throughout the state's history, Texas had attracted a number of adventurers, social misfits, and even criminals. In order to provide a suitable law enforcement organization, the Texas Rangers were created to make the state a safer place to live. The state's greatest assets were its vast acreage and cattle. Consequently, the cattle industry thrived and the population had increased dramatically by the turn of the century. Unfortunately, at the time, only ten percent of the school-age children in the state attended school, and the first compulsory attendance law was not passed until 1915.

By the beginning of the twentieth century, the state's economy had bounced back, thanks to the cattle industry and the growing cotton market. In addition, agricultural developments in the Rio Grande Valley and sizable oil discoveries created enormous fortunes and also aided the state's economy. During the decade starting in 1908, prohibition was a major topic of discussion in Texas, and the state ratified the national prohibition amendment in 1918.

Unfortunately, the state's schools were segregated racially until well after the *Brown v. Board of Education* decision, resulting in drastically inferior schooling for African-American children. Also, Latino children suffered greatly from the same educational problems. Texas was also suffering from the influences of conservatives who were successful in undoing the meager public education beginnings which occurred during Reconstruction.

During World War II, the state was able to turn around the economic setbacks suffered during the Great Depression. Following the war, Texas was the site of a landmark Supreme Court decision, with the *Sweatt v. Painter* case. The University of Texas was still racially segregated in 1950 when the plaintiff, Sweatt, attempted to enroll in the University's law school. Due to the state's segregation practices, the University refused to allow his entry to the "whites only" law school, but attempted to create a special school just for him. As can be expected, the facilities were decidedly inferior and violated the concept of "separate but equal," which was established during the 1896 *Plessy v. Ferguson* Supreme Court decision. The University of Texas was ordered to enroll him in their existing law school because the new school for Sweatt was not "equal" to the segregated school for European-Americans. It was one of the key decisions which led up to the *Brown v. Board of Education* decision of 1954.

The last half of the twentieth century saw numerous changes in Texas. The state's economy continued to grow and the population became more diversified with the arrival of new microcultures from around the world. However, the progress in race relations has tended to be somewhat slow. The natural resources in the state helped to create a more diversified economy as well.

THE EDUCATIONAL SYSTEM

A landmark Texas court case occurred in March, 1985, over the issue of home schooling. The Texas Education Agency announced that home instruction did not qualify for the private or parochial school exemption to the compulsory education law. About 150 truancy prosecutions were initiated against the families who refused to send their children to school. When the case finally reached the Texas Supreme Court, the ruling of the lower court was affirmed on the grounds that the Texas Education Agency's prosecutions constituted arbitrary enforcement and violated the fourteenth Amendment rights to due process and equal protection.

Presently, Texas requires school attendance between the ages of six and seventeen. Exceptions include children who are enrolled in private or parochial schools, which include a course in good citizenship. Also exempted are handicapped children, or children with a mental condition. Home schooling is presently allowed.

In order for teachers to become certified, it is necessary for them to pass a basic skills examination and be observed in successful in-class performances with children. The state has no statutory provisions related to the use of corporal punishment in the schools. Students have the absolute right to individually, voluntarily, and silently pray or meditate in a nondisruptive manner.

The per capita expenditures for elementary and secondary education in Texas are $951.31, compared to the national average of $931.76. While the state enjoys substantial wealth, it ranks as one of the ten lowest states in terms of the poverty status of children between the ages of five and seventeen. Compared to the national average of 19 percent, 23.1 percent of Texas children between those ages are below the poverty level.

Texas has a policy on year-round schools and a number of these exist. The state provided both full and half-day kindergartens. While 42 percent of the nation's teachers hold a master's degree, just 26.8 percent of Texas teachers have a master's degree. The state commissioner of education in Texas is appointed by the governor.

MULTICULTURAL EDUCATION EFFORTS

Responses to the authors' multicultural education questionnaire revealed that Texas has no multicultural education program, nobody is in charge of such enterprises, no state funding exists, and no leadership is provided to school districts in multicultural education.

The predominant microcultures in Texas are Latinos, African-Americans, Asians, and Native-Americans. No special coursework and/or multicultural experiences are required for teacher certification, and, for the most part, the state's curriculum tends to stress a cultural assimilation approach. Bilingual education programs are available for teaching students in their native language, whenever necessary.

Texas is under court order for desegregating their school districts. This is referred to by the name of Civil Action 5281, and it was originally issued in 1971. The Court Order required Texas to act at once to eliminate by positive means all vestiges of the dual school structure throughout the state and to compensate for the abiding scars of past discrimination.

During the past five years, the racist incidents have increased in Texas schools. This conclusion was based on the number of reported incidents, many of which were racist epithets. The respondent also reported that inadequate accounts of Native-American history are included in the state's regular curriculum.

The Texas Office of Education does evaluate curriculum materials, library materials, and textbooks for racist and/or sexist statements.

The respondent replied that the biggest problem facing multicultural education in Texas is the fear of the non-European-American microcultures by European-American Texans. Another major problem was reported to be the changing demographics, namely the growing number of persons of color throughout the state.

It was felt by the respondent that the biggest improvement in the state's multicultural education program would be to require multicultural education coursework for teacher certification. Other needed improvements included requiring multicultural inservice training of all prospective teachers and requiring that teachers employ multicultural teaching approaches in their classrooms.

REFERENCES

Council of Chief State School Officers, *The Council.* Washington D.C.: Council of Chief State School Officers, 1998.

Dorsey, George, *Traditions of the Caddo.* Washington D.C.: Carnegie Institute of Washington, 1905.

Frantz, Joe B., *Texas: A Bicentennial History.* New York: W. W. Norton, 1976.

Fuermann, Conner George, *The Reluctant Empire.* Garden City: Doubleday, 1957.

John, Elizabeth A., *Storm Brewed in Other Men's Worlds; The Confrontation of the Indians, Spanish, and French in the Southwest, 1540–1795.* College Station: Texas A & M University Press, 1975.

Leiter, Richard A., (ed.), *National Survey of State Laws.* First edition. Detroit: Gale Research, 1997.

Meredith, Howard, *Southern Plains Alliances.* Lawrence: University Press of Kansas, 1994.

Richardson, Rupert N., et al., *Texas: The Lone Star State.* Englewood Cliffs, NJ: Prentice Hall, 1970.

Sweatt v. Painter, 339 U. S. 629, 70 S. Ct. 848 94L. Ed.1114 (1950).

United States Department of Education, *Digest of Educational Statistics.* Washington D.C.: United States Department of Education, 1997.

United States of America v. State of Texas, et al., Civil Action No. 5281, 1971.

Whitebead, Irving, and Meredith, Howard, "Nuh-Ka-Oashun: Hasinal Turkey Dance Tradition." In Smyth, Willie (ed.), *Songs of Indian Territory: Native-American Music Traditions of Oklahoma.* Oklahoma City: Center of the American Indian, 1989.

Zirkel, Perry A., "Home Sweet School." In *Phi Delta Kappan*, Vol. 76, No. 4 (1994), pp. 332–333.

UTAH

STATE HISTORY

Utah's history is unique because of its religious background, which makes it more like a theocracy than any of the other states. The region has also been referred to as "sagebrush country" by some writers, due to the fact that the *artemisia* is the single most widespread plant. And while the Church of Jesus Christ of Latter-Day Saints (Mormons) exhibited enormous influence in the State's history, prior to the time of the arrival of this European-American group, the state was inhabited with Native-Americans, particularly the Utes and Shoshones.

It is believed that as early as 9000 B. C., the area was inhabited by a nomadic desert culture. It is thought that originally, these people had no agricultural knowledge and only primitive tools. Eventually, these early inhabitants had contacts with more advanced groups from northern Mexico and a new culture commenced to unfold about the time of Christ. Referred to as the Anasazi by anthropologists, these residents acquired the techniques of agriculture and learned how to build permanent structures like the fabled apartment buildings of Mesa Verde and Chaco Canyon.

Members of the Uto-Aztecan language group, the Utes were nomadic hunters and gatherers who traveled in extended family groups. Their residences were usually brush huts or tipis whenever large game were available. Considered to be rather aggressive and warlike, the Utes were led by chiefs who were chosen on the basis of their hunting and raiding prowess.

The first contacts with Europeans were with the Spanish in New Mexico during the seventeenth century. These interactions were advantageous for the Utes, since they were able to acquire horses and arms in return for buckskins and their own Native-American captives. These captives often became slaves of the Spanish adventurers.

In addition to the Shoshone, who resided in the Salt Lake regions, other tribal members occupied much of Nevada, southern Idaho, and western Wyoming. Originally they resided in California's Death Valley regions. Generally they enjoyed peaceful relations with their Uto-Aztecan neighbors and quite cleverly made use of the available food supplies, such as plant seeds and the camas. In addition, they were skilled hunters and trappers of bighorn sheep and small game. They were forced to travel mostly by foot because food supplies were not available in large enough numbers to feed horses, due to the arid nature of the region.

While it is believed that Spanish explorers came to present-day Utah as early as 1540, the first known were Franciscan fathers Francisco Antonasio Dominguez and Silvestre Velez de Escalante, who, in 1776, headed a party searching for an overland route to Monterey, California. They provided historians with the first written description of the people and lands which comprise the present boundaries of the state.

Between 1820 and 1840, Canadian fur trappers came searching for skins and a number of "mountain men" arrived in the region as well. One of these mountain men was Jim Bridger, who may have been the first European-American to see the Salt Lake after its discovery by Native-Americans.

Further European-American involvement in Utah occurred in 1849 when the Mormons arrived in Utah, dubbing the area "State of Deseret." A constitution was drawn up, officials were elected and the State of Deseret applied for admission to the Union. However, as had been the customary practice in earlier times, the United States government designated the region as a Territory.

The Mormon religion was started by Joseph Smith. He was born in 1805 and grew up in New York State. His parents had occasionally worked as teachers, and the family tended to be somewhat economically challenged. By the time he was about fifteen years old, he had his first reported vision. At the time he had been mostly educated by his parents and was able to read. However, he had almost no formal education. In 1823 he reported another vision in which an angel visited him. A replica of this angel now adorns the Mormon Temple in Salt Lake City.

The church formally began in Fayette, New York. However, friction with their neighbors motivated a move to Kirtland, Ohio. After two stops in Missouri, they migrated to Nauvoo, Illinois. However, the murder of Joseph Smith motivated the Mormons to move again, this time to Utah under the leadership of Brigham Young. The move stemmed from a number of the Mormon's religious beliefs, particularly their adoption of polygamy.

When the Mormons arrived in Utah, the land had just become part of the United States as a result of the Treaty of Guadalupe Hidalgo, which granted the region to the United States. After their arrival, conflicts with the federal government ensued. Suspicious of their religious ideas, in 1857 President Buchanan replaced Brigham Young as governor with Alfred Cummings from Georgia. Also, 2,500 soldiers were sent to the region in order to monitor the actions of the Mormons. The troops remained at Fort Floyd until the Civil War and were later replaced by several hundred California volunteers. Their mission was to watch the Mormons and guard against troubles between the Native-Americans and the Mormons.

The turbulent history of the state centered around conflicts between the Mormons and Gentiles, Mormons and Native-Americans, and Mormons and federal government. These conflicts were partly political, partly religious, and partly economic. One incident which stirred up more anti-Mormon sentiment was an event known as the Mountain Meadow Massacre. The Mormons, not being particularly cordial toward Gentiles moving into the region, attacked the Fancher wagon train, which entered the Deseret State in 1857. Mormon militiamen, supposedly dressed up as Native-Americans, joined with Native-Americans and almost annihilated the members of the expedition. And while Protestant ministers, federal officials, and Gentiles found the Mormons to be frugal, mostly moral, and industrious, they were repulsed by the religious principle of plural marriage, which was sanctioned by the Mormon Church in 1852.

In 1852 the U. S. Congress passed a law disincorporating the Latter-Day Saints Church, preventing it from holding more than $50,000 worth of property, excluding their houses of worship. In this same piece of legislation, polygamy was made a crime. By 1890 the church yielded and announced the termination of plural marriages. The federal government then softened its anti-Mormon posture and statehood was granted in 1896.

Education in Utah had been mostly denominational until 1890. At that time, religious and public schools combined into one unit, which created a free and uniform public education system for the first time in history. The dominant Latter-Day Saints religious body created religious institutes which were located next to high schools and colleges. This practice still occurs in Utah, as well as other nearby states with large Mormon populations.

Another facet of the Mormon education program is the missionary requirement for young men. They are expected to spend two years of their lives in an attempt to recruit people to the Mormon religion. Special efforts take place in Central and South America, as well as South Sea Island locales such as American Samoa and Hawaii. In addition to the United States, special efforts at conversion to Mormonism occur in other Spanish-speaking locales, such as Mexico and the Spanish-speaking regions of the United States. Interestingly, this practice has come under criticism by a number of non-Mormon universities, which argue that this two-year commitment provides an athletic advantage for predominantly Mormon universities such as Brigham Young, since their student-athletes often are two years older than the athletes in non-Mormon schools.

During the early part of the twentieth century, the Republican party dominated Utah politics. The state's politics were controlled by Senator Reed Smoot, a Republican. He won out over Senator Thomas Kearns, a Catholic mining millionaire. Then, in 1916, a Jewish businessman held forth for a short time. After Democratic New Dealers controlled the state's politics for a time, they were defeated by such conservatives as Governor J. Bracken Lee, who became a champion for the repeal of the nation's income tax laws.

THE EDUCATIONAL SYSTEM

Utah requires children to attend school between the ages of six and eighteen. Exceptions to this requirement include children who have completed all the work for graduation from high school and children who are at least sixteen years of age, who may be excluded from the requirements in certain circumstances. Also, it is possible for children to be excluded from the compulsory education requirement if they are home-schooled or if their physical and/or mental condition makes public school attendance impracticable. Also excluded from attendance are children whose employment provides proper influences and adequate educational opportunities. Interestingly, Utah does not require children to attend school if they are unable to profit from it because of a negative attitude toward discipline.

The state has no statutory provisions regarding the use of corporal punishment in the schools and likewise, no statutory provisions are in place relative to the use of prayer in the schools.

In order to become a certificated teacher in Utah, it is first necessary to be observed in successful in-class teaching performances. Utah's per capita expenditures for elementary and secondary school education are $874.29 somewhat below the national average of $931.76.

Utah has a state policy on year-round schools and many schools in the state have such programs in operation. School districts are required to provide half-day kindergarten programs and special education services for all students between the ages of three and twenty-one.

Utah's state superintendent of education is appointed by the State Board of Education. Compared to the national average of 42 percent, just 23.5 percent of Utah's teachers hold a master's degree. Only four other states have a lower percentage.

MULTICULTURAL EDUCATION EFFORTS

Utah's questionnaire respondent stated that the state had no multicultural education program. Nobody is in charge of such programs, and no funding is available for multicultural education. However, it was reported that the State Office of Instruction conducts training sessions in race, cultural, and bias awareness for teachers and administrators. Also, the respondent reported that bilingual/ESL endorsement classes included multicultural elements. The predominant microcultures in the state were reported to be Latinos, Asians, Pacific Islanders, and Native-Americans.

Another requirement for Utah teacher certification is a special course in multicultural education. Prospective teachers must complete a course entitled "Teaching Minority Students in Public Schools."

Regarding the issue of cultural pluralism versus cultural assimilation, the respondent replied that most school districts tended to require a cultural pluralism approach to the curriculum. However, it was stated that in the more rural areas there was still a tendency to subscribe to a cultural assimilation emphasis.

It was stipulated in the 1998 questionnaire responses that Utah had no special programs for teaching children in their native languages, when appropriate.

The issue of racial segregation in Utah has been almost a nonissue throughout the state's history because of the predominant European-American population. However, when necessary, it was stated that Utah has been able to comply with the 1954 *Brown v. Board of Education* Supreme Court decision by simply adjusting the boundaries.

It was reported that Utah had an increase in racist incidents in recent years. The history of Native-Americans is included in the state's regular curriculum, particularly in the fourth and seventh-grade social studies textbooks. Also, it was reported that Utah's Office of Education evaluates curriculum materials, textbooks, and library materials for the possible inclusion of racist and/or sexist statements.

In response to the last two questions, the respondent felt that the biggest problems facing multicultural education programs in Utah was the lack of a state policy on diversity and/or multiculturalism in the core curriculum and in teacher education requirements.

The greatest improvements in Utah's multicultural education efforts would be to find ways to get more teachers and administrators to understand the difference between multiculturalism and ethnocentrism, in order to increase the number of educators who advocate for the proper philosophical approach in infusing the existing core with multicultural concepts and strategies.

REFERENCES

Arrington, Leonard J. and Bitton, Davis. *The Mormon Experience: A History of the Latter-Day Saints.* New York: Alfred A. Knopf, 1979.

Council of Chief State School Officers, *The Council.* Washington D.C.: Council of Chief State School Officers, 1998.

Delaney, Robert, *The Ute Mountain Utes.* Albuquerque: University of New Mexico Press, 1989.

Fradkin, Philip, *Sagebrush Country: Land and the American West.* New York: Alfred A. Knopf, 1989.

Larson, Gustive O., *The Americanization of Utah for Statehood.* San Marino, CA: The Huntington Library, 1971.

Leiter, Richard A., (ed.), *National Survey of State Laws.* First edition. Detroit: Gale Research, 1997.

Markowitz, Harvey, (ed.), *American Indians.* Pasadena, CA: Salem Press, 1995.

Peterson, Charles S., *Utah: A History.* New York: W. W. Norton, 1977.

Rockwell, Wilson, *The Utes: A Forgotten People.* Denver: Sage Books, 1956.

Stegner, Wallace, *Mormon Country.* Lincoln: University of Nebraska Press, 1981.

United State Department of Education, *Digest of Educational Statistics.* Washington, D.C.: United States Department of Education, 1997.

VERMONT

STATE HISTORY

The Algonquian tribes, along with other tribal groups who were members of the Iroquois confederacy, were the original residents of Vermont. They were there to greet Samuel de Champlain when he became the first known European to see the lake which has his name. Originally the Algonquians populated the regions, which became eastern Canada, along with the northeastern regions of the United States, including the present boundaries of Vermont.

The Algonquians were also enemies of the Iroquois confederacy groups and sided with the French in their military alliances and trade enterprises. On the other hand, the members of the Iroquois confederacy tended to ally themselves with the British. Consequently, the history of Native-Americans in Vermont must include the involvement of both groups.

However, the Algonquian groups declined dramatically by the colonization efforts by the British, and the aggressiveness of the Iroquois caused this group to decline in strength by the end of the seventeenth century. And 100 years later, much of the Algonquian culture had undergone dramatic changes.

One of the earliest forts in Vermont was constructed by the French in 1666. Fort Ste. Anne was erected on the Isle La Motte. Later in the same century, a small fort was created by Captain Jacobus de Warm of Albany, at Chimney Point in Vermont's Addison County. These French Forts prevailed until the British prevailed in the French and Indian War, which ended in 1763.

After Montreal fell in 1760, many European-Canadians commenced moving into Vermont, and England took control of the region in 1763, as a result of their victory over France in the just concluded war. Governor Benning Wentworth offered land grants west of the Connecticut River in an area which was then called the New Hampshire grants by New Hampshire. Resistance to these grants became organized when Ethan Allen organized the Green Mountain Boys, who were strong enough to defend their region and also brazen enough to punish persons who had acquired these grants.

When word of the conflicts at Lexington reached Vermont, Ethan Allen, aided by Benedict Arnold, captured Fort Ticonderoga. Unfortunately, Vermont forces took part in an ill-advised expedition into Canada, resulting in the capture of Allen near Montreal. The British concocted a plan to separate New England from New York and were successful in moving toward that goal when General Burgoyne recaptured Fort Ticonderoga and commenced driving toward Albany. This led to the only battle in the Revolutionary War, which was fought on Vermont soil, the Battle of Bennington.

The Green Mountain Boys recorded a major victory when they defeated the British and captured many military supplies at Bennington. Also participating in the victory for the colonists was Brigadier General John Stark's New Hampshire command, as well as elements of the Massachusetts militia.

When Vermont declared its independence from Britain in 1777, it called itself "New Connecticut" but soon after, the name "Vermont" was adopted and a constitution was drawn up which excluded the enslavement of African-Americans and granted universal suffrage for men only. In those days, Vermont carried on a great deal of trade with Canada. At this time, the state provided for a school or schools in each town and a grammar school in each county. Vermont's first school law was enacted in 1782 and school districts were created at that time.

For a while, it was thought that New York and New Hampshire would divide Vermont, with each state taking over certain portions. However, in 1791, Vermont was admitted to the Union as the new nation's fourteenth state. It formerly had been an independent republic and was admitted, along with Kentucky, in an attempt to balance the northern and southern interests.

During the War of 1812, Britain attempted to divide New York from New England by creating a wedge between the two regions through the Champlain Valley. Vermont was saved from British occupation when Thomas MacDonough put together a fleet which achieved a major victory over the British at Plattsburgh in 1814. After that period, the state began to develop a rather strong antislavery stance and displayed very little interest in the Mexican War.

Between the end of the War of 1812 and the beginning of the Civil War, the Champlain Canal created a new transportation system by connecting the Champlain valley with the Hudson River. Also during this era, Vermont's transportation system was expanded with the development of turnpikes and the state's rail system. Much of the rail labor was supplied by Irish-Americans.

During the Civil War, Vermont responded by sending 34,328 men to fight with the Union armies. But in spite of the dedication of the Vermont soldiers, no Civil War battles were fought on Vermont soil. However, Vermont's soldiers were highly regarded and received many commendations for their participation in the victorious effort.

After the war, immigrants from Scotland and Italy came to Vermont, along with a small number of Poles. They followed the early settlers who came from Connecticut, New Hampshire, Massachusetts, and New York.

In 1881, Chester A. Arthur was the first vice-president to be elected from the state of Vermont. Shortly afterward, President Garfield was assassinated and Arthur became Vermont's first president of the United States. During the Spanish-American War, Vermont Admiral George Dewey from Montpelier, became famous because of his victory at Manila Bay.

During World War I, some 16,000 Vermonters served in the armed forces and about 642 of them were killed in battle. Shortly later, Calvin Coolidge became the second Vermonter elected to the presidency. The state has always been considered to be mostly Republican, but in 1958, Vermont elected its first Democratic congressman in 106 years. And in 1964, the state voted for its first Democratic presidential candidate since 1824, when its electoral votes went to Lyndon Johnson. In 1985, Madeline Kunin was elected the first female governor of Vermont.

THE EDUCATIONAL SYSTEM

Vermont is one of the New England states which historically has placed a high value on its citizens becoming highly educated. In order to accomplish this, the concept of education for everyone grew up with its early history. Today, the state's educational system is directed by the state commissioner of education, who is appointed by the State Board of Education.

School attendance is compulsory between the ages of seven and sixteen. Exceptions to the requirement include children who are physically or mentally incapable of attending and children who have completed at least the tenth grade. Also, school superintendents have the capacity to excuse students from school attendance. Home schooling is also allowed.

Vermont does not allow the use of corporal punishment in the schools as a means of disciplining students. However, necessary and reasonable force may be utilized in order to quell a disturbance or obtain possession of a weapon. Reasonable and necessary force can also be used in self defense or for the protection of persons or property. Vermont has no statutory provisions related to the issue of prayer in the schools.

In order for teachers to become certified to teach, they must complete a teacher education program and be observed in successful in-class teaching performances.

Vermont enjoys one of the nation's lowest percentages of children under age 17 who are in poverty. Compared to the national average of 19 percent, just 13 percent of Vermont's children in this age group find themselves in poverty circumstances. Only twelve other states have a lower poverty rate. The state spends $955.41 per capita on elementary and secondary education, slightly above the national average.

More than 47 percent of Vermont's teachers hold a master's degree. This compares with the national average of 42 percent. Nearly 9 percent of the state's residents over the age of twenty-five have completed graduate or professional degrees, compared with the national average of just over 7 percent. Only six other states have a higher percentage. The national average is 7.2 percent.

MULTICULTURAL EDUCATION EFFORTS

Vermont does not have a formal multicultural education program and nobody is responsible for such efforts. No funding for multicultural programs is available. However, it should be noted that the respondent to the authors' 1998 questionnaire stipulated that the state provides technical assistance, consultation, training, and materials/resources for schools. These services are funded by federal monies (Title IV Civil Rights, and Title VII Bilingual Support Services).

Vermont does provide leadership in multicultural education to school districts in specific kinds of multicultural education programs. This usually takes the form of Title IV services, which have focused on gender/race equity activities. However, because of Congressional funding cuts during 1996–1997, these have not continued.

The predominant microcultures in Vermont were said to be Franco-Americans, Vietnamese-Americans, Bosnian- and Russian-Americans, and

Latinos. No mention was made of the Native-American and other European-American groups.

While the state does not have special coursework and/or other multicultural experiences for multicultural education, the Vermont State Board of Education gave approval to an English as a Second Language (ESL) K-12 endorsement, which requires coursework and/or multicultural experiences for those persons teaching limited English proficiency students. The Vermont respondent also stated that the state has certain competencies that are required of all educators. The candidate must understand how individuals and groups differ. Also, they must be able to create equitable instructional opportunities that respond to the needs of all children. It is up to the teacher training institutions as to what special coursework and multicultural experiences are required in their teacher preparation programs.

Vermont does not stress cultural pluralism in its curriculum and instruction efforts and there are no special programs to teach children in their native language. Also, it was stipulated that school desegregation is not much of an issue in Vermont.

Racist incidents were reported to have increased throughout the state in recent years. A possible reason given for the increase is that there is more diversity in Vermont and several newspaper articles have focused on racist incidents that have occurred in school settings. While the respondent also replied that the history of Native-Americans was not included in the state's regular curriculum, it should be pointed out that there is no specific "state curriculum" in Vermont. Rather, there is a Framework of Standards and Learning Opportunities which schools use in developing their own curriculum.

Vermont's Office of Education evaluates curriculum materials and textbooks for racist and sexist content. These materials must coincide with Vermont's Framework of Standards and Learning Opportunities.

In response to the question asking what are the biggest problems facing multicultural education in Vermont, the reply was that it is not seen as something that needs to be infused into the curriculum of the schools. Also, there is little emphasis on the development of multicultural competencies for multicultural teaching.

The respondent felt that the biggest need in multicultural education programs was to create an emphasis on diversity (race, gender, language, and national origin), which would become a part of all the state's school reform efforts.

REFERENCES

Ballantine, Betty, and Thomas, David Hurst, (eds.), *The Native-Americans: An Illustrated History.* Atlanta: Turner Publishing, 1993.

Council of Chief State School Officers, *The Council.* Washington D.C.: Council of Chief State School Officers, 1998

Jellison, Charles A., *Ethan Allen: Frontier Rebel.* Syracuse; Syracuse University Press, 1969.

Jones, Matt Bushnell, *Vermont in the Making , 1750–1777.* Cambridge: Harvard University Press, 1939.

Leiter, Richard A., (ed.), *National Survey of State Laws*. First edition. Detroit: Gale Research, 1997.

Ludlum, David M., *Social Ferment in Vermont, 1791–1850*. New York: AMS Press, 1966.

Morrissey, Charles T., *Vermont,* New York: W. W. Norton, 1981.

Newcomb, William W., *North American Indians: An Anthropological Perspective*. Pacific Palisades, CA: Goodyear, 1974.

Trigger, Bruce, (ed.), "Northeast." In *Handbook of North American Indians* Volume 15. Washington, D.C.: Smithsonian Institution Press, 1978.

United States Department of Education, *Digest of Educational Statistics*. Washington D.C.: United States Department of Education, 1997.

VIRGINIA

STATE HISTORY

Virginia's colorful history commences with the Powhatan confederacy, which consisted of about thirty tribes located throughout the state. Some of the more prominent groups were the Chickahominy, Gingaskin, Mattaponi, Nansemond, Nottoway, Pamuniey, Patawomeck (Potomac), Rappahannock, Weyanoke, and the Wicconcomicos. These Powhatan groups, under the leadership of their famous chief, Powhatan, met Captain John Smith and his Jamestown settlers in 1607. After his brother Opechancanough captured Smith, Powhatan chose not to execute him for reasons that are not clearly understood.

Moreover, Powhatan allowed Pocahontas, his favorite daughter, to visit the British settlement. Smith claimed that she actually saved his life. When his daughter was later taken prisoner as a hostage, she converted to the Anglican Church of England and married John Rolfe.

When the Europeans arrived, the members of the Powhatan confederacy had already acquired their skills in agriculture. The women were responsible for planting crops, while the men hunted and foraged. While each one of the confederated groups had their own chief (Weroance), they all swore their allegiance to Powhatan.

However, Powhatan's brother Opechancanough became disgruntled with the British encroachments and their attempts to assimilate the Powhatan confederacy members into the dominant British culture. After the English murdered a highly regarded warrior in 1622, Opechancanough successfully prevailed upon the members of the confederacy to launch an attack on the British, resulting in the deaths of nearly one third of Virginia's English-American population. However, successful English counterattacks resulted in the destruction of crops and the burning of villages, which ultimately led to the defeat of the Native-Americans. While a truce was consummated in 1632, hostilities broke out again in 1644, when Opechancanough, estimated to be 100 years old, prevailed on the Confederacy once again. Again the English were victorious, having about 8,000 English-Americans in Virginia by this time. The old chief was murdered by a guard after his capture, and a new treaty was negotiated two years later.

These English victories ended the hostilities between the Native-Americans and the English settlers in Virginia. The Powhatan confederacy deemed further resistance to be futile, since by 1670 the English-American population was estimated to be about 40,000.

Ten years later, the English settlers commenced importing African slaves to work in the tobacco fields, which were becoming one of the area's staple crops. John Rolfe had observed the Native-Americans using tobacco, but their leaves did not quite satisfy the English-Americans. After securing the large-leaf *Nicotiana tabacum* plants from the West Indies, the new industry generated an interest in Europe, and the industry was on its way. Of course, as the industry grew, so did the need for cheap labor in order for the tobacco entrepreneurs to maximize their profits.

By 1670, the Virginia colony, presided over by governor Sir William Berkeley, had an estimated population of better than 40,000, including 6,000 indentured servants and 2,000 African slaves. This compares with the 1642 slave population of about 600.

During the eighteenth century, large numbers of Irish, Scotch-Irish, and German persons commenced to arrive in the state of Virginia, causing the population to acquire a slightly more multicultural flavor. Gradually, Virginia began to develop an aristocratic society, which was patterned after the English country-gentry society. These aristocrats lived well and amassed large fortunes through land speculation and the acquisition of increasing numbers of African slaves.

By 1753, incompatible claims between the British and French motivated Virginia's governor Robert Dinwiddie to send young George Washington to warn the French away from the region. However, Washington's attempts did not result in any significant changes in the situation. A number of conflicts between the French and Indians, which heavily involved the Native-Americans as well, led up to the beginning of the American Revolution against Britain.

In 1775, during the Second Continental Congress, George Washington was elected commander in chief of the Continental Army. However, at this time, most Virginians opted for a reconciliatory action with the British, not wishing to become involved with the radical pronunciations of Thomas Jefferson, Patrick Henry, and others.

And even though Virginian Thomas Jefferson's Declaration of Independence was adopted in 1776, the colony had little involvement with the Revolution except for supplying troops. But after the Revolution, Virginia supplied more than its share of fine statesmen, including such stalwarts as Benedict Arnold, George Rogers Clark, not to mention its presidents.

But by 1780, Virginia was so short of troops for the Revolutionary cause, that Benedict Arnold was able to destroy Virginia's capital at Richmond in 1781. However, after Cornwallis was unable to defeat Lafayette's army later that year, he finally surrendered at Yorktown.

For the first four decades of the new national period, Virginia dominated the political scene. Washington served the first two terms as president and between 1801 and 1825, Jefferson, Madison, and Monroe served presidential terms. Also, for more than three decades in the first half of the 1800s, Virginia's John Marshall served as chief justice of the United States Supreme Court.

Virginia's actions during the Civil War are quite well documented. Leading up to that event, the Nat Turner revolt led to the death of some sixty Virginia-Americans, and this became one of the important events leading up to the Civil War. While Virginians tended to view the action as a despicable and unprecedented slave uprising, abolitionists tended to regard it as yet another example of the evils of slavery.

Virginians were hostile to the northern abolitionists, even though they tended to disagree with the strong proslavery stance of South Carolina and a few other southern states, which also were strongly proslavery. And even though the

John Brown raid on Harper's Ferry actually occurred in West Virginia, this and other incidents motivated most Virginians to reluctantly secede from the Union.

During the Civil War, Virginia found itself right in the middle of many Civil War confrontations. Serious fighting erupted in the Battle of Bull Run and Ball's Bluff. The state also was the site of such famous battles as Bull Run, Antietam, Fredericksburg, Chancellorsville, and Gettysburg. And when the hostilities finally were over, Virginia was devastated. It had been the center of military operations for the Confederacy and gave one of its favorite sons, General Robert E. Lee, to the Confederate effort.

The end of the war and the era of Reconstruction saw Virginia reeling from deflated land prices and other economic hardships. In addition, many of its traditional mores were changing, and it was estimated that the war and the Reconstruction period following the termination of hostilities cost the state some 150 million dollars in damages. At that time, Virginia's population was about 700,000 European-Americans and about 500,000 African-Americans. The state was readmitted to the Union in 1870.

However, by the end of the nineteenth century, Virginia had commenced to recover economically and spiritually. But in spite of agricultural diversification and a new rail economy, Virginia still lagged behind the nation in per capita income until World War I revitalized the economy even more.

Virginia maintained a racially segregated society in its social institutions, particularly the schools, until after the 1954 *Brown v. Board of Education* Supreme Court decision. In spite of the desegregation edict, the state fought for illegally-segregated schools until finally meeting the demands for school integration, which occurred minimally in the late 1950s. However, Virginia adopted a plan to fund private "white" schools through the issuance of tax credits. This practice was declared to be unconstitutional in 1964 (*Griffin v. County School Board*, 377 U. S. 218 (1964). By the same year, the poll tax for federal elections was ended and two years later the poll tax requirements for state elections met the same fate, thanks to a United States Supreme Court decision.

During the last half of the twentieth century, Virginia grew faster than the nation and maintained its strongly conservative posture. Christian conservatives, such as Jerry Falwell and Oliver North, attracted large followings and the state's economic development was enhanced by the growth of military and federal agencies.

THE EDUCATIONAL SYSTEM

Since its early days of colonization, Virginia has had a strong history of private schools. This lasted throughout much of the nineteenth century. Thus, it is interesting that Thomas Jefferson, a Virginian, was an advocate for the development of public schools in the United States. It was not until the mid-1800s that some state funds were finally made available for public schools. However, there was no constitutional legislation until 1869 and due to political bickering, no adequate public school funding was made available until the 1902 constitution.

Virginia's state superintendent of schools is appointed by the governor. Teacher certification requires candidates to acquire a passing score on the National

Teacher Examination, exhibit basic skills competency, and be observed in successful in-class teaching performances.

Children must attend school between the ages of five and eighteen. Exceptions to this requirement include children who are enrolled in private or parochial schools, and children who are involved in home instruction taught by a qualified tutor. However, in order for parents to home school their children, they must hold a baccalaureate degree, be a certificated teacher, or use an approved correspondence course or other approved programs. Approved achievement tests must be administered to the home-schooled children.

Special education services are provided by the public schools for Virginia children between three and twenty-one years of age. Corporal punishment is prohibited in Virginia schools. Schools may establish the daily observance of one minute of silence and voluntary student-initiated prayer is allowed.

The state provides funding for elementary and secondary education at the rate of $880.16 per capita. This compares to the national average of $931.76 per capita, placing Virginia somewhat below the national level.

Although Virginia has no policy regarding year-round schools, there are such entities in some of the state's school districts. Virginia provides both half-day and all-day kindergartens and attendance is required.

More than 9 percent of Virginians over the age of twenty-five have attained graduate or professional degrees, which places them sixth in the nation in that category. Compared to the national average of 42 percent, 64.4 percent of Virginia's teachers hold a master's degree. Only seven other states have a higher percentage.

Virginia does not have a major poverty problem among its youth under the age of seventeen years. Compared to the national average of 19 percent, 14.5 percent of Virginia's children find themselves in this predicament.

MULTICULTURAL EDUCATION EFFORTS

While Virginia does have a program director for educational equity, the state has no multicultural education program, nobody in charge of such ventures, and no state funding is provided. However, the state does provide leadership in specific kinds of multicultural education through Title IV funding, which allows the Equity Education Office to assist school districts as requests are made for multicultural assistance.

The state's predominant microcultures were listed as African-American, Latino, Asian/Pacific Islanders, and Native-Americans. The respondent stipulated that special coursework and/or other multicultural experiences were required for teacher certification, but these were limited to English as a Second Language programs.

Virginia's curriculum tends to stress a philosophy of cultural pluralism rather than assimilation. There are no special programs designed to teach children in their native language when needed, except when special circumstances warrant it.

In order to racially desegregate schools, Virginia now provides limited busing, magnet schools, boundary changes, and incentives to attract students into predominantly minority districts. Some school districts in Virginia are under court order to become racially desegregated.

The respondent replied that racist incidents had increased during the past five years, and the history of Native-Americans is included in the state's regular curriculum, Virginia does evaluate curriculum materials, library materials, and textbooks for racist and sexist statements.

The biggest problems facing multicultural education programs in Virginia were reported to be the conservative political climate and the pervasive attitude that multicultural studies are not viewed as being necessary for student achievement or success in life. The biggest improvement would be to have multicultural education become a major part of the Virginia Standards of Learning Curricular Design and to be valued, supported, and endorsed by the top educational and political leadership.

REFERENCES

Ashe, Dora J., (ed.), *Four Hundred Years of Virginia, 1584–1984: An Anthology.* Lanham, MD: University Press of America, 1985.

Council of Chief State School Officers, *The Council.* Washington, D.C.: Council of Chief State School Officers, 1998.

Dabney, Virginius, *Virginia: The New Dominion.* Garden City: Doubleday, 1971.

Leiter, Richard A., (ed.), *National Survey of State Laws.* First edition. Detroit: Gale Research, 1997.

Moger, Allen W., Virginia: *Bourbonism to Byrd, 1870–1925.* Charlottesville: University Press of Virginia, 1968.

Morton, Richard L., *Colonia Virginia.* Chapel Hill: University of North Carolina Press, 1960.

Roundtree, Helen C., *Pocahontas's People: The Powhatan Indians of Virginia Through Four Centuries.* Norman: University of Oklahoma Press, 1990.

Roundtree, Helen C., *The Powhatan Indians of Virginia: Their Traditional Culture.* Norman: University of Oklahoma Press, 1989.

Rubin, Louis D. Jr., *Virginia: A Bicentennial History.* New York: W. W. Norton, 1977.

United States Department of Education, *Digest of Educational Statistics.* Washington D.C.: United States Department of Education, 1997.

Williams, Walter L., (ed.), *Southeastern Indians Since the Removal Era.* Athens: University of Georgia Press, 1979.

Zirkel, Perry A., and Richardson, Sharon Nalbone, *A Digest of Supreme Court Decisions Affecting Education.* Bloomington: Phi Delta Kappa Educational Foundation, 1988.

WASHINGTON

STATE HISTORY

Like the other Pacific states, Washington is geographically really two states. The Cascade range created not only two separate climates, but different life styles as well. On the eastern side of the state live the Yakimas, Cayuse, Nez Perce, Okanogan, Spokane, and Cayuse, while the numerous coastal tribes consist of the Chinook, Clallam, Clatsop, Nisqually, Nooksack, Lummis, and Puyallup.

The Lummi, members of the Salishan language group, resided on the San Juan Islands and the northern Puget Sound mainland regions. Their tribal economy was based on various types of seafood, which provided the tribe with an extremely tasty diet, as well as a good livelihood. They fished for sockeye salmon, which they caught in their nets from canoes. Herring, dogfish, codfish, and silver salmon were also caught, as were ducks in underwater nets, and clams, and crabs as well.

The Lummi were also famous for their use of the longhouse for living quarters. They traded with other tribes from the White River to the Fraser River in Canada. One of the first known Europeans in Washington was Bruno Heceta, a Spanish navigator, who sailed up the Pacific coast from California and around the mouth of the Columbia River in 1775. Many historians refute the claim of Juan de Fuca as being the first European to have discovered the famous strait that is named after him.

By 1827 a Hudson's Bay post was established in the region and by the 1850s, European-American settlers commenced encroaching on the Lummi territories. These European-Americans participated in the usual episodes that robbed the Native-Americans of their homeland. Also, they brought diseases for which the Lummis had no immunity.

The tribe was provided a reservation near Bellingham and has experienced a cultural renaissance in recent years. In addition, the Lummi tribe has created an aquaculture program which is designed to raise selected seafoods which are in short supply. During the past two decades, part of their aquacultural efforts has centered around an attempt to grow Maine lobsters. Also, the Lummis' self-governing program has enabled them to break away from their control by the Bureau of Indian Affairs.

An example of one of the eastern tribes are the Spokanes of northeastern Washington. Members of the Salishan language group, the Spokanes are actually a relatively small tribe with a population of just 2,118, based on the 1990 census. The tribe was first mentioned in the writings of Captains Meriwether Lewis and William Clark, in their famous trek to the mouth of the Columbia River in 1805, and David Thompson of the Northwest Fur Company. They were excellent fishermen, taking advantage of the Kettle Falls on the Columbia River and the Spokane Falls in present-day Spokane, Washington. And in addition to gathering food products, they were also known to travel clear to the plains areas in search of bison, even before the introduction of the horse. Culturally, the tribe was known for its sweathouse activities, as well as shamanism, vision quest, and tutelary spirits.

Uncontrolled encroachments by adventurous European-American miners and other settlers eventually resulted in warfare. Unfortunately, this incurred the wrath of Colonel George Wright, who attacked the tribe, destroying their livestock, horses, farms, and crops. As a result of Wright's actions, nearly a quarter of a century later, the Spokane Indian Reservation was established a few miles northwest of the city of Spokane.

While the tribe was originally able to maintain many of their original tribal practices, events in 1911 (construction of Little Falls Dam), and 1935 (construction of the Grand Coulee Dam), negated a substantial portion of their cultural practices, due to the end of the annual migration of salmon to their spawning ground.

The Spokane reservation has become organized around a tribal council with headquarters, museum, community center, and tribal store located in Wellpinit, Washington. Most of the tribal children attend school in the Hunters School District. Pauline Flett, a member of the Spokane tribe, has been attempting to record the Salish language. Both Catholic and Protestant churches are located on the reservation. In addition to Flett, other prominent members of the Spokane reservation include Sherman Alexie, author of *The Lone Ranger and Tonto Fistfight in Heaven, Reservation Blues,* and *Indian Killer.*

The first known European-American settlement in present-day Washington occurred in 1791 at Neah Bay. The European settlers were a group of Spanish colonists. However, their efforts at colonization were rebuffed. And in 1810, the next group of would-be European settlers involved in fur trading established the Spokane House, a few miles northwest of Spokane's city boundaries. The trade involved John Jacob Astor's Pacific Fur Company.

After the fur traders, the missionaries followed. Marcus Whitman established one of the most famous missions near the present city of Walla Walla, in southeastern Washington. However, the Cayuse tribe, thinking that the Whitmans had brought their diseases with them, murdered Marcus and Narcissa Whitman.

By 1825 the Hudson's Bay Company had established Fort Vancouver, located just north of the Columbia River, in the present state of Washington. The earliest settlement north of the Columbia River was established at Tumwater in 1845. And just eight years later, the area north of the Columbia River and the 46th parallel was organized as the Washington Territory.

By 1867 the territorial legislature sent a message to the United States Congress pressing for statehood into the Union. However, it was not until 1889 that Washington was finally admitted to the Union. Due to the relatively isolated location of the state, growth was slow to come. For the west side, the pioneering and entrepreneurial efforts of Arthur Denny were instrumental in the founding of Seattle, on Elliott Bay in the Puget Sound. The site was chosen because of the water depth, which would allow larger ships to dock there. Denny arrived there after following the Oregon Trail to Portland in the mid-1800s.

Eastern Washington settlement by European-Americans occurred largely because of gold discoveries in 1855. Naturally, this influx of gold-hungry

European-Americans caused great consternation among the Native-American residents in the area between 1855 and 1859. The Cayuse War of 1847–1850 and the Yakima War of 1855, constitute two of the more major confrontations between the Native-Americans and the European-Americans, who were uninvited guests to their territories.

The Yakima War resulted from the large numbers of European-Americans who encroached upon Yakima lands in southcentral Washington. After an early victory by the Yakimas, Colonel George Wright entered the fray with his superior numbers and a truce was consummated in 1856. At the present time, Washington has twenty-six Reservations. Only California, Arizona, New Mexico, and Oklahoma have more. The Yakima Reservation is the state's largest.

When Oregon became a state in 1859, the Washington Territory was enlarged to include the portions of the Oregon Territory which were not included in the new state's boundaries.

During the Civil War, sentiment in Washington for statehood grew and in 1867, the territorial legislature sent a resolution to Congress urging admission. However, eleven years passed before a constitution was finally drawn up and Washington was finally admitted to the Union in 1889. By this time, the Great Northern rail line connected Washington with the East Coast.

Much of the growth in eastern Washington occurred because of the mineral deposits in northern Idaho. Spokane became known as a center for banking and investment operations. Pioneers such as James Glover became wealthy because of their banking, investing, and development operations. South of Spokane, the rich volcanic soil known as the "palouse", had the capacity to produce choice wheat at the rate of forty to fifty bushels an acre.

By 1910 Seattle had a population of nearly 250,000. The city had developed a solid industrial base and African-Americans had been moving into the region. At that time, there were seventy-seven African-American farms in the state and increasing numbers of African-Americans in the Puget Sound areas. Also, a substantial number of Asian-Americans were moving to the Puget Sound region, giving it a more multicultural flavor. Some of these residents were Chinese-Americans who had a history of working on the railroads.

However, throughout its history, eastern Washington has not had the multicultural populations that the west side of the state enjoys. It is highly rural and conservative politically and culturally, creating an interesting contrast with the residents from the western side of the state.

The two World Wars caused an enormous increase in the state's industrial potential and resulted in substantial growth throughout the state. The shipbuilding industry blossomed, along with military aircraft industries. The Boeing plant became an enormous economic factor in the state, and, in recent years, Bill Gates' computer enterprises turned him into one of the richest men in the world. During World War II, the atomic energy plant at Hanford brought thousands of workers to the Pasco/ Kennewick/Richland area and Richland became known as having the largest number of Ph.D.s per capita of any U. S. city.

Even though a school was established for children of the Hudson's Bay Company in Vancouver and in Spokane for Native-American children in the

1830s, the state's educational system was not clearly established until 1854. At that time, the first territorial legislature provided for the common schools. At the present time, the state constitution requires the provision of education for all children, regardless of race, color, caste, or sex.

THE EDUCATIONAL SYSTEM

Washington's schools are under an elected state superintendent of public instruction and a State Board of Education. Free education is provided through high school for all individuals between the ages of six and twenty-one, and the compulsory attendance ages are between eight and eighteen.

Exceptions to the compulsory attendance requirement include children who are at least fifteen and legally employed; children who are proficient through the ninth grade; children who have met the graduation requirements; and children who have received a certificate of educational competence. Special education services are provided between the ages of three and twenty-one.

Washington has provisions for home schooling, as long as certain curricular topics, such as spelling and appreciation for art and music are included in the content. Persons who home school must be supervised by a certificated person or a parent with at least forty-five college level credit hours.

In order for teachers to become certified in Washington, it is necessary to perform successfully on the National Teacher Examination or other special tests designed for prospective Washington teachers. Successful in-class observations are also required. The state has no statutory provisions pertaining to prayer in school.

The state has the nation's highest percentage of citizens who have completed their bachelor's degree. Nearly 16 percent of the state's population have attained this level, compared to the national percentage of 13.1. Of the state's children, 16.5 percent are below the poverty level, compared to the national figure of 19 percent. Compared to the national per capita level of $931.76 for elementary and secondary education school expenditures, Washington spends $1,132.45, ranking the state sixth in that category. Of the state's teachers, 64.5 percent have completed their master's degree, well above the national average of 42 percent.

MULTICULTURAL EDUCATION EFFORTS

While Washington does not have a planned program in multicultural education, there is an equity education program. Also, the respondent stipulated that there was a person in the state office who is responsible for multicultural education programs. However, there is no specific funding for such ventures.

Washington does provide leadership to school districts for specific kinds of multicultural programs. The state coordinates an equity network and makes information available to school districts. A number of publications are also available to school districts.

The state's predominant microcultures are Native-Americans, Asians, Pacific Islanders, African-Americans, Russian immigrants, and Southeast Asians. Washington does require special coursework and other multicultural experiences for teacher certification. Teachers must take a diversity course. For example, one such course offered for teacher candidates at Eastern Washington University is "Teaching in a Pluralistic Society," a course in multicultural education. In addition, prospective teachers must have experiences working with children from a racial background other than their own.

Washington's school districts tend to utilize a philosophy of cultural pluralism in developing curriculum content. This function is carried out at the local level. Washington does have special programs designed to teach children in their native language when necessary. Funds are available for qualified students in order for school districts to implement such undertakings.

Washington does have a number of strategies available for ensuring that schools do not become racially segregated. In Spokane, with a small minority population, this is accomplished through boundary changes. However, in urban regions of the Puget Sound area, this is accomplished through the use of busing, magnet schools, theme schools, and boundary changes.

The respondent replied that racist incidents have increased during the past five years.

While the state school office provides guidelines for school districts to use, state law requires that the evaluation of curriculum materials for possible racist and/or sexist statements be carried out in the local school districts.

In response to the question pertaining to problems facing multicultural education in Washington, the respondent replied that the "far Right" and "religious fundamentalists" objections to the notion of multicultural education constituted the greatest barrier to such efforts. Another problem related to the lack of access to such information and the provision of strategies for incorporating such efforts into the curriculum.

Finally, the respondent stated that the biggest improvements in multicultural education would be the concept's formal recognition in order to provide better assistance to the state's school districts.

REFERENCES

Avery, Mary W., *Washington: A History of the Evergreen State.* Seattle: University of Washington Press, 1965.

Castile, George Pierre, *The Indians of Puget Sound.* Seattle: University of Washington Press, 1985.

Chalfont, Stuart A., "Ethnohistorical Reports on Aboriginal Land Use and Occupancy." In *Interior and Salish Eastern Washington Indians* Volume 4. New York: Garland, 1972.

Clark, Norman H., *Washington: A Bicentennial History.* New York: W. W. Norton, 1976.

Leiter, Richard A., (ed.), *National Survey of State Laws.* First edition. *Detroit:* Gale Research, 1997.

Meany, Edmond S., *History of the State of Washington.* New York: Macmillan, 1909.

Nelson, Gerald B., *Seattle: The Life and Times of an American City.* New York: Alfred A. Knopf, 1977.

Ross, John Alan, *An Ethnoarchaelogical Survey of the Spokane Indian Reservation.* Wellpinit, WA: United States Bureau of Indian Affairs and United States Department of Forestry, Spokane Tribal Council, 1993.

State Superintendent of Public Instruction, *Organization and Financing of Washington Public Schools.* Olympia: Office of the State Superintendent of Public Instruction, 1996.

Taylor, Quintard, *In Search of the Racial Frontier: African-Americans in the American West, 1528–1990.* New York: W. W. Norton, 1998.

United States Department of Education, *Digest of Educational Statistics.* Washington D.C.: United States Department of Education, 1997.

WEST VIRGINIA

STATE HISTORY

Nicknamed the Mountain State, West Virginia is located between the eastern and the midwestern states, and its mountainous regions have created a quite different history compared to Virginia, its neighbor to the east. The mountainous terrain made the growing of tobacco impossible, and, whereas Virginia belongs to the South, West Virginia has always been more closely related to the North.

These mountainous lands were the homes of various Native-American groups, particularly the Hopewell, who were in the area for an estimated 1,000 years, disappearing about 800 years before the arrival of the Europeans. However, for reasons which are not well understood, only their mounds remained after the Europeans came to the region. Their prehistoric earthworks can still be seen in the Charleston region.

Their successors were members of the Iroquois confederation, who had driven the weaker tribes out of the area by the time that the first known European-American, John Lederer, arrived in the western Virginia region in 1669. At that time, this unpopulated country was actually being used for hunting grounds by the Cherokee, Tuscarora, Mingo, Delaware, and Susquehana. These Native-American groups put up strong resistance to the European settlers who came to the region across the Appalachian mountains in the early part of the eighteenth century.

The new colonists created a different order from the slave-holding settlers in Virginia. Due to the many mountainous regions, they started small farms so there was little need for cheap labor. Consequently, West Virginia's history was not the history of a southern slaveholding state. Germans from Pennsylvania in search of religious freedom came to the region, as did Scotch-Irish Americans. During these times, they were definitely not welcomed by the Native-Americans in the region, and many skirmishes occurred. These settlers constructed a number of forts and blockhouses, which sometimes became the cities that are located within the present boundaries of the state.

In 1742, the discovery, which would later become both a blessing and a curse to the state, occurred when John P. Salley discovered a coal deposit near Racine. However, it was not immediately developed. The Coal River gets its name from this discovery, since the deposit was located near that body of water.

In an attempt to avoid further conflicts after the French and Indian War (1754–1763), King George III decreed that no colonists would be allowed to settle west of the Alleghenies unless a peaceful agreement could be reached with the Native-American groups residing in the region. However, since a substantial number of these early settlers were illiterate, many could not read his decree, and the others simply ignored it.

Finally, in 1769, a treaty was signed with the Cherokee and Iroquois Native-Americans, causing them to give up all of their native lands between the

Allegheny Mountains and the Ohio River. This motivated large numbers of new European-American settlers to enter the region, resulting in attacks by the Shawnee. Retaliation by the settlers came in the form of a day-long battle at Point Pleasant in 1775.

While the Native-Americans agreed to be neutral at the beginning of the Revolution, two years later they sided with the British. However, by 1794 the Native-Americans finally left the area and West Virginia became a relatively safe place for all to live.

Throughout its history, there have been two distinct sections of Virginia's original large colony. The east side had the power and financial edge because of the lucrative tobacco industry. The western Virginians were industrious, hard working frontier persons who farmed and raised livestock for a living. Gradually, this breach between the two areas began to widen.

West Virginians first petitioned the Continental Congress for forming their own government in 1776. During the execution of the Jacksonian program of democracy and expansion, the interests of present-day West Virginia were primarily political and economic. When the federal government would not provide banks for their economic development, more pressures were exerted by the West Virginians.

At the outset of the Civil War in 1861, the westerners repudiated the action of the Virginians, who seceded from the Union. The westsiders refused to follow them, and finally the new state of West Virginia was born in 1863, when Abraham Lincoln approved the separate statehood bill. West Virginia's free school system came into existence during that year, and, by 1872, tax funds became available for the support of schools. Since slavery was quite minimal throughout the region's history, West Virginia did not develop a racially segregated school system on the order of Virginia's.

The acquisition of statehood resulted in a number of disputes with neighboring states. For example, a suit by Virginia sought to recover Berkeley and Jefferson counties, but West Virginia prevailed. Another argument erupted over the Hatfield and McCoy feud, which was resolved in favor of Kentucky in 1888. But litigation initiated by Maryland in 1910 was settled in favor of West Virginia.

After the Civil War, West Virginia went through a reconstruction period, which was similar to that experienced by the Confederate states. And in 1872, the state constitution was adopted. Thirteen years later, Charleston became the permanent capital. Another critical development for West Virginia was the expansion of the state's rail system, which allowed industrial development to expand in the mountainous regions.

West Virginia experienced a long era of turmoil between 1877 and 1935. During this period, industrial strife was rampant, as the mine owners resisted the attempts of the miners to create unions. These labor problems reached a climax in 1921, when a four-day battle erupted between the union members and the owners, who were backed by United States troops. This confrontation, known as the Battle of Blair Mountain, resulted in a major defeat for the miners. Finally, in 1935, the Labor Relations Act was passed during the Roosevelt administration. By this time, the state had become the nation's leader in the production of coal.

Another key incident occurred in 1915, when a United States Supreme Court decision ruled in favor of the state of Virginia, resulting in a financial award of $12,393,929.50, which West Virginia was forced to pay because of what was owed Virginia at the time of their separation.

The political history of the state became controlled by the Democrats from 1933 to 1954, thanks to the Roosevelt programs, which helped the nation extricate itself from the ravages of the Great Depression. In 1957, the country turned to the conservative policies of the Republicans, which resulted in a high level of unemployment, the state's most nagging problem. That condition prevailed until the 1970s, when West Virginia experienced substantial economic gains, a decrease in the unemployment rates, and increases in the per capita income levels.

THE EDUCATIONAL SYSTEM

The common schools of Virginia gave West Virginians many of the ideas for their own system of education. The original schools often were located in barns, lofts, and private homes. Most of the early teachers were men, and some of the common schools were organized by schoolmasters who contracted with parents. Also, in those early days, many of the common schools were used for the education of poor children. Some of the teacher payments were in the form of room and board or farm produce. Secondary education got underway in the public sector in 1908. Prior to that time, high-school education was only available at the private academies.

Presently, West Virginia's educational system is supervised by a state superintendent, who is appointed by the state's Board of Education. The state provides textbooks through the use of public funds for students who are not able to afford them. The administration of the state's schools is carried out in county units, which are administered by county superintendents and their assistants.

Compulsory attendance ages in West Virginia are from six to sixteen. Exceptions include enrollment in private, parochial, or other approved schools; instruction in the home; physical or mental incapacity; residence in excess of two miles from a school or school bus route; conditions rendering school attendance to be impossible or hazardous; the granting of work permits; serious illnesses or death in the home; and destitution in the home.

Home-schooled children must have up-to-date records detailing their progress. If a child's education is suffering, a superintendent of schools may seek a court order denying home instruction. Instructors must have graduated from high school or had formal education four hours higher than the most advanced student. Also, children must take the required standardized tests.

West Virginia allows a designated brief time for students to exercise their right to personal and private contemplation, meditation, or prayer. There is a state policy on year-round schools, and half-day kindergartens are provided.

In order for teachers to become certified in West Virginia, they must perform successfully on basic skills exams, specialty area exams, and be observed during successful in-class teaching observations. Unfortunately, West Virginia is last in terms of the percentage of the state's citizens who have completed their bachelor's degrees. Just 7.5 percent of the state's citizens over twenty-five years of age have reached that level, compared to the national percentage of 13.1 percent.

West Virginia has one of the highest percentages of children under the age of seventeen who are below the poverty level. Compared to the national average of 19 percent, 25.9 percent of West Virginia's children suffer from that problem. Only New Mexico, Mississippi, and South Carolina have a higher percentage. On the other hand, the direct expenditures per capita for elementary and secondary education place West Virginia slightly above the national average.

MULTICULTURAL EDUCATION EFFORTS

West Virginia's respondent replied that the state has no multicultural education program, nobody in charge of such ventures, and no funding. Moreover, the state provides no leadership to school districts in specific kinds of multicultural education programs. However, the counties provide opportunities for multicultural training for both professional and associate staff in the various school districts.

The state's predominant microcultures were reported to be African-Americans, Native-Americans, Latinos, and Asians. The respondent stated that racist incidents had increased during the past five years.

The history of Native-Americans is included in the state's regular curriculum. West Virginia students study the history of the state and the Native-American groups, which were part of that development. The heritage of West Virginia is traced through the people who have contributed to the culture.

There is no special course work and/or other multicultural experiences for teacher certification, but West Virginia's schools attempt to teach the importance of the contributions of the various cultural groups in the state's development, growth, and history. There seems to be no emphasis on assimilationist philosophy in the curriculum, since the respondent stipulated that West Virginia schools stress the importance of the microcultures all contributing to the state's macroculture.

West Virginia does have programs in place which attempt to teach children in their native language when necessary. This is undertaken in the state's bilingual education programs. English as a Second Language (ESL) programs are provided to children in order for them to acquire English proficiency.

When turning to the greatest problems facing multicultural education programs in West Virginia, the respondent replied that there are no state programs that provide technical assistance to local school districts in the area of multicultural education. The biggest improvements in multicultural education efforts would be to acquire such assistance from the state.

REFERENCES

Cometti, Elizabeth and Summers, Festus P., *The Thirty-Fifth State*. Morgantown: West Virginia University Library, 1966.
Council of Chief State School Officers, *The Council*. Washington D.C.: Council of Chief State School Officers, 1998.

Leiter, Richard A., (ed.), *National Survey of State Laws.* First edition. Detroit: Gale Research, 1997.

Markowitz, Harvey, (ed.), *American Indians.* Pasadena, CA: Salem Press, Inc., 1995.

Rice, O. K. *West Virginia: A History.* Lexington: University Press of Kentucky, 1993.

Sullivan, Charles, *Coal Men and Coal Mines.* New York: Garland, 1989.

United States Department of Education, *Digest of Educational Statistics.* Washington D.C.: United States Department of Education, 1997.

Williams, John A., *West Virginia.* New York: W. W. Norton, 1984.

WISCONSIN

STATE HISTORY

Known as the "Dairy State," Wisconsin owes its unique topography to glaciation, which occurred some 1,500 years ago. Also, the state owes much of its storied history to its original Native-American residents, the Winnebagos, Menominees, and several other regional tribes.   Of Siouan origin, the Winnebagos are believed to have arrived in the part of the United States which became Wisconsin during the second of four main Siouan migrations. Present-day Winnebagos tend to argue that their tribe was originally from Wisconsin, particularly around the Green Bay regions.

It was in this area that the Winnebago encountered their first Europeans, namely, Jean Nicolet, an agent for the Quebec Governor Champlain, who first mentioned interactions with the Winnebagos in the Green Bay area about 1634. By 1763, the Winnebago influence in the region disappeared when the French were unable to maintain their dominance in Canada, and Britain became the controlling force in the region until after the independence of the fledgling nation, the United States.

However, Winnebago resistance to the incursions of European-Americans remained strong and reached its peak during the Blackhawk War of 1832. Following that incident, there was a thirty-year period of U.S. imposed treaties, which essentially put an end to Winnebago claims in Wisconsin.

The first of the early visits by the Europeans occurred in 1634, when Jean Nicolet arrived in the region in an attempt to create better relations between the Native-Americans and the French. And during the next century, the area was visited by Pierre Esprit Radisson and Medart de Groseilliers, Jacques Marquette, and others. By 1763, control of the region gave way to British influences, but the actions of the fur traders still continued.

After 1783, the Wisconsin region became part of the Northwest Territory from 1783 to 1800, and also was part of the Territories of Indiana, Illinois, and Michigan. During this period of time, the Winnebago resisted the incursions of these European intruders, and, in their first peace treaty of 1816, they were invited to accept the protection of the United States government and to agree that any of their lands, which had been given up to the French or British, were now part of the new United States government.

In 1828, President John Quincy Adams agreed to pay the Winnebagos and neighboring tribes approximately twenty thousand dollars in goods to compensate for their losses of land by European-American settlers.   Later, President Andrew Jackson agreed to compensate the Winnebagos a fixed sum over twenty-seven years for what was considered to be the true value of the lands ceded by the Native-Americans.

The Menominee, part of the Algonquian language group, occupied the Great Lakes regions before recorded history. They had a rigidly defined social system which required strict adherence to gender roles. While they were matriarchal, only the men could become tribal chiefs. They prized individual rights for all of their tribal members, including children. Two of their main food sources were sturgeon and wild rice, as well as other fresh water fish and shellfish from the rivers that flowed into Lake Michigan.

For a time, the Menominee believed in witches and sorcerers, although they were not necessarily considered to be evil. They did not believe in one onmipotent being, but believed in a number of gods at different levels, including gods of humor and violence. Their first encounters with Europeans were with the French and later the British, who bought their loyalty with firearms and alcohol.

During the War of 1812, the tribe fought with the British against the Americans. But in 1856, a treaty was signed with the Americans, and the Menominee lived on 235,000 acres. By 1980 the tribe had started a new school district, complete with a community college.

Treaties between the European-American settlers and the Native-Americans were negotiated between 1829 and 1833 and resulted in the European-Americans acquiring most of the lands comprising the present state of Wisconsin. The Territory of Wisconsin was formed in 1836. Just twelve years later, the state's constitution was accepted and Wisconsin became the thirtieth state in the Union.

With the acquisition of statehood, Wisconsin also got serious about establishing its system of public education. Native Protestants saw public education as the hope of the future. They envisioned the schools as a means of teaching English, patriotism, and Protestant values. And while the state's constitution clearly prohibited sectarian instruction, the early superintendents were all Protestants who bent the constitution to coincide with their values, allowing many schools to use the Bible and prayer in the curriculum. The first public elementary school was founded in Kenosha in 1845.

By this time, lead miners had been migrating to Wisconsin from the southern state,s and, during the last half of the 19th century, European-Americans from Germany helped Milwaukee become one of the largest German-American cultural centers in the United States. Also, immigrants from Norway, Canada, Austria, Ireland, and Sweden came to the region.

During the Civil War, Wisconsin contributed more than 91,000 soldiers to the Union cause. In addition, the state provided millions of bushels of wheat to the Union effort. However, by 1870, the wheat production had diminished and Wisconsin commenced to be known as the dairy state, with an increase in production of milk products.

The turn of the century saw Wisconsin's primary economic thrust also start turning toward industrial products. The state became the nation's leading producer of dairy products and the labor unions grew substantially as Wisconsin's industries continued to grow, necessitating a need for more laborers.

Politically, the years after 1900 saw the growth of the Republican party's progressive wing under the leadership of Governor Robert M. LaFollette. During his era of leadership, a number of progressive measures were passed, including rail taxes, workmen's compensation, and the direct primary. After mainline Republicans returned to power during the World War I era, the

Progessives returned to power until just before the United States involvement in World War II.

During this period, Wisconsin war plants produced more than twelve billion dollars worth of war materials and Wisconsin farmers produced record quantities of dairy products. More than 300,000 men and women served in the armed forces. Another 132,000 served during the Korean-United States hostilities.

During the last half of the twentieth century, Wisconsin was forced to deal with problems related to a rapidly increasing population, the need for improved roads and urban improvement, and a procedure to meet the rising costs to operate the state. During that time, they acquired the Braves from Boston and lost them to Atlanta. The new St. Lawrence Seaway brought cargo clear to Wisconsin ports. And the National Football League's Green Bay Packers successes brought a new kind of pride to Wisconsin.

THE EDUCATIONAL SYSTEM

Compulsory attendance laws in Wisconsin were first established in 1849, when children between the ages of seven and fourteen were required to attend school. Presently, the compulsory school attendance ages are between six and eighteen. Exceptions include children who have graduated; children with physical/mental conditions which render them incapable of learning; and children attending private schools or children who are home schooled. Children may attend vocational or technical schools when they reach the age of sixteen.

Wisconsin's home schooling program requires that the parents or guardians must meet the same requirements for a private school, such as a minimum of 875 hours of instruction each year. This instruction must include reading, language arts, math, social studies, science, and health. While the use of corporal punishment as a disciplinary measure is prohibited in Wisconsin, reasonable and necessary force is allowed for self defense and to protect others. The state has no provisions related to the issue of prayer in the schools.

In order to become certified to teach in Wisconsin, candidates must pass a basic skills test and be observed in successful classroom teaching performances. Thirty-eight percent of the state's teachers hold a master's degree, compared to the national average of 42 percent.

Wisconsin has no policy on year-round schools and kindergartens are not required by law. However, both exist in Wisconsin.

The per capita expenditures for education in the state are $1,078. This compares nicely to the national average of $931.76. And Wisconsin fares quite well as to the percentage of children under the age of seventeen who fall below the poverty level. Eleven percent of them must face this problem compared with the national average of 19 percent.

MULTICULTURAL EDUCATION EFFORTS

According to the respondent, Wisconsin has no multicultural education program, nobody in charge of such efforts, and no state funding is available. Presently, the state offers no leadership to school districts in multicultural education. However, it should be noted that Wisconsin does have a number of laws and administrative rules related to equity and multicultural education. These relate to such issues as pupil non-discrimination; the provision of instructional materials which reflect cultural diversity and pluralism; human relations; bilingual/bicultural education; provisions for reducing racial imbalance; and several others.

The respondent stipulated that the predominant microcultures in Wisconsin were African-Americans (11 percent), Latinos (3.5 percent), Asian/Pacific Islanders (3 percent), Native-Americans (1.6 percent), and European-Americans (84 percent). These figures come from a document which relates to pupil nondiscrimination provisions.

It was reported that Wisconsin requires special coursework in multicultural education. This occurs as part of the state's human relations regulations for professional school personnel. These regulations include such human relations issues as the history, customs, social institution values, lifestyles, and contributions of women and various racial, cultural, and economic groups in the United States. Another phase of the requirements relates to the constitutional and legal bases related to the status of women and the various racial and cultural groups in the United States.

Another section of these requirements relates to the manner in which racism, discrimination, and prejudice can be reflected in instructional materials. Prospective teachers must also have opportunities to examine their own feelings and attitudes about issues of racism, prejudice, and discrimination. There are many other requirements of a similar nature which delve into the key multicultural education issues which affect children from all racial and ethnic backgrounds in American society.

In regard to the issue of whether schools and states tend to stress cultural pluralism or cultural assimilation in the state's curriculum, the respondent stipulated that such decisions are made by local school boards and there is no total state policy regarding the matter.

Wisconsin has programs designed to teach children in their native language. The state legislature in Wisconsin has found that there are Wisconsin students who enter elementary and secondary school with limited or nonexistent English speaking ability, due to the use of another language in their family. Obviously, classes taught in English may not provide adequate instruction for children with limited English-speaking proficiency. Therefore, Wisconsin has decided that in order to provide equal educational opportunities, it may be necessary to ensure that appropriate programs are available for Wisconsin students who exhibit such language deficiencies.

Most of these provisions have been bilingual/bicultural education programs. The state definition describes such efforts as being designed to improve the comprehension and the speaking, reading, and writing ability of a limited English-speaking student in the English language so that he or she will be able to perform ordinary class work in English. Teachers of bilingual education receive a certificate from the state which authorizes them to perform ordinary classroom work in English.

School segregation efforts in Wisconsin have attempted to ensure that children will not be assigned to specific schools based solely on their racial or ethnic background. Consequently, the state has stipulated that certain programs which attempt to reduce racial imbalance may be implemented by the state's public-school districts. Moreover, children are entitled to transportation in order to ensure such racial desegregation outcomes.

Based on the reported complaints by local school districts and the accounts of such incidents in the media, the respondent replied that racist incidents have increased in Wisconsin during the past five years.

The history of Native-Americans is included in Wisconsin's regular curriculum. In fact, the state requires the state superintendent to establish standards for certifying the abilities of teachers participating in American Indian language and culture education programs.

Wisconsin's state Office of Education does not evaluate curriculum materials, library materials, and textbooks for racist and sexist statements. That function is carried on at the local level.

The biggest problem facing multicultural education programs in Wisconsin was felt to be the lack of a requirement for the creation and continuance of such efforts. There is no state leadership, no models, and no funding. Nor is there any clearing house for local educators. The biggest improvement in Wisconsin would be to have such an effort in place.

REFERENCES

Blegen, Theodore, C., *The Land Lies Open.* Westport: Greenwood Press, 1975.

Council of Chief State School Officers, *The Council.* Washington D.C.: Council of Chief State School Officers, 1998.

Current, Richard Nelson, *Wisconsin: A History.* New York: W. W. Norton, 1977.

Jones, John Alan, *Winnebago Ethnology.* New York: Garland, 1974.

Leiter, Richard A., (ed.), *National Survey of State Laws.* First edition. Detroit: Gale Research, 1997.

Nesbit, Robert, *Wisconsin: A History.* Madison: University of Wisconsin Press, 1973.

Ourada, Patricia K., *The Menominee Indians: A History.* Norman: University of Oklahoma Press, 1979.

Peroff, Nicholas C., *Menominee Drums: Tribal Termination and Restoration, 1954-1974.* Norman: University of Oklahoma Press.

Radin, Paul, *The ulture of the Winnebago.* Baltimore: Waverly Press, 1949.

Radin, Paul, *The Winnebago Tribe.* Lincoln: University of Nebraska Press, 1990.

Wisconsin Department of Public Instruction, *Wisconsin Laws and Administrative Rules Related to Equity and Multicultural Education.* Madison: State of Wisconsin Department of Public Instruction, 1993.

Wisconsin Department of Public Instruction, *Pupil Population in Wisconsin Public Schools Protected by Pupil Nondiscrimination Provisions.* Madison: Wisconsin Department of Public Instruction, 1993.

WYOMING

STATE HISTORY

Wyoming's early history can be likened to the vintage western novel. Indeed, it is fraught with Native-Americans, miners, cattle, western towns, cattlemen, ranchers, and even gunslingers. Its initial history, however, centered around the activities of the Native-American residents, namely the Crow, Cheyenne, Arapaho, Shoshone, and Sioux.

The Arapaho were one of the more significant tribes in Wyoming's history. They were a plains tribe with a classical buffalo economy. Members of the Algonquian language group, they also resided in the present-day state of Oklahoma. They were closely associated with the Cheyenne and the Utes. Shoshones and Pawnees were their enemies a great deal of the time. It is believed that they were pushed west by the Sioux. It is not exactly known when they first arrived in the Wyoming plains.

Originally, the Arapaho killed buffalo by either driving them over cliffs or chasing them into enclosures, where they were slaughtered with spears and arrows. However, about the middle of the eighteenth century, they acquired horses from some of the southwestern tribes and their lives were changed dramatically. Not only did their buffalo-hunting strategies change, but they used the travois, a sort of horse-drawn trailer, as a means of moving rapidly from place to place.

The Arapaho were a deeply religious tribe and significant ceremonies were held for nearly every type of human endeavor. For example, special rituals were conducted for each stage of life, buffalo hunts, and an individual's pledge for service. Moreover, music and dance were important parts of these ceremonies. Vision quests were also significant elements of personal religious undertakings.

While the great Civil War was being fought in the East, a critical between natives and European-Americans occurred at Sand Creek, Colorado, in 1864. After a treaty had been negotiated with the federal government, Colonel Chivington attacked the encamped Arapaho and Cheyenne, killing some 300 Native-American people. Most were women and children. According to the records, the Chivington forces mutilated many of the bodies after the massacre. In 1869 the Arapaho were assigned to the Shoshone Reservation in western Wyoming.

It is believed that the first two Europeans to reach the present-day Wyoming region may have been Francois and Louis Joseph de la Verendrye, who traveled southwest from the Mandan villages in 1742 and 1743. Other Frenchmen traveled on the North Platte River, reaching the Wyoming area in the latter part of the eighteenth century. Later, John Colter, a veteran of the Lewis and Clark expedition, reportedly spent the winter of 1807–1808 in northwestern Wyoming, on a visit to an area just west of the present-day city of Cody. He also became the first known European to travel through Yellowstone Park.

Three years later, a fur trading expedition composed of European-Americans, traveled through northern Wyoming on their way to Astoria, Oregon. During the next several decades, other European-American travelers passed through the region and by the 1840s, Fort Laramie became one of the primary stops along the way. Located in eastern Wyoming near the North Platte and Laramie Rivers, it began first as a fur-trading post and later was sold to the U.S. government in 1849. The first school in the present state of Wyoming was established there in 1852.

The other popular stopping point was Fort Bridger, which was located in the southwestern part of the state. It was named after its famous founder, Jim Bridger, who gained fame as a mountain man, fur trapper, guide, and storyteller. It is estimated that 150,000 European-American settlers passed through the region between 1841 and 1853. Some of the travelers were on their way to the California gold fields, while others, such as the Mormons, were headed to other far western territories in search of places to settle down.

These encroachments were unnerving to the original Native-American residents, who were experiencing a rapidly depleting supply of game. Consequently, they were involved in numerous disputes with the European-Americans, who had little understanding of or sympathy for the Native-Americans they encountered. This culminated in a treaty council, which provided the Native-Americans with an annual annuity of $50,000 in goods if the various tribes would allow the settlers to pass through the area freely.

However, this settlement did not prove to be entirely satisfactory. A number of conflicts still took place, and, in 1868, in a treaty at Fort Bridger, the Wind River Reservation for Native-Americans was established for the Shoshone. The Arapaho moved there in 1878.

During this period of time, the railroads were also coming to Wyoming. The Union Pacific Railroad entered southern Wyoming in 1867 and, two years later, had crossed into Utah. In Wyoming, cities such as Cheyenne, Laramie, Rawlins, Rock Springs, Green River, and Evanston emerged. As they grew in population, the argument for the creation of a territory emerged, and in 1868 the region finally became the Wyoming Territory. Women were given the right to vote and became able to run for office. The 1870 census revealed a population of 9,118 people.

During the next two decades, Wyoming's population experienced rapid growth. Yellowstone became the first national park in the United States in 1872, and the state's first oil well was drilled in 1883. Also during that era, hundreds of thousands of Texas longhorns were driven into the territory and much of the state's power lay in the hands of the Wyoming Stock Growers Association. In 1890, Wyoming became the forty-fourth state of the Union.

During this era, the new residents' thoughts turned once more to the education issue, and a school in Cheyenne opened in 1868. A territorial school law was enacted a year later, and, by 1875, the first high school had opened its doors to students.

During the twentieth century, Wyoming experienced steady growth, although compared to other states, it always remained rather sparsely populated. In fact, the 1990 census revealed that Wyoming was the nation's least populated state. During the Spanish-American War, Wyoming far exceeded its quota of volunteers, and, during World War I, some 12,000 young men were in uniform. This figure jumped to approximately 30,000 during World War II.

Following the war, Wyoming attempted to lure industries to the state in order to diversity its economy, which had theretofore relied primarily on ranching/farming, raw materials production, and tourism. Uranium production increased and defense preparations led to the establishment of an intercontinental ballistic missile base at Cheyenne in 1958.

A significant racial issue centering around fourteen African-American student athletes on the University of Wyoming football team occurred in 1969, when the players went to the office of football coach Lloyd Eaton. They were wearing black armbands and asked permission to wear them against Brigham Young University to protest BYU's alleged racist religious practices. The coach refused and dismissed the young men from the team, a decision which was upheld by the University of Wyoming Board of Trustees. The team managed to defeat Brigham Young without the fourteen African-American players. However, they went on to lose all the rest of their games that year.

During the past three decades of this century, it seemed that the effort to establish a greater industrial base was largely unsuccessful. The petroleum industry waned, although a natural gas discovery near Gillette helped the state's economy. And as the century drew to a close, Wyoming maintained its mostly European-American population.

THE EDUCATIONAL SYSTEM

Wyoming's public elementary and secondary schools are supervised by a state superintendent of schools, who is elected by popular vote. The State Board of Education was established in 1919 and, presently, this nine-member body is appointed by the governor with approval from the state's senate. Most of the funding for Wyoming's public education comes from property taxes. Wyoming's compulsory attendance requirement is for children between the ages of seven and sixteen. Exceptions include children who have completed the eighth grade; children for whom the local school board feels that school attendance would be detrimental to the child's or other children's mental or physical health; children for whom attendance would create an undue hardship; and children who attend a private school or are home schooled. In Wyoming home schooling must meet the requirements of basic education and academic programs. Parents must submit the curriculum to the local board of education.

Local Wyoming school boards may adopt rules for teachers to use reasonable forms of punishment and disciplinary measures. There are no statutory provisions related to prayer in school. There are no provisions pertaining to the privacy of school records.

In order for people to become certified as Wyoming teachers, they must be observed in successful classroom teaching performances. At the present time there are no special test-taking requirements. Just 26.5 percent of Wyoming's school teachers have achieved the master's degree, compared to a national average of 42 percent. Only Hawaii, Idaho, Montana, North Dakota and South Dakota have a lower percentage.

Wyoming provides special education services for children between the ages of three and twenty. There is no policy on year-round schools and school districts are required to provide half-day kindergartens. Just 10.6 percent of Wyomings' children under the age of seventeen are below the poverty level. Only four other states have a smaller percentage of children in this category. The per capita expenditures for elementary and secondary education are $1,264.73. This compares quite favorably with the national average of $931.76. Only Alaska, New Jersey, and New York have a higher percentage.

MULTICULTURAL EDUCATION EFFORTS

The respondent stated that Wyoming did have a planned multicultural education program in the state. It was commented that "foreign cultures" was one of the knowledge areas in a common core for which school districts must develop student performance standards locally. However, no one in the State Office of Instruction is responsible for such efforts, and there is no funding provided. The state offers no leadership to school districts in specific kinds of multicultural education programs.

The predominant microcultures in the state of Wyoming are Latinos, Native-Americans, African-Americans, Japanese, Chinese, Vietnamese, Thai, and Basque. However, the great majority of Wyoming residents are of European-American descent.

In order to become certified teachers, candidates must demonstrate an adequate knowledge of the historical and cultural values, customs, and social institutions of both western and nonwestern cultures.

Wyoming does have special programs designed to teach students in their native language when necessary. Students on the Wind River Reservation have a program designed to teach their native language. However, the response to this question stipulated that seldom did teachers actually teach in any language other than English.

Due to the small population of the state, the respondent stipulated that school desegregation by race has not been a large problem. Based on the best available evidence, racist incidents have remained about the same in Wyoming's schools during the past five years. The Office of Education does not evaluate curriculum materials, library materials, and textbooks for racist and sexist content.

Finally, the respondent replied that the greatest problems facing multicultural education programs in Wyoming have been a lack of resources and support from the state's educational agency. The greatest needs reported were for more ethnic teachers and aides in classrooms and some sort of exposure for students in the isolated rural areas.

REFERENCES

Bass, Aletha, *The Arapaho Way*. New York: Clarkson N. Potter, 1966.

Coel, Margaret, *Chief Left Hand: Southern Arapaho*. Norman: University of Oklahoma Press, 1981.

Larson, T. A., *History of Wyoming*. Lincoln: University of Nebraska Press, 1978.

Larson, T. A., *Wyoming: A History*. New York: W. W. Norton, 1977.

Leiter, Richard A., (ed.), *National Survey of State Laws*. First edition. Detroit: Gale Research, 1997.

Murray, Robert A., *Military Posts in the Powder River Country of Wyoming, 1865–1894*. Lincoln: University of Nebraska Press, 1968.

United States Department of Education, *Digest of Educational Statistics*. Washington D.C.: United States Department of Education, 1997.

Zdenek, Salzmann, *The Arapaho Indians: A Research Guide and Bibliography*. New York: Greenwood Press, 1988.

SELECTED BIBLIOGRAPHY

Alexander, Kern and Alexander, M. David, *American School Law.* Belmont, CA: West/Wadsworth, 1998.

Ambler, J. Richard, *The Anasazi: Prehistoric People of the Four Corners Region.* Flagstaff: Museum of Northern Arizona, 1977.

Bullough, et al., *The Elusive Eden: A New History of California.* New York: Alfred A. Knopf, 1987.

Bureau of Administration and School Improvement Services, *Guidelines for the Development of Multicultural, Non-Sexist Education Plans.* Des Moines: Iowa Department of Education, 1998.

Carr, Audrey T., *Program Guidelines for Multicultural Education.* Lexington: Kentucky Department of Education, 1992.

Corkran, David H., *The Cherokee Frontier: Conflict and Survival, 1740 - 1762.* Norman: University of Oklahoma Press, 1962.

Council of State School Officers, *The Council.* Washington D.C.: Council of Chief State School Officers, 1998.

Cremin, Laurence A., *American Education: The Colonial Experience, 1607–1783.* New York: Harper and Row, 1970.

Dorsey, George, *Traditions of the Caddo.* Washington D.C.: Carnegie Institute of Washington, 1905.

Fischer, Louis, Schimmel, and Kelly, Cynthia, *Teachers and the Law.* New York: Longman, 1995.

Florida Department of Education, *Multicultural Education in Florida.* Tallahassee: Florida Department of Education, 1993.

Foreman, Grant, *The Five Civilized Tribes.* Norman: University of Oklahoma Press, 1934.

Green, Michael D., *The Politics of Indian Removal: Creek Government and Society in Crisis.* Lincoln: University of Nebraska Press, 1982.

Heizer, Robert F., (ed.), *California.* In *Handbook of North American Indians* Volume 8. Washington D.C.: Smithsonian Institution, 1978.

Josephy, Alvin M. Jr., *Five Hundred Nations.* New York: Alfred Knopf, 1994.

Leiter, Richard A., (ed.), *National Survey of State Laws.* First edition. Detroit: Gale Research, 1997.

Lumpkin, Henry, *From Savannah to Yorktown: The American Revolution in the South.* New York: Paragon House, 1981.

Markowitz, Harvey, (ed.), *American Indians.* Pasadena, CA: Salem Press, Inc., 1995.

Mitchell, Bruce, et al., *The Dynamic Classroom: A Creative Approach to the Teaching/Evaluation Process.* Dubuque, IA: Kendall/Hunt, 1996.

Mitchell, Bruce and Salsbury, Robert, *Multicultural Education: An International Guide to Research, Policies, and Programs.* Westport, CT: Greenwood Press, 1996.

New Hampshire Department of Education, *Equal Education Access for Students with Limited English Proficiency.* Concord: New Hampshire Department of Education, 1998.

New Jersey Department of Law and Public Safety, *Bias Incident Report* (1994). West Trenton: Department of Law and Public Safety, 1994.

New Jersey State Department of Education, *Guidelines for Education That Is Multicultural.* Trenton: Office of Educational Opportunity of the New Jersey State Department of Education, 1993.

New Mexico State Department of Education, *Bilingual Multicultural Education: Guidelines for Compliance with Existing Federal and State Law.* Santa Fe: New Mexico State Department of Education, 1995.

New Mexico State Department of Education, *Procedures for Identification and Assessment of Limited English Proficiency (LEP) Students.* Santa Fe: State of New Mexico Department of Education, 1994.

Noon, Christine, (ESL Coordinator, NH Department of Education) *Memo Regarding National Study of Multicultural Education.* Concord: State of New Hampshire, Department of Education, 1998.

Puckette, John L., *Foxfire Reconsidered: A Twenty-Year Experiment in Progressive Education.* Urbana: University of Illinois Press, 1989.

Raft, Herbert C., *The Lenape: Archaeology, History, and Ethnography.* Newark: New Jersey Historical Society, 1986.

Rippa, Alexander, *Education in a Free Society: An American History.* New York: Longman, 1992.

Salsbury, Robert and Mitchell, Bruce, *Multicultural Education in American Schools.* Cheney, WA: Eastern Washington University (Monograph), 1991.

Schwantes, Carlos A., *The Pacific Northwest: An Interpretive History.* Lincoln: University of Nebraska Press, 1989.

Takaki, Ronald, *A Different Mirror: A History of Multicultural America.* Boston: Little, Brown, 1993.

Taylor, Quintard, *In Search of the Racial Frontier: African-Americans in the American West, 1528–1990.* New York: W. W. Norton, 1998.

United States Department of Education, *Digest of Educational Statistics.* Washington D.C.: United States Department of Education, 1997.

Walthall, John A., *Prehistoric Indians of the Southeast.* University of Alabama: University of Alabama Press, 1980.

Williams, Juan, *Eyes on the Prize: America's Civil Rights Years, 1954 - 1965.* New York: Viking, 1987.

Wilson, Terry P., *The Osage.* New York: Chelsea House, 1988.

Zirkel, Perry A., and Richardson, Sherry Nalbone, *A Digest of Supreme Court Decisions Affecting Education.* Bloomington: Phi Delta Kappa Foundation, 1988.

INDEX

About the Authors

BRUCE M. MITCHELL is Professor Emeritus of Multicultural Education at Eastern Washington University. He is the co-author of *Multicultural Education: An International Guide to Research, Policies, and Programs* (1996) and the *Encyclopedia of Multicultural Education* (1999), both available from Greenwood Press.

ROBERT E. SALSBURY is Professor of Education at Eastern Washington University. With Bruce M. Mitchell, he is the co-author of *Multicultural Education: An International Guide to Research, Policies, and Programs* (1996) and the *Encyclopedia of Multicultural Education* (1999), both available from Greenwood Press.

ISBN 0-313-30859-4

90000>

EAN

9 780313 308598

HARDCOVER BAR CODE